Improving Supervisors' Effectiveness

How Organizations Can Raise the Performance of Their First-Level Managers

Jack J. Phillips

Improving Supervisors' Effectiveness

Jossey-Bass Publishers
San Francisco • Washington • London • 1985

IMPROVING SUPERVISORS' EFFECTIVENESS
How Organizations Can Raise the Performance
of Their First-Level Managers
by Jack J. Phillips

Copyright © 1985 by: Jossey-Bass Inc., Publishers
433 California Street
San Francisco, California 94104
&
Jossey-Bass Limited
28 Banner Street
London EC1Y 8QE

Library of Congress Cataloging in Publication Data

Phillips, Jack J. (date)
Improving supervisors' effectiveness.

(The Jossey-Bass management series)
Bibliography: p. 403
Includes index.
1. Supervision of employees. 2. Supervisors—
Training of. I. Title. II. Series.
HF5549.P459   1985   658.4'071245   84-43032
ISBN 0-87589-647-2

Manufactured in the United States of America

JACKET DESIGN BY WILLI BAUM

FIRST EDITION

Code 8517

The Jossey-Bass
Management Series

Consulting Editors
Human Resources

Leonard Nadler
Zeace Nadler
College Park, Maryland

To Johnnie,
my wife and great friend,
who inspires me to be at my best

Preface

Whether they are called foremen, superintendents, managers, or section leaders, the people in the front-line management team—the supervisors—can make the difference between success and failure for an organization. The supervisor's job is to carry out management's goals and plans through the employees who actually do the work. By any measure, this is a challenging and difficult task—so much so that many organizations tolerate less than exceptional performance from supervisors.

A few years ago an *Industry Week* article (Overbeke, 1975, p. 39) captured the situation in a summary comment: "Pressure from above with little understanding. Pressure from fellow foremen. An often embarrassing position with little group identity. Pressure from the union. An ax over your head which could thrust you back into the ranks of the blue-collar workers with seniority lower than practically every man you used to lead. All this adds up to the foreman's job."

Although the situation may not be that serious in every organization, the job is indeed one that has its share of problems. It sometimes includes unrealistic challenges that are difficult even for a super performer to achieve. Neither manager nor worker, the supervisor takes much of the heat while receiving little of the credit.

Each year new surveys are conducted to try to identify and assess the frustrations and difficulties facing supervisors. One of the most thorough of these surveys, involving 8,000 supervisors, was highlighted in the *Harvard Business Review* (Bittel and Ramsey, 1982). This study found that some 29 percent of the first-level blue-collar supervisors and 21 percent of the first-level white-collar supervisors would return to the rank and file if they could do so without a pay reduction or loss of face. One of the most distressing findings was that only 40 percent of the supervisors regard themselves as part of management. These conclusions are alarming, yet they represent a realistic picture of what exists today.

How an individual becomes a supervisor is another area of concern. The transition from hourly employee to supervisor is a difficult one, yet many organizations require employees to make this transition with little or no preparation and almost no explanation of what is expected of them or how they will be measured. This condition alone causes many supervisors to give up in the early stages of their supervisory career.

The Changing Role of the Supervisor

Although many changes have occurred in the workplace in the past few years, one of the most important is the subtle and gradual erosion of the role of the supervisor in the organizational structure. There was a time when the supervisor's job was relatively simple. The supervisor knew the employees and they knew the supervisor. Employees knew what was expected of them, and there was little doubt what would happen if they did not do what was asked. If something went wrong, the supervisor was immediately aware of it and could take proper action. The supervisor commanded respect and had the authority to carry out responsibilities with little concern for unions, government agencies, corporate policies, and staff support. And most of all, the supervisor had the support of upper management.

Today the supervisor's role is very different. Technological and social changes have brought new dimensions to the job. The supervisor must be a manager, counselor, cost accountant, social worker, coordinator, human resources specialist, lawyer, production scheduler, public relations specialist, and sometimes an engineer. In short, the supervisor is responsible for more now than in the past, yet often with less authority to meet those responsibilities. While few jobs in today's work force are as important as those of supervisors, according to Peter Drucker (1983, p. 32), "no job is going to change more in the next decade than that of the first-line supervisor in both factory and office. And few people in the work force are less prepared for the changes and less likely to welcome them."

Improving the Supervisor's Job

Organizations need to make changes to improve the supervisory role so that the job will be more attractive and the supervisor will be more effective. Perhaps Drucker (1983, p. 32) said it best: "For forty years now . . . American business—with some exceptions—has taken the first-line supervisor for granted. But in the next decade the supervisor will again become central to industrial relations. Indeed the status, authority, and responsibility of the supervisor—as well as his compensation and promotional opportunities—may become our most pressing and difficult problem in the management of people at work."

Revamping the supervisory role will require organizations to do the following:

- Change assumptions about supervision and try to understand the frustrations and anxieties that are inherent in this difficult job.
- Invest in the selection, training, education, and development of supervisors.
- Implement programs to recognize and reward supervisors adequately so they will continue to be motivated to do their best.
- Provide ample support from management and from staff groups so that the supervisor's job is accomplished effectively.
- Give supervisors freedom to manage their work unit and hold them responsible for the results.

- Let supervisors know what is expected of them straightfor-wardly and keep them informed about the organization, its plans and goals.
- Recognize supervisors as key participating members of man-agement.

More specifically, a comprehensive plan of action must be implemented to meet these challenges and increase the effec-tiveness of supervisors. This book helps managers and organiza-tions to tackle the most needed improvements, with a chapter devoted to each. It shows organizations how to do the following:

- Select the most qualified candidates for supervisory vacancies.
- Develop training and education programs for supervisors.
- Implement realistic supervisory performance standards and appraisals.
- Maintain an adequate and competitive compensation system.
- Implement an effective communications program for super-vision.
- Give supervisors ample authority to accomplish the job.
- Enhance organizational support and recognition for supervi-sion.
- Prepare supervisors to participate in decisions that affect them.

Taking these actions will result in vast improvements in supervisory jobs, which in turn will have an immediate, positive impact on an organization. Supervisors will be more effective in their jobs since many of the impediments to success will be re-moved. Supervisors will remain in their jobs longer since there will be less difficulty and frustration. Also, employees in the or-ganization will be more likely to actively seek the job of super-visor when it is more attractive. This should help ensure an am-ple supply of qualified candidates for future vacancies.

Not every organization will need improvement in each of these areas. Some items are more important and carry a higher priority than others. Each organization must assess its current posture and develop new policies, programs, and management practices to make the necessary improvements.

Purpose of This Book

Why another book? This question faces every author in developing a new book, particularly when there seems to be an overabundance of published material for management and staff professionals to read and digest. This book had its beginnings a few years ago when I examined the status of supervision in an organization. As a result of this review, I realized that although many organizations had supervisory problems, little published information was available. I found that the vast majority, if not all, of the books on supervision are aimed at the supervisor and thus provide little help for organizations. Some define the supervisor's job and outline its basic responsibilities, functions, and duties. Others present basic supervisory principles and the skills necessary for success, all directed at the supervisor. Still others are written in a "how-to" format and serve as handbooks or problem-solving guides. These provide supervisors with step-by-step solutions to immediate problems and show them how to accomplish routine tasks. Finally, there are a few books on job enrichment and job redesign that describe techniques to make jobs more challenging and rewarding. These are usually theoretically based and cover a broad range of jobs, including the supervisor's.

But these categories of books leave a large void. To my knowledge, until now, no one has addressed the problem of how the organization can improve the job of the first-level supervisor. This book is directed at the organization because, after all, it is the organization that makes changes in policies, procedures, and practices that affect the supervisor.

This book should be a useful guide for several groups, and the audience for this book should be very broad. Human resources professionals should find this work to be a very useful tool, since they are responsible for designing and implementing personnel policies, compensation practices, and selection procedures for supervisors. This will be a practical guide to designing systems and to providing support services to supervisors. Human resources development (HRD) staff members will also find this book very helpful. It is their job to identify training needs, develop training programs, and provide training for supervisors.

Almost without exception every HRD department is involved in supervisory training to some extent. This book will help HRD staff members develop effective programs while providing support to supervisors.

Another important audience is middle and top management. These groups must participate in developing practices and policies to make supervision more attractive and supervisors more effective. Also, they must provide direct support to supervisors as they perform their duties. Although this book will be an asset for all key decision makers, it should be required reading for every manager with first-level supervisors who report directly to him or her. Finally, the book should give supervisors some insight into the areas where improvement is needed and prepare them to accept responsibility for making the system work.

Experience and Theory

The conclusions and recommendations in this book are based on a combination of practical experience and an examination of recent publications and supervisory studies. In the last twenty years, I have had the pleasure of working with over 5,000 supervisors in a variety of industries and organizational settings. This exposure has left me with some strong impressions about the problems and challenges faced by the supervisor and some of the potential solutions to these problems. My full-time experience with organizations in four industries (aerospace, textiles, metals, and construction materials), coupled with occasional consulting for nonprofit organizations and public seminar presentations to supervisors, has provided me with unusual opportunities to gain insight into the job of supervisor. In addition, I have implemented improvement programs in each of the areas outlined in this book. Some of these were highly successful while others required a certain amount of modification. In any case, I have had the opportunity to see what works and does not work in attempting to improve the job of supervisor.

Important input has also come from recent professional publications on the supervisor's job. These include articles published in the major management, supervisory, and human resources periodicals over the last five years. Valuable input was also secured from studies about the job of supervisor conducted by various organizations. Fortunately, there have been many such studies, and the most significant ones are referred to throughout the book. Although this book could have been written solely on the basis of my experiences, the thoroughness and credibility of the final product have been enhanced by this input from management literature and supervisory studies.

Overview of the Contents

The first chapter introduces the basic problems facing the supervisor. It traces how the supervisor's role has changed, outlines causes of the problems, and indicates what must be done to improve the job and make it more attractive.

Next, a chapter is devoted to each of the action areas already mentioned—selecting supervisors, developing training programs, and so forth. Each of these core chapters begins with a discussion of the importance of the particular action—to both the supervisor and the organization. This can help the organization set priorities for which actions are needed right away. Then, each core chapter sets forth useful approaches, techniques, and ideas that can be used to make the necessary improvements. Many examples and illustrations are presented to reinforce the approaches. Results of surveys and research are presented to support conclusions. Each chapter, except for the first, ends with a list of suggested readings.

The last chapter illustrates how to implement a plan of improvement for the supervisor's job. It presents ways to assess an organization's current posture, set priorities, develop an action plan to make improvements, and check the progress of the plan.

This book should prove useful in a variety of settings. Although many of the studies and examples presented are from business and industry, other settings are well represented, including nonprofit, health care, and government institutions. There is a balance of coverage between plant-oriented supervisors and office supervisors. The majority of supervisors do, of course, come from business and industry; accordingly, the illustrations and examples lean toward that particular group.

In summary, this is meant to be a practical guide for middle and top management, personnel and human resources managers, and HRD professionals to implement new policies and programs to make the supervisor's job more attractive. If this is done, individual supervisors will be more effective, command the respect they deserve, and increase their contribution to the organization.

Acknowledgments

No book represents the work of the author alone. Many colleagues have shared their thoughts, which have been refined, developed, and ultimately presented here as the final product. Several organizations have supplied material for this book and are given credit at various points.

The individuals who have influenced, supported, or encouraged me in this effort are almost too numerous to mention, but some deserve special attention. Perry Given and Herbert Stockham helped convince me of the tremendous importance of first-level supervisors and encouraged me to develop and implement programs to increase their effectiveness. The Human Resources Management faculty of the University of Alabama provided helpful suggestions and was very supportive of this effort. But most of all, this project would not have been possible without the support and encouragement of my boss, Carl Register, president of the Southern Division of Vulcan Materials Company. Carl is an outstanding executive, who places a high priority on the development of employees, particularly those at the first level of management.

Much gratitude goes to Leonard and Zeace Nadler for their meticulous review of the manuscript and very thoughtful suggestions for improvement, the vast majority of which were implemented. Both have extraordinary insight into the field of management and supervision.

Special appreciation goes to Debra Rousseau, who not only typed the manuscript but provided valuable input for improvement. Without her untiring efforts, the manuscript would not have been completed on time. Sharon Oswald and Hugh Bryant, who reviewed the manuscript and offered many important comments, were also instrumental in developing the book.

And finally I owe much appreciation to my wife, Johnnie, who provided encouragement, support, and assistance throughout the effort. She made many sacrifices to make this book a reality.

Birmingham, Alabama   Jack J. Phillips
February 1985

Contents

Tables, Figures, and Exhibits

Tables

Figures

Exhibits

The Author

Jack J. Phillips has twenty years of experience in human resources, culminating with his present assignment as manager of human resources and administration at Vulcan Materials Company, Southern Division, Birmingham, Alabama. Prior to this appointment, he was training and development manager and personnel manager at Stockham Valves and Fittings, also in Birmingham. He was training director for American Enka Company, a textile fiber producer in Tennessee, and has served in various capacities in training and production for nine years at the Lockheed-Georgia Company.

A native of Georgia, Phillips received his associate degree in electrical engineering technology from Southern Technical Institute, his bachelor of science degree in physics, summa cum laude, from Oglethorpe University, and his master's degree in decision sciences from Georgia State University.

A frequent contributor to management literature, Phillips has authored the *Handbook of Training Evaluation and Measurement Methods* (1983) and a chapter in the *Handbook of Human Resource Development* (1984). Phillips has written more than fifty articles for professional publications, including *Training* magazine, *Training and Development Journal, Personnel*

Journal, Personnel, Supervisory Management, Supervision, Manage Magazine, and the *Advanced Management Journal.* He serves on the editorial advisory board of *Personnel Journal* and the contributing editors board of *Personnel.*

Phillips is an active member of several professional and technical organizations including the American Society for Training and Development, the American Society for Personnel Administration, and the Academy of Management. In addition, he has served on the board of directors of the National Management Association.

Improving Supervisors' Effectiveness

How Organizations Can
Raise the Performance of
Their First-Level Managers

1

Rethinking the
Supervisor's Role:

Responding to Today's Challenges

Definitions

To enhance the readability of this work and to improve the reader's understanding of its concepts, consistent terminology will be used. Thus, the definition of some basic terms is necessary here before we begin to examine the problems, frustrations, and concerns facing supervisors and to explore what must be done to improve their work and the payoffs to be derived from these efforts.

To begin with the most general term, *organization* refers to an employing entity in which various groups and levels of employees perform tasks to meet goals or objectives. (See Figure 1 for an outline of a typical organizational structure.) Organizations include businesses, industries, governments (federal, state, and local), hospitals, nonprofit institutions, associations, and virtually all other organized bodies of employees. Organizations have missions, goals, and monetary resources, provide services or products, and employ workers.

The terms *supervisor* or *supervision* refer to the first level of management in an organization. This group supervises nonmanagement employees. Supervisors are judged on how well they can motivate others to work effectively. Although definitions of supervision can vary, there seem to be at least four common characteristics of first-level supervisors:

- They have several employees working directly for them.
- They accomplish the work of the organization through their employees instead of performing the work themselves.
- They strive to meet the performance goals set for their work unit by higher management.
- Their activities are narrowly focused when compared to those of higher-level managers in the organization.

The job titles used for this first level of management vary considerably among organizations. Typical job titles of first-level supervisors include:

Supervisor	Captain	Superintendent
Foreman	Coordinator	Assistant superin-
Manager	Group leader	tendent
Department head	Section leader	Head clerk
District director	Lead engineer	Head teller
Assistant manager	Head nurse	Head waitress/
Assistant director	Section chief	waiter
Project leader	Unit chief	Chief technician
Branch manager	Crew chief	Chief dietician
Office manager		

This list shows the variety of titles used in several diverse organizations. One conclusion to be drawn is that there is no consistency as to which title clearly represents the job of first-level supervision. Indeed, the terms *supervisor* and *foreman* seem to be common, while the words *head, lead,* and *chief* are typical descriptive parts of the title. It is important to understand that in some organizations these job titles represent different levels of management. For example, consider the title *superintendent.* A building maintenance superintendent in a hospital is usually a first-level supervisor responsible for perhaps one or two employees. Again, in the crushed stone industry, the work unit typically consists of about fifteen to twenty employees who work in a rock quarry. The superintendent usually represents the first level of management. Contrast these examples with the steel industry, where the superintendent may manage a complete steel-making facility employing several thousand workers. Regardless of the title, every organization has a first level of management, and for the remainder of this book, the words *supervisor* or *supervisory* will be used to refer to this level of management.

The *work unit* includes the facility, employees, and work process under the control of the supervisor. It is the lowest boss/subordinate team in the organization. The supervisor and employees work together to produce a product or provide a service for the organization. The work unit may be a section, an area, a small plant, a small division, a department, a store, or a functional part of the organization.

Above supervisors are *middle managers* or the *middle-management* group, which may involve more than one level. Middle managers are sandwiched between the supervisors reporting to them and the executives above them. They have limited policy-making ability and are more involved in the traditional management functions of planning, organizing, directing, and controlling. They set departmental goals and quite often manage a function or part of a function in the organization, such as marketing, production, engineering, personnel, or accounting. While the supervisor can expect to work with or near the unit being supervised, the middle manager may be physically removed from the supervisors. Throughout this book the words *manager* or *middle manager* will be used to denote the immediate superior of the supervisors in the organization.

At the top of the organization is the *executive management* group. The *executives* include the top- or senior-level managers in the organization. Typical job titles are those of vice-president, division manager, executive vice-president, executive director, administrator, as well as president and chairman. Executives have middle managers reporting to them and typically have one or more functions of the organization under their con-

Figure 1. Typical Organizational Structure.

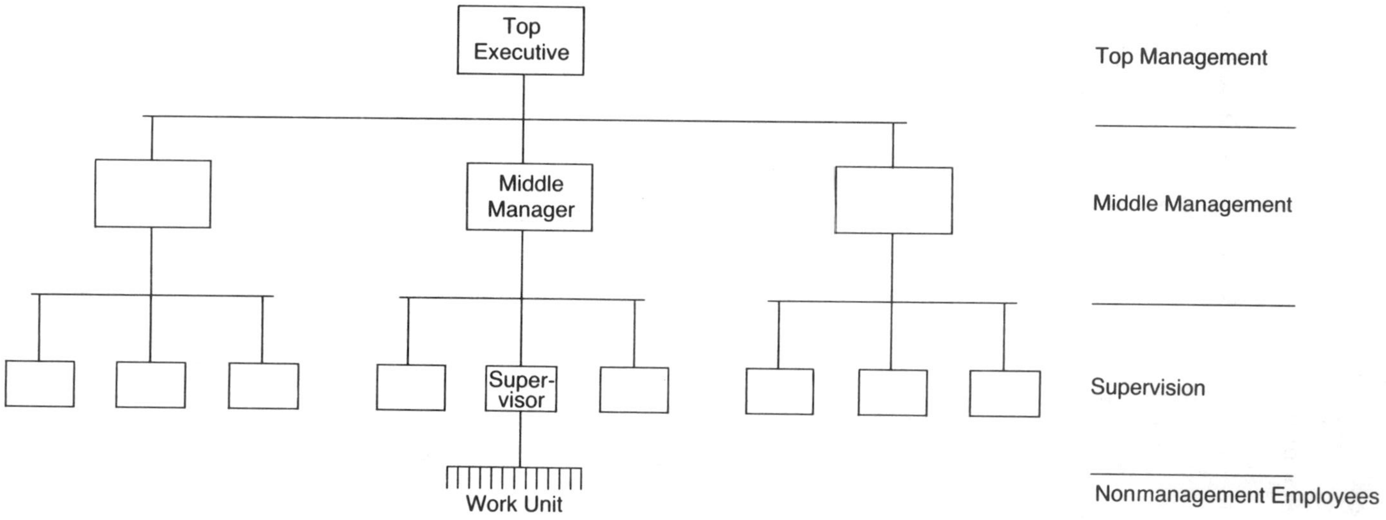

Top Management

Middle Management

Supervision

Nonmanagement Employees

Top Executive

Middle Manager

Super-visor

Work Unit

trol. This is the policy-making group that sets the goals and determines the mission of the organization. They make the major decisions in the organization and are held accountable for the overall results. In practice the executive management group may include more than one level, and for very large organizations it may represent three or four levels. Throughout this book the terms *top management* or *executive management* will be used to refer to this senior-level management group at the top of the organization. The term *upper management* will refer to both the middle and top management groups.

Together these three groups of management—executives, middle managers, and supervisors—form the entire management of the organization. The remaining employees are the *nonmanagement* group and represent the hourly workers, clerical employees, or professional salaried employees. They form the bulk of the work force and are responsible for performing a clearly defined job, the output from which can be easily observed and measured. They do not supervise others but are responsible for their own performance. They are sometimes called employees, workers, or subordinates. The term *employees* will be used to refer to this group.

The Dilemma of Today's Supervisor

Few jobs in organizations have changed as much as that of the supervisor. Supervisors have become critical to the organization's success, yet their status does not always reflect their importance.

Evolution of the Supervisor's Job. In the early part of this century, the supervisor's or foreman's job was relatively simple. With almost no interference, the foreman gave orders to employees who were performing simple tasks. No one disputed or questioned those orders. The person selected for the job was tough, mean, loud, and usually big; in fact, he was often chosen on the basis of size, strength, and ability to physically handle the work crew. He (yes he, there were no female supervisors in those days) knew what had to be done and how to get it done. By any measure, he was boss.

Near the middle of the century the role of the supervisor gradually began to change. Technological and social changes added unprecedented demands to his job. Unions, personnel departments, support departments, government regulations, employment laws, and changes in worker attitudes all presented new challenges for supervision. The authority of supervisors gradually eroded, while their status deteriorated. Yet management had come to expect more and more from supervisors. Additional duties and responsibilities were added, all to be carried out within the increased constraints. Changes in technology and automation brought additional dimensions, and gradually the supervisor's job evolved into a very complex one, now requiring skills and abilities never before demanded.

Unique Role of Supervisors. The functions of supervision and the skills required of a supervisor are similar to those found in other levels of the management hierarchy. However, the role of the supervisor is also unique, as is illustrated in Figure 2, since it is the level in the organization between upper management and the employees. Top management requires supervisors to carry out the plans and goals of the organization. They are looking for performance without problems. Employees, who must do the work, look to supervisors for leadership, direction, and rewards. In their eyes, supervisors are management. Supervisors thus provide a vital link in the upward and downward flow of information and very little can be accomplished in the organization without them. Since they typically supervise several employees, they must possess good interpersonal skills. In this unique role the supervisor is faced with pressures and problems different from those present in other levels of management.

Many studies have been conducted that detail the job requirements and the skills needed for successful supervision. These skills usually fall into three major categories: technical, administrative, and interpersonal. Technical skills include a grasp of the technology or processes of the work unit, the content of the jobs of the employees, and technical job standards related to the output of the unit. Administrative skills include

Figure 2. Supervisors: Caught in the Middle.

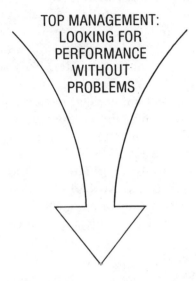

TOP MANAGEMENT:
LOOKING FOR
PERFORMANCE
WITHOUT
PROBLEMS

SUPERVISORS

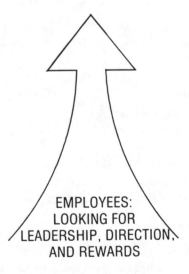

EMPLOYEES:
LOOKING FOR
LEADERSHIP, DIRECTION,
AND REWARDS

an ability to understand and process the information and paper work necessary for the unit to run smoothly and efficiently. Interpersonal skills, which some believe to be the most important of all, include the supervisor's ability to interact with employees, peers, staff groups, and upper management. Most supervisors possess the necessary technical skills, but administrative and interpersonal skills are another matter. This situation is confirmed by the employees who work for supervisors. In a significant study of government employees, most employees indicated that supervisors were technically competent, but gave them less satisfactory marks for administrative skills and even lower ones for interpersonal skills (Siegel, 1980).

One extensive study conducted by the American Telephone and Telegraph Company (AT&T) identified job duties for first-level supervisors (Macdonald, 1982). The duties, listed according to the percentage of time spent on each, were

- controlling the work
- solving problems
- planning the work
- providing informal oral communication
- providing performance feedback
- coaching employees
- providing written communication and documentation
- creating and maintaining a motivated atmosphere
- managing time
- attending and conducting meetings
- self-development
- career counseling employees
- representing the company

Duties will vary somewhat with the organization, but there will be a few duties common to all supervisory jobs. As is evident from this list, most duties involve interactions with employees.

Status of Supervisors. Surveys and research studies also have revealed the dilemmas faced by today's supervisors and have identified problem areas where supervisors need assistance and support to improve their status. The most significant of these studies was conducted by Bittel and Ramsey (1982). Their National Survey of Supervisory Management Practices gathered responses from over 8,000 supervisors in 564 different organizational units in thirty-seven states. (The survey will be referred to often in this book since it provides considerable insight into the problems faced by supervisors.) Although the survey revealed some positive trends, it confirmed many of the problems of supervisors that had been identified in earlier studies:

- Only 40 percent of the supervisors felt that they were a real part of company management.
- Supervisors were dissatisfied with their pay scales; 61 percent said their pay was not quite enough or that it was far too little.
- Almost 50 percent of the supervisors who moved from a nonmanagement job to supervision said their crossover experience was difficult or very difficult.
- Twenty-one percent of the supervisors would go back to their old jobs if they could do so without reduction in pay or loss of face.
- Only about one in five supervisors was content to stay in the same job or at the same level while nearly three fourths of them (71 percent) had their sights on either their boss's job or some other high-level management job.
- Seventy-five percent said that paper work was either very heavy or moderately heavy on their jobs.
- Nearly two thirds (64 percent) of all supervisors said they felt a great deal of pressure to cut costs and hold expenses in line.

Other disturbing conclusions were:

- Supervisor selection systems were poorly planned and implemented.
- Pay differences between hourly employees and supervisors were narrow.
- Hourly jobs were viewed as more secure while supervisory work was seen as full of frustrations.

- Supervisors were nervous about their ability to handle the perplexities of day-to-day interpersonal relationships.

Finding out what supervisors want from their jobs is another source of insight into supervisory problems. One study, involving 300 first- and second-level supervisors over a three-year period, analyzed this issue (Abboud and Richardson, 1978). In this study the top eight items that first-level supervisors wanted from their job, listed in order of importance, were (1) interesting work, (2) salary, (3) chance for promotion, (4) appreciation for work done, (5) good working conditions, (6) job security, (7) loyalty of supervisor (middle manager), and (8) filling in on things. Many of these needs of supervisors have been ignored by management, but they provide a framework for developing, as Abboud and Richardson suggest, "a meaningful plan of action for using supervisory talents in any organization" (p. 334).

The impact of the supervisor's status on his immediate family is another area of concern. One study (Schoenfeldt, 1980), conducted with 208 wives whose husbands were foremen in manufacturing and chemical-processing plants, gave some insights into this problem. The following is a list of six work-related problem areas commonly associated with the foreman's job that appear to be of high concern to wives:

- Sixty-nine percent of the wives in this study felt that shift work was disruptive to normal family life.
- Forty-two percent of the wives felt that the individuals who worked for their husbands had more job security than their husbands.
- Thirty-six percent of the wives definitely felt their husbands had to satisfy too many people in carrying out the day-to-day activities of their jobs.
- Twenty-eight percent of the wives felt that management did a poor job of solving day-to-day problems and that consequently the problems recurred.
- Twenty-five percent of the wives felt their husbands' pay was not related (to any great extent) to how much they contributed to the overall success of the company.

- Twenty-five percent of the wives felt management did little to find out from their husbands how they thought things might be done better on the job.

The questionnaire was also distributed to the 208 foremen. They, like their wives, reported that shift work, job security, unity of command, problem solving, monetary compensation, and participative management were problem areas of high concern. Of those responding, 32 percent felt management did not treat them as important members of the management team. Twenty-five percent felt management did not provide them with enough information to do their jobs efficiently, and the same number believed the structure of the organization did little to encourage foremen to do their best work. Thirty-one percent said they definitely did not want their children to earn their living in positions similar to theirs.

In addition to these studies, the literature is laced with statements about the dilemma of supervisors. For example, Sasser and Leonard (1980, p. 113) have provided this synopsis of the supervisor's situation: "Being a first-level supervisor is one of the most difficult, demanding, and challenging jobs in any organization. Buried in an organizational web, this person must be adroit at administering a unit and at perceiving which, among all the daily tasks delegated downward, are the most important to accomplish. Through such administrative competence, he or she must be able to link the unit's accomplishments to the functioning of other organizational subunits." Cook (1981, p. 74) has summarized the problems of the supervisor this way: "Neither manager nor worker, [the foreman] takes all the heat while receiving none of the light. The manner in which many employees treat their foremen makes one wonder who would want the job. And for all the complaints about foremen that one hears from top management very little is being done to upgrade the position, to even its former vitality." Drucker (1983, p. 32) has provided this comment: "In most of American business, the supervisor is very much what he or she was many years ago—a boss, though little is left of the authority and responsibility a boss had a few years ago before unions and powerful staffs and personnel functions."

The above-mentioned studies and articles represent only a small sampling of the information available about the current status and dilemma of supervisors. To add to this convincing data many accounts of a typical day of a supervisor have been published. One such account is presented in Appendix A. But what does all this mean? It means that the status of supervisors in today's work force is in serious jeopardy. The reasons for this situation are summarized next.

Causes of Problems

My discussion of the major causes of the problems of supervisors is primarily based on the significant studies and research available on the supervisor's job. In addition, it is supplemented by my experience with over 5,000 supervisors in a variety of settings and organizations.

Improper Selection Methods. Sometimes it appears that the problem of inadequate and frustrated supervision could be avoided completely if more emphasis were placed on getting a good match between the candidates and the skills and abilities needed for the job. Selections are usually made on the basis of technical competence, prior experience, and attitude. These are all important factors, but they should not be the complete basis for selection. Studies from the University of Pennsylvania (Bittel and Ramsey, 1983) show that many organizations are likely to promote the wrong individuals to supervisory ranks. There appears to be a lack of objective criteria for selecting candidates for supervisory roles. Unfortunately, family ties, considerations of friendship, and seniority are strong factors in the selection process. Selecting the best employee in a work unit to be supervisor is also a common and dangerous practice. The skills required to be an effective supervisor are vastly different from those required of a top-notch employee. The attraction of more money, prestige, and status often entices good employees to accept supervisory jobs; because many are ill equipped for the job, however, they perform marginally or poorly. Some quit, some are terminated, while others stay on the job to save face with their friends or fellow employees. The net result is a drain on the performance of the organization. Solutions to selection problems are presented in Chapter Two.

Inadequate Training and Education Programs. Another concern is the training and education provided to supervisors. One area often neglected is the training received soon after promotion. A bank would be reluctant to put a new teller on the job without prior training and education. No manufacturing company would put a machine operator on the job without thorough preparation in how to operate the equipment. Yet, many organizations feel comfortable asking an employee to switch roles—usually over the weekend, leaving the job on Friday as an operator and showing up on Monday morning in the new role of supervisor—without any prior training. The consequences can be disastrous. Without initial training, supervisors can lose confidence in their ability and lose respect for the organization.

Too often organizations leave the growth of supervisors to chance, hoping they will eventually acquire the skills to be effective. Supervisors must grow to meet the challenges of the job. They need opportunities to learn new skills and generate profitable ideas. This does not mean that every organization must have an array of training and education programs for supervisors, although many of them do. To be effective, an approach does not have to include formal, classroom-type efforts. It may involve several different types of activities, including on-the-job coaching, special projects, and job rotations. Additional information on approaches to supervisory training and education is presented in Chapter Three.

Ineffective Performance System. Managers had been setting goals and objectives even before Peter Drucker advocated them in the early fifties (Drucker, 1954). However, supervisors are probably the last management group to have had management by objectives (MBO) implemented at their level. The goals developed for supervisors appear to have several weaknesses:

• They lack specificity in many cases.

- They are not tailored to the supervisor's individual needs.
- They are unrealistic, often impossible to accomplish by the supervisor.
- They are frequently outside the supervisor's scope of responsibilities.
- There is little or no input from supervisors in developing these goals.

Most of the goals focus on production targets, quality ratings, and efficiency measurements as a basis for supervisory performance. A more effective approach is to develop a complete system of performance measurements that not only involves the critical responsibilities of production, quality, and efficiency but also such other factors as customer service, administrative duties, employee relations, and communications. With this approach, measurable performance standards can be established for all key areas of responsibilities, and the supervisor's performance can be evaluated on objective criteria. Chapter Four outlines a comprehensive performance system involving job descriptions, performance standards, and performance appraisal.

Uncompetitive and Unrewarding Compensation. The compensation of supervisors is another area of concern. Here, it is a question not only of developing a system that is competitive with other organizations but of maintaining internal equity and rewarding performance. Compensation data are readily available with which organizations can compare their supervisors' salaries and keep them competitive. However, problems can surface when pay policies produce internal inequities. Understandably, supervisors become irritated when their salaries are significantly less than those of their staff counterparts, particularly when supervisors have backgrounds similar to those of the staff employees. Also, in basic industries, where wages have been increased significantly through aggressive collective bargaining efforts, it is not unusual to find employees who are earning as much as their supervisors. When the employees work overtime, the problem is compounded since supervisors usually work the same hours without overtime pay.

Another serious problem is the relationship of rewards to

performance. Although most organizations regard their merit pay programs as pay for performance, in reality they are only modified cost-of-living programs. Supervisors have different goals and objectives and should be rewarded for their individual contributions. Finally, organizations have been too secretive with their compensation programs. Supervisors need to understand the compensation package and how their salaries are administered. Otherwise, an organization's pay policies will be met with criticism and skepticism. This type of communication puts the salary system out in the open and removes many of the concerns and fears of supervisors. Solutions to supervisory compensation problems are presented in Chapter Five.

Inadequate Communication. It is often said that lack of communication is the root of all our problems. Communication is the nervous system of any organization. A communication breakdown somewhere in the chain can be blamed for many of the problems in organizations. A supervisor's effectiveness is impaired when the necessary information on which to base decisions is not available. Management must depend on the supervisor to communicate to it the attitudes, feelings, and problems of the work unit. And managers must also rely on the supervisor to communicate the plans and goals of the organization to its employees. Yet, many organizations still leave their supervisors in the dark. Quite often, through rumor mills and the grapevine, employees learn about important items before the supervisors do. And, in many organizations, supervisors are unprepared to communicate effectively with their employees.

There has been much improvement in organizational communication in recent years. An awareness of the need to communicate is the first step to making improvements. Progressive organizations have recognized the importance of supervisors in the communication process and have developed special media to make supervisors an integral part of that process. Chapter Six outlines some of the approaches that can improve supervisory communication.

Lack of Decision-Making Authority and Ability. Too often supervisors have had their authority stripped away by policies, procedures, labor contracts, government regulations, and employment laws. Unions and personnel departments have probably done more harm to the effectiveness of supervisors than of any other group. Supervisory rights have slowly been negotiated away with every renewal of collective bargaining agreements, often without input from supervisors. Company policies and procedures have slowly inhibited the supervisor's ability to function effectively and efficiently. Personnel policies hamper the supervisor's ability to hire, discharge, transfer, or promote employees. In more than one organization, supervisors are reluctant to make any personnel moves unless they first consult a representative of the human resources department of that organization.

One cause of the serious erosion of the supervisor's authority lies in the additional layers of management that have been placed between the supervisor and top management. Managers with responsibility for systems, quality control, product lines, methods engineering, and production control all have steadily chipped away at the supervisor's authority. The supervisor has become simply the implementer of the policies developed by these new experts. This is not to imply that a supervisor should be allowed to ignore policies, procedures, and other controls. However, such controls should be kept to a minimum and provide enough flexibility for the supervisor to manage the work unit efficiently.

In addition, supervisors are rarely provided training and coaching on how to make effective decisions. A formal process for making decisions does not exist in most organizations. Hence, successful approaches to increasing decision-making authority and ability are presented in Chapter Seven.

Insufficient Participation in Decisions. Employees at every level want to be a part of the decisions that affect their jobs. Supervisors are no different. Nevertheless, middle and upper management routinely make decisions for supervisors without their active input and involvement. They change work methods, purchase equipment, adjust standards, and make personnel decisions without consulting their supervisors. In addition, supervisors are not encouraged, and in some cases not allowed, to seek input from employees on decisions affecting the work unit.

The concept of participative management has been around for some time. As it relates to the supervisor, this practice involves getting input, ideas, and suggestions from employees on major decisions affecting their jobs or their departments. Letting supervisors participate in this process and encouraging them to secure participation from their employees help stimulate creativity and initiative while making both groups feel more a part of the organization. Supervisors and their employees are more committed to the outcome of decisions when they are part of the process leading to that decision. For these reasons alone, organizations should develop systems and procedures that will require supervisory input in key decisions. However, many have been slow to change from the autocratic, dictatorial style of management that was dominant in the 1940s and 1950s to a more democratic, participative style. Chapter Eight explores participative management and how it can be successfully implemented in an organization.

Ineffective Organizational Support and Recognition. Another important area of concern is lack of organizational support and recognition for supervisors. This includes job security, staff support, organizational recognition, and identification with the management group. An employee moving into a supervisory job is stepping out of a traditional, comfortable, low-risk situation into a high-risk, demanding job. The supervisor's performance is evaluated almost daily, and it may appear that his or her job is always on the line. Traditionally, employees in the work unit are protected by their seniority and union contracts. They cannot be fired at the whim of their bosses and are usually guaranteed fair and equitable treatment during periods of layoffs or when their performance is not completely satisfactory. Moving into the supervisory ranks puts them into a different ball game. Job security is often uncertain and may depend on how well the supervisor is liked by the manager. This concern for job security is one of the reasons for the growing interest in unions for supervisors. They want the same protection as their employees.

Staff groups have slowly stripped away the supervisor's effectiveness by making excessive demands on him or her and failing to provide genuine, helpful assistance. Supervisors often regard the staff as an adversary group that only gets in the way of the primary mission of the organization. Supervisors perceive themselves as victims of staff overload and as being caught in the middle of a complex arrangement of corporate staff departments.

Moreover, positive recognition and reinforcement of supervisors from management and the organization are sometimes lacking. Supervisors need to know that their actions have the support not only of their immediate manager but of top management as well. Simple expressions of appreciation can mean a lot to a hard-pressed supervisor, but this happens too infrequently. Also valuable are written records of a supervisor's accomplishments, but few organizations follow this policy.

Another persistent problem affecting organizations is the failure of supervisors to consider themselves as part of the management team. Without proper management alignment, supervisors cannot fulfill their responsibility of being management's representative on the front line. In most organizations supervisors are part of the management team and must be recognized and supported in this role. They must be given the full rights, status, and privileges of management. Specific techniques for improving organizational support and recognition are presented in Chapter Nine.

Rethinking the Supervisory Role

It is obvious, then, that the status and effectiveness of today's supervisors must be improved. The transition from their present status to a more effective, productive one cannot be left to chance. Organizations, and particularly middle and top management of those organizations, must pursue a carefully planned program to bring about the necessary changes, as Chapter Ten explains in detail. In other words, a systems approach is necessary to bring about improvement in the various elements that can lead to increased supervisory effectiveness. It may not be productive to improve certain parts of the job without addressing the other parts. At this point, however, let us review the factors influencing supervisory performance and the new role that will be necessary for supervisors, along with the potential benefits for the organization.

Supervisory Performance Model. At the heart of improving supervisory effectiveness is improving supervisory performance. This is often a complex and confusing issue since there are a number of factors that contribute to supervisory performance. As shown in Figure 3, there are four major influences that determine the total performance of the supervisor.

Figure 3. Supervisory Performance Model.

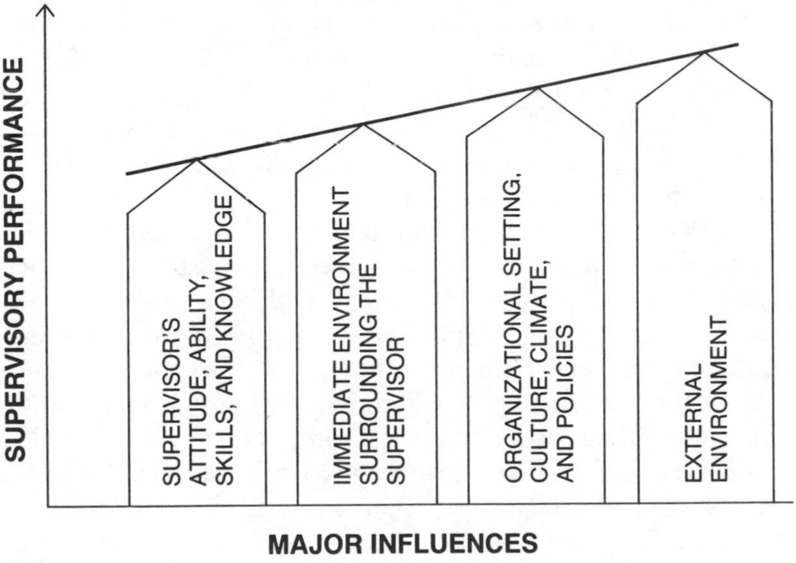

The first influence is one over which the supervisor has a good deal of control. Attitudes may be defined as consistent reactions to certain persons, objects, or concepts. Supervisory attitudes are based on beliefs, perceptions, and values, and they affect performance, satisfaction, and learning. Positive attitudes can strongly motivate a supervisor to apply his or her knowl-

edge, skills, and ability to constructive efforts, while negative
attitudes can have just the opposite effect. Ability refers to the
mental capacity to perform tasks and assignments. It is the
power to perform an act, either physical or mental, whether in-
nate or acquired by education and practice. Skills refer to how
effectively tasks are handled. They are acquired aptitudes. A
skillful supervisor is one who handles situations effectively and
thus reaches the desired outcomes. Skills may be conceptual (as
in problem solving), interpersonal (as in counseling an employee), or motor (as in adjusting equipment). Behavior modeling, skills training, coaching, and behavior modification are all
approaches that can develop and improve supervisory skills.
Knowledge refers to facts, data, logic, principles, and generaliza-
tions related to the job. Specific knowledge of work processes,
technical standards, management principles, administrative procedures, and organizational policies is necessary for success on
the job. Attitudes, skills, knowledge, and ability are all factors
that will affect the individual output of the supervisor. These
factors can be either developed or enhanced through supervisory training and education programs. Also, they form part of
the basis for the selection of supervisors.

The next significant influence is the immediate work
environment that surrounds the supervisor. A supervisor's performance is greatly affected by items such as job structure, performance standards, interpersonal relationships, job freedom,
and immediate management support. The job structure, which
defines the constraints, restrictions, work flows, communication channels, and work rules of a unit, can enhance or inhibit
supervisory performance. Performance standards are an essential
part of supervisory performance. Supervisors must know the
standards for the job they are expected to accomplish, and
these standards should be understood by both the manager and
the supervisor. The interpersonal relationships that can affect
the supervisor's performance most are those involving the employees supervised, the peer group, and middle managers. A
productive, cooperative relationship is necessary to motivate
and develop drive within the employees. Supervisors must work
effectively with other supervisors and staff support groups to

create a smoothly functioning organizational team in which work conflicts and confusion are minimized. And, of course, the relationship with the middle manager is extremely important since the supervisor must win the trust and confidence of the manager to be successful on the job and to advance in the future. The ability and authority to make decisions, as well as the extent of the supervisor's participation in decisions affecting the work unit, are additional factors that affect supervisory performance. Along with freedom must come authority if the supervisor is ultimately to be responsible for results. And, finally, support and feedback from management are significant factors affecting performance. Supervisors must receive positive reinforcement to help them accomplish the work unit's goals and missions.

The third major area of influence is the organizational setting, culture, climate, and policies. These are organization-wide factors and include such items as general policies and procedures, organizational goals, organizational support, organizational commitment, human resources systems, and management styles. Usually, the fewer policies and procedures the greater the potential for performance, since excessive controls and restrictions can stifle productivity. The goals and missions of the organization and the dedication to accomplish them are important factors that contribute to the supervisor's performance. Human resources systems covering items such as selection, training, compensation, and employment security are important to performance. These help to ensure that supervisors are properly selected, trained, compensated, and provided with assurances that they will have employment as long as their performance is satisfactory. Open communications, progressive management styles, and a trusting organizational climate set the proper stage for a productive atmosphere.

The last area of influence on supervisory performance is the external environment. Particularly in recent years, it has become increasingly difficult for supervisors to function because of external influences in three basic areas: government, unions, and the general public. Everyone is aware of the tremendous influence of government regulations on organizations. Fair employment, safety and health, labor relations, and a host of other areas are the target of laws and regulations that affect the decisions supervisors must make about their employees. These factors can have a strong impact on the supervisor's ability to act or react swiftly. The influence of unions is certainly well known, although it is beginning to diminish. Restrictive union contracts can dampen or inhibit the supervisor's ability to control the output of the work unit. Such contracts can also absorb precious supervisory time with grievances, disputes, and arbitrations that may not exist in a nonunion environment. The public is another factor that must be taken into account by most organizations, particularly consumer-oriented organizations that must deal directly with the public. Quite often an organization's actions are shaped by the attitude and perceptions of the public community. Many of the decisions made by supervisors must take into consideration the impact they will have on the public.

This book explores each of these major influences. Virtually every factor that can affect supervisory performance is addressed in the chapters ahead. Practical approaches to improve supervisory performance are present in each chapter.

Redefining the Supervisor's Role. The concepts, ideas, and principles presented in this book reinforce the need for a rethinking of the supervisory role. They move the supervisor from a traditional authority-oriented role to one of a team leader who provides support and encouragement to employees as they work toward accomplishing the goals of the work unit. As depicted in Figure 4, the new posture of the supervisor is one in which he or she coordinates the activities of the work group, providing assistance, encouragement, and support as necessary. This will require the supervisor to assume six distinct roles in the future:

1. *Provide adequate resources.* Employees in the work group need adequate information to accomplish the job, funds to purchase the necessary resources, sufficient tools and supplies to perform the tasks, and a tolerable work environment. A future role of the supervisor is to ensure that employees have the resources necessary to work effectively and to remove any

Figure 4. Comparison of Supervisory Roles.

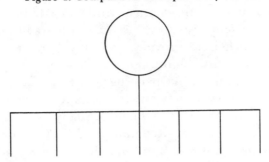

AUTHORITY-ORIENTED SUPERVISION

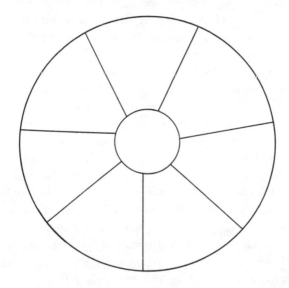

TEAM LEADERSHIP AND RESOURCE SUPERVISION

impediments to success in the work unit. This does not mean that every work unit must have the latest equipment and technology to be successful. However, the organization, through the supervisor, must provide the resources that will keep the work unit productive and competitive with other organizations. As long as employees understand that the organization is supplying them with the best resources that it can afford, they will usually try their hardest to be productive within that framework. This new role of the supervisor contrasts with the traditional role of supervisors, which is to provide employees with minimum resources and very little information. This older approach attempts to get the most by spending the least. Although in the short run this approach may be satisfactory, it has some serious and negative long-range consequences. Many organizations are recognizing that, although providing funds to upgrade the work environment may not add any immediate return, there are intangible improvements such as increased morale and job satisfaction that should ultimately have a positive impact on the growth, stability, and productivity of the organization.

2. *Resolve or mediate differences and conflicts.* Every work unit will develop differences and conflicts because it is made up of individual employees. A future role of the supervisor is to serve as a mediator to resolve these differences and conflicts and to increase the spirit of cooperation and teamwork among employees. This requires the supervisor to isolate the causes of conflicts and try to eliminate them from the work unit. Also, the supervisor must recognize that some conflict will always exist in a work unit where there is a competitive spirit. The traditional method of dealing with the problem of individual differences and conflicts is to eliminate the individuals involved. Although this approach may sometimes work, it may also mean the removal of the most productive employees. Most differences can be resolved, or at least minimized.

3. *Provide frequent performance feedback.* Employees in a work unit need to know how they are doing individually and collectively. A future role of the supervisor is to let employees know on a continuous basis the progress they are making as individuals and as a work unit team. When mistakes are made, employees should learn from them and not necessarily be punished because of them. Performance discussions must be conducted in a positive manner and must focus on the problem, not on the individual. The traditional approach is to discuss performance only when there are problems and save the discussion of good performance for the annual performance appraisal. Few attempts

are made to provide periodic feedback on the success of the work unit.

4. *Give visibility to organizational goals, purposes, and mission.* Employees in the work unit must have a clear understanding of what the organization is trying to accomplish. This improves their understanding of how the work unit fits into the organization, and it also provides a foundation for establishing work unit goals. A future role of the supervisor is to ensure that employees are involved in setting work unit goals and relating them to departmental, divisional, and organizational missions and objectives. Employees will more closely identify themselves with the work unit goals when they have helped in developing them. The traditional approach of supervisors is to provide little information on what the organization wants to accomplish other than make a profit (for profit-oriented organizations). And, traditionally, work unit goals are established with little or no input from employees. For example, the overall objective that is typically established by companies is to make an adequate return on their investment. However, this does not fully define the mission of the organization in terms of markets, product lines, and growth possibilities, as well as other important issues not directly related to profits, such as impact on environment, employment stability, research and development, and product innovation.

5. *Allow employees to learn and grow on the job.* Most employees want to learn more about their organization, their work unit, and their job. A future role of the supervisor is to ensure that employees are allowed to learn as much as they possibly can and to advance their careers in the organization. This requires productive coaching and counseling of employees, along with assistance and support of them. Supervisors must look at job assignments as a means of providing job satisfaction and fulfillment for their employees, as well as an opportunity to learn more about the organization. They must recognize that most employees want to grow and develop in the organization and have aspirations for other jobs. The traditional role of supervision is to teach employees their immediate jobs, with minimum attention to career advancement possibilities. But it is in the

long-term best interest of the organization if supervisors provide maximum learning opportunities to prepare employees for additional assignments even if these are outside the supervisor's work unit.

6. *Give employees freedom to manage their work.* Employees do not respond well to close supervision. They need freedom to perform their work in a productive and effective climate. The days of the dictatorial foreman who harasses employees on a daily basis are over. Also, the tendency to break jobs down into simple, dehumanizing tasks is disappearing. A future role of supervision is to redesign jobs to be more meaningful and fulfilling for employees. Activities such as planning and control can be added to allow employees to manage their own work. Thus, employees can be involved in scheduling, coordinating, and prioritzing their work, and they can be made responsible for their own inspection, record-keeping, and quality control. Supervisors must routinely encourage employees to use their minds and abilities to improve the work flow and their jobs. The traditional role of supervision was to limit activities, in the name of efficiency, to a few repetitive ones so that employees were not required to think.

The "new" future role of the supervisor outlined in the preceding paragraphs is not in fact all that new. It has been advocated by many researchers and organizational change experts. Some fifteen years ago, Myers (1970) advocated a new role for supervisors similar to the one developed here. Unfortunately, few organizations have required, allowed, or even encouraged their supervisors to adopt new roles. Role changing is a very slow process but one that is greatly needed today if organizations are to meet the challenges facing the supervisor. The important point here is that, among the actions necessary to improve the job of supervisor, the role of supervisors should not be overlooked and can be changed only through planned effort. Through selection, training, and communication, along with encouragement, support, and coaching, the organization can gradually move supervisors from their traditional role to the helping and supportive role outlined in this chapter.

Payoff Potential. There is a limit to what top and middle management can do to improve an organization. It is obvious that effective supervisors are necessary to develop a productive work force and to bring about needed improvements. These supervisors motivate employees to contribute their maximum efforts, and they solve problems at the first level of management rather than pushing them up the organization where time is more expensive. Developing an effective supervisor can generate a significant return on the organization's investment.

The profit contribution of an improvement program has been documented in many studies. In one such study—involving a large food-processing facility—a program to improve supervisors was the single most important factor in improving operational performance (Doud and Miller, 1980). Productivity increased, while turnover, absenteeism, and accident rates all decreased markedly. In this one plant alone, during the five years after the improvement was begun, the organization had realized measured savings in administrative costs of $819,000 and calculated benefits of improved operating performance of $3,128,000 for a total of almost $4,000,000. This study involved improvements in the role of supervisors, implementation of performance standards, recognition for participation in the development process, and the enhancement of the responsibility levels of supervisors through increased authority.

On the other side of the coin, an organization must look at the cost of not having effective supervisors. Such an organization will probably suffer from inefficiency, low output, and poor quality. In addition there are intangible consequences of ineffective supervision. One noted labor relations expert cites ineffective supervisors as a major reason for labor strikes (Imberman, 1981).

Measuring the effectiveness of supervisors is necessary to gain an appreciation for the potential return on investment. Although there are several approaches, two methods are most frequently used. One is to consider the assets managed by the supervisor. To a large degree, the supervisor's effectiveness will determine whether or not the assets are used efficiently. The assets managed by supervisors vary greatly. Office supervisors typically have small amounts to manage, while supervisors may have large investments in capital-intensive industries under their care. The investment may include physical assets, inventory, and in some cases accounts receivable. To illustrate, consider a supervisor who manages assets with a value of $1 million in an organization that wants an annual return on those assets of at least 15 percent before taxes. The average supervisor in the organization should achieve the expected return of 15 percent, or $150 thousand unit-level earnings for the operation. An exceptional supervisor with above-average performance might be able to return 20 or 30 percent. In effect, the supervisor could possibly double the unit-level profit margin by producing $300 thousand.

Does a supervisor really have that much control over assets? Most managers will agree that they do. They can achieve this control through a carefully planned program of maximum utilization of assets. They can schedule the production processes efficiently, install preventive maintenance programs to make sure the equipment does not break down unnecessarily, and control costs in all areas. Supervisors can ensure that equipment is cared for properly and scheduled to achieve optimum efficiency.

A second approach to examining the potential for supervisory improvement is to analyze the expenditures controlled by supervisors. This is a typical approach for office supervisors in a labor-intensive production area where the assets may be low but the expenditures are high. In this case, labor costs are significant. To calculate the potential return on investment to improve supervision, annual costs, which are usually the budget for the work unit, are projected. Suppose, for instance, that the annual budget for a supervisor is $400 thousand. Even an office supervisor with only fifteen employees could easily have an annual budget of this much. An average supervisor would be expected to meet that budget; however, an exceptional supervisor might be expected to beat the budget by 10 percent or more. Most of this savings would go straight to the bottom line because it represents a reduction in operating costs compared to what was anticipated. These expenses are usually directly under the control of the supervisor. It is not unreasonable to expect effective supervisors to operate more efficiently—in a more cost-conscious manner—and exceed the expectations of a planned budget.

While there might be other approaches to evaluating the opportunity for return on investment in supervisory improvement, these two appear to be realistic and readily accepted by management. In other situations, however, the number of employees supervised, the technical complexity of the work, the potential for problems or catastrophes, the sensitivity of the work to customers or the community are additional areas in which the potential improvement of supervisors could be measured. However, they are more subjective, and, consequently, in these instances it is more difficult to convince management that a significant, measurable return has been realized.

Summary

This initial chapter outlined many of the problems and opportunities facing supervisors and introduced the major topics in this book. From all the evidence at hand, the supervisor's job has changed dramatically in recent years to the point where it has become a very difficult, challenging, and frustrating assignment. Many factors have caused the current problems, and each was briefly discussed. The solutions to these problems are contained in the remaining chapters of this book. Making improvements that will lead to the increased effectiveness of supervisors will call for a rethinking of the supervisor's role. An important part of this process, as described in this chapter, is to isolate those factors that influence supervisory performance and to define the new role desired for the supervisor. Finally, the potential for payoff was highlighted: It has become convincingly clear that organizations stand to gain much from an investment in the improvement of supervisors.

2

Selection:

How to Find the Right People

The task of selecting new supervisors is a challenging and difficult one for any organization. Yet, too often this task is taken lightly by middle and top management. Selections are frequently made on the basis of who is the best performer in a group, many times without the use of objective criteria. Unfortunately, the best performer in a unit does not always make the best supervisor. The result can be a frustrated supervisor who is ineffective and possibly damaging to the organization.

Many of the problems of ineffective supervision can be traced to poor selection (Bittel and Ramsey, 1982). Training programs cannot overcome all the limitations supervisors bring to the job. Training can compensate for some deficiencies, but a few employees will never be effective as supervisors, no matter how much training they receive. Also, no amount of leadership skill at the middle-management level can make a real "winner" out of a "loser." At best it can bring slightly below-average employees up to satisfactory levels. The first step in maintaining a productive organization is selecting top quality individuals for supervisors.

There are four distinct areas where the quality of supervision has a visible impact on the organization.

First, improperly selected supervisors can increase costs,

reduce productivity (or not increase productivity to acceptable levels), increase scrap and waste, and lower the overall efficiency of the organization. This loss of efficiency will place a direct financial burden on the organization by lowering its profitability and stunting its potential growth.

Second, ineffective supervisors are a liability to the organization. Their actions (or inaction) can result in major problems or possibly even a catastrophe for the organization. For example, ineffective and arbitrary supervision is one of the major causes for employee strikes. Many discrimination suits are tied in some way to comments or actions by supervisors in regard to employee promotions, transfers, and hiring. Recently there have been a growing number of employee lawsuits against supervisors and their organizations as a result of accidents caused by unsafe situations not corrected by supervisors. Any of these actions can be devastating to an organization.

Third, supervisors form a very important source of middle and upper managers for an organization. An organization with effective supervisors will have a steady flow of candidates to assume more responsibility. Organizations with ineffective supervisors will have to bypass this source and go directly to the outside to get qualified individuals for middle and top management. This can be demoralizing to the remaining supervisors and jeopardize the continuity of the organization. Another consideration is the costs and disruption due to the turnover of supervisors who must leave their jobs because they cannot handle them. The cost of selecting and training new supervisors is also very high.

Fourth, probably no group affects employee morale more than supervisors. An employee's image of the organization is largely shaped by the actions and attitude of the boss, and for the great majority of the work force, this image maker is the first-level supervisor. To the employees, supervisors are management, and how they conduct themselves is a reflection of management within that organization. Whether or not the employee will have a sense of commitment to the organization will depend on the commitment the supervisor has demonstrated to the employee.

Proper selection of a supervisor is as important to the individual selected as to the organization. An organization can create a serious problem for an individual improperly placed in the job of supervisor. There are three distinct areas of concern—from the individual's viewpoint—if the organization has made an improper selection.

First, finding oneself in the wrong job is a frustrating experience. An ineffective, improperly placed supervisor will not be able to accomplish the objectives and goals of the organization and meet the standards required for the job. Also, an ineffective supervisor will be unable to spark a cooperative spirit among the employees. There will be resentment, conflict, and dissension in the work group. This can be very demoralizing, and the additional stress could possibly cause health problems for the supervisor.

Second, an improperly placed supervisor often resigns or is terminated. Some supervisors, in a fit of frustration, see the handwriting on the wall and leave the organization to assume another job, with the hope of securing one where they will be more effective. Others, in an organization that may not be so tolerant, find themselves being dismissed from their jobs. This can be a devastating setback for individuals and their families, but one that could be avoided in many cases if supervisors were properly selected for their jobs and given the necessary tools to be effective.

Third, in some organizations, improperly placed supervisors are demoted to their previous jobs or transferred to lower-level jobs where they do not have to supervise people. This failure can be a painful experience and cause individuals to lose complete confidence in their abilities. Typically, they lose the respect of other employees and will probably find the way barred to any future career advancement in the organization.

From the viewpoint of both the organization and the individual, then, it is easy to see the tremendous importance of having a good process for selecting supervisors. Although a proper selection will not guarantee success on the job, it is a very important first step in the process, one that must be taken with care and caution. This chapter will explore the key issues, factors, and components of selection systems. It will cover current practices and present what is needed if organizations are to have more objective criteria on which to base selection decisions.

Legal Considerations in Supervisory Selection

Before discussing the key issues of supervisory selection, however, let us briefly review some legal considerations. Employee selection has come under close scrutiny by the federal government, as well as by state and local governments, in recent years. Laws have been enacted to prevent employment discrimination and provide fair employment opportunity for all residents. The groups protected by various laws include, as a minimum, minorities (blacks, Spanish-surnamed Americans, Asian-Americans, American Indians), women, individuals over forty, and disabled individuals. Strengthened by court decisions and presidential orders, these laws have had a tremendous impact on organizations. Although they affect many basic terms and conditions of employment, much of their impact has been on the selection procedures used in organizations. Northrup and others (1978) have even argued that the recent trends toward more objective supervisory selection procedures are a result of governmental pressure rather than of a desire on the part of organizations to have better selection systems.

It is still true that in some organizations prejudice prevents some candidates from being given a fair and equal opportunity for promotion. For example, managers may prefer to choose Caucasian men over women or minority group members. Their prejudiced feelings may be the result of years of acculturation and may be very difficult to change. It is not an easy task to ask these managers to hire people whom they have always believed to be inferior in intellect and ability. Usually these managers have had very limited experience working closely with women or minorities and in some cases may not have prejudices themselves but may think that the employees in their work units or fellow supervisors are prejudiced. They, therefore, prefer not to create a difficult situation by bringing a woman or a member of a minority group into the unit. Prejudice in supervisory selection appears to be diminishing, but it still exists. And for the majority of managers who make supervisory selection decisions, special training is needed to remove their prejudices and to make them capable of fair and equitable decisions.

Discriminatory Practices. It is the result of a selection procedure, not the intent, that determines whether discrimination exists. Courts usually consider supervisory selection procedures discriminatory when they produce an adverse impact on protected groups such as minorities and women. An exception is allowed only when an organization can show that it is a business necessity to continue with the discriminatory selection procedure. In this case, the selection procedure must be related to job requirements and usually must be validated. Business necessity has been defined very narrowly by the courts; they have required overriding evidence that a discriminatory practice is essential to safe and efficient operation of the business and/or that there will be an extreme, adverse financial impact without the practice.

The courts and agencies have frowned on rigid hiring standards such as minimum education or physical requirements. The requirement of a high school education has been found unlawful in several cases where such a requirement resulted in an adverse impact on protected groups and the employer did not show that it was sufficiently related to job performance. Policies that automatically exclude candidates because of police or arrest records, or even convictions, have been ruled illegal because of their adverse impact on minority employment. Where it has been shown that such a policy is justified on the basis of business necessity, however, the policy has usually been upheld. Even promotions from within can result in employment discrimination. In these cases courts have noted that the organizations had few, if any, minority candidates in entry levels and decided that affirmative action was required to break the chain of discrimination.

Employee tests for promotion have come under fire by the Equal Employment Opportunity Commission (EEOC) and other enforcement agencies. Basically, the selection guidelines from the EEOC require that any tests used for employment decisions be related to the job sought by the applicant or the employee. Because of the difficulty in validating tests and showing their job relatedness, however, many organizations have abandoned testing procedures.

Court-Ordered Remedies. The extent to which the government dictates an organization's procedures varies widely. In some cases where organizations have been found guilty of discrimination, remedies have taken the form of imposing hiring goals or quotas for certain job classifications in which the class in question is underrepresented. Supervisory positions are common targets for such quotas. In addition, the courts have awarded expensive assessments for back pay and legal costs. The type of court action that sets forth the most specific goals and the most specific procedures for achieving those goals is the consent decree, which is an agreement between an organization and the EEOC or other government agency. The consent decree is filed in federal court. Conciliation agreements between organizations and government agencies, which are not enforceable through the courts, also frequently call for hiring goals for certain job classifications. They also outline the selection procedures an organization promises to follow. Going beyond the principle of equal opportunity, laws and court rulings have also established affirmative action plans as a means of correcting the effects of past discrimination. These affirmative action plans, which are required of a government contractor, may pinpoint areas of underutilization of minorities and suggest recruiting programs or selection methods aimed at improving the situation.

Making a System Legally Defensible. For an organization whose promotion policies have not been investigated by the fair employment agencies, the best approach is usually to minimize the extent to which its overall selection process results in adverse impacts on protected classes. If there is an adverse impact, the organization must make sure that its selection techniques are job related.

The Uniform Guidelines on Employee Selection Procedures, issued in 1978 by the EEOC, have been the subject of much disagreement and litigation. While some specifics of the selection process have yet to be established as far as the law is concerned, there are several basic issues that have been resolved and do provide a framework for supervisory selection within the law. It is clear that any employer subject to federal equal employment opportunity laws must:

1. Design the selection system so that all components of the system measure characteristics and skills actually needed for successful performance of the supervisor's job. Only entry-level characteristics and skills can be required, since some skills can be enhanced through supervisory training.
2. Ensure that all applicants or candidates for supervisory jobs are handled consistently in each step in the selection process. An applicant need not be taken through all steps if sufficient grounds for rejection are discovered at an early stage.
3. Determine whether the overall selection process results in an adverse impact on the selection of any group protected under the law. Where there is an adverse impact, the employer must find out what specific steps or techniques used in the selection process are contributing to it.
4. Prove that any selection technique resulting in an adverse impact is job related and thus complies with the requirement of business necessity.

The validation of selection systems is an important issue with organizations, although in practice much progress is still needed. In one study (American Society for Personnel Administration, 1983), less than one out of five firms (16 percent) had validated any of their selection procedures in accordance with the federal guidelines. Also, according to the study, nonbusiness establishments and large organizations were more likely to have conducted validation studies of their selection techniques than were businesses and small organizations in general.

Sources for New Supervisors

An important factor to consider in the overall supervisory selection system is the source for new supervisors. This is important because the source, in many cases, will determine the quality and quantity of candidates available. Organizations typically develop promotion policies around one or more supervisory sources: promotion from within the work unit, promotion from other parts of the organization, promotion from formal, full-time management trainee programs, and outside recruiting. The advantages and disadvantages of each source will be described in this section.

Candidates Within the Work Unit. Probably the most important source for new supervisors is the work group itself. The work group has long been advocated as the best and most reliable source of supervisors. Some thirty years ago Drucker (1954, p. 324) voiced a strong opinion about promotion from within: "Supervisors should be recruited from the rank and file. Denying the rank-and-file worker opportunities for promotion to supervisory jobs undermines his motivation. It is as incompatible with our social beliefs as is the denial of promotional opportunities for supervisors. Such a recruitment policy is also the only way to get good supervisors. There exists no acceptable substitute in the preparation of a supervisor for the actual experience of working as one of the team."

Promotion from within appears to be the most common source of new supervisors. In one study involving the personnel policies of large nonunion companies, promotion from within was found to be a fundamental principle among all the companies studied (Foulkes, 1980). In another study spanning several industries, the primary source of replacements for supervisors was employees who were promoted from the ranks (Northrup and others, 1978). There are some specific advantages to promotion from within:

- It rewards employees who have demonstrated their ability to assume additional responsibility. This can be a highly motivating force that can lead to superior performance by employees and boost their morale.
- It provides a clear path of promotional opportunities from the lowest level of employment to the management level. This means that an employee has a chance to rise to management on the basis of ability, performance, and effort.

- It will usually produce a very knowledgeable, competent supervisor who is familiar with the operation of the work unit and the employees. This valuable experience is difficult and time consuming to develop in someone who has not worked in the area.
- It will, in the long term, develop a group of managers who know the operation because they have been in one or more of the jobs they supervise. Organizations take pride in the fact that a large number of their managers were actually hourly employees at one time. This can be important in a stable business that changes slowly and in which past knowledge and experience are very important.
- It can provide a smooth transition by allowing organizations to move top candidates into assignments where they can learn the supervisor's job. Some organizations create the jobs of leader, assistant foreman, and utility operator, usually at the top of the wage and salary scale, for just this purpose. Employees in these jobs are given partial leadership responsibilities and have an opportunity to apply limited supervisory skills and be evaluated on how well they perform.

Although promotion from within has been popular, it has also been the subject of misuse. Too often, promotions have gone to those at the top of the seniority list, the best skilled craftsmen, or the most popular employees. Although these may be important factors, they are not necessarily related to the skills and abilities required to be a successful supervisor. In addition to these misuses, there are some disadvantages to promotion from within:

- There may not be an adequate supply of individuals with the skills and characterstics needed for the job of supervisor. A completely different set of skills is required to be an effective supervisor from those needed to be a good operator.
- An employee promoted from within may experience difficulty when supervising former fellow employees. There may be built-in resentment from other employees who thought they should have been given the opportunity. Employees

may feel that their supervisor knows little more than they do, and the supervisor's credibility may suffer.

- Promotion from within does not allow the organization to develop new ideas and approaches. Frequently an outside candidate can bring in cost-saving methods, a fresh approach to old problems, or changes needed to spark new life into the work unit. This will rarely happen when the promotion occurs from within the work unit.
- It will usually create a vacancy in the work unit that might be difficult to fill. Often the employee selected for promotion is a key individual with skills critical to the functioning of the group. This may cause a temporary disruption in the work unit.
- A strict promotion-from-within policy will reduce the depth of management, particularly at the higher levels. There may not be enough candidates who can rise from the nonmanagement level to the top management jobs in the organization.

It appears that this practice of promotion from within may become more difficult to implement in the future because of the increasing importance of specialized knowledge obtained in other jobs, the need for more formal education, and the requirements imposed by equal opportunity laws. In any case, an organization that relies on promotion from within as an exclusive source of talent can be guilty of tunnel vision. For promotion from within to remain viable, it will require high entry standards and sound management development programs (Foulkes, 1980).

Candidates in Other Parts of the Organization. A variation on the policy of promotion from within is to allow candidates to be selected from other parts of the organization. These are usually nonmanagement employees who work in areas related to the department with the supervisory vacancy. For instance, an insurance sales representative with supervisory potential is promoted to be supervisor of the customer service function. In another case, an industrial engineer is promoted to be supervisor of a group of warehouse employees. Previously, the engineer designed and developed material-handling systems for the warehouse. In another case, a production scheduler is named supervisor of a production unit. The scheduling experience had given the new supervisor extensive knowledge of the production processes. These are just a few of the types of promotions that can occur when employees from one department are considered for supervisory positions in another.

This approach broadens the scope of promotional opportunities beyond those of an employee's work unit. Theoretically, an employee with supervisory potential can be considered for almost any supervisory vacancy as long as the experience requirements are met and the move is feasible. As with promotion from within, this approach has the advantages of rewarding individuals and producing supervisors who know something about the organization. But there are also some disadvantages. The new supervisor may lack experience with and knowledge of the technology of the work unit. Also, he or she may be at a disadvantage because of unfamiliarity with the department's equipment and the jobs now being supervised. Finally, it may be demoralizing to the employees in the work unit to have a person from another unit promoted to be their supervisor.

Formal Trainee Programs. Another common approach to filling supervisory vacancies is to select participants from formal management trainee programs. These programs take many shapes but are typically full-time education efforts in a structured, on-the-job setting. Some candidates, typically those with college degrees, are recruited for the program from outside the organization. After an extensive six-month, one-year, or even two-year program, they are available for supervisory jobs. The program involves a combination of on-the-job assignments, rotations in different departments, seminars, workshops, self-study, and special projects. Participants are exposed to company operations and gain the skills necessary for the supervisory job. Ideally an organization should recruit candidates who range from high-potential nonmanagement employees to graduate engineers with MBAs, and some should have the potential to assume increased responsibilities in the near future. The selection of candidates for these programs should be as thorough as the selection process for supervisors since the objective of these programs is to supply the organization with new supervisors.

This source for supervisory candidates has several advantages:

- The candidates receive excellent preparation for their new assignments. The program should develop the skills necessary for successful job performance.
- Since candidates from this source may have a variety of backgrounds, it enables the organization to recruit high-potential, fast-track employees who are destined to move to middle and top management jobs in a short time. They can move quickly to supervisory jobs and, as they prove themselves, move on to higher levels of management.
- If a variety of backgrounds is required for these programs, employees see another clear path to supervisory responsibilities. This can be particularly motivating when employees are allowed to apply for the formal program.
- Candidates can voluntarily resign from the program if they decide not to take the job or continue the preparation. This can prevent a potential supervisory failure in the future.

As with the other approaches, this one also has some disadvantages:

- Typically, the participants from these programs lack the direct knowledge of the various jobs they will supervise. There seems to be an inherent value in having worked in one or more of the jobs under the control of a new supervisor. Without this experience, employees may lose respect for, and may eventually come to feel resentment toward, their supervisor.
- This approach is a very expensive way to recruit and develop new supervisors. Typically, the participants are on the payroll for a year or more and are usually less than fully productive during that time. Although they may be involved in special projects and fill-in assignments, their contribution is limited.
- This approach may cause employee resentment, since the

supervisor comes from outside the work unit. Many of the participants in this program will have college degrees, while the majority of the work unit usually tops out at the high school level. There may be some inherent resentment for the fast-track whiz kid.

Outside Candidates. The fourth source of new supervisors is outside candidates. Outside recruiting for supervisory vacancies is a common practice. Organizations usually require supervisory experience in the area where the supervisory vacancy has occurred. This approach has several advantages:

• Outside candidates with excellent work experience, and particularly those from well-respected organizations, can bring in new ideas and approaches that will add to the vitality and productivity of the organization. This approach will enable the organization to pick up the best ideas, techniques, and practices of other organizations.
• Training time is significantly reduced since outside candidates usually have supervisory experience in the field where they will be assigned. After a short transition period to adjust to the organization's policies, procedures, and processes, the new supervisor should be a contributing member of management.
• Outside candidates, with a variety of background experiences and skills, can give the organization more depth from which to choose candidates for middle-management jobs.
• Outside recruiting will allow an organization to obtain specialized experience when it is necessary but is not available within the organization. However, an organization may have to pay dearly for this specialized experience, and as a result those with high salaries may create problems with the salary administration program.
• In some cases an outside candidate may be accepted more easily than an employee promoted from the work group. Although this issue may be debatable, the selection of an outside candidate is one way to circumvent the problem of having an employee supervise former fellow employees.

But this approach is not without its disadvantages:

- Overall, it can be demoralizing for the lower-level employees in the organization. They may see little opportunity for advancement if most of the supervisory positions are filled from the outside. It will usually result in frustrations and the loss of high-potential employees.
- Outside candidates may not be familiar with the tasks and individuals of the work unit. It will take some time before this experience is gained, and this may hamper initial productivity.
- An organization will frequently have to pay more for highly qualified, experienced supervisors than it would have to pay for internal, entry-level supervisors without previous experience. Going outside the organization has a tendency to raise the average salary of supervisors, resulting in greater than desired average salaries for the organization.

Which Source Is Best? Every potential source of new supervisors has its advantages and disadvantages, which will vary considerably with the organization's requirements for the supervisory job and the ability and educational level of nonmanagement employees. A progressive organization will exercise flexibility and not exclude any particular source. Certainly, if they meet the qualifications, preference should be given to current employees. Otherwise the organization is misusing its human resources and doing an injustice to its employees. However, there may be times when qualified, capable candidates are not available within the work group. Then the organization must look for candidates either internally, through formal trainee programs, or through outside recruiting. A healthy, growth-oriented organization will consider all four approaches with the ultimate goal of selecting top quality people for this important job, because no organization can function well without an effective supervisory force.

Other Factors Affecting Supervisory Selection

In addition to the sources of supervisors and the legal considerations involved in selecting them, other factors can also have a significant impact on their selection.

Formal/Informal Processes. The vast majority of the selection systems in place today are informal. In one recent study, seven eighths of the respondents indicated that they had informal rather than formal procedures for selecting supervisors (Rendero, 1980). Many organizations—particularly the smaller ones—have been reluctant to develop policies, selection guidelines, or written procedures that spell out how supervisory candidates are chosen. Larger organizations, which are more likely to be the targets of discrimination suits, have slowly developed formal procedures to handle the selection of supervisors. An example is the New York City Department of Transportation, where positions are filled permanently through written civil service examinations.

Informal procedures have come under the watchful eye of the courts and fair employment agencies. In one case an organization was found guilty of discrimination as a result of an informal approach to selecting employees for promotion. Vacancies were not posted, and the managers were given no written guidelines for making promotion decisions. As a result the procedures were found to be biased. In another case the court ruled that a company could not rely solely on the recommendations of company foremen in selecting employees for promotion since the standards used by the foremen were vague and subjective (Miner and Miner, 1978).

Formal procedures include statements of company policy about equal opportunity and selection and written procedures that spell out in detail the various components of the selection system. This could include how selection procedures are administered, who is responsible for each part, and more importantly how employees can be considered for promotion. Formal procedures may include guidelines to aid managers in the selection process. Examples are interviewing techniques, evaluation forms, and procedures to identify potential supervisors. Also, a formal approach may include applications or requests that give employees the chance to indicate that they want to be considered for a promotion and to outline their qualifications for the supervisor's job.

Group/Individual Decisions. The extent to which various levels of management are involved in selecting supervisors is another important consideration. There may be several levels of management, as well as other departments, that should be involved in this process.

The human resources department of an organization usually has the major input in supervisory selection decisions. Often it tracks candidates, helps in the interviewing process, and in many cases monitors and maintains the complete selection system. Also, its judgment and evaluations are often an important factor in determining who gets the job. The middle manager with the supervisory vacancy also has an important part in the selection process. This manager is involved in the interview process and possibly participates in other components of the selection system as well. And since this manager must live with the results, he or she frequently makes the final decision of who should get the job, particularly when there are several candidates. The candidate's present and former supervisors may provide important information on previous work performance. A recommendation from these individuals can be a strong factor in the decision-making process.

Top management, division management, or the plant manager may be involved in the decision. The extent of such involvement depends on the individual organization but is often limited to an informal interview of candidates. Upper management usually wants to meet the candidates face to face and have some limited input into the decision. In some organizations a selection committee screens and interviews candidates for promotion to supervisor. The committee is usually composed of line and staff managers, but it also receives considerable input from the human resources department and in some cases from an equal employment opportunity specialist.

There can be much variation in the extent to which different management levels, as well as different staff support groups, are involved in the supervisory selection process. The extent of each group's involvement will depend on the organization and its philosophy toward supervisory selection.

Organizational Factors. A number of organizational factors should be considered when an organization is developing a selection system. The nature of the work is an important factor. Supervisory jobs differ significantly from one organization to another. Some require very specific technical backgrounds while others do not. For example, it would be difficult for a maintenance supervisor to function effectively without prior maintenance experience in one or more of the crafts or trades in the work unit. The supervisor would lack understanding of the craft and would find it hard to gain the respect of employees and peers in the organization. Conversely, it would not be necessary for a supervisor of a word-processing center to have been a word processor (or typist) in the past. It would be more important to have someone with good planning and interpersonal skills.

The internal availability of supervisory vacancies is another consideration. For example, in some plants it is not unusual for supervisors to be on the job ten to twenty years. The technology, and the industry, may change slowly, and there would be little need to have a supervisor ready at all times. But if there is rapid growth and new jobs are created frequently or if there is unusually high turnover among supervisors, there will naturally be more vacancies for a selection system to fill. Under these circumstances, a system must be able to turn out the required number of potential candidates quickly. In a chain of fast-food restaurants, for example, the average supervisory tenure may be one year, and new candidates need to be readily available.

Another consideration is the size of the plant or office. Smaller operations will have fewer vacancies, and the supervisory jobs are more likely to require a variety of skills. A selection system might not have to be as formal and structured as in the case of a large plant with 4,000 employees where supervisory vacancies occur often, many of them requiring similar skills.

Environmental Factors. Just as there are organizational factors to consider, there are factors outside the organization that may have an influence on the selection system. The local labor market is an important consideration, particularly for organizations that recruit outside candidates to fill most of their supervisory vacancies. In a small, rural community it may be difficult to locate qualified supervisory candidates, while in an industrialized, larger city the local labor market may include an ample supply of qualified candidates. The existence of educational institutions and technical training centers is another important consideration. A community college with a degree program in supervision or industrial management can be a tremendous asset to local organizations seeking supervisory candidates.

The growth of the industry is another factor. High-growth industries attract attention, and this attention may help bring in outside candidates to fill supervisory vacancies. In highly competitive situations, recruiting battles may develop to fill specialized supervisory vacancies. Unless selection systems are properly planned and functioning effectively, the net result may be a shortage of supervisors, and supervisory pay scales may soar above the national or regional average. Therefore, an organization must consider its strategic recruiting position relative to competitors and other organizations in the community.

Presupervisory Education Programs. Another important factor in developing a supervisory selection system is the availability of presupervisory education programs. These programs can help identify supervisory talent, develop future supervisors, and provide input into the final selection decision. Typically, these programs combine classroom sessions with on-the-job visitations and can usually be integrated into an employee's regular work schedule. In one company, the program spans fifteen full-day sessions over a fifteen-week period. The objectives of presupervisory education usually are to:

- provide employees with an overall knowledge of the organization's people, products, and processes.
- show employees opportunities for advancement in the organization
- stimulate employees to develop a program to accomplish their career goals

- provide management with a reliable source of supervisory candidates

Part of this program involves an evaluation of the participants as they visit different departments. They are usually given department tours and are provided small projects to complete while they visit the departments. The evaluation is based primarily on the employee's perceived ability, eagerness to learn, attitude, and other related areas. This approach gives the organization additional input on prospective supervisors and enables managers to observe the employee under a variety of settings.

Another approach is to use the organization's cooperative education (co-op) program to prepare new supervisors. Most organizations have a co-op program in which college students alternate work and study from their sophomore through senior years. Typically, the rotating assignments give the students full exposure to the organization and the career opportunities that may exist after graduation. For years, these programs have been used for technical and engineering occupations. However, the number of formal co-op programs in management and supervision is increasing. Many junior colleges offer degree programs in supervision technology while most four-year institutions offer degree programs in business administration or industrial management. A co-op arrangement provides an organization with an opportunity to observe candidates in a variety of settings. Students can rotate to different assignments that increase in difficulty each term. Near the end of the program, they can be given temporary supervisory assignments in a work unit and have their performance evaluated.

Components of the Selection System

At the heart of every selection system are the key components used to evaluate the candidates' skills and abilities. It is a relatively easy task to identify the candidates who appear to have the potential for supervision. It is more difficult to establish the selection criteria necessary to make a final decision. In almost every department, managers can identify employees who are dependable, have a positive attitude, and possess extensive job knowledge. Overall they may be considered promotable to supervisory positions sometime in the future. The difficulty arises in deciding which of those candidates will make the most effective supervisor when actually placed in the job. There are a variety of techniques available for gathering data and making the final selection decision. A study conducted by the American Society for Personnel Administration (ASPA) in 1983 gave some insight into the procedures used to select first-line supervisors. The report was based on responses from 437 personnel executives selected from the members of ASPA. Data from the survey were reported by three industry groups and by two company-size categories. Table 1 shows the selection procedures

Table 1. Procedures Used to Select Supervisors in 430 Organizations.

Procedure	Outside Candidates (percent)	Internal Promotion (percent)
Background information		
• Reference/record checks	93	65
• Weighted application blank	8	5
• Investigation by outside agency	13	2
Interviews		
• Unstructured	71	64
• Structured	36	26
Ability testing		
• Skill performance test/work sample	2	3
• Mental ability test	6	3
• Job knowledge test	4	5
• Assessment center	3	5
Other screening techniques		
• Medical examinations	40	4
• Polygraph test/written honesty test	2	*
• Personality test	4	2
No answer/none used	1	10

*Less than 0.5 percent

Source: American Society for Personnel Administration, 1983.

used for both outside applicants and internal candidates for supervisory jobs. Background checks, structured and unstructured interviews, and medical examinations were the most im-

portant selection procedures used for outside applicants. For internal candidates, previous work records, along with structured
and unstructured interviews, were the most frequently used
methods to gather information for the selection decision. Figure
5 shows a system used to select office supervisors from internal

Figure 5. Supervisor Selection System.

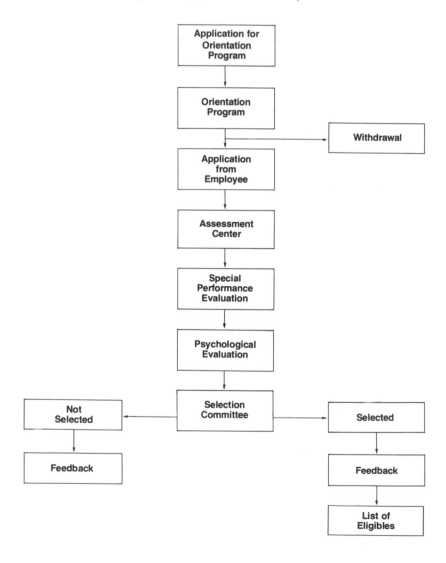

candidates at a medium-size organization. It features an orientation program, an assessment center, a special background check, and a psychological evaluation. Although systems vary with organizations, the components common to them will be presented next.

Background or Reference Checks. Any selection system will include reference checks on outside applicants and a review of past performance for internal candidates. Reference checks can provide useful insight into candidates' preparation for a supervisor's job. The reference check will usually include confirmation of the candidate's educational and training background. This is a must, particularly with the growing number of fraudulent degrees and fake transcripts used by candidates to secure supervisory and professional jobs. A transcript should be located even if the candidate produces a copy of his or her diploma. If the institution is unknown, it might be helpful to check the credentials and accreditation of the institution. There are many diploma mills granting degrees to individuals for a price.

A check of past work experience should center on job-related requirements. Work habits, skills, abilities, and characteristics necessary for the job should be thoroughly checked with previous employers. If possible, reference checks should be made directly to the former supervisors of the outside candidates or to fellow employees if supervisors are not available. Personnel departments are very cautious in what they say and may limit their comments to job classification, pay, and date of termination. It is important to stick to job-related questions. This will keep both the reference checker and the former employer within the limits of the law. Also, only job-related information is necessary in making the decision on the candidate. The reference check should be conducted in the same way as an interview and should seek specific examples of on-the-job behavior related to the supervisory position.

For internal candidates, the past work record is usually the most important component in the selection system. An examination of the candidate's work record should include a review of performance appraisals, commendations, attendance records, disciplinary reports, and any other job-related performance indicators. Out-of-date information should be excluded, as well as any information not related to the job of the supervisor. An important input should come from the candidate's current and previous supervisors in response to questions about the candidate's ability to function in the supervisor's job. If leadership skill is one of the job requirements, questions might be centered on situations where the employee has demonstrated leadership skills. Examples might include representing the department in a charitable fund drive, serving as coach of the department's softball team, assuming a leadership role in a company-sponsored professional or social club, acting as group leader in the work unit, or representing the department on a company committee.

Physical Examinations. According to the results of the American Society for Personnel Administration survey (1983) shown in Table 1, 40 percent of the organizations require a physical examination for outside supervisory candidates. However, these organizations probably require physical examinations for all new employees. This practice is reasonable and justifiable since an organization must have employees at all levels who can function effectively on the job. The supervisor's job can be very stressful and demanding. In many organizations the job requires high levels of physical energy. An unhealthy person may not be able to withstand the tremendous physical pressures involved. In an office setting, of course, the physical requirements may not be so stringent. The examination should focus on the requirements of the job. A supervisory prospect should not be disqualified unless the organization can show that a physical impairment or deficiency would prohibit him or her from functioning in the job. The examining physician should understand the physical requirements for the job and establish a dialogue with the company's medical coordinator so that potential problems can be eliminated. These requirements vary with the type of job, the environment in which the work is performed, and the organization's policies and procedures.

It is important to keep in mind that a representative of

the organization who asks questions about health and physical ability may be in danger of breaking the law. Legislation dealing with the hiring of handicapped employees forbids organizations to ask general questions concerning physical ability and forbids them to equate past with present medical problems. It is illegal, for example, to assume that a person who has a history of heart problems still has a heart condition. Thus, judgments in this area should be made by a licensed physician and not by the organization. In the ASPA survey, about one third (32 percent) of the firms that require pre-employment physicals have a medical professional make the judgments about the applicant's fitness for the job. In some organizations the physical examination records are kept with the physician.

For internal candidates considered for a promotion to supervisory jobs, physical examinations are not normally required since employees usually have had previous physical examinations and the company may be aware of any health problems they have. Nevertheless, if the job requires an unusual level of energy and stamina, it may be appropriate and justifiable to conduct physical examinations as part of the selection process. If so, it is customary to have these examinations as a last part of the selection system since they are time consuming and expensive.

Interviews. Another important component of a supervisory selection system is the interview. Interviews vary considerably with the organization, the job, and the objectives of the selection system. Some organizations use structured interviews (26 percent in the ASPA survey). A structured interview, sometimes referred to as a pattern interview, contains a predetermined list of questions that the interviewer asks each applicant. However, more organizations (64 percent in the ASPA survey) use unstructured interviews that allow the interviewer to ask additional questions as information is uncovered. Unstructured interviews are developed around specific objectives, all related to the job. For convenience, selection interviews have been grouped into three categories: preliminary or screening interviews, campus recruiting interviews, and detailed job-related interviews.

The *preliminary or screening interview* is a brief interview used to eliminate casual applicants. Its objective is to determine if the candidate meets very basic qualifications and has a genuine career interest in supervision. For instance, an outside candidate may not meet a requirement of having two years of previous supervisory experience to be considered for a supervisory vacancy. Or, an internal candidate may not meet a requirement of having worked for five years in retail sales. Very few job-related questions are asked, and the interviewer has an opportunity to explain the job and the selection process and to discuss the candidate's potential for that job.

The interview situation that perhaps requires the greatest skill on the part of the interviewer is the *college campus interview*. College recruiting has become a common source of trainees destined to be supervisors. The initial interview is conducted on campus usually within a thirty-minute or one-hour time frame. Initial screening is usually performed by the college placement office, but this is traditionally limited to scheduling only those students who have certain majors and an interest in supervision. The backgrounds of the students will vary, and most of them will not have job experience. The age, language, or appearance of the student may create a barrier between the student and the interviewer. Usually full-time interviewers conduct these interviews, although it is an increasingly common practice to have line and other staff managers involved. When this is the case, they must be fully prepared and properly trained to conduct the interviews. They must, for example, know the skills and characteristics needed for the job. At best the campus interview will serve as a screening device to check the student's interest in and basic qualifications for supervision. This interview is important since the decision to go to the next step usually involves the expense of a visit to the employer's facilities.

The most important interviews in selection systems are the *detailed job-related interviews*. These are typically conducted by professionally trained interviewers who ask candidates questions relating to the characteristics, skills, and abilities (usually called dimensions) required for successful performance on the job. An interviewer will ask for specific examples of behavior, both good and bad, related to each of the job dimensions. Interviewers then rate the candidates on a sliding scale for each dimension. This makes it possible to compare the various candidates being considered for the job. Usually more than one person conducts job-related interviews. A representative from the human resources department, along with the manager with the supervisory vacancy, make an ideal pair for conducting them.

The primary objective of this interview is to predict the candidate's future behavior on the basis of his or her past behavior. It is generally accepted that an employee's past behavior is a good predictor of behavior in the future. Most of the job-related dimensions will be behaviorally oriented. They describe what a person should do to be successful in the job of supervisor. Behavioral data may have to be collected from previous jobs that are different from the target job. Although candidates may not have held supervisory positions, they have probably had opportunities to demonstrate some of the skills required in the supervisory job. For instance, initiative, which is a common skill required of supervisors, can show up in a candidate's experience in almost any type of job.

The interview has come under fire as a valid selection tool because of discrimination suits. Much of the attention has been on the types of questions asked, and thus some organizations have developed interviewing guides that list questions that should not be asked. Because of these legal concerns, there has also been increased emphasis on other methods of arriving at the final selection decision. The interview then becomes just one input into the total selection system. A job-related approach, in which questions are specifically related to the job, can prevent many problems. However, there is no magic formula for conducting interviews that will ensure infallibility in selecting the best candidate. Interviewing is not a science and does have significant weaknesses. Moffatt (1979, pp. 2–3) has listed six of them:

- lack of uniformity in the nature, length, and content of the interview

- lack of objectivity in the interview process
- failure to recognize the limitations of the interview
- time constraints on the interview
- the interviewer's feeling that he or she lacks authority
- lack of training on the part of the typical interviewer

Even with these weaknesses, the interview is still an important and popular component of selection systems in use today to determine who should move into the supervisor's job.

Testing. Organizations abandoned selection tests in large numbers when they were challenged by discrimination suits in the 1960s and 1970s. Many of the tests in use could not be validated while others were of questionable validity. The safest course of action appeared to be the elimination of testing altogether. Now, however, psychologists, lawyers, and personnel specialists are increasingly being asked to provide opinions as to whether testing programs will be acceptable to the EEOC and/ or the Office of Federal Contract Compliance (OFCC). Both of these federal agencies have published guidelines and other documents in an effort to reduce uncertainty and to assist employers in complying with legislation and executive orders that bear on testing. Yet nothing has been published to date that would provide a sure guide to employer action; many uncertainties and ambiguities remain. Faced with the prospects of terminated federal contracts and sizable awards for damages, some organizations have decided to forgo further testing until the situation clears. Such a strategy may require a long wait. Both the EEOC and the OFCC have taken the position that they will not approve individual testing programs as being fair and nondiscriminatory. They argue in part that they lack the manpower to carry out the many investigations this would require. Even more important, however, is the government's position that under existing law it is up to the employer to establish that employment practices do not discriminate, and that government certification of testing programs would be wholly inconsistent with this particular legal strategy (Miner and Miner, 1978, p. 216).

On the positive side, there has been a general improvement in the quality and quantity of validated tests available for employee selection. The difficult task is to find reliable criteria to relate the results of the selection test to supervisory performance. Considering the variable nature of people, performance, and tests, it is easy to see the problems organizations have faced in test validation. It is beyond the scope of this book to identify the available tests and their applications. A comprehensive listing is contained in Yoder and Heneman (1979, pp. 4-143–4-145). However, it would be helpful to review one example of test validation. One successful approach can be found in the testing program used by Honeywell (a large manufacturer of computers, electronics, and control systems) to select factory supervisors (Northrup and others, 1978). Honeywell's testing program is based on the convictions that (1) discrete performance for a particular job can be defined and, with some degree of accuracy, measured; (2) information related to performance in a specific job can be obtained from a job applicant; and (3) information collected from a job applicant through interest tests and pattern interviews can be used to judge objectively the applicant's relative suitability for the job. The process used by Honeywell in developing the testing program involved three phases: performance standards development, predictor validation, and interest profile development.

In developing performance standards, personnel specialists captured the thoughts of managers concerning their expectations of an employee's performance in a supervisory position. These ideas were used to develop a set of performance categories that applied to the job of a factory supervisor. Performance comments were then generated for each category. The comments were intended to be descriptions of supervisory behavior—good, bad, or neutral—for each category.

In the next step, Honeywell developed a predictor (selection test) that can be used to predict performance using the previously developed performance standards. Several tests were used and checked for their ability to predict the performance of employees who were incumbents in the factory supervisor's job. The product of this phase was a battery of selection tests.

As a final step in the process, Honeywell conducted tests to measure occupational interest and how it related to tenure. In this case the predictor for the interest profile had to identify with the interest of probable high performers.

In all instances where this testing and selection program has been implemented at Honeywell, the results have surpassed initial expectations. One division that had a history of difficulty in locating and encouraging people to accept supervisory positions in the factory had over 150 people sign up to take the test. In almost every instance the final pool offered enough women and members of minority groups to meet the division's equal employment opportunity goals. Another division, which usually took three months to fill factory supervisory vacancies, now fills them within a week. Managers and employees feel that the selection of supervisors is open and objective and that anyone may try. For more information on this program, see Northrup and others (1978, pp. 123-152).

Job Simulations. Job simulations, or work samples, are another effective technique for evaluating a candidate's ability to handle a supervisory job. These simulations are usually behaviorally oriented, since the supervisor's actions and behavior are correlated with job success and can easily be observed and documented. By definition, a behavioral simulation is a controlled situation in which supervisory candidates display behavior related to success on the job. For example, if supervisors must frequently conduct disciplinary interviews, a simulation can be developed to allow the supervisory candidate to conduct an interview, given the appropriate facts and information. The candidate's behavior would be directly observed by a trained representative, who might even play the role of the person being disciplined. In some cases it might be a third-party observation. The behavior exhibited would then be placed in categories or dimensions as described earlier.

Job simulations are particularly appropriate in situations where it is difficult to evaluate the candidate's background because he or she has had little or no opportunity to demonstrate supervisory behavior. For example, planning is usually a job dimension for supervisors. It might be difficult to observe strengths and weaknesses in planning skills in an hourly employee's previous job or jobs. Therefore, a simulated exercise in which the candidate has an opportunity to demonstrate planning ability could give the organization some additional insight into the candidate's skills in this area. Several types of job simulations are commonly used to supplement the other components of the overall selection system. *In-basket exercises* require supervisors to handle the accumulated memos, notes, letters, and other written items found in a simulated in-basket for supervisors. The candidate must make decisions, ask for cooperation, write letters and reports, and plan, organize, and schedule activities based on the information supplied in the in-basket. This type of job simulation is well suited for measuring job dimensions such as problem analysis, sensitivity, initiative, planning and organizing, written communication, judgment, and decisiveness.

An *analysis exercise* evaluates the candidate's ability to sift through data, come to a conclusion, and present a logical argument to back up the conclusion. Supervisory candidates are given data on the situation and asked to recommend appropriate courses of action. This type of exercise is particularly suited for measuring such dimensions as written communication, judgment, and analysis.

Interview simulations require meetings with employees, either one-on-one or as a group. A job simulation is developed in which the supervisory candidate is given an opportunity to conduct interviews with employees, staff members, or other individuals with whom there is frequent contact. This type of simulation is particularly effective in dealing with difficult situations such as conflict resolution, disciplinary discussions, and problem solving. It enables the organization to evaluate a candidate on the dimensions of planning and organizing, leadership, sensitivity, oral communication, and tolerance for stress.

Scheduling exercises require the candidate to schedule the work assignments of employees. This may include planning for work flow, arranging for resources, and laying out special work projects. Scheduling exercises simulate problems faced by supervisors and allow an organization to evaluate the dimensions of planning and organizing, analysis, judgment, and decisiveness.

There are a number of other types of job simulations or work samples that can be applied as part of the selection process. They are usually an integral part of the assessment center process that will be described later.

On-the-Job Tryouts. Another selection system component is the use of supervisory candidates in temporary assignments in the supervisor's job. In this case, the candidate fills in for the supervisor during vacation, periods of excessive overtime, jury duty, or other short-term vacancies. The supervisory candidate is given complete responsibility for the work unit, and is evaluated on how well the assignment is handled. Several useful guidelines can help make this process work. Supervisory candidates must have a clear understanding of what is expected of them and how they will be evaluated during the assignment. They must have all the responsibility and authority that normally is assumed by the supervisor, and word of the assignment must be given to all members of the work unit.

The status of the candidates should be changed to reflect their new role. In some organizations they are temporarily promoted from hourly to salaried status and given a pay differential. In one aerospace company their identification badges are changed to indicate their supervisorial role. They should be provided with all the privileges normally given to supervisors. This includes the use of special locker facilities and dining rooms and the enjoyment of other status symbols available to supervisors.

This approach allows the organization to assess the candidate's ability to perform the job for relatively short periods. Objective short-term performance criteria can be developed with little difficulty. It provides an excellent learning experience without putting the candidate under excessive pressure. This approach has little risk since it would be difficult for supervisory candidates to cause much harm to the organization if they proved to be ineffective in this short-term assignment.

A variation of this approach is to promote supervisory

candidates to the job of supervisor for a predetermined trial period. This is done with no binding commitment from either the employee or the organization. After the trial period, the employee can elect not to go into supervision and suffer no consequences or future damage to career opportunities in other areas. Also, at the end of the trial period, the organization can decide to promote or not to promote the employee, ideally without any animosity on the part of the supervisory candidate. The same guidelines that apply to temporary assignment apply here. In this case, however, it is more important that there be a clear understanding between management and the supervisory candidate as to what is expected during the trial period. This approach can be expensive and may not be feasible for all organizations. It works best when there is a large pool of supervisors, and they can be shuffled to make room for the temporary supervisor.

Explaining the Job and Selling the Organization. Another component of the selection system is to explain the job to candidates and to sell them on the organization and the supervisory opportunity. This is usually integrated into the various steps of the selection system, although it may be accomplished as a separate step, particularly when outside candidates are being recruited. For outside candidates, this component should include information about the typical items used to sell the organization to any job applicant: pay, working conditions, benefits, location, and opportunities. Also, pertinent job information should be disseminated. Reprints of company publications describing a day in the life of a supervisor make excellent handouts to supervisory candidates. Individuals involved in the selection process should be prepared to answer questions about the nature, scope, duties, and requirements of the job. In addition, they should be able to answer questions about working conditions, salary, benefits, work schedules, basic policies, procedures, and required personal equipment, if applicable.

Decision Making. All the previous components of the selection system provide data for making the decision to accept or reject the candidate for a present or future supervisory vacancy. This decision, which should be made by key management in the organization, is often a group decision. It is important that all the data from the selection system be processed and summarized into a meaningful format for the key decision makers. Most selection systems provide several decision points at which a candidate can be rejected before all the data are collected. This is efficient since it allows an organization to save the time and expense of taking all the candidates through all the steps.

Which Components Are Best? The previously discussed components are common in selection systems today. In a particular setting there will be variations of these components and possibly additional ones. There is no ideal selection system. It must take into account all the factors outlined in this chapter, but it must also be tailored to the organization's needs and to the supervisor's job. One very effective method is found in the assessment center. The assessment center is growing in popularity and is used in a variety of organizations, including the EEOC. If developed properly and operated effectively, it can provide a very objective, unbiased process for identifying and selecting first-level supervisors. The remainder of the chapter will describe the assessment center.

Assessment Center Method for Selecting Supervisors

An assessment center is a formal system of management and supervisory simulations used to evaluate the dimensions of managerial success that have been established as important for a particular position within the organization. Its foremost application has been in the selection of supervisors. It differs from other evaluation techniques in three major ways:

- Multiple job simulations are used to elicit behavior.
- Groups of individuals are evaluated at the same time.
- Assessment is conducted, and evaluations are made, by trained observers (or assessors) who are familiar with the job for which candidates are being selected.

History. In comparison with other selection methods, the assessment center method is relatively new. Yet it has been used to select managers for over thirty years. It had its beginning in the military during World War II when it was used to select individuals who could successfully undertake hazardous intelligence-gathering missions. At the same time, assessment centers were developed by the British War Office Selection Board and the British Civil Service Selection Board for choosing military and civil service officers.

Assessment centers were first applied to the industrial environment in the 1950s by AT&T. In 1958 the first operational assessment center designed to select supervisors was implemented in one of the Bell System units of AT&T. Since then AT&T and its former subsidiaries have been the foremost users of the assessment center process, although organizations with early implementations of the method include Standard Oil (Ohio), IBM, General Electric, Sears, and Caterpillar Tractor. Internationally, early programs were developed at IBM World Trade, Shell Oil (Brazil), and the Canadian government (Moses and Byham, 1977, pp. 10-11). Today over 2,000 organizations are using the assessment center process, not only for employee selection but for individualized counseling, management development, and organizational development. It is a process with much potential and is ideally suited to select supervisors.

Advantages. Several factors have produced growing interest in the use of the assessment center process in the selection of supervisors:

- *Accuracy of the technique.* Studies conducted by AT&T, IBM, Sears, General Electric, and Standard Oil (Ohio) have substantiated the accuracy of the assessment center process. Candidates selected by the process have been found to be two to three times more likely to be successful at higher-management levels than those promoted strictly on the basis of supervisory judgement.
- *Learning experience for participants and assessors.* Managers who serve as assessors in the assessment center gain insight

into their own skills and develop new, improved job-related skills. They are more aware of what contributes to success on the job. Also, the participants in the assessment center claim that their involvement in the exercises is a learning experience, particularly when they receive feedback on how well they handled the exercises.

- *Nondiscriminatory.* The assessment center method has been found to be accurate for all protected groups. It has been accepted as a valid selection technique in discrimination suit settlements and is used by several government agencies, including the EEOC.
- *Positive impact on morale.* With this approach, employees can readily see that they have an opportunity for advancement and a fair chance to display their abilities. It removes much of the secretiveness of supervisory selection.
- *High acceptance by management.* The assessment center method is a logical process, and higher-level managers are impressed by how the exercises simulate the challenges an employee will face in a supervisory position.

Qualities Assessed. Defining the criteria to use in selecting supervisors in an assessment center is a very important task. It is completed as an initial part of the implementation of a center. With so many responsibilities, a successful supervisor must possess a variety of characteristics, skills, and abilities (dimensions). These dimensions emerge from a logical, rational analysis of the supervisor's job, usually involving several steps:

- a review of all job descriptions and other documents related to the supervisor's job
- direct observation of supervisors on the job at various time periods
- interviews with supervisors to determine how they spend their time and to identify the critical and challenging parts of their jobs
- a questionnaire describing the major job activities of supervisors that is administered to all incumbent supervisors
- interviews with all middle-management personnel to whom

the supervisors report to collect specific examples of their effectiveness or ineffectiveness
- data analyzed and combined to generate a tentative list of dimensions
- a questionnaire used with middle managers as the final determinant of which dimensions will be included in the selection system

Although these steps may vary slightly, their purpose is to isolate the most important dimensions that relate to success. If executed on a planned and controlled basis, with the help of outside experts if necessary, they should provide a valid, defensible basis for supervisor selection.

Typical Supervisory Job Dimensions. The dimensions for a supervisor's job will vary considerably with the organization and its policies and procedures and the type of work and work setting. It is difficult, if not impossible, to suggest a group of supervisory dimensions that would be appropriate for all organizations. Nevertheless, to illustrate the use of dimensions, here is a brief description of the dimensions developed for the supervisor's job in one organization (Phillips and others, 1980a, pp. 35-40):

- *Oral communication*—effectiveness of verbal expression in individual or group situations
- *Initiative*—originating action rather than just responding to events
- *Leadership*—use of appropriate methods in guiding individuals or a group toward a goal
- *Sensitivity*—understanding the needs and feelings of others
- *Tolerance for stress*—stability of performance under pressure and/or opposition
- *Planning, organizing, and scheduling*—establishing a course of action for self and for others; scheduling proper assignment of employees to machines and tasks
- *Management control*—establishing procedures to monitor responsibilities, delegated assignments, or projects

- *Problem analysis*—identifying problems, gathering information, and determining possible causes of problems
- *Judgment*—making decisions based on logical assumptions and factual information
- *Management identification*—achievement of personal satisfaction from supervisory responsibilities
- *Energy*—maintaining a high activity level
- *Technical knowledge*—understanding of and ability to perform technical activities related to the supervisor's job

How the Process Works. A typical assessment center involves six participants and lasts approximately two days. The participants take part in exercises developed to give them an opportunity to display their skills under each of the supervisory job dimensions. Usually three assessors observe the participants' behavior. From this point on, there may be slight variations in the details of how a particular assessment center works. The following is a brief description of how one center functioned to select first-level production supervisors (Phillips and others, 1980b, p. 100).

Each assessor is assigned to record notes on the performance of one or two candidates. After each behavioral simulation has been completed, the assessors review their notes and write a report on how their assigned candidate(s) performed relative to the dimensions required. It is important that each candidate be observed by each of the assessors at some point in the assessment process so that any biases or rating tendencies of individual assessors affect all candidates equally. The extensive training provided for assessors eliminates most rating difficulties.

After all exercises have been completed by all candidates and assessors have finished their reports, the assessors meet to discuss each candidate individually. The meeting is called an assessor integration discussion because the assessors each have seen a particular candidate in a different simulation and must combine or integrate all their individual pieces of information.

Assessors read their reports to each other and, after all reports have been reviewed, weigh the information presented by all assessors. They then arrive independently at an overall numerical rating of how they feel the candidate performed on each dimension. Assessors present their overall ratings, explain their reasoning (ratings must be justified through specific examples of behavior), and reach a consensus on the rating. When all dimensions have been discussed, the final product is a profile of each candidate that displays the candidate's strengths and weaknesses relative to the target job of supervisor.

At this point, some organizations ask assessors to make one final judgment and come to an agreement regarding the candidate's overall acceptability to be promoted to the supervisor's job. Other organizations use a system that combines the assessment center with additional components, such as an interview targeted toward the supervisor position and a performance evaluation from the candidate's supervisor. A trained committee from upper management usually weighs data from all sources and determines the candidate's potential for supervision.

Assessment Techniques. The techniques used in an assessment center to measure supervisory potential can vary. As a general rule, no single technique is designed to provide information on all the dimensions indicated for the job. Considerable research has shown that certain techniques provide information that is highly relevant to specific dimensions (Moses and Byham, 1977, p. 6). For example, the most effective way of evaluating interpersonal behavior is simply to have a candidate interact with others. Asking an individual to select a preferred leadership approach in a given setting is not as effective as simulating an actual situation that requires leadership capabilities. What is needed is a variety of exercises or job simulations, as described earlier, that give the assessment center participants an opportunity to display their skills and abilities relative to each of the supervisory job dimensions. Although there are many different types of exercises, typically only four are used in a particular center. Figure 6 shows types of exercises that can be used to solicit behavior relative to specific dimensions.

Assessment Center Personnel. An important part of an assessment center is the staff. Since the assessment is a judgmental

Figure 6. Guide for Selection of Categories of Exercises.

This chart will aid organizations in identifying which dimensions can be typically observed from a particular category of simulations (indicated by checkmarks). As an additional refinement, if the exercise category is particularly well suited in eliciting a particular dimension, a star (★) is used instead of a checkmark. An (X) indicates that although that dimension may be observable in that exercise category, only specific exercises within that category can elicit that dimension.

Job-related DIMENSIONS	Business Game	In-Basket & Interview	Leaderless Group Discussion (Assigned Roles)	Leaderless Group Discussion (Non-assigned Roles)	Analysis	Scheduling	Targeted Selection Interview	Fact finding & Decision Making	Interview Simulation	Written Presentation	Analysis/ Oral Presentation
1. Impact			✔	✔			✔		✔		★
2. Oral Communication Skill	✔	✔	★	★					★		
3. Oral Presentation Skill			★		X						★
4. Written Communication Skill		★			✔					★	
5. Creativity		✔			X			✔			
6. Tolerance for Stress					X[1]	X[1]		✔	✔[2]		
7. Work Standards		✔			X			✔	✔	X	
8. Leadership	✔		✔	★					★		
9. Persuasiveness/Sales Ability			✔		✔			✔	X	X	★
10. Sensitivity		★	✔	★					✔		
11. Behavioral Flexibility	X		✔					✔	✔		
12. Tenacity			✔					✔	✔	X	
13. Risk Taking	✔	✔			X	✔		✔			✔
14. Initiative	✔	★	✔	★				★	X		
15. Independence		✔						✔	X	X	
16. Planning and Organizing	✔	★			X	★		✔			
17. Delegation		★						✔		X	
18. Management Control		★						✔	✔		
19. Analysis	✔	★			★		✔	★	✔	X	★
20. Judgment		★		X	★	★	✔	★	✔		★
21. Decisiveness		★		X	★		X	★	✔		★
22. Development of Subordinates		.X						✔	★	X	
23. Adaptability	✔							✔			
24. Technical Translation		X			X					★	✔
25. Organizational Sensitivity		X			X			✔		X	X

1. Time Stress
2. Interpersonal Stress

Source: Development Dimensions International, P.O. Box 13379, Pittsburgh, Penn. 15243.

process, the quality of the judges is no doubt a key ingredient to the success of the process. The judges in this case are the assessors. They must be able to assimilate a great deal of information rapidly, be relatively free of personal bias, and be perceived by the organization as effective individuals. They must be carefully selected and trained in assessment techniques in a very controlled environment. Typical assessors come from the next level above the supervisor's job, which is usually the middle-management group. In addition, staff managers are sometimes selected to be assessors. Usually there are many assessors involved because of the many demands on each one's time and the organization's desire to expose large numbers of managers to the assessment center process. Probably the most important argument for using a large number of managers is their increased ability to use the results of the assessment center.

Each assessment center also requires an administrator. The program administrator is an individual who has responsibility for the coordination, administration, and operation of the assessment center. The administrator may be full time or may be assigned this responsibility in addition to regular duties. The administrator's functions are to

- select and train assessors
- write assessment reports
- administer assessment exercises
- maintain appropriate records and files
- maintain inventory forms and exercises
- ensure that all assessment centers are standardized

The administrator should be selected from the management group and must be familiar with the job of the supervisor. Like the assessors, the administrator must be trained in assessor skills, as well as in the requirements and techniques for proper program administration.

Implementation Concerns. Although the assessment center process has many positive features, it is not without its disadvantages. First, there is the cost, which varies depending on the size of the organization and on how much outside assistance is needed, if any. Several consulting firms are available to assist organizations in developing assessment centers. For a company with 100 supervisors, the cost for a consulting firm to implement an assessment center could be as high as $30 thousand. The cost thereafter might run to $500 per candidate in the assessment center. Another factor is time. Assessment centers are time consuming for the administrator as well as for the assessors. Assessor training usually takes three to five days, while it requires nearly a week to conduct the assessment center. A third factor is the legal issue. The assessment center process is a fair, objective, and legally defensible system for selecting supervisors —but only if the system is properly designed and is implemented under controlled conditions. This adds to costs and to the amount of time required. However, this legal issue alone may justify the cost of implementing the system when the cost of defending the present system, should it be challenged, is taken into account. A fourth factor is the size of the operation. It is difficult to establish a cutoff point at which the system would cease to work effectively. It has been shown to work well in medium-size organizations, employing less than 2,000 employees. It should also work well for smaller companies. In fact, the system is currently used to select employees in organizations where the total number of people in the target jobs numbers fewer than 50.

There is a final area to consider, namely, the cost of having ineffective supervisors. As noted earlier in this chapter, the selection of capable supervisors is extremely important to an organization. An ineffective supervisor can easily cost the organization thousands of dollars every month. An organization would do better to spend money up front to ensure proper selection, thereby reducing the chances of supervisory ineffectiveness and failure.

Summary

This chapter explored the important issue of supervisory selection. If organizations gave more attention to proper selections, many of the problems caused by inadequate and unprepared supervisors could be prevented. The chapter focused on legal considerations, sources of new supervisors, components of selection systems, and other factors affecting selection. Organizations are left with the challenge to

- Examine the current supervisory selection system to see if it is legally defensible considering the applicable laws and regulations.
- Review the sources for new supervisors to see if alternative sources are appropriate. Progressive organizations develop a variety of internal and external sources.
- Evaluate the selection system design to see if its various parts are functioning effectively. A comprehensive system will contain several components, ranging from reference checks to job simulations, with each supplying valuable information for the selection decision. This chapter discussed eight major components.
- Examine other factors, both internally and externally, that can have an impact on the effectiveness of the selection system to see if changes or improvements are necessary.

In addition, an important and promising technique for selecting supervisors—the assessment center method—was described in some detail. Although it has been around for over thirty years, it is still in its infancy when compared with other major selection systems. It shows great promise in providing an objective process for supervisory selection.

Suggested Readings

Carroll, S. J., and Schuler, R. S. (Eds.). *Human Resources Management in the 1980s.* Washington, D.C.: Bureau of National Affairs, 1983, chap. 4.

Cascio, W. F. *Applied Psychology in Personnel Management.* (2nd ed.) Reston, Va.: Reston Publishing, 1982, 11–33, 177–250.

Dessler, G. *Personnel Management: Modern Concepts and Techniques.* (3rd ed.) Reston, Va.: Reston Publishing, 1984, 27–217.

Foulkes, F. K. *Personnel Policies in Large Nonunion Companies.* Englewood Cliffs, N.J.: Prentice-Hall, 1980.

Holley, W. H., and Jennings, K. M. *Personnel Management: Functions and Issues.* New York: Dryden, 1982, 97–220.

Keil, E. C. *Assessment Centers: A Guide for Human Resource Management*. Reading, Mass.: Addison-Wesley, 1981.

Lorentzen, J. F. *The Manager's Personnel Problem Solver*. Englewood Cliffs, N.J.: Prentice-Hall, 1980, 1-54.

McBurney, W. J., Jr. *College Recruiting: Effective Programs and Practices*. New York: AMACOM, 1982.

Miner, M. G., and Miner, J. B. *Employee Selection Within the Law*. Washington, D.C.: Bureau of National Affairs, 1978.

Moffatt, T. L. *Selection Interviewing for Managers*. New York: Harper & Row, 1979.

Moses, J. L., and Byham, W. C. (Eds.). *Applying the Assessment Center Method*. Elmsford, N.Y.: Pergamon Press, 1977.

Northrup, H. R., and others. *The Objective Selection of Supervisors*. Manpower and Human Resources Studies, No. 8. Philadelphia: Industrial Research Unit, Wharton School, University of Pennsylvania, 1978.

Thain, R. J., and others. *The Campus Connection: Effective College Relations and Recruiting*. New York: Brecker and Merryman, 1979.

Yoder, D., and Heneman, H. G., Jr. (Eds.). *ASPA Handbook of Personnel and Industrial Relations*. Washington, D.C.: Bureau of National Affairs, 1979, pt. 4.

Yoder, D., and Staudohar, P. D. *Personnel Management and Industrial Relations*. (7th ed.) Englewood Cliffs, N.J.: Prentice-Hall, 1982, 101-293.

3

Training, Education, and Development:

Designing Programs for Results

Throughout this book the term *training and development* or *development* has been used to refer to learning experiences for supervisors. This is common terminology; increasingly used, however, is the term *human resource development* (HRD), which encompasses the three activities of training, education, and development. It is important to understand the conceptual differences among these three terms, particularly as they relate to the supervisor. One description of the differences is presented by Nadler (1980, p. 23), who suggests that training, education, and development be differentiated by the three areas shown in Table 2.

Training prepares a supervisor to better perform his or

Table 2. Differentiation of Learning Experiences.

Label	Focus	Economic Classification	Risk Level
Training	Present Job	Expense Item	Low
Education	Future Job	Short-Term Investment	Medium
Development	Organization	Long-Term Investment	High

her present job. It is usually regarded as an expense item that is needed to make the organization more effective and increase productivity. This effort represents a very low risk to the organization because it has an immediate payoff. It is the principal focus of most HRD departments.

Education represents learning experiences that prepare supervisors for future jobs. Many of the approaches to learning outlined in this chapter meet the educational needs of supervisors by preparing them for future job assignments. Education represents a short-term investment on the part of the organization and carries only medium risk. Although they do not provide an immediate return, educational programs are important to the organization in periods of both growth and downturn. In growth periods there is a need to prepare supervisors for other promotional opportunities to meet the challenges brought on by expansion. During periods of economic downturn educational programs may be needed to prepare supervisors to take on other jobs.

Development focuses on the organization and future organizational activities. It is based on the assumption that organizations must grow and change in order to remain viable. Developmental programs prepare individuals to move in the new directions that organizational changes may require. They are investments for which it is almost impossible to calculate a return, and, because of this, they are high-risk ventures. Developmental activities are long range in scope and are provided without reference to a particular job. True developmental experiences are not common in most organizations, at least on any formal basis.

Although the learning experiences for supervisors in an organization may not always carry the labels of training, education, and development, it is recommended that such programs be analyzed and placed in one category or another. This can help management decide which programs are needed at what time and for what purpose. In practice most of the programs presented will fall in the category of either immediate job training or educational programs that are preparing supervisors for other jobs.

Few executives will dispute the importance of providing

opportunities for supervisors to participate in HRD. But many organizations still fail to invest adequately in this important resource in the organization. According to one recent survey conducted by the American Management Associations (Levine, 1982), only half of the organizations surveyed had formal HRD programs for their supervisors. However, many of those that did not have formal programs reported that they used such informal methods as on-the-job coaching, self-study, and rotational assignments.

Although there may be room for additional emphasis on supervisory training, it now receives the biggest slice of the training pie, according to another study. *Training* magazine's 1983 "Organizational Census" queried organizations to determine what types of programs are priorities and to whom those programs are delivered ("Training in Organizations," 1983, pp. 41–44). The study revealed that, on the average, 16.8 percent of the total training effort is devoted to first-level supervisors. This compares to 14.8 percent for professional employees and 14.1 percent for middle managers. Production employees, who significantly outnumber supervisors, account for only 8.4 percent of the total effort. The same study revealed that 80.9 percent of the organizations conduct training for supervisors and foremen.

Supervisory HRD is important for many reasons for both the organization and the supervisors. First, supervisory training can improve the skills of supervisors and increase their effectiveness and efficiency. This training can equip supervisors with the skills necessary to handle critical job situations properly and to motivate their work group to achieve more output. In one study, supervisory training produced significant results for a group of supervisors at an international company. Lost-time accidents were reduced by 50 percent, formal grievances were reduced from an average of fifteen per year to three, and productivity goals were exceeded by $250,000. In another study involving seventeen supervisors at a financial institution, these results were achieved with a supervisory training program:

- number of new loans written, up 300 percent

- number of credit life insurance additions to loans, up 233 percent
- new business referrals, up 300 percent
- overtime per employee, down 92 percent

Results of this kind are not uncommon for supervisory training programs when they are implemented properly.

Second, supervision is a tough and challenging job by anyone's estimate. Effective supervisory training can improve supervisors' ability to cope with job stress and increase their confidence by teaching them how to handle situations effectively and how to assume their responsibilities in an efficient manner. Many reports from supervisory training evaluations, particularly those involving new supervisors, have revealed how initial skills training has improved their ability to handle problems associated with the job. One major study—conducted by Development Dimensions International, Pittsburgh—covered 22,000 supervisors trained with the Interaction Management (IM) Training Program from 1978 to 1982. The results: 93.5 percent of the trained supervisors expressed confidence and satisfaction with the program, indicating that they were likely or very likely to use IM skills on the job. In another study at Brown & Williamson Tobacco Corporation in 1982, managers evaluated supervisory skills after training. They found improvement in supervisors' listening skills and self-confidence. Supervisors handled conflicts positively and learned a system for dealing with problems.

Third, given a world of scarce resources and increasing costs, organizations are limited as to the amount of HRD they can provide employees. Since supervisors usually have several employees reporting to them, allocating additional investment for their training can diffuse the influence of this training throughout the organization. Some organizations have adopted the philosophy, "Train supervisors and they will train the employees." Consider this example. An organization is interested in getting employees to explore ways of simplifying their jobs, develop cost-savings methods, and improve the efficiency of their departments. It may be impractical and too costly to train every employee in the principles of work simplification. As an alternative the organization trains supervisors so that they will fully understand the steps involved in simplifying work and finding cost-savings ideas. Supervisors are also trained to conduct meetings with employees to explain work simplification and secure input and ideas from the employees. They are charged with the responsibility of implementing a target number of work simplification methods. Since they know their employees best and can relate to them on an individual basis, it is the supervisors who conduct training sessions with employees. As a result, the organization has multiplied its training investment tenfold by ensuring that supervisors are prepared to teach employees.

Fourth, supervisors are charged with enforcing the policies of the organization and ensuring that procedures are followed correctly. One effective approach to enable supervisors to understand this responsibility and to handle it effectively is to provide them with training on policies and procedures. Without this training, supervisors will learn policies and procedures at their own pace—with their own interpretation—and there will be little chance of uniform understanding and consistent application throughout the organization. Supervisors may not use manuals properly unless they have had an opportunity to examine and discuss the contents of the manuals in a learning environment.

Fifth, training helps supervisors keep up with the job. Many changes occur in work settings, not only in the technical processes involved but in the techniques of management and supervision. Supervisors must stay up-to-date so they will be able to keep employees abreast of the latest technology. Supervisory training can provide a way for supervisors to stay abreast of changes and keep current on what they need to know.

Sixth, many experts in the field contend that training supervisors is the key to improving productivity. Gellerman (1981, p. 2) has reported from his research that the difference between superior supervisors and below-average supervisors is that the former group has found a way to apply the textbook principles of management—planning, organizing, and controlling—to the work schedule. This can best occur through supervisory training. In one study involving sixty supervisors, quality and productivity measures for work groups were compared before and after supervisors of the work groups were trained. The average productivity level before training was 95 percent of the target. After training it was 109.8 percent of the target. Before training, when the manpower level was reduced by 10.34 percent, quality level went down 5.5 percent. After training, when the manpower level was reduced 10.47 percent, quality level went *up* 6.37 percent.

While the preceding list shows the importance of supervisory training to the organization, the supervisor also has a very important stake in this issue. Each of the six areas discussed has a direct impact on the supervisor. Without training, the supervisor will suffer as much as the organization. Some capable, high-potential employees will become effective supervisors without training. They will learn from their mistakes and develop the skills needed in their jobs. However, this is not an efficient approach, and the toll may be heavy on those who are not star performers (and every organization has them). It is members of the average group who, without proper training, may become ineffective, demotivated, and fail at their work.

Training New Supervisors

Much has been said about how difficult it is—technically and emotionally—for employees to move from a nonmanagement job into a supervisory position. The culture and value systems of the two roles are vastly different, and the skills and insights required in supervision are rarely required in nonmanagement work. Yet many organizations still pay little attention to supervisory training at the time of promotion. It is still common to find organizations in which supervisors make the transition from employee to a member of management over the weekend with little or no instruction on how to perform the job of supervisor. These same organizations would be reluctant to let a new employee operate equipment or machinery without receiving prior instruction and training. Organizations are aware that new employees at the nonmanagement level need training to do their jobs, but they somehow regard supervisory jobs differently. They sometimes think that supervisory skills and knowledge are present at the time of promotion. It is true that there are specific personality traits in some individuals that make the acquisition of supervisory skills relatively easy, and it is also true that some selections are made on that basis. However, effective supervisors are developed. There are no natural-born supervisors, managers, or leaders.

New supervisors expect initial training and are usually surprised when they do not receive it. They recall that in previous, lower-level assignments they received initial instructions and in some cases very extensive training. When they assume supervisory responsibilities with little or no preparation, they are left frustrated and in some cases dismayed by what they have gotten themselves into. They can easily be overwhelmed by these new responsibilities and the impact that their actions have on the organization as a whole. They now have responsibility for many individuals, and the results of their decisions are clearly visible and reported to almost everyone.

In summary, it is a serious injustice for organizations to allow new supervisors to move into the job unprepared and to be forced to learn supervisory skills through trial and error. This approach is illogical and unprofessional; fortunately, it is becoming increasingly rare in today's organizations.

Timing of Initial Training. There are three basic options for the training of new supervisors: educate them before they are promoted, train them as soon as they assume their supervisory responsibilities, or train them after a few months on the job. Each of these approaches has certain advantages and certain shortcomings. Appropriate timing will depend on the ability of the individual, the skills, knowledge, and ability needed in the job, the nature and scope of the specific supervisory assignment, and the organization's resources for training and education.

Education prior to promotion may be provided after a selection decision has been made, or it may be provided to potential supervisory candidates. In either case, it typically includes an explanation of the job and the skills necessary for successful supervision. Presupervisory education has several advantages:

- It prepares supervisors before they face the problems of supervision and thus helps ensure against potential failure or significant mistakes.
- It can make employees aware of what to expect in a supervisory job and thus eliminate those who are not prepared or who feel they cannot handle the job.
- It can build the confidence of potential supervisors so that they will exhibit the necessary leadership, authority, and positive attitude.
- It can create a positive image for the organization that may attract more candidates to the supervisory jobs—possibly some who would not pursue it otherwise.

Presupervisory education has the following disadvantages:

- It is expensive and time consuming to provide this education to candidates before they assume their jobs.
- It is inefficient, since some participants may be prepared for but never receive a supervisory promotion. Also, this approach can build false hopes in those who are not promoted.
- Some of the value of the education may be lost because of the length of time that elapses before the participants have a chance to use their new skills.
- Participants may not be able to relate the education to the supervisory setting since they have not yet occupied the job.

Even with these disadvantages, organizations, in increasing numbers, are conducting education programs for supervisors prior to their assignments. As far as costs are concerned, many organizations regard these programs as investments that will yield a prepared, effective supervisory work force.

Some organizations wait until supervisors have received their promotions before providing them with initial training. In addition to the advantages mentioned earlier, this approach has the added attraction of eliminating the time lag from training to job assignment. Also, this approach is efficient in that only those actually selected for supervision are trained. But it is not without its flaws. In addition to most of the disadvantages of presupervisory education, this approach contains a potential timing problem in that most organizations do not have training programs in place at all times. Thus, some organizations find this approach impractical. It is, nevertheless, an important option to consider when planning initial training.

Most organizations train supervisors soon after they have been assigned to the job of supervisor, typically within three to six months. This gives supervisors an opportunity to see the problems facing them in the light of the skills, examples, and situations discussed in the training program. From a scheduling standpoint, it is more practical to have the flexibility of attending programs in a three- to six-month period. There are, however, problems with this approach. Some supervisors, particularly the marginal performers, may become frustrated and give up prior to receiving the training. Others may flounder and make mistakes that lower their self-esteem and lessen their employees' respect for them. Supervisors may develop bad habits that will be difficult to change, particularly if they have as yet suffered no adverse consequences from them. Also, this approach is incompatible with the usual approach to training employees for other jobs (for example, as machine operators and bank tellers), where training is provided as soon as the employees are assigned to the job. But even with these disadvantages, most organizations tend to postpone supervisory training until some period of time after promotion.

Types of Training. The training of new supervisors can be accomplished in a variety of ways. The specific approach will depend on the organization, the type of job, the level of employees, and the individual skills of those employees being supervised. The approaches described later in this chapter apply equally well here. However, there are several approaches unique to training new supervisors. Some organizations assign a new supervisor to a seasoned, experienced supervisor. The new supervisor receives regular coaching, is allowed to handle limited assignments, and receives feedback from the experienced supervisor. These on-the-job assignments can vary from one month to a year in length depending on the organization and the nature of the work. A variation of this approach is to select supervisors from a formal supervisory trainee program. These programs are designed to prepare individuals for supervisory positions and usually involve rotational assignments to related departments or functions. They may also involve special projects and fill-in supervisory assignments that give these future supervisors an opportunity to see at first hand some of the problems they will face.

Another approach is to consider a tryout in a supervisory role. This was discussed in more detail in Chapter Two as part of the selection method for new supervisors. In this approach supervisors are given the opportunity to assume the supervisory role during a trial period with no commitment from the organization or the employee as to whether or not there will be a permanent placement. This approach is often criticized because of the lack of immediate training and complete instructions for the supervisory job.

Still another way to prepare new supervisors is to provide courses for employees interested in becoming supervisors. These programs can be offered on the employees' own time or on company time. They serve to explain the job of the supervisor and to begin developing the necessary supervisory skills. One disadvantage of this approach is that some employees may never become serious candidates for the job; thus, if they are allowed to participate, they may develop false hopes. Nevertheless, this can be a viable approach and one that is inexpensive if employees learn on their own time. Also, it can be an aid to supervisory selection since high-potential supervisory candidates can be identified.

Objectives and Content. The specific objectives of a training program for new supervisors will vary with the organization. The objectives for one program for recently promoted supervisors are presented in the following list. After completing the program, the new supervisor will be able to:

1. understand the job of the supervisor, including functions, expectations, responsibilities, and authority
2. plan, coordinate, and organize the work of his or her employees
3. use company policies, procedures, services, and resources effectively
4. set and achieve goals
5. understand his or her employees and what motivates them
6. improve his or her own leadership ability by examining and practicing effective ways to handle employees
7. communicate more effectively with employees, fellow supervisors, and middle managers
8. train, and conduct an orientation for, new employees
9. understand work unit costs and budgets
10. understand and work within the company and union agreement
11. handle the unpleasant situations that will arise with employees, including administering discipline, handling complaints, and resolving grievances
12. develop a systematic and logical approach to solving problems and making decisions
13. establish a plan of self-development in both technical and managerial areas

This program is broad in scope and comprehensive; it lasts two full weeks—off the job—with about a one-month interval between the two weeks.

Although the specific content can also vary, training programs for new supervisors will usually address six areas:

- *Job duties and responsibilities.* The training program will explain the detailed responsibilities of the job and allow supervisors to develop a thorough understanding of it. It will cover the important functions of planning, organizing, controlling, communicating, and problem solving, among others. It is important for supervisors to have a full awareness of job duties and responsibilities in order to successfully accomplish what is expected of them.

- *Policies and procedures.* Supervisors are charged with the enforcement of company policy and must ensure that procedures are properly followed. In addition, supervisors are typically the source of information about company policies and procedures for their employees. Therefore, they must understand and know how to interpret them.
- *Employee familiarization.* A supervisor must quickly get acquainted with the employees of the work unit. A training program can show a new supervisor how to get to know the employees as soon as possible. It can provide specific instructions on how to review job descriptions, performance standards, personnel files, and other employee records. In addition, it will show supervisors how to obtain information about employees from previous supervisors and how to conduct interviews and group meetings with employees to secure important information.
- *Attitudes and confidence.* Moving into supervision requires an individual to develop new attitudes toward the job, employees, and the manager. The new supervisor has taken on a completely new role, one for which he or she may be qualified but has not been trained. An effective training program for new supervisors can help develop these attitudes as well as build the confidence necessary if supervisors are to be effective on the job.
- *Handling employee interactions.* One of the most critical aspects of a new supervisor's job is to be able to handle interpersonal problems effectively. In recent years there has been much improvement in the supervisory training processes for building the necessary skills. Behavior modeling, described later in this chapter, is proving to be a very effective approach to building these skills. It is important that new supervisors develop these skills and have them reinforced early in their careers; otherwise, they will develop bad habits that will be difficult to change.
- *Career development.* Most new supervisors have worked hard to get to their new position, and they may have thought very little about where they can go from there. It is not too soon to discuss career advancement at promotion time, although admittedly this would probably have the lowest priority

among the six areas discussed here. Such a discussion can give new supervisors a good feeling about the organization and its approach to developing human resources. Potential career opportunities and specific career development paths should be discussed if feasible. Otherwise, some supervisors may feel that they are assuming a dead-end job. Ideally, supervisors should see the movement into the supervisory ranks as the beginning of their management career, one that is only limited by their own desire to achieve.

Designing Supervisory HRD Programs

Supervisory training is usually planned to correct performance deficiencies or to improve performance above an average level. Supervisory performance, at the individual level, is a function of the supervisor's attitudes, skills, ability, and knowledge, all of which can be improved or enhanced through properly designed training programs. An important part of this process is to correctly determine training needs, set program objectives, and establish appropriate content.

Needs Analysis. Some human resource development managers make the mistake of attempting to use programs from other organizations—or packaged training programs—for their own organization whether they are appropriate or not. A more professional approach is to conduct a detailed analysis to determine the specific needs of an organization and develop or purchase programs to meet those needs. The programs developed or purchased must be relevant to the supervisors' needs, their jobs, and the organization. A needs analysis will result in programs that supervisors can apply and put to use immediately. All supervisors may not need training in communication or improvement in leadership skills. In fact, no two supervisors will need exactly the same training. However, it is possible to find some common needs among all the supervisors in an organization, and these usually form the core program for internal supervisory training. Other programs are specialized and are provided only to those supervisors with specific needs.

Common techniques that organizations use to uncover deficiencies and identify training needs include:

- *Examining supervisory performance records.* Performance measures are available in every organization, and a quick analysis of them will reveal the areas in which supervisors are not performing as well as they could. Typical performance measures are presented in the next chapter.
- *Administering training needs surveys to supervisors.* Surveys can collect detailed information on supervisory performance, the performance of the employees in the work unit, the type and frequency of use of supervisory skills, and perceived areas of training needs.
- *Administering training needs surveys to middle managers.* Although similar in scope to surveys with supervisors, surveys with middle management can provide input on the performance of supervisors, specific supervisory training needs, and practical approaches to training supervisors.
- *Conducting interviews with each supervisor.* Face-to-face interviews are a common information-gathering technique and, if conducted properly, can uncover problem areas, specific behavioral examples, experiences, and performance deficiencies.
- *Conducting interviews with middle managers.* To complement interviews with supervisors, interviews with middle managers can provide information about acceptable and unacceptable supervisory performance, supervisory strengths and weaknesses, and possible approaches to correct deficiencies.
- *Conducting group discussions with supervisors.* Group discussions can identify areas of perceived training needs, important obstacles to excellent supervisory performance, and other issues related to supervisory training.
- *Administering an attitude survey.* Attitude surveys measure a supervisor's attitude toward specific aspects of the job, the organization, and the employees in the work unit. Unacceptable attitudes can possibly be changed in a training program.
- *Administering standard supervisory inventories.* Supervisory inventories on subjects such as communication, human relations, safety, discipline, and labor relations are available for supervisors. Scores on these inventories can reveal individual

training needs, and group results can be compared with normative data.
- *Directly observing supervisors on the job.* Direct observation can provide much information about how supervisors perform their jobs and handle critical situations. It also helps determine the difference in the approaches of low and high performers.

Each of these approaches has its advantages and limitations, and variations of these may be used to secure the desired information. A comprehensive analysis may include input from all these sources, while a single technique may be appropriate in another case.

The results of a needs analysis will yield training needs that are probably unique to the target group. One analysis, involving 805 first-level supervisors in city and state government in North Carolina, revealed the following major needs (Jerdee and Calhoon, 1977, p. 24):

- decision making and problem solving
- methods improvement
- keeping abreast of new developments
- setting goals for subordinates
- motivating subordinates
- planning, organizing, and scheduling the unit's work

More detailed information on training needs analysis can be found in Zemke and Kramlinger (1982).

Objectives. Developing objectives for supervisory training programs is extremely important. There are two major categories of objectives. One includes specific objectives for each program, and the other represents broad, overall objectives for the entire human resource development system for supervisors. For each specific program, objectives are developed to show what the course is designed to accomplish. According to Kirkpatrick (1983, p. 50), there are four kinds of objectives for training programs:

- *attitude* objectives that focus on the supervisor's attitude toward the training program, some aspect of the job, employees, management, or the organization
- *knowledge* objectives that focus on specific parts of the job and include policies, procedures, processes, and technical aspects of the work unit
- *skill* objectives that focus on the identifiable changes in how a supervisor performs a task or assignment
- *job behavior* objectives that focus on measurable results obtained back on the job after completing the training program

Ideally, objectives should be developed for the skill and job behavior categories of each program in the organization. Specific objectives are important for several reasons. If objectives have been defined, both supervisory participants and discussion leaders will know what is expected of them. The HRD staff and middle and top management will know what should be accomplished with the HRD function. Also, it is objectives that form the basis for evaluating the effectiveness of supervisory HRD programs.

Broad objectives are commonplace in policy manuals or company procedures. For example, in the Methodist Hospitals of Memphis, the following broad objectives were outlined for their supervisory training and education effort (Simpson, 1983, p. 56):

- Identify and describe expected specific supervisory behaviors.
- Assess the developmental needs of all first-line supervisors individually (annually or semiannually).
- Provide managers with a process whereby they can systematically assist their supervisors in developing their skills and competencies.
- Assist supervisors in establishing specific measurable development plans (annually or semiannually).
- Provide training programs that address the developmental needs of supervisors and managers.

These objectives provide a general framework on which the total supervisory training and education effort can be focused. Broad objectives are important in establishing an integrated and comprehensive system to train and educate supervisors. Also, these objectives can be linked to career ladders or paths in the organization.

Content. The specific content of programs varies considerably with the organization and the supervisory jobs. The content is developed after the needs are determined and objectives have been set. Table 3 shows the content from a sampling of supervi-

Table 3. Subjects Covered in Formal Supervisory Training Programs in 34 Organizations.

Subject	Number of Programs
Human relations skills	34
Evaluating and appraising others	31
Understanding human behavior	29
Leadership	28
Motivating others	28
Counseling and coaching	28
Discipline	27
Oral communication	27
Developing and training subordinates	26
Avoiding discrimination charges	26
Written communication	22
Selecting employees	21
Managerial skills	32
Role of the manager	30
Meeting objectives and priorities	26
Managing time	25
Organizing and planning	24
Technical skills	21
Safety procedures	19

Note: Most companies include more than one of the these subjects in their programs.

Source: Levine, 1982, p. 9.

sory training programs from thirty-four organizations (Levine, 1982, p. 9). Although the needs vary, there is much common ground in the content of the programs from these organizations. The variety of content of supervisory training can best be illustrated by examining the approach used at General Electric. In order to meet the challenges of training 8,000 supervisors in over 100 locations worldwide, General Electric developed a modular approach to supervisory training. Figure 7 shows the modules developed, along with their target group—either pre-supervisors, new supervisors, or experienced supervisors. These modules provide a building-block approach to supervisory development. By choosing from the available modules, each manager can tailor a course for his or her own supervisors. The result is an individually tailored training program for each location. Each module is self-contained and freestanding while at the same time it is capable of interfacing with other modules. This variety of modules enabled General Electric to meet its objective of providing training for the varied and diverse needs of all its departments.

Approaches to Supervisory HRD

There are many approaches available to train supervisors and make them more effective. While there are specific advantages and disadvantages to each, their effectiveness will depend on the organization, the supervisor, and the nature of the job.

Internal Classroom Programs. One of the most common types of supervisory training is the internally presented classroom training program. In one recent survey (Levine, 1982, p. 6), almost half the respondents used internal classroom programs as an approach to training supervisors. Almost every organization with a formal HRD department will offer internal supervisory training programs whose subjects range from principles of supervision to effective writing. It is an approach that is almost synonymous with supervisory training.

The "classroom" ranges from onsite training rooms and conference rooms to elaborate training and education centers situated some distance from regular facilities. One such center is IBM's Management Development Center, a campuslike facility located on twenty-six acres at Armonk, New York. The heart of the campus is a multipurpose building that contains administrative offices, the company's archives, separate sets of classrooms, a personnel resources library with video playback rooms, a lounge, and a formal dining room. Other organizations use local hotels, college campuses, or conference centers for their supervisory training programs.

Specific training methods used in internal classroom programs are varied. They include lectures, group discussions, exercises, case studies, films, video tapes, and skill practices. Most supervisory training programs use several different methods that are tailored to the training setting and the supervisors being trained. Some methods are more effective than others, depending on the subject matter, previous experience of the learners, and the effectiveness of the program leader.

Behavior Modeling. A particularly effective and relatively new approach to internal classroom training is called behavior modeling. While the HRD field has had its share of new fads with fancy names, this approach to training seems to be producing significant results. Many companies, including AT&T, General Electric, and IBM, have used behavior modeling with much success. A number of consulting and publishing firms have sprung up in the last few years with packages of behavior-modeling programs that produced outstanding successes.

Behavior modeling develops supervisory skills, usually through interactions with employees. A typical modeling sequence embraces six stages (Bittel and Ramsey, 1983, p. 43):

1. a presentation of the concept
2. step-by-step demonstration (on cassette or film) of the key steps a supervisor must take to handle the situation
3. the supervisor's behavioral rehearsal in a supportive environment
4. supportive feedback from peers and/or trainers
5. an action plan or performance contract to transfer learning to the actual job setting
6. follow-up to assess the problems encountered and to suggest ways to overcome them

Because they normally deal concretely with common in-

Figure 7. Modular Supervisory Training Programs at General Electric.

Module	Length in Hrs.	Content	Suitable for:		
			Pre-Supervisor	New Supervisor	Experienced Supervisor
Elements of Foremanship	2	Foreman/Supervisor role as seen by foreman/supervisor, his/her manager, and his/her manager's manager	X	X	X
Styles of Leadership	4	Comparison of leadership styles and their results	X	X	X
Two-Way Communication	8	Concepts and techniques of effective one-on-one verbal communication in the business environment	X	X	X
Listening Awareness	2	The need for active listening in daily work activities	X	X	X
Instructing and Developing People	6	Conducting job analyses, making work assignments, job coaching, developing and administering job training programs	X	X	
Dealing with People	6	Improving communications, motivating work teams appraising employees, resolving conflicts, counselling	X	X	
Grievance Handling	4	The foreman/supervisor's role in anticipating, preventing, investigating, and resolving employee grievances	X	X	X
Constructive Discipline	4	Using discipline as a positive, constructive force to stimulate an atmosphere of willing cooperation	X	X	X
Facilitating Change	3	Techniques for introducing change and anticipating possible problem areas		X	X
Interpersonal Relationships	4	Avoiding or minimizing day-to-day conflict situations		X	X
Job Instructing Training	6	Techniques for analyzing skills of work force, preparing detailed job breakdowns, effective job instruction		X	X
Cost and Waste Control	2	Focuses attention on responsibility for cost and waste control and provides techniques for gaining active employee support and cooperation		X	X

Module	Length in Hrs.	Content	Pre-Supervisor	Suitable for: New Supervisor	Experienced Supervisor
Work Station Control	3	Technique for analyzing a work station to determine cause of a problem		X	X
Labor Relations - I	4	Foreman/supervisor responsibility for administration of local labor agreement		X	X
Handling Work Assignments	4	Principles and techniques of effective job assignments		X	X
Improving Employee Performance	4	Use of positive reinforcement to stimulate employee productivity		X	X
Setting Performance Standards	4	Technique for developing objective, measurable performance standards		X	X
Industrial Alcoholism	4	Role clarification and technique for handling alcohol-and drug-related performance problems	X	X	X
Controlling Absenteeism	2	Techniques for dealing with employees with absenteeism problems		X	X
Transactional Analysis — A Communication Tool	4	Using TA techniques to overcome or prevent communication barriers	X	X	X
Increasing Personal Effectiveness	3	Enlarging the scope of the job effectiveness by testing perceived constraints		X	X
Influencing Job Performance	4	Effect of foreman/supervisor expectations on employee job performance		X	X
Planning, Organizing and Controlling for Contingency Situations	6	Tools and techniques for anticipating and handling contingency situations		X	X
Effective Time Management	4	A look at time management techniques with particular emphasis on distinction between "urgency" and "importance" in setting priorities	X	X	X
Preventing and Handling Insubordination	4	Identification of insubordination situations according to legal definition of term. Techniques for preventing and handling insubordination	X	X	X

Source: Richard D. Colvin, General Electric Company.

terpersonal problems with employees, both experienced and in-
experienced supervisors can benefit from these types of programs. Some typical behavior-modeling sessions are shown in
Table 4. A complete description of this approach can be found
in Robinson (1983).

Table 4. Typical Modules for a Behavior-Modeling Program.

Conducting the hiring interview	Resolving employee conflicts
Setting job standards	Counseling on employee problems
Teaching a new job	Averting discrimination problems
Conducting the work progress interview	Handling employee complaints
	Communicating with confidence
Improving employee performance	Listening with understanding
Improving employee performance —follow-up	Creating your own key actions
	Delegating
Correcting problem behavior	Handling emotional behavior in
Taking disciplinary action	discussions
Terminating an employee	Keeping your boss informed
Overcoming resistance to change	Presenting an idea to your boss
Giving recognition	Confronting issues with your boss
Holding the Performance Appraisal Interview	

Source: Adapted from the Training Program for Supervision, developed and marketed by Zenger-Miller, 10061 Bubb Road, Cupertino, Calif.
95014.

Outside Seminars. Outside seminars represent another important approach to training for supervisors. In smaller organizations, because of their limited budgets and staffs, the total training effort might rest on what is available in the outside market.
In larger organizations, outside seminars are usually integrated
into the overall supervisory training, education, and development system to complement what is offered internally. The
HRD staff should identify a core of outside programs with
proven track records.

Much care must be exercised in selecting an outside seminar since there has been an overabundance of poorly developed
and presented seminars. The HRD staff should carefully evaluate these programs before using them. This means gathering

detailed information, checking the references of speakers, and contacting previous participants. In addition, these programs should be monitored and evaluated routinely to make sure their quality is being maintained. Specific techniques for developing an effective approach to using outside seminars are found in Phillips (1983a).

Self-Study. Much of the supervisor's learning is individually focused. From any point of view, self-directed learning or self-development is a growing requirement of the supervisory job. The supervisor must be motivated to learn new skills, technology, and methods of supervision. Most organizations recognize their obligation to make learning opportunities available and to stimulate interest in those opportunities. At the same time, they recognize that most learning is self-directed, and because of this they are placing increased emphasis on self-study as an approach to supervisory training. Highly motivated supervisors, eager to learn more about their jobs, will take advantage of this approach to training. Others will follow suit if encouraged or required to do so.

Organizations have used several approaches to self-study. Some provide a suggested reading list for supervisors. Others develop their own "great books" program with assignments and follow-up meetings to see if the supervisors have read the material. This reading material must be related to the supervisor's job and written so that it can be easily understood by the supervisor. This approach seems to work best if top management sets the example and develops its own reading schedule. Programmed instruction courses are commonly used as a self-teaching technique. This approach allows the learner to proceed at his or her own pace. The participant must learn one topic before going to the next, and reinforcement and repetition are used to ensure that the supervisor fully understands the material. A variety of supervisory courses are available in this format from the major publishing companies. Home study courses are another approach to self-study. They help supervisors sharpen their skills as well as build expertise in a variety of management topics. There are many courses available from commercial correspondence schools, industry and trade groups, and local colleges and universities.

Job Rotation. A few organizations use a formal job rotation program to improve the performance of supervisors in present assignments and prepare them for future assignments. Several effective approaches to job rotation are available, each with its own limitations and advantages. The most common type is the one in which two or more people simply exchange places, with each taking on new responsibilities either permanently or temporarily. For example, the inspection department in one manufacturing firm has several supervisors in charge of the employees who inspect the work at different stages in the process. These supervisors are rotated systematically to give them exposure to different types of inspection and quality control problems. One hospital has an extensive rotation program in which new department supervisors rotate through all major departments and stay for one-month intervals. A variation on this approach is internal lateral replacement, which involves filling vacancies with a transfer from within the department. Filling the job from within eliminates the need for the extensive orientation that would be required for someone brought in from outside the organization.

A part-time or temporary job rotation allows two people to swap activities for a week or more to train each other in certain duties of their jobs. For example, one organization temporarily assigns district sales supervisors to headquarters positions when corporate staff supervisors are on vacation. This not only provides additional training for district supervisors but also improves the cooperation and working relationship between the field staff and the headquarters staff.

Finally, if budget and organizational setting permit, an extra employee can be allocated for a permanent learning slot. This may involve keeping one person in the work unit to learn as many jobs as possible in a learning slot. This "extra employee" is usually preparing for the next opening that occurs. There is some flexibility in this approach because the extra employee can be involved in cross-training or can be used to relieve others who are involved in cross-training activities. One manufacturer has an extra production supervisor for each major department. This slot is usually staffed with a newly promoted supervisor who fills in when someone is on vacation, jury duty, or a short leave of absence.

Job rotation has several advantages both for the organization and for managers who initiate it. A manager has more flexibility to make assignments when more than one person can do a job. This flexibility keeps the operation running smoothly while preparing supervisors to assume other jobs and helping them to develop their careers. Job rotation prepares replacements for jobs that will eventually have to be filled. It can even allow a supervisor to develop a replacement for his or her own job and thus eliminate the anguish of a promotion deferred because a prepared successor is not available. Also, for the organization, job rotation can help identify those supervisors who have the ability and skills to move to higher-level jobs. It provides a valuable opportunity for determining how supervisors perform in a variety of settings and represents very objective input into the promotion decision.

In addition to the advantages for the organization, the individual benefits greatly from job rotation. Taking on new assignments with new responsibilities provides a challenge for supervisors. It prevents them from becoming stale in the job, while also providing them with opportunities for learning more about other positions and other aspects of the organization. Since different experiences teach different lessons, supervisors may be given a chance to develop skills and abilities not required on current assignments. Overall, job rotation can raise self-esteem, increase skills, help develop careers, and increase the respect that supervisors receive from other employees in the organization. For more information on specific techniques for job rotation and the requirements for successful implementation, see Phillips (1981).

On-the-Job Coaching. A practical and sometimes informal approach to training supervisors is through on-the-job coaching, which is usually conducted by the middle manager. This technique is based on the premise that the vast majority of a supervisor's learning will occur on the job as a result of guided experience under the direction of effective managers. When using this approach to develop supervisors, middle managers should remember that coaching is not a one-time effort. Rather, it is a continuous process that involves discussions between the manager and the supervisor. The manager (coach) observes supervisors, gives feedback, and plans specific actions to correct performance deficiencies. The process is repeated regularly, and because of this supervisors feel less anxiety toward coaching than toward the typical performance appraisal. Realistic performance feedback is critical, but somehow managers have confused coaching with criticism and consequently have avoided the process. Supervisors must have a thorough understanding of their duties and the standards by which they are evaluated. They must know and understand the goals, targets, and mission of their department, division, or organization. Performance feedback must be frank, open, and straightforward. Supervisors must know when their performance is good and when it is unacceptable.

Another important point is that coaching should not be confused with cheerleading. It is, of course, important for the coach to provide encouragement and help to supervisors. Positive reinforcement is essential, and motivation is an important part of coaching. However, a coach will attempt to raise the morale of supervisors only when low morale is a critical issue. Also, there is a mistaken belief that only fast-track supervisors or marginal performers need coaching. In reality, all supervisors need coaching, including the large group of average performers. Coaching is important for new supervisors since it will help them become more productive in a short period of time. Coaching will help marginal performers improve their performance to an acceptable standard. It helps average supervisors identify strengths and weaknesses and develop skills necessary to move above an average level of performance. And for the super performers, coaching is important in helping them maintain their outstanding performance records and advance to other jobs in the organization.

Although supervisors may come to view their coach as a

role model, the coaching process is not one of providing leadership to the supervisors. A coach does not carry the ball. The coach may help the supervisor with a performance problem but does not solve the problem for the supervisor. A coach is an observer who does not get too involved in the actual problems and difficulties encountered by the supervisor. It is best for the supervisor to handle it himself or herself with the aid of some advice from the coach. It is important to understand that good, effective coaching will not happen by itself. It must be encouraged by top management, and examples must be set up and down the organization. An organization would do well to train the middle-management group to be effective coaches.

Mentor Relationships. An intriguing and increasingly common approach to supervisory development is mentoring. Although this process may be at work informally in almost every organization, some organizations capitalize on this principle and encourage the practice, particularly for supervisors. A mentor is a person in the organization who takes on the responsibility to train and educate another individual and assist him or her in career advancement. Specifically, mentors teach, guide, advise, counsel, and sponsor the supervisor while serving as role models. The mentor may or may not be in the same department, division, plant, or location as the supervisor. For supervisors, mentoring involves establishing a relationship with an experienced, influential manager, who is usually at a higher level. There must be a good match between the mentor and the supervisor. Otherwise, the relationship will not be productive. They must both be willing participants in the process and realize that the supervisor needs assistance and help from the mentor. In addition, the mentor must enjoy helping supervisors achieve their goals in the organization. According to one report of this process (Lea and Leibowitz, 1983, p. 35): "An awareness of what constitutes mentoring will allow many veteran managers to utilize consciously their experience and knowledge in their daily interactions to develop employees. The impact can be far greater than many expensive formal management or employee development efforts."

A word of caution is in order, however. Supervisors learn

from poor role models as well as good ones. It seems important to have a variety of mentors rather than a single mentor, regardless of the competence of the mentor. In practice, most successful managers have worked for several memorable bosses and have learned what *not* to do from role models almost as often as they have learned what to do.

Special Projects and Assignments. An infrequent approach, but still one that can be effective, is the use of special projects and assignments to develop supervisors. This approach involves assigning special, nonroutine job duties to supervisors that will build skills needed in the current job as well as prepare supervisors for assignments in the future. Typical projects are:

- *Short-term assignments.* Examples are special investigations, an analysis of a problem, exploring the feasibility of a new method, procedure, or technique, or installing new equipment.
- *Task forces.* These may be involved in implementing a new management information system in the organization, tackling a serious quality problem, or designing a program to train new employees.
- *Special assistance to schools and colleges.* A supervisor might assist a local vocational school to develop a new curriculum, serve on an advisory committee, or teach a business course in high school.
- *On-loan assignments for volunteer and nonprofit organizations.* Examples are the United Way annual fund drive, the National Alliance of Business, the Chamber of Commerce, and Junior Achievement.

The full range and scope of activities are almost unlimited. Projects or assignments should be selected on the basis of the training and educational needs of the supervisor and the supervisor's willingness to participate in such activities.

Professional Societies and Associations. A final approach to supervisory training and education is the use of professional organizations. These come in two varieties, one expressly for management and supervision and the other for technical or professional specialties. For managers and supervisors, two organizations offer local chapters. The National Management Association and the International Management Council of the YMCA have chapters virtually all over the United States, both in cities and in individual companies. A third organization, the Society for the Advancement of Management, has local chapters on college campuses only. These associations, through their regular meetings, seminars, courses, and other involvement programs, can enhance supervisory skills. They give supervisors a forum in which to exchange information and learn from others, all through a self-imposed, voluntary effort. More information on these associations is presented in a later chapter.

The other types of associations include the many technical and professional organizations available for individual memberships. For almost any type of work there is a professional association or society connected with it in some way or another. A few typical organizations are the Purchasing Management Association, American Marketing Association, American Society for Production and Inventory Control, Public Relations Society of America, Hospital Personnel Association, American Society for Quality Control, and National Association of Accountants.

A membership in the appropriate organization can improve technical expertise and thereby assist in the training and education of supervisors. It also develops peer contacts that can be useful in solving technical problems. Many organizations support the participation of supervisors in these organizations by paying their expenses and encouraging them to become actively involved through taking an office, serving on a committee, or working on a special project. This active involvement benefits both the individual and the organization.

Factors Influencing Supervisory HRD

Although a properly designed HRD program conducted in an effective manner is an indispensable condition for the ultimate success of the supervisory HRD effort, indirect factors such as

commitment, support, involvement, and results also play important roles.

Supervisory HRD is not the single responsibility of any
individual or group of individuals in the organization. To a large
degree, supervisors must accept some responsibility for their
own improvement. As noted earlier, most of the supervisor's
learning is a highly individualized matter. Because of this, supervisors should take the initiative in improving their skills, increasing their knowledge, and preparing for future assignments and
responsibilities. Unfortunately, some supervisors will not assume this responsibility. They sometimes look to other groups
in the organization to provide them with programs, opportunities, encouragement, and support for their development.

HRD departments have a very significant responsibility
in providing effective programs. They develop—or purchase—
and implement high-quality programs appropriate to the organization's needs. They obtain results from those programs and
communicate them to management. They develop effective and
productive relationships with the primary users of supervisory
training, who are usually members of the line organization. In
addition, the top HRD officer must establish an open and productive relationship with the chief executive officer. This can
ensure that the chief executive has a clear understanding of the
training and educational needs of the organization and at the
same time is able to communicate his or her expectations to the
HRD department.

It is only through shared responsibilities that an organization will develop and implement effective supervisory HRD programs. Some organizations outline these multiple responsibilities in policy manuals. Others develop an informal understanding
of the responsibilities. Still others place more emphasis on the
line organization's responsibility, as is the case with the General
Accounting Office (GAO). One of the six guiding principles for
training supervisors and middle managers at GAO is: "Management development is the responsibility of the line organization,
not exclusively a personnel function. GAO managers must perceive that management development is important to their unit's
success" ("Management Development: How GAO Does It,"
1983, p. 58).

To further emphasize the importance of the line responsibility, some argue that staff trainers should report to senior line managers, not to an HRD manager (LeFlufy, 1983). The rationale? Anyone hired to help a manager with supervisory training should report to that manager, not to a staff department.

Defining responsibilities will not alone ensure success for supervisory training. It takes a combination of factors working simultaneously to achieve maximum return for the training expenditures. There are four primary factors that can influence the success of these programs:

Commitment of Top Management. As mentioned earlier, top management shares an important responsibility for supervisory HRD. Its actions have tremendous impact on the success of HRD efforts. According to Phillips (1983b, p. 232), strong top management commitment to the function requires the chief executive officer or other top officials to

- develop a mission for the HRD function
- allocate the necessary funds for a successful effort
- allow employees time to participate in programs
- get actively involved in the process and require others to do so
- support the HRD effort and ask other managers to do the same
- place the HRD function in a visible and high-level position in the organization, close to the chief executive
- demand that each program be evaluated in some way
- insist that programs be cost effective and require supporting data
- set an example in self-development
- create an atmosphere of open communication between top management and HRD personnel

It would be difficult to achieve all these goals in any one organization. However, more and more chief executives are increasing their commitment to this function and beefing up the resources and staffs of the HRD department.

Middle-Management Support. Middle managers usually discharge their responsibilities for supervisory HRD through the support provided to their supervisors. They are the most important determinant of whether or not supervisors will put into practice what they have learned. The type of support given by middle managers typically varies considerably with the organization. An ideal supportive environment exists when the middle manager

- gives enthusiastic endorsement and approval of supervisory involvement in HRD programs
- volunteers personal services or resources to assist in the HRD effort
- makes a commitment with the participant prior to attending the program that outlines what changes should take place or what tasks should be accomplished after the program has been completed
- reinforces behavior changes resulting from the program
- conducts a follow-up of the results achieved in the program
- gives positive rewards for participants who have outstanding accomplishments as a result of attending the program (Phillips, 1983b, p. 234)

Utopia? But it is precisely this kind of support that HRD departments should strive to create. Specific details on how to improve support for supervisory training programs are found in Phillips (1978).

Management Involvement. This refers to the active participation of all levels of management in the HRD process. There are almost as many opportunities for management involvement in the process as there are steps in the design and development of a complete program. One recent survey (Lashbrook, 1981, pp. 53-55) showed that managers are involved in evaluating program effectiveness, determining program content, determining the size of the HRD budget, allocating the HRD budget, and selecting outside suppliers. It appears that the most important—and practical—approaches for obtaining management involvement are to

- *Use managers on advisory committees.* Many organizations have established committees to improve the input to the HRD department. These advisory committees are very common and can be developed for individual programs, specific functions, or for multiple functions. They can be one-time committees or standing committees, depending on the duration of the program. And they can be used in many stages of the process, from needs analysis to communication of program results.
- *Select managers to serve as discussion leaders.* In many organizations, managers at different levels are involved in conducting HRD programs. Although this approach can have several benefits, it also presents unique challenges for the HRD staff. Not everyone has a flair for leading a discussion in a training program. Discussion leaders must be carefully chosen and in some cases trained to handle their assignments.
- *Use managers on a training task force.* A task force is sometimes given the responsibility for developing a major training program. This approach is particularly useful for a program that lies outside the scope and capabilities of the HRD staff. Also, the time required to produce a program may prohibit the HRD staff from developing it through their efforts alone.
- *Encourage managers to attend HRD programs.* Some organizations require managers to attend HRD programs ahead of their supervisors. This firsthand experience can improve the managers' perception of the program and prepare them to effectively support their supervisors after the program is completed.

These four approaches are very effective ways to get management involved in the HRD process. The results may be surprising. The credibility of the program will be enhanced. Managers will feel that the program is theirs, since they have been involved in the process of developing, conducting, or evaluating it. Management involvement also increases the interaction between supervisors and managers while sharpening the skills of managers. In some cases, moreover, it is more economical to use managers in lieu of the HRD staff. Finally, these approaches reward good managers for their contributions to the HRD effort. With all these advantages, more organizations should utilize the skills, abilities, and influence of managers in supervisory HRD programs.

Results. Last, but not least, results must be achieved if a supervisory HRD effort is to continue. The staff must take steps to evaluate each program and, if feasible, to show its contribution to the bottom line of the organization. Fortunately, the technology and methods to show the worth of any training and educational program are available. This sometimes requires a reorientation of the HRD department's philosophy, so that the concern for results is considered in the program design all the way from the needs analysis to program implementation. One HRD program design model that places emphasis on results is presented in Figure 8. This model devotes no less than eleven of its eighteen steps to getting results. These results will no doubt attract the attention of top management and thereby increase its commitment. In fact, each of the four factors mentioned earlier—commitment, support, involvement, and results—has a direct relationship to all the others. As one is improved or increased, it has a positive impact on the other factors. Working together, these four factors will ensure that the right kind of supervisory HRD effort is in place in the organization.

Career Development

Supervisors are concerned about their careers. One study, involving almost 1,000 foremen and supervisors, revealed that some 59 percent of foremen and 84 percent of white-collar supervisors were interested in changing jobs (Keavenly and Jackson, 1977, p. 15). The percentages were even higher for younger foremen: 67 percent of those under thirty-one were interested in changing jobs, while 85 percent of the white-collar supervisors in the same age group were interested in relocating. In a study of supervisors by Bittel and Ramsey (1983), only about one in five indicated that he or she was content to stay in the same job or at the same level. Nearly three quarters had their

Figure 8. Results-Oriented Human Resources Development Model.

1. Conduct a Needs Analysis
▽

2. Identify Purposes of Evaluation
▽

3. Establish Baseline Data
▽

4. Select Evaluation Method/Design
▽

5. Determine Evaluation Strategy
▽

6. Develop Program Objectives
▽

7. Estimate Program Costs/Benefits
▽

8 Prepare and Present Proposal
▽

9. Design Evaluation Instruments
▽

10. Determine and Develop Program Content
▽

11. Design or Select Development Methods
▽

12. Test Program and Make Revisions
▽

13. Implement or Conduct Program
▽

14. Collect Data at Proper Stages
▽

15. Analyze and Interpret Data
▽

16. Make Program Adjustments
▽

17. Calculate Return on Investment
▽

18. Communicate Program Results

sights on either their boss's job or on a higher-level management job. But they did not appear to be very mobile in this regard. Only one in ten was willing to leave the organization to move upward.

Given this concern for career development, organizations need to focus attention on providing formal career development programs and career-planning assistance for supervisors. Apparently, organizations are growing increasingly aware of the need for a broad range of career development programs for their supervisors. Three fourths of the 203 midwestern and national companies responding to a Midwest College Placement Association survey have planned or are currently planning such programs ("Corporate Career Development . . . ," 1984). These programs vary widely but usually take the following forms:

Career Resource Center. The least expensive approach to providing career information is the establishment of a career resource center. This may be part of the management and supervisory library and contain resource material on career planning and development. There has been a proliferation of books and self-study programs on this subject in recent years. Organizations make this material available to interested supervisors. Some provide questions and exercises, as well as encouraging words, to help supervisors understand career development possibilities. A number of companies have provided employees with copies of career-planning books such as *What Color Is Your Parachute?* (Bolles, 1978). Some have even created their own career-planning workbooks that contain company-related information about resources available, career options, and contacts for counseling (Carroll and Schuler, 1983, pp. 5–8). This simple approach can develop positive feelings among supervisors because it demonstrates that the organization is interested in their careers.

Individual Development Plans. Since much of the development of supervisors is individual in nature, career development can be most efficiently accomplished on an individual basis. One such approach involves the use of individual development plans

(IDPs) for supervisors. These plans are developed around what the supervisor needs to know to handle his or her job more effectively and/or to prepare for advancement to a higher position. They may be developed for all supervisors or restricted to selected groups. One organization, for example, limits this approach to those supervisors who are considered to have high potential for advancement, high potential being defined as the ability to advance two job levels in five years.

Individual development plans outline various experiences, specific training and educational programs, special projects, and other learning activities planned for a predetermined period of time. Ideally these plans are developed with the help of staff support personnel, usually personnel from the human resources function. These individual plans are most effective when:

- Supervisors have direct input into determining what should be contained in the IDP.
- The middle manager is directly involved in the assessment of the supervisor's education and training needs and in the preparation of the IDP.
- Supervisors are given some responsibility for monitoring their own progress related to the IDP.
- Supervisors receive immediate, objective feedback on their progress.
- Staff support is provided to ensure that the IDPs are developed and reviewed on a timely basis and that the process is accomplished in a consistent manner.
- The IDP is modified as necessary after periodic progress reviews.
- The IDPs remain confidential and are available for review by those in the chain of command above the supervisor.

Individual development plans come in a variety of formats. One such format is shown in Exhibit 1; it is for a supervisor who has shown excellent potential and is being prepared to assume a department manager's position. The plan has a number of target dates and is reviewed every six months. The

Exhibit 1. Example of an Individual Development Plan.

Name   Bill Jones

Current Job   Supervisor, Claims Section

Time Period   Six Months

Last Review Jan. 10, 1986

INDIVIDUAL DEVELOPMENT PLAN
PERSONAL & CONFIDENTIAL

AREAS FOR DEVELOPMENT	DEVELOPMENTAL ACTIVITIES	TARGET DATE(S)
Finance and Accounting	Attend three-day workshop on Finance and Accounting for Non-Financial Managers conducted by AMA.	02-21-86
	Visit the headquarters General Accounting Department to become familiar with their functions that are related to the Claims Department.	03-14-86
	Assist the Data Processing Department in the development of the new claims tracking system.	05-30-86
	Prepare the 1987 Preliminary Departmental Budget and have it ready to be reviewed by the Division Manager.	06-30-86
Leadership Skills	Represent the department on the Company's Employee Benefits Advisory Committee and report significant changes to the department.	During 1986
	Prepare and deliver a presentation on "Computerized Claims Processing" at the Annual Agents Conference.	04-24-86
	Serve as coordinator for departmental group meetings.	Continuous for Six Months
	Attend seminar on "Leadership Skills for Department Heads" conducted by Corporate Human Resources. (Continued)	06-16-86

VULCAN MATERIALS COMPANY - SOUTHERN DIVISION

VMC-3506

specific items are initiated and monitored by either the middle manager or the human resources department.

The primary benefit of this approach is that it recognizes individual differences in the training and education needs of supervisors and subsequently provides a tailored plan to meet those specific needs. In the places where this approach has been used, the reaction has been extremely favorable (Luthans, Lyman, and Lockwood, 1978, p. 5).

Career Paths or Ladders. Some organizations have taken a more formal approach to the career development of their supervisors by developing potential career paths or career ladders. By means of flow charts, diagrams, and tables, the most likely career paths are outlined for supervisors who have the ability to move upward in the organization. Although this emphasis on career possibilities may create anxieties about advancement in some supervisors, the mere presence of a career path gives many others a comfortable and satisfied feeling about their organization. Even those who are not presently interested in moving up may take some pride in knowing there is a direct path for advancement if they should someday become dissatisfied with their current jobs. Effective career paths for supervisors should be developed along the following lines:

- They should represent typical job moves that have occurred in the past.
- The paths should represent a likely sequence of job assignments for a typical supervisor in the area where the paths are developed.
- Special conditions or unusual requirements should be clearly communicated along with other information on the career paths.
- Career paths should be discussed with supervisors, particularly those who have expressed an interest in career advancement.
- Supervisors aspiring to move along a path should receive regular feedback on their performance and frank discussion about why they are not advancing to their desired position, if that happens.

Some organizations provide career path information through postings on bulletin boards and in company publications. A few organizations—particularly the larger ones—have established elaborate career-planning and control departments. The purpose of these departments is to provide regular management reports regarding career development activities. Career path coordinators are available to discuss possible career paths and provide the additional information that supervisors might need to move along those career paths.

Career Counseling. Another approach to supervisory career development is to assign someone to provide counseling to supervisors. Although some organizations consider it the manager's duty to offer supervisors career advice, the manager sometimes lacks the time, motivation, and skills to provide effective career counseling. For years, organizations have provided counseling for drug abuse, family problems, legal matters, and even psychological disorders. Organizations are now providing counselors who can answer questions and assist supervisors in achieving their career goals. These counselors can be deployed in a variety of ways. Some organizations have full-time people assigned to the human resources function. In smaller organizations, human resources professionals may have career-counseling duties along with employment, recruiting, training, or salary administration responsibilities. In other organizations, capable staff and line managers provide advice and information to supervisors on a part-time basis, usually after receiving training on how to perform this task effectively.

To be most effective, career counselors should have the following characteristics:

- They should be aware of the content of the jobs that they will be discussing with supervisors.
- They should be well respected and credible in the eyes of the supervisory group.
- They must be available as needed to provide advice and assistance to supervisors.
- They should be visible, their names should be known, and

their function should be clearly communicated to the supervisory group.
- They should be rewarded for their efforts when they get results, particularly if career counseling is not their full-time
assignment.

Some organizations track career-counseling activity and monitor
its results. The number of counseling sessions, the time spent on
the effort, and the outcomes help show the effectiveness of
counseling. The result of this effort is usually subjective, however, since it is dependent on the counselor's decision as to
whether a satisfactory resolution has been achieved.

In summary, the interest in career development in organizations is growing significantly. Perhaps it is the most significant
development in the field of human resources in the past few
years. Career development efforts are most effective when they
start small and are allowed to grow as the organization is able to
enhance the process. Career planning and development can provide a focus for coordinating various types of training and education efforts, especially for supervisory groups. There are a
variety of approaches available, and an investment in career development for supervisors should reap a handsome return for
the organization.

Summary

This chapter presented the various approaches to providing supervisory training, education, and development, or human
resource development as it is usually called. It focused on the
training of new supervisors, the design of successful programs,
approaches to supervisory HRD, and career development for
supervisors. To develop its human resources effectively, the organization must

- Evaluate the way it provides training to new supervisors near
the time of promotion. The content and quality of this initial training can be very critical to the success of supervisors.
- Review the design process for supervisory HRD programs to

see if improvements are necessary in determining needs, selecting objectives, and developing content.

- Examine the potential approaches to supervisory HRD for applicability in the organization. The approaches presented in this chapter range from internal classroom programs to the use of professional societies and associations.
- Analyze the factors that influence the success of supervisory HRD and make adjustments as needed. Securing management commitment, support, and involvement, as well as achieving measurable results, are all important factors.
- Explore the career development issues facing supervisors and develop practical approaches to satisfying their needs in this important area. This chapter presented four proven ways to tackle the issue.

Supervisors are concerned with their internal growth and developmental opportunities. An investment in the training, education, and development of supervisors can both ensure their success and produce significant results for the organization.

Suggested Readings

Belker, L. B. *The First-Time Manager: A Practical Guide to the Management of People.* New York: AMACOM, 1978.

Boyd, B. B. *Supervisory Training: Approaches and Methods.* Washington, D.C.: American Society for Training and Development, 1976.

Broadwell, M. M. *The New Supervisor.* (2nd ed.) Reading, Mass.: Addison-Wesley, 1979.

Gardner, J. E. *Training the New Supervisor.* New York: AMACOM, 1980.

Goldstein, A. P., and Sorcher, M. *Changing Supervisor Behavior.* Elmsford, N.Y.: Pergamon Press, 1974.

Kirkpatrick, D. L. *A Practical Guide for Supervisory Training and Development.* (2nd ed.) Reading, Mass.: Addison-Wesley, 1983.

Laird, D. *Approaches to Training and Development.* Reading, Mass.: Addison-Wesley, 1978.

Michalak, D. F., and Yager, E. G. *Making the Training Process Work.* New York: Harper & Row, 1979.

Nadler, L. *Corporate Human Resources Development: A Management Tool.* New York: Van Nostrand Reinhold, 1980.

Nadler, L. *Designing Training Programs: The Critical Events Model.* Reading, Mass.: Addison-Wesley, 1982.

Nadler, L. (Ed.). *The Handbook of Human Resource Development.* New York: Wiley, 1984.

Phillips, J. J. *Handbook of Training Evaluation and Measurement Methods.* Houston: Gulf, 1983.

Ray, C. M., and Eison, C. L. *Supervision.* New York: Dryden Press, 1983, 208–309.

Robinson, J. C. *Developing Managers Through Behavior Modeling.* Austin, Tex.: Learning Concepts, 1983.

Warren, M. W. *Training for Results.* (2nd ed.) Reading, Mass.: Addison-Wesley, 1979.

Wexley, K. N., and Latham, G. P. *Developing and Training Human Resources in Organizations.* Glenview, Ill.: Scott, Foresman, 1981.

Zemke, R., and Kramlinger, T. *Figuring Things Out.* Reading, Mass.: Addison-Wesley, 1982.

4

Performance:

How to Set Standards and Appraise Results

Regardless of the nature of the supervisor's job, successful performance is essential to employment stability, as well as to preparation for future assignments. Since performance determines effectiveness, supervisors must know what kind of performance is expected of them. Few executives will argue with this point. Unfortunately, many supervisors do not know what is expected of them or how they will be evaluated. Performance evaluation is often mysterious, confusing, and complex, but it does not have to be that way. The process can be simple, logical, and methodical. What is needed is a formal supervisory performance system in place in the organization.

A formal supervisory performance system encompasses four basic elements, three of which directly involve the supervisor. First is the *job description,* which defines what the supervisor should be doing. Second, *written performance standards* indicate how well a supervisor should be performing the job. Third, the *performance appraisal* provides supervisors with a complete review of how well they are performing the job. Fourth, there must be *goals and objectives* set for the organization, as well as for the various departments and divisions. These goals and objectives help determine in which direction the organization will move and what must be accomplished by the different parts of the organization. The need for a formal system is emphasized because in reality a supervisory performance system does exist in every organization. It may be informal and left to chance and as a result may be somewhat ineffective. A formal approach includes a specific program with policies and procedures, and it enlists the support and commitment of the management group to ensure that it works the way it was designed to work.

A sound and complete supervisory performance system will require an accommodating work climate and the appropriate organizational commitment. The supervisory performance checklist below lists ten very basic requirements that are necessary if a performance system is to work effectively in an organization. The first three items, which are probably the most important, are fully discussed in this chapter. The other elements are covered briefly in this chapter and in more detail in other chapters. The last item—compensation—is presented in detail in the next chapter.

An organization contemplating changes in the supervisory performance system should briefly examine this checklist and answer each of the questions, before proceeding further:

1. Do supervisors have a complete understanding of what they should do (detailed job description)?
2. Do supervisors know how well they are expected to perform their jobs (written performance standards)?
3. Do supervisors receive periodic feedback on how well they are actually performing their jobs, along with suggestions for improvement (performance appraisal)?
4. Are organizational goals and departmental (divisional) objectives clearly defined and written in a manner so that supervisors know what their organization plans to accomplish?
5. Do supervisors avoid spending an excessive amount of time fighting fires and solving crises and instead prevent them in the first place?

6. Do supervisors avoid spending too much time on diverse activities and avoid losing sight of the results-oriented aspects of their work?
7. Do supervisors have a strong sense of urgency to complete their assignments on time and also a willingness to accept the responsibility for deficiencies?
8. Is there an open atmosphere between supervisors and managers that allows them to discuss problems and mutually agree on solutions?
9. Is there an atmosphere of trust within the organization so that a certain number of errors and mistakes are allowed without undue criticism?
10. Does the organization have a formal compensation plan that clearly rewards supervisors for their performance?

Although there can be many interpretations of the responses, a possible scoring for the checklist is as follows: A score of eight to ten Yes responses describes an organization with an excellent approach and attitude to supervisory performance. The performance of supervisors in this organization should be very high, and there is little or no room for improvement. A score of five to seven Yes responses indicates some room for improvement. Supervisors are not performing as well as they could or should. The organization needs to redirect its efforts and focus on performance. A score of less than five Yes responses indicates an unsatisfactory attitude toward supervisory performance. Supervisors are stifled and reduced to mediocrity, and the success of the overall organization is probably in jeopardy.

Supervisors should know the full scope of their responsibilities, and the job description is the basic document that describes these responsibilities. It outlines the areas of accountability, the scope of the job, and the various relationships that must be cultivated to successfully perform the job.

It is important that supervisors know what is expected of them as they carry out their responsibilities. This is accomplished with performance standards. Even if they are not written, standards of performance exist for all supervisory jobs.

Every manager must periodically make decisions about a super-visor's performance, growth, and career advancement. Should the supervisor get a raise? Should the supervisor be assigned more responsibility? Should the supervisor be promoted? Should the supervisor be transferred or replaced? Every decision of this type is made on the basis of a series of observations on the part of the manager. Each observation automatically be-comes an evaluation when it is compared with what is expected of that manager. For instance, a 10-percent quality reject rate may be judged good if 6 percent was expected, whereas a 10-percent quality reject rate may be judged poor if 15 percent was expected. The key to establishing clear expectations of su-pervisors is to develop written, precise, measurable standards for each job.

However, the performance process is not complete when written performance standards have been established. There must be a formal discussion of performance at a predetermined time. This performance appraisal is an opportunity for the man-ager and supervisor to discuss and reach agreement on recent performance as well as to identify the strengths and weaknesses of the supervisor. Ideally this discussion will include input from both parties, and it should result in a clear understanding of how the supervisor has performed and which areas must be im-proved to enhance his or her performance in the future.

Detailed job descriptions, written performance standards, and effective performance appraisals will enable the supervisor to improve individual and group productivity. Clearly defined targets with constructive feedback enable supervisors to work more intelligently and accomplish more. The supervisor will fo-cus on the most important aspect of the job, thereby increasing the contribution of individuals and the work unit as a whole. A complete system of performance improvement will ensure that the organization is utilizing supervisors to their maximum ex-tent. Supervisors will no longer be judged on the basis of activ-ity levels but rather on that of results achieved.

A formal performance system improves communication between manager and supervisor. With a clear understanding of what is expected, the morale of supervisors will be improved, and the relation between boss and subordinates will be enhanced. There will be few, if any, surprises. In fact, an effective performance system will enable supervisors to review and appraise their own work prior to a formal review process. Supervisors will know how well they are doing at almost any time during the appraisal period. Moreover, frustration among supervisors can develop when they are judged on factors over which they have little or no control or that they know nothing about. A formal performance system should eliminate that kind of frustration.

Job effort will be balanced when a formal supervisory performance system is in place. All key areas for which the supervisor should be expected to perform will be identified, not just one or two. Sometimes supervisors are judged on work output alone, and other factors are deemed secondary. This is particularly true in manufacturing or service-oriented organizations where the work unit is producing a product or providing a service. There is a tendency to require maximum output at the expense of other important items. Supervisors must be judged on all the factors that are important to the success of the work unit. A properly designed and implemented supervisory performance system will help ensure that this overall job effort is balanced.

Supervisory Job Descriptions

A supervisor's job description, sometimes called a position description, primarily consists of statements about the important responsibilities and duties of the job. It describes what supervisors should do and the areas for which they are held accountable.

Purposes and Issues. Although during the past twenty years job descriptions have been becoming more and more standardized, still their form, content, scope, uses, and procedures vary considerably with the organization and the basic purpose of the job description program. These purposes include:

- *Organizational design.* Job descriptions are used to structure or restructure operations. Such descriptions are used in long-range planning, operational planning, work flow review, and methods improvement, as well as job design.
- *Compensation administration.* Job descriptions are used as the basis for evaluating supervisory jobs and placing them in the appropriate salary grade.
- *Recruitment, selection, and placement.* Job descriptions are used to accurately reflect the content of jobs for recruiting new supervisory candidates.
- *Individual career planning.* Job descriptions allow potential supervisors to understand the opportunities and challenges of supervisory jobs in the organization.
- *Performance standards and appraisals.* The job description is used to develop written standards of performance that provide the primary basis for the performance appraisal of the supervisor.

In actual practice, a job description program may be designed for some or all of these purposes. Because of its importance to performance, the last purpose listed will be emphasized in this chapter. For a more complete description of the uses of job descriptions, see Wortman and Sperling (1975, pp. 34–48).

A number of issues must be addressed in developing job descriptions for supervisors. One involves the responsibility for the original development of the description. Typically the human resources staff is charged with the responsibility of developing, revising, and maintaining job descriptions in the organization. It is best for one part of the organization to have this responsibility to ensure that consistent and standardized procedures are followed. Another issue is the extent of input from incumbents of the jobs being described. Ideally organizations should seek supervisor input to make sure the description accurately reflects what the supervisor is doing or is supposed to be doing. Input should also come from middle managers and related staff. Still another requirement is a mechanism for continually updating the job descriptions. Some organizations review jobs on a periodic basis, perhaps every two years. This review period is a function of how fast jobs change in the organization. High-growth, high-technology organizations may need to review job descriptions every six months, whereas a stable company with little growth may wait five years. Some organizations require supervisors to notify the job description coordinator whenever job duties are changed significantly either through a planned realignment of responsibilities or a gradual change in job content. A final issue is determining who has access to the information. Supervisors should have access to their job description. Otherwise, this whole process would be virtually meaningless, particularly if one of the premises of the program is to let supervisors know what they should be doing. Sharing this information with supervisors can help improve their commitment to and acceptance of the supervisory performance system. Also, in most organizations middle managers and other levels of managers above them have access to the job descriptions of their supervisors. Still other members of the organization will usually have access to supervisory job descriptions if they have a need to know. This need could be a result of career-planning discussions, organizational problems, or personnel-related issues concerning transfer, promotion, and placement of supervisors.

Preparing Descriptions. There is no one right way to write a job description. The format may vary with the type of supervisory job, the basic purposes of the program, and the organization's policies and procedures. However, when job descriptions are used as the basis for developing performance standards, there are several steps that may be helpful in simplifying this process. The description should contain a statement of responsibility with an action verb. For example, one basic responsibility for most supervisors is to train new employees. Here, *train* is the action verb. Some job descriptions stop there. However, a performance standard will require a measure of each responsibility. Because of this, the statement should be extended to explain why supervisors have this responsibility. This adds an extra dimension that makes it easier to measure the result achieved for the area of responsibility. The "responsibility" portion of the statement is linked to the "results" part by the words *so that*:

Responsibility		*Results*
Maintain a safe and healthy work place	so that	job-related accidents and injuries are kept to a minimum.

This combined statement appears as one statement in the job description. This process enables performance standards to be easily developed. Additional information on how performance standards are developed will be presented later in the chapter. At this point it is simply recommended that job descriptions be written in the "responsibility" and "results" format if they are to be used as a basis for developing performance standards. Exhibit 2 shows a complete supervisory job description that was developed by using this process, and Table 5 provides a listing of common action words used to develop job descriptions.

In addition to the "responsibility" and "results" statements, some job descriptions contain more detailed information involving a variety of aspects of the supervisor's job. The use of so-called scope data is common. These data show the magnitude of the job by stating the assets managed, the number of employees supervised, or the annual budget under the control of the supervisor. This information reflects the importance of the job and its potential for contributing to the organization. Some descriptions include information about the authority delegated to supervisors. This approach outlines decisions that can be made by supervisors within their normal scope of responsibilities. Some even detail specifically which decisions they can make and which will involve other levels of management. Still other job descriptions show the relationships of supervisors with peer groups, staff support personnel, suppliers, customers, or government agencies. Finally, some descriptions provide information on working conditions, on the assumption that a challenging environment should be differentiated from a less demanding one. For example, a coal-mining firm might describe working conditions on job descriptions since its supervisory

Exhibit 2. Job Description for a Supervisor.

Position Title: Foundry Supervisor _____ Division: Production _____

FLSA Class.: Exempt _____ Job Grade: 11 _____ Department: Foundry _____

EEO-1 Job Category: Officials and Managers _____ Location: Milwaukee _____

SCOPE DATA (Complete only where applicable to position)

- Assets Managed $ 2,750,000   • Total Employees In Dept.:   20
- Budget Managed $ 950,000   • No. Employees Supervised: Exempt   -
- Sales Value $ 2,100,000   Non-Ex. 20
- Annual Payroll Suprvsd. $ 350,000   Total   20

- Other Qualitative/Quantitative Data: _____
  _____

REPORTING RELATIONSHIPS

- Reports to (Title):   Production Manager

- Subordinates (Titles):   Iron Pourers, Molders, Laborers

SUMMARY DESCRIPTION OF POSITION (In a brief, concise statement explain the overall purpose/function of this position. Answer why this job exists.)

Supervise the production activities of unskilled and semiskilled employees in the production of all types of iron castings, maintaining quality production on a daily schedule at a minimum cost.

PRINCIPAL DUTIES

1. Direct the production activities of molders, iron pourers, and service laborers so that maximum production tonnage is achieved at the least possible cost.

2. Produce castings at the highest level of quality so that customer complaints can be minimized and our competitive position can be maintained.

3. Inspect castings produced so that necessary corrections can be made to eliminate casting defects when they arise.

4. Requisition and maintain required amount of supplies so that the unit operates efficiently and within the approved budget.

5. Coordinate with other departments so that required patterns and cores are at the proper machines when needed in order to reduce downtime and unnecessary production delays.

Approved By: _____ Date:_____   Prepared By: D. Rousseau

Approved By: _____ Date:_____   Date Prepared: May 8, 1985

Incumbent's Signature: _____ Date:_____   Revised: _____

PRINCIPAL DUTIES

6. Arrange for proper maintenance of all departmental equipment, which includes operating machinery and patterns, so that downtime can be decreased and operating efficiency increased.

7. Develop and maintain a working knowledge of molding sands and metal temperature requirements needed to produce quality castings.

8. Coordinate the movement and transportation of raw material through the department and the movement of castings to the inspection areas so that production schedules are met.

9. Maintain a safe and healthy work place so accidents and injuries are kept to a minimum.

10. Communicate effectively with employees so that they are kept informed, understand their jobs, and errors and misunderstandings are kept to a minimum.

11. Create and maintain high morale and motivation in the work unit so that employees are able to operate effectively and satisfactorily in their jobs.

12. Perform administrative duties as outlined in the Procedures Manual so that errors, mistakes, delays, and misunderstandings can be kept to a minimum.

13. Acquire a working knowledge of the Company-Union Agreement and Company Policy Manual so that company policy is always administered correctly and equitably.

14. Assign employees to the various jobs so that each employee is matched to the best of his or her ability.

15. Select, train, and develop and provide orientation for employees so they can effectively handle their jobs and prepare themselves for better jobs in the future.

16. Keep abreast of new methods and techniques in foundry technology and supervisory management so that the most effective methods and processes are used on the job.

Table 5. Action Words for Supervisory Job Descriptions.

Develop	Approve	Supervise	Maintain	Publicize
Prepare	Control	Produce	Operate	Write
Assist	Plan	Coordinate	Direct	Reject
Perform	Administer	Evaluate	Select	Program
Recommend	Determine	Schedule	Establish	Hold
Review	Counsel	Requisition	Execute	Identify
Supply	Allocate	Analyze	Test	Correct
Assign	Improve	Organize	Initiate	Compare
Provide	Ensure	Interview	Inform	Purchase
Terminate	Issue	Compile	Screen	Protect
Process	Negotiate	Authorize	Disburse	Give
Meet	Formulate	Arrange	Investigate	Guide
Train	Account	Cooperate	Propose	Report
Change	Forecast	Contract	Serve	Create
Justify	Appraise	Promote	Design	Extend
Consider	Anticipate	Acquire	Interpret	Collect
Release	Activate	Contribute	Request	Delegate
Upgrade	Select	Transfer	Discharge	Distribute
Handle	Remove	Furnish	Recruit	Replace
Sell	Audit	Service	Contact	Manufacture

work settings vary from underground mining to barge loading for customer shipments.

Performance Standards: Basic Concepts

Although the steps to develop written performance standards from job descriptions are not difficult, they sometimes cause considerable confusion for supervisors. This section presents a few basic concepts about performance standards and shows how they are developed.

Definition and Purpose. Performance standards represent a type of goal-setting process. (The difference between standards, objectives, and goals is discussed later.) In simple terms, a written performance standard is defined as a statement of the conditions that will exist when a job has been or is being satisfactorily performed. It is stated in terms of the desired outcome. The U.S. Office of Personnel Management defines performance standards for federal agencies as "the expressed measures of the level of achievement established by management for the duties and responsibilities of a position or group of positions. . . . [They] may include, but are not limited to, elements [measurement factors] such as quantity, quality, and timeliness" (Pajer, 1984, p. 82). A performance standard should be quantitatively expressed and should not include ambiguous language such as "prompt," "sufficient," "maximum," "minimum," "efficient," "aggressive," or "rare exception." It should be feasible and attainable yet at the same time should represent a challenge for the supervisor. Finally, the standard must have the commitment of the supervisor and the acceptance of the middle manager. In the absence of these conditions, it will be difficult to achieve properly designed performance standards.

For convenience, assume that each performance standard is preceded by the following statement (even if it is not written next to the standard): "Satisfactory performance has been achieved when. . . ." An example of a performance standard is: "The error rate for claims processing will not exceed _____." This simple statement provides a measure of performance for the quality of processing insurance claims. The desired level of error rate for claims is entered in the blank. This level could change from time to time. Other examples of performance standards are:

- Total loans and acceptances are increased by *20* percent by June 30.
- Machine downtime is less than *35* hours per month.
- Production output exceeds *150* units per month.
- Project is complete within *+ 5* percent of budget.
- Customer service calls are answered in less than *2.5* hours.

Developing Standards. Performance standards can easily be developed to cover almost every area of supervisory responsibilities, particularly if the job description is developed in the format described earlier. Consider the example of the supervisor's responsibility for safety from the previous section. It is reproduced in Exhibit 3 with the desired standards. This example focuses on the number of accidents, the severity of accidents,

Exhibit 3. Example of a Complete Performance Standard.

Responsibility		Results	Standards
Maintain a safe and healthy workplace	so that	Job-related accidents and injuries are kept to a minimum	Accident frequency rate is less than ___. Accident severity rate is less than ___. Industrial health exposure monitoring reveals *no* overexposures.

and the outcome of industrial health monitoring. Other safety and health standards appropriate for the organization could be used. This process provides a logical sequence of steps to get to the desired standard. The responsibility and result are in the job description and are separate from the standard. The procedure of using three columns is recommended in the early stages of developing performance standards. After this, it is only necessary to work with the standards in the last column, which may be put on a separate form. Exhibit 4 shows completed performance standards for a supervisor.

Once an organization is fully committed to using performance standards, every supervisor should develop them. Initially they should be developed for the major job responsibilities. These are sometimes called key result areas and represent the areas most important to the success of the supervisor's effort. Standards should be jointly developed and accepted by both the supervisor and the middle manager. New standards and changes in existing standards can be initiated by either one of the parties but should be agreed to by both. Standards should be reviewed on a regularly scheduled basis. In some organizations this is done quarterly, in others it is done semiannually or once a year.

Relation to Objectives and Goals. A note on terminology is in order. Three terms are used to represent the targets set for individuals and groups: goals, objectives, and standards. Sometimes used interchangeably to mean the same thing, they grew out of the management by objectives (MBO) process that became popular in the 1950s (Drucker, 1954). To keep the terms from causing confusion and to conform to generally accepted terminology, the following distinctions are made. Goals refer to broad statements and reflect the desires and mission of the organization. They are strategic in nature and are usually long range in outlook. Improving relationships with customers might be a goal of an organization. It represents a desire or direction but is not specific and measurable as stated.

Objectives, in contrast, are more precise statements that are specific and measurable. They relate to departments, divi-

Exhibit 4. Complete Performance Standards for a Supervisor.

MANAGEMENT PERFORMANCE STANDARDS

NAME   Ken Rousseau

CALENDAR QUARTER   BEGINNING January 1, 1985   ENDING March 31, 1985

Key Result Areas	STANDARDS	Not Met	Met	Exceeded
PRODUCTION & QUALITY	1. Average production per week on each product is within ____% of target production per quarter.			
	2. Tons per employee hour is at least ____.			
	3. Scrap rate is less than____%.			
INVENTORY & PRODUCTION CONTROL	1. Total missed schedules do not exceed ____% of total number of open orders per month.			
	2. Inventory adjustments do not exceed ____% each year.			
EFFICIENCY	1. Incentive bonus averages ____ per month.			
	2. Overtime hours are less than ____% of total hours worked.			
	3. Manufacturing cost/ton is within ____% of target for quarter.			
SAFETY	1. Accident frequency rate is less than ____.			
	2. Accident severity rate is less than ____.			
	3. OSHA incident rate is less than ____.			
	4. At least ____ safety meetings are conducted each quarter.			

Key Result Areas	STANDARDS	Not Met	Met	Exceeded
MORALE & MOTIVATION	1. Absenteeism rate is less than _____.			
	2. Turnover rate is less than _____.			
	3. No. of employee complaints less than _____ per month.			
	4. At least _____ suggestions are submitted by employees each month.			
ADMINISTRATIVE DUTIES	1. Time card corrections are less than _____% per week.			
	2. No. of reports returned for correction does not exceed _____% per month.			
	3. No. of reports submitted late do not exceed _____ per month.			
TRAINING & DEVELOPING EMPLOYEES	1. All job vacancies are filled within _____ days with a trained replacement.			
	2. A potential replacement is identified for my job by _____.			
	3. Average time until new employees meet standard production is reduced by _____% in the next quarter.			
COMMUNICATION	1. At least _____ group meeting(s) are held with employees every month.			
	2. An average of _____ coaching and counseling sessions are conducted with employees each month.			
SELF-DEVELOPMENT	1. At least _____% of meetings of the National Management Association are attended.			
	2. _____ self-study programs are completed per year.			
	3. At least _____ outside training programs are attended per year.			

AGREEMENT BETWEEN _____ and

(Name)

_____

(Name)

sions, plants, or other organizational units. They are operational and are set for medium time frames, usually a year. When this period is over, new objectives are set. For example, a plant-level objective might be to reduce defective products reaching customers by 10 percent during the year. This particular objective would support the organizational goal mentioned in the previous paragraph.

Finally, performance standards apply to individual managers and supervisors and are developed from the job description. They identify the conditions that must exist if satisfactory performance is to be achieved. They are usually continuous and remain in place until some external condition causes a change. Each supervisor might have performance standards that contribute toward departmental, divisional, or organizational goals and objectives. For example, a standard for a production supervisor might include keeping the reject rate of products below 2 percent in the next three months. This would support the plant objective and organizational goal mentioned in the previous examples. This differentiation in terminology is summarized as follows:

Term	Focus	Nature	Time Frame
Goals	Organization	Strategic	Long Range
Objectives	Department/ Division	Operational	Medium Range
Standards	Manager/ Supervisor	Individual Performance	Short Range

Although the definitions of goals, objectives, and standards given here provide a framework for understanding the remainder of this chapter, they may vary with organizations and with other literature on the subject.

Measuring Supervisory Performance

Performance measurement is an important issue for the leading organizations and institutions in the United States. The White House recently sponsored what was probably the most significant conference on improving productivity ever assembled. The participants included leading representatives from business, labor, academic, consulting, and research organizations. The scope was not limited to any particular group or type of employees. According to the final report (American Productivity Center, 1983a, p. 15), measures of performance form one of the five key issues concerning rewards systems and productivity: "The measurement of performance is critical to an effective reward system that pays for performance improvement. Difficulty in developing measures has been one of the barriers to innovative reward systems. In addition, the lack of accounting systems which reflect productivity improvement on the profit and loss statements often lead management to ignore the impact of improvement."

The report noted that measures should be meaningful to the work groups covered, as well as to those collecting the data, and that there should be greater balance in the long- and short-term measures of performance. The report concluded with four recommendations for organizations in the area of measurement and reward systems:

1. Reward systems should be based on measures of productivity, quality, and other indicators of organizational health in addition to the traditional reliance on measures of financial performance.
2. Measurement systems should reflect both the short- and long-term effectiveness of the organization.
3. Firms should develop measurement systems that reflect the value of productivity improvement as well as its costs.
4. The Financial Accounting Standards Board should develop accounting standards for productivity reporting in addition to those for financial accounting systems.

Types of Measurements and Data. For convenience, a distinction is made between two general categories of data: hard data and soft data. Hard data are the primary measures of supervisory performance and are presented in rational, undisputed numbers. They are easy to measure and quantify and are objectively based. They are usually the most desired type of supervisory performance data since they represent common measures of organizational performance and are very credible in the eyes of management. Table 6 shows examples of hard supervisory performance data. They are grouped in the categories of

Table 6. Examples of Hard Data.

Output	Period costs
Units produced	Fixed costs
Accounts booked	*Time*
Productivity	On-Time shipments
Items shipped	Equipment downtime
Items assembled	Training time
Items sold	Processing time
Money collected	Overtime
Forms processed	Work unit efficiency
Tasks completed	Time to completion
Loans approved	Lost-time days
Patients visited	*Quality*
Inventory turnover	Scrap
Rooms cleaned	Rework
Applications processed	Rejects
Costs	Waste
Labor costs	Error rates
Raw material costs	Product failures
Budget variances	Shortages
Overtime costs	Accidents
Accident costs	Inventory adjustments
Variable costs	Variance from standard

output, cost, time, and quality. Some of these are related directly to cost savings, while others are in a noncost category. The latter, however, can be readily placed in cost-savings categories. All these data relate to the results of the supervisor's work unit and can be easily monitored and measured. Ideally these should be used in developing supervisory performance standards.

When hard data are not available, the organization must resort to using soft data, which are more difficult to measure and quantify, at least directly. They are usually subjectively based and behaviorally oriented. Table 7 shows examples of soft performance data for supervisors. Although they may not be as

Table 7. Examples of Soft Data.

Product mix	Discrimination charges
Customer complaints	Employee complaints
New equipment installation	Employee attitudes
Methods changed	Counseling sessions held
Calls made	Decisions made
Technological improvements	Meetings conducted
Procedures changed	Problems solved
Employee turnover	Conflicts avoided
Absenteeism	Communication breakdowns
Grievances	New ideas implemented
Suggestions submitted	

desirable as hard data, soft data usually represent important factors related to supervisory performance and are appropriate for performance standards.

How data are measured and presented is another area of concern. They may be given as absolute numbers, ratios, percents, time spans, or dollar amounts. The various ways in which performance data may be developed and presented for performance standards include:

Type of Measurement	Example
Absolute number	The number of loan applications processed exceeded fifty per week.
Ratio	Accident frequency index was less than 3.2.
Percentage	The monthly turnover rate was less than 1 percent.
Time span	New milling machine will be installed and operating by December 31, 1986.
Dollar amounts	Project completed with a total expenditure of less than $10,000.

It is important to distinguish again between objectives and standards, particularly in terms of the examples shown above. A department may have the objective of installing a new machine or completing a project. This project may involve several supervisors, and their efforts could be specified in their individual performance standards. In this case the performance standard is not a routine or ongoing target but a one-time effort for the specific time period for which the performance standards have been developed. It measures each supervisor's effort toward achieving the overall departmental objective.

A performance standard may also be expressed as a variance to allow limits on a planned target. For example, a standard may be stated as follows: "Actual costs at year-end will be ±3 percent of approved budget." This leaves some room for uncontrollable factors and eliminates the need to hit an exact target. If the standard had been stated in terms of "meeting the approved budget," the outcome would have been uncertain unless the actual costs were exactly equal to the budgeted costs. Would a $100 overrun on a $300 thousand budget be considered unacceptable performance? Probably not, just as a $100 favorable variance would not be considered exceptional performance.

Basis for Measurement. A performance standard will usually be compared to one of three general conditions: past performance, performance of other groups, and organizational goals or commitments. Supervisors and managers examine past performance and plan future performance levels based on what has been accomplished. For example, an error rate may be set on the basis of a previous error rate. The specific rate may vary, depending on whether conditions will be better or worse in the future or whether specific efforts are aimed at improving the standard. Some standards are based on what other departments, groups, or even organizations have been able to accomplish in supervisory responsibility areas. For example, the standards for accident frequency rates and turnover data may be established on the basis of the performance of other departments, plants, divisions, companies, or the industry as a whole. Data are usually available from which supervisors can make these comparisons. Finally, performance standards may be developed to show the work unit's effort toward achieving departmental, divisional, or organizational objectives. Many deadlines and targets are set at the top of the organization. These, in turn, could become performance standards for individual supervisors. For example, suppose an organization plans to step up its equal employment opportunity efforts and through an affirmative action plan has developed some very ambitious targets for the coming year. This action could easily translate into individual performance standards for all supervisors.

Basically a performance standard will focus on work unit results. When results are not directly observable, standards may be established to monitor the symptoms of problems or conditions. For example, the absenteeism rate, turnover rate, and number of grievances may reflect the level of morale in a particular work unit. These are symptoms that relate to the supervisor's responsibility for maintaining a high level of morale among the employees. In some instances, standards may measure the effort expended toward completion of a project. This is particularly true in service and staff support areas, such as engineering, market research, systems development, and construction support. A specific number of employee hours may be contributed during a predetermined time period to assist with the implementation of a project.

As measurements are developed, the supervisor should keep these questions in mind for each area of responsibility:

- How much can be accomplished?
- How well should it be done?
- What are the quality limits?
- Is time a factor or is it continuous?
- Is cost a factor?
- Is it a controllable item?
- What is the desired accuracy?
- What is the basis for comparison?

The most challenging part of developing performance standards is selecting the precise way to measure the results of the supervisor's efforts. It need not be a difficult process, although it sometimes is. Because of this, a few organizations have developed this philosophy: "If there is really no way to determine whether an activity is being or has been satisfactorily performed, then why should it be done at all?" This may seem a little cold and unrealistic, but it presents a challenge for supervisors, particularly in the service and support areas. It emphasizes the point that if all possibilities are explored, supervisors with the help of their managers can usually arrive at some means of measuring the results of their efforts, at least for the most important areas.

Implementing Performance Standards

The implementation of performance standards for an organization goes beyond the mechanical process of developing the standards. A program's success will depend on the type of organization, the capability of the supervisory group, and the degree of management commitment to the process. The following is a brief discussion of the conditions that must exist and the steps necessary to successfully complete this implementation.

Management Support. Very few things can be accomplished without the full support of the management group. The implementation of performance standards is no exception. This will not be done successfully unless management pledges its full support. For some organizations this process is new, making it all the more crucial for management to get behind it. This means that managers must develop a good understanding of the process, set an example in developing their own standards, and require their supervisors to develop standards as part of the official policy of the organization. In addition, managers should be well enough acquainted with the process that they can give advice and assistance to their supervisors to help them develop these standards. This personal support will make it even clearer to supervisors that their managers are part of the program and are committed to making it work.

Policies and Procedures. The actual mechanics of a performance standards program will vary with the organization. Policies, procedures, and guidelines should be developed to keep all the management group on the same course and to improve the consistency of the effort. In addition, these become tools for discussion meetings and training programs to help the supervisors learn the system. Some organizations develop manuals, booklets, and brochures to explain the need for performance standards and to outline the process in detail with examples from a variety of settings. These are very helpful, although they will not guarantee success by themselves. Lack of knowledge of how to develop standards is often a difficult stumbling block. Many supervisors, particularly the longtimers, will have difficulty in adapting to such a process. They will need all the assistance they can get, and good documentation can help.

Selling Process. Supervisors must be sold on performance standards. One of the most critical steps in implementing performance standards is to get the supervisors to buy into the process. A flashy sales gimmick will not do the job. Supervisors need to see what is in it for them and the advantages of their becoming involved. Issuing a policy statement will not get the desired results, although a few supervisors will develop performance standards if they are required to do so by company policy. The organization needs the enthusiastic participation of supervisors and their determination to make the process work. This can only be accomplished if supervisors understand the need for standards and see the benefits for both themselves and the organization. Because of this, the initial communication of this system is extremely important. An otherwise positive campaign initiated by top management can be short-circuited by negative comments from middle management. The whole management group must be united. Communication must be very clear, to the point, and utilize a variety of media. Every attempt should be made to remove the impression that performance standards represent a new fad or technique that the organization is trying. Instead, it should be communicated as a proven, sound philosophy to which the organization is dedicated, and it should be emphasized that standards will become a way of life in the organization.

Job Description Review. The initial activity on the part of supervisors will probably be a complete review of the job description. Unless they have been reviewed recently, job descriptions may be out of date, incomplete, or presented in a manner that may make it difficult to develop performance standards. The process described earlier in this chapter is an efficient approach to writing job descriptions. It is particularly important with implementation of performance standards that job descriptions accurately reflect all the current duties and responsibilities. This complete review will probably require the assistance of the human resources staff or other section assigned to keep track of the job descriptions in the organization.

Initial Standards Development. Once a job description has been developed, specific measurements must be worked out that will define the conditions that will exist when the job has been satisfactorily performed. Ideally these measurements should involve quantity, quality, time, or costs. When these are not available, soft data are appropriate to indicate desired performance for a particular responsibility. It is best to deal with a small and manageable number of performance standards, at least in the early stages of the process. Although there should be at least one standard for each key result area, there is a limit to the number of standards that can be effectively reached. A level should be established that reflects what the organization considers to be acceptable performance for the supervisor.

Mutual Agreement. An essential part of this process is for the manager and supervisor to reach mutual agreement on the desired level of performance. Ideally, a performance level is suggested by the supervisor, and the middle manager concurs. If there is a difference in opinion, there must be a give-and-take relationship that will ultimately lead to a mutual agreement. This point cannot be overemphasized. If standards are set too high and forced upon the supervisors, the process will take on negative connotations. At the other extreme, if levels of performance are established that would be achieved without any extra effort on the part of supervisors, the process will become a meaningless exercise.

Review. Obviously the supervisor's performance must be reviewed against the planned level of performance at a predetermined time. While this review period may vary considerably with the organization, it should not exceed one year. Quarterly reviews seem to be very popular. This review should be a two-way discussion between the supervisor and the middle manager. The discussion should focus on whether the supervisor met, did not meet, or exceeded the standards. At this time new levels of performance may be set, or new standards may be added, particularly if departmental, divisional, or organizational objectives have changed. Also, standards involving time limits will no longer be operative if that time has passed and the project or task has been completed.

Overall, these factors and steps can provide a smooth transition from an organization in which written performance standards are not required to one in which they are integrated into the normal management process and become a routine part of the job. More detailed steps may be needed for some organizations, or possibly some of the steps could be omitted depending on the degree of supervisor familiarity with this process.

Misconceptions About Performance Standards

For most organizations, performance standards will be a significant departure from previous attempts at measuring and evaluating supervisor performance. And with changes come forms of resistance that cannot be overcome simply by establishing policies, procedures, or guidelines. It takes all the factors described in the previous section to make the implementation of performance standards successful, and it will also be necessary to remove numerous misconceptions about such standards.

Many organizations have implemented performance standards. They have experienced the difficulties that will occur with the implementation of any major program, but they have managed to overcome the misconceptions and misgivings of supervisors. Other organizations contemplating performance standards can learn from their mistakes and the problems they encountered, namely:

1. *Failing to realize the advantages of standards.* Super-

visors must understand the inherent advantages of having performance standards. When that happens, the implementation will go much more smoothly, and standards may actually be welcomed at the supervisory level. It is difficult for supervisors to make a sincere effort to achieve something for which they see no reason. An organization will do well to spend much time up front convincing supervisors that they will be better off with this program.

2. *Becoming too involved in administrative requirements and forgetting their purpose.* As with many new programs, supervisors can get hung up on the question of how they are supposed to do something rather than why they are supposed to do it. This chapter has presented some guidelines and suggested forms for implementing the program. They all involve additional paper work. But the technique and procedure should not be confused with the overall purpose. The fundamental rule is, Do not let the mechanics stand in the way of the process.

3. *Considering standards a tool for identifying failure.* No group wants to develop a club that will eventually be used to beat its members to death. Supervisors will not accept standards if they think they will be used to remove them from their jobs. On the evidence of previous implementations, performance standards will identify few failures. They should, in fact, identify more successes than have been identified in the past if the standards require supervisors to focus on those aspects of the job that are most important and that can improve performance.

4. *Failing to negotiate realistic levels of performance.* The supervisor and manager must reach an agreement on the expected levels of performance. It is extremely important that this negotiation take place honestly and sincerely and that a mutual agreement be reached. Without a challenge, standards are meaningless. Also, it is sometimes a temptation for the middle manager to set the standards at a level that is almost impossible to achieve instead of one that represents satisfactory performance. This should be avoided, and realistic standards set so that the program will function as it has been designed.

5. *Taking shortcuts to "beat" the system.* Often a super-

visor will develop standards that are just sufficient to satisfy policy or the middle manager. And a supervisor can find loopholes in a system, regardless of how well it is designed. It will always be possible to beat the system, but this should not deter implementation of standards. Supervisors must take this task seriously and develop realistic standards to adequately reflect their jobs.

6. *Developing too many standards.* Sometimes, particularly with a new implementation, eager supervisors will develop too many standards that minutely detail every responsibility and job duty. This "overload" will reduce the effectiveness of supervisors, not allowing them to focus on the key result areas. This can be as dangerous as taking shortcuts. Supervisors should be encouraged to develop an achievable number of standards.

7. *Hoping standards are a fad and will go away.* Many new programs, particularly those initiated by a human resources department, stay for a while, and are then replaced with a new fad or gimmick. But performance standards, when properly developed and implemented, can produce significant improvements in supervisory performance. The process is not a fad. It has shown excellent results in some of the best organizations and is now being implemented in the federal government. For example, the Civil Service Reform Act of 1978 requires managers to set performance standards before evaluating performance as a basis for merit pay, promotion, training, and performance improvement. It is a very logical and sensible way for organizations to approach supervisory performance.

In summary, each organization can learn something from the mistakes and failures of others. They need not be repeated as performance standards are implemented in other organizations.

Supervisory Performance Appraisal: Basic Concepts

Performance appraisals for supervisors can be defined as a communication process between a manager and a supervisor through which an organization determines how effectively the supervisor is performing his or her job, establishes the appropriate rewards for the supervisor, and identifies areas for improvement. Performance appraisal goes by several names, including those of performance evaluation, performance review, performance ratings, merit ratings, job review, and performance assessment. There are many aspects of performance, and, as a result, performance appraisals can be designed to meet one or more of the following objectives:

1. Review the performance of a supervisor over a predetermined period of time.
2. Determine the amount of salary increase and/or other rewards that should be based on performance.
3. Document a supervisor's performance to satisfy administrative and legal requirements.
4. Identify the strengths and weaknesses of a supervisor as they bear on job-related performance and potential.
5. Determine the training and educational needs of a supervisor.

Because of this variety of objectives, performance appraisals appear in many formats. They exist in every organization, and few aspects of the employment relationship are as controversial as the performance appraisal system. Yet, it is possibly management's most powerful tool in controlling human resources and productivity. According to one study (Bureau of National Affairs, 1983), 91 percent of the firms surveyed had formal appraisal programs for supervisors. Even without a formal process, informal judgments are made about an individual's performance, and those judgments are used to arrive at decisions about that individual's career. A formal process attempts to minimize errors and ensure that information is gathered efficiently and is used to meet the objectives. But there are problems with these formal programs: According to the Bureau of National Affairs study, about half of the organizations surveyed are either making improvements or planning improvements in their formal appraisal system.

Individuals being appraised are not necessarily happy with the process and typically approach it with the same anxiety as that experienced by someone undergoing an IRS audit.

The manager conducting the appraisal, often looking for a totally objective system—something that is impossible to find—is
not convinced the time required is worth the effort. Another
study provides some reasons why appraisal systems do not always work (Fombrun and Laud, 1983, p. 24). Using a sample
of firms drawn from the *Fortune* 1300 (a list of the 1300
largest industrial companies compiled by the editors of *Fortune*
magazine), this study revealed four key reasons for failure:

1. managers' psychological resistance and emotional conflict
    when giving negative evaluations to subordinates
2. evaluators' political interest in "looking good" by not caus-
    ing problems
3. the perceived invalidity of evaluating complex jobs
4. evaluators' fear of reprisal—from either individuals or gov-
    ernment—for "discriminating" among employees

Nevertheless, most organizations do have formal performance appraisal systems, and it appears that many of them are
seeking potential improvements in the process. Specific approaches for revitalizing a performance appraisal program will
be presented later.

Relationship with Performance Standards. In the Bureau of National Affairs study, 87 percent of the performance appraisal
programs for supervisors were used to determine salary adjustments. However, because of the last two objectives outlined earlier the performance appraisal may be kept separate from the review of performance standards, although in reality this review is
an appraisal of performance against those standards. A few organizations prefer to use the performance appraisal as a developmental tool instead of as a review of actual performance to determine pay increases or bonuses. In the study based on the
Fortune 1300, only 12 percent of the firms did not tie performance appraisal to salary increases in any way. When it is not so
tied, the performance appraisal is scheduled at a time other than
the planned salary increase date and is separate from the review
of standards.

Still other organizations combine the standards review

with the formal performance appraisal process. This can be accomplished in two ways. One approach is to include all items in the appraisal with the standards review in one performance discussion. The other approach is to conduct two discussions: one devoted to a summary review of performance standards for the appraisal period and the other devoted to the remaining items in the formal appraisal process. The latter approach is recommended since it allows all items directly related to past performance and compensation to be discussed at one time while developmental issues are considered in a separate discussion, possibly at another time. This is consistent with current trends in performance appraisals. A study of 267 firms by the human resource consultants Drake, Beam, and Morin ("Performance Appraisals Reappraised," 1983) revealed a back-to-basics theme in appraisals. The most important trend that they discovered was the use of "redesigned appraisals that emphasize specifics in individual performance criteria" (p. 5). This reduces the emphasis on development, an item that concerns many professionals. However, a separate discussion on developmental issues can help give the proper attention to both areas.

Inasmuch as all organizations have not and will not develop and implement performance standards, the remaining material in this chapter is devoted to the performance appraisal process in general. The ideas presented may be integrated with performance standards or used independently of them.

Types of Performance Appraisals. Performance appraisals are based on three major categories of information: traits, behavioral examples, and standards (or objectives). Early performance appraisals were limited to evaluations based on traits that were considered important to supervisory behavior and usually included intelligence, attitude, cooperation, reliability, personal appearance, and integrity. Supervisors were evaluated on the basis of these traits and were assigned a rating, either descriptive or numerical. Typically, this rating involved checking boxes labeled "poor," "below average," "average," "above average," and "excellent." This approach is very simple and easy for evaluators to complete, but it has many shortcomings. It is subjective, it is highly unreliable, and its validity is questionable. The same supervisor could be evaluated by two managers and end up with completely different ratings. What one manager considers to be an excellent attitude might be considered a poor attitude by another. It is difficult, if not impossible, to link traits to job performance. Because of these problems, trait-based appraisals are less and less used by organizations, although they still show up on quite a few forms.

To overcome the deficiencies in trait-based appraisals, many organizations adopted a more objective results-oriented appraisal process, such as written performance standards or management by objectives (MBO), described earlier in this chapter. This approach gained its popularity in the 1960s and continues to be successful. It is objective and is directly related to job performance. According to the survey of *Fortune* 1300 companies, objectives- or standards-based appraisals were the dominant approach used for supervisors (Fombrun and Laud, 1983). The Bureau of National Affairs study (1983) found that almost half the supervisory performance appraisals used an MBO approach.

These two approaches represent extremes that range from a very subjective basis to a very objective basis for performance. Both extremes have critics. Critics of performance standards argue that this type of evaluation neglects to explain what has caused success or failure and what other factors may have materially contributed to the actual outcome. They claim that numbers are not everything and that this approach neglects the human element. To fill the gap between these extremes, researchers and practitioners have attempted to develop behaviorally related descriptions of performance outcomes to focus attention on what behavior is desired. The Behaviorally Anchored Rating Scale (BARS), originally published in the early 1970s, is one successful example (Plachy, 1983, p. 59). BARS addresses the problem of describing behavior objectively and is derived from critical incidences of effective and ineffective job-related supervisory behavior. It emphasizes development because it takes into account how results are achieved. It is job specific because job-related information is used to develop the ratings scale. Also it identifies measurable job-related behavior that is critical to the success of the supervisor's job. Table 8 shows an example of a Behaviorally Anchored Rating Scale de-

Table 8. Behaviorally Anchored Rating Scale.

Position: Supervisor	Skill: Conducting Small Group Meetings
Rating	Behavior Description
10	This supervisor thoroughly plans and schedules at least one small group meeting each week. This supervisor always distributes an agenda, communicates clearly during the meeting, sticks
9	to the agenda, and gives employees every opportunity to provide feedback in an open and trustworthy climate. This supervisor handles all employee questions and comments effectively,
8	and follows up on every item for which additional information is needed.
7	This supervisor conducts the required number of meetings, on schedule, as planned. This supervisor distributes an agenda in about half the meetings, usually sticks to the agenda, occasion-
6	ally allows employees to voice their opinions, handles most of the questions and comments effectively, and follows up on the most important items.
5	
	This supervisor conducts meetings only when prompted. This supervisor is usually not prepared for meetings, does not pre-
4	pare or distribute an agenda, rarely ever allows employees to voice their opinions, handles a few questions and comments effectively on them while avoiding others, and follows up on
3	items only when reminded to do so by the group.
	This supervisor will conduct meetings only when forced to and
2	then with much resistance. He or she avoids them at all costs. This supervisor does not plan for the meeting, does not allow open discussion, and does not follow up on the items discussed.
1	This supervisor will openly voice disapproval of the requirement to conduct meetings.

veloped for the supervisory skill of conducting small group meetings: A rating between one and ten is selected, depending on which number best describes the supervisor's behavior. This approach to performance appraisal is not yet common in organizations, but its popularity is growing. In one study, behaviorally anchored ratings were used for supervisory appraisals in 25 percent of the firms surveyed (Fombrun and Laud, 1983, p. 26). For supervisors, scales must be developed around each of the job dimensions that were described in Chapter Two. Because of this, behaviorally anchored ratings are time consuming, difficult to develop, and very costly to administer. Nevertheless, this approach shows some promise as an alternative to the two extremes of traits and standards. It also enables an organization to bring behavior into the appraisal process.

Revitalizing a Performance Appraisal Program

Since an organization probably already has some type of supervisory performance appraisal program, its first task is to take a fresh look at the existing program and then upgrade it to meet legal, administrative, and economic needs. (There appears, in fact, to be much concern about, and dissatisfaction with, performance appraisal programs in many organizations.) In the past, this upgrading process primarily focused on forms design and the development of procedures and ignored the need to integrate the program into the organization's philosophy, culture, mission, and structure. But failure to attain this integration is a major reason for the failure of many appraisal systems (Butler and Yorks, 1984). In short, changing an appraisal system is a problem of organizational change. The following steps are recommended for review and revision of an existing performance appraisal program. Many of the steps also apply to organizations developing a program for the first time.

1. *Consider using a task force approach.* A task force, made up of representatives of major departments, may be appropriate for the design and implementation of a new appraisal system. The task force members must be very familiar with the organization and speak with authority for their departments. This may be a nontraditional approach since human resources specialists usually design performance appraisals and then adjust them to secure management support. At any rate, the task force approach has several inherent advantages. It taps some of the best thinking from all areas of the organization, and it enhances

management acceptance and support for the final product. It helps to ensure that a realistic and workable process is developed. There are also some disadvantages, however. The group can become unwieldy and difficult to manage. Also, the time required to develop the new system will usually be longer with a task force. Nevertheless, the advantages may outweigh the limitations, particularly for larger organizations. For example, the task force approach has worked very successfully at General Electric (Butler and Yorks, 1984).

2. *Interview the management group.* The first task is to assess the effectiveness of the current performance appraisal program. This will involve interviews either with all supervisors and managers or with a sample of them. The primary purpose of this step is to determine how well the program is working and to find out if both managers and supervisors know how performance is measured. They should be asked to identify weaknesses in the existing system and suggest ways to overcome them. The questions should address the typical elements of a performance appraisal program, including program objectives, policy, procedures, appraisal form(s), appraisal training, communications, appraisal discussion, developmental plan, performance standards, and monitoring and follow-up. Also, straightforward questions concerning the climate under which the appraisal is conducted are very important.

3. *Audit performance appraisal records.* An audit of the files, records, and other documents related to the performance appraisal program should provide additional information on the effectiveness of the program. Most organizations have copies of performance appraisals, either in personnel files or in special confidential files for appraisals. When the individual charged with administering the program receives these, she usually reviews them and then files them for future reference. But this continuous review may not uncover long-range inconsistencies, errors, or incomplete appraisals. A complete or at least a sample audit of the files can give much insight into how well both managers and supervisors are meeting their responsibilities in the performance appraisal process. Also, it provides a way to compare the actual documentation with legal and administrative requirements.

4. *Survey the supervisory group.* It is important to collect the reactions of supervisors to the performance appraisal
process. Negative reactions may reflect serious problems and an
ineffective program, whereas positive reactions may indicate
that the process is working well. An attitude survey (or opinion
survey) is an excellent way to measure supervisory attitudes.
Standard instruments are available or can be developed that will
provide insight into how supervisors think or feel about various
aspects of their jobs. Questions should be asked about the
supervisor's perceptions of various elements of the performance
appraisal program mentioned earlier. In addition, they should
assess the functional impact of the program on the supervisor's
individual work. Typical statements for this type of survey are:

	Strongly Disagree	Dis- agree	Agree	Strongly Agree
I am thoroughly familiar with the objectives of the performance appraisal program.	☐	☐	☐	☐
During the appraisal discussion, my manager is open to comments about my performance.	☐	☐	☐	☐

This survey should be conducted in confidence, and all participants should remain anonymous. In addition, it should follow
the guidelines for conducting effective attitude surveys.

5. *Determine and secure support needed for the performance appraisal process.* An appraisal program must be consistent with organizational goals and philosophy. Part of the review process should involve discussions with top and middle
management concerning its reasons for supporting or not supporting the current performance appraisal program. Penetrat-
ing questions are appropriate to determine if the current appraisal process is consistent with the organizational goals and
philosophy, method of operation, and policies. When major
reasons for lack of support are uncovered, each should be ad-

dressed vigorously. An effective program will require top management to demonstrate the importance of the performance appraisal process by actually making use of the results of the appraisal process. Anything short of full commitment and support from middle and top management is unacceptable, and this commitment and support should be secured prior to program implementation.

6. *Examine the objectives.* An important part of revitalizing a performance appraisal program is to examine the program's objectives and/or basic purposes. This requires the organization to ask, What does management want to accomplish with this process? Typical objectives of appraisals were discussed earlier. Others may be appropriate for a particular organization. The importance of this step cannot be overstated. Too many organizations are conducting performance appraisals for the wrong reasons. The objectives must be clearly understood, approved, and supported by top management.

7. *Redesign the appraisal system.* The next step is to redesign the system on the basis of information collected up to this point, if it in fact needs to be redesigned. The users of the system, both supervisors and managers, must make the system work and therefore should have some input into the design process. A task force or committee may be the most effective approach to secure this input. This involvement will increase the commitment of supervisors and managers to make the system function effectively. The redesign could involve changes in all or only part of the elements of a performance appraisal program.

8. *Implement the program.* After redesign, the new performance appraisal program should be implemented. A major part of the implementation is thorough training and communication for both managers and supervisors. More information on these aspects is presented in the next section.

9. *Monitor and evaluate the program.* Once implemented, a performance appraisal program should not become a permanent fixture. It must change as the organization changes and as internal and external conditions that affect the appraisal process change. The program must be monitored regularly to ensure consistent administration and be reviewed periodically to see that it is meeting its objectives. An audit of the program in

view of the legal and administrative considerations may be appropriate for some organizations, particularly if there is a strong possibility that the performance appraisal program has had an adverse impact on protected groups.

Special Issues in Performance Appraisal

The remainder of this chapter explores a variety of issues in the design and implementation of a supervisory performance appraisal program. These include timing, policies and procedures, training, degree of supervisory involvement, employee ratings of supervisors, legal considerations, critical incident files, documentation, and communication. Each can have an impact on the success of a program.

Timing. The timing of performance appraisals is an important issue that must be addressed early in the planning stage of a performance appraisal system. Establishing the appropriate interval between appraisals represents a trade-off between the time the staff can devote to the process and the time that is necessary to give adequate feedback to improve performance and develop employees. Most plans operate on an annual basis, although some have semiannual reviews and a few have quarterly reviews. Some analysts argue that frequent appraisals are needed to give an accurate account of an individual's performance and make improvements in the future. While this is important, the formal performance appraisal is no substitute for the routine and almost daily feedback a supervisor must have in order to successfully accomplish his or her job.

Another timing issue concerns the time at which one supervisor's appraisal is conducted relative to that of other supervisors. Some organizations conduct all appraisals at the same time and rank supervisors according to how well they perform relative to each other. This approach ensures consistent application of policies. Other organizations, however, give performance appraisals at the supervisor's anniversary date or in some cases the mid anniversary date (six months away from the anniversary).

Another issue is the timing of the appraisal relative to pay increases. If the primary objective of the performance appraisal is self-development instead of a review of past performance, then the appraisal should not be conducted at the time merit increases are initiated. However, if the principle purpose of the performance appraisal is to improve past performance, then the appraisal should be conducted at salary review time and used as a basis to determine the amount of increase.

Policies and Procedures. Policies and procedures are needed to ensure consistent application of the performance appraisal process. They are often regarded as necessary evils, since they require timely action by management. Organizational policy outlines what is expected or required from those in the organization with active roles in the process of appraisal. Procedures not only spell out what must be done by managers and supervisors but also provide forms, charts, tables, and other tools that will enhance the understanding of the system and ensure its consistent application. Policies and procedures should be brief, precise, and easy to understand. Otherwise, the organization will be burdened by an unnecessarily heavy work load while creativity and initiative are stifled. Also, even the best policies and procedures will *not* ensure that the system will be followed precisely. This is only one element in the performance appraisal process that must work in harmony with the other parts if the system is to be successful.

Training. Another important issue is the training provided for the appraiser and in some cases for the supervisors being appraised, if they have a formal role in the process. Effective performance evaluation requires many skills in the areas of communicating, counseling, problem solving, and planning. Training is important to ensure that managers acquire these skills. Surveys indicate that more organizations are providing appraisal training than they did formerly. A few years ago, less than half the companies with appraisal programs provided training at all (Lazer and Wikstrom, 1977, p. 39). More recently, another survey revealed that 65 percent of organizations provide appraisal training (King, 1984, p. 66). Appraisals can be enhanced through training that focuses on the techniques of appraisal and ways to evaluate performance. Some programs extend beyond this scope and include skill practice sessions in which middle managers have an opportunity to conduct simulated performance appraisals and receive feedback from experienced observers. If practical, operating management should conduct these training sessions to increase acceptance of the program and keep it from becoming a human resources program. Also, for some organizations it may be appropriate to train the supervisors being appraised, particularly if they are highly involved in the appraisal process. This training gives them an understanding of the process, outlines what is expected of them, prepares them to be meaningful participants in the discussion, relieves some of the anxiety connected with the appraisal process, and should provide far better feedback and ultimately better results from the process. Also, retraining may be necessary to reaffirm the program in the minds of the supervisors.

Degree of Supervisory Involvement. Another trend in performance appraisals is to increase the involvement of supervisors in their own performance appraisals. In traditional systems, the manager completed the appraisal and reviewed it with the supervisor. There was little, if any, opportunity for the supervisor to provide feedback in the discussion. Today, organizations are giving supervisors an opportunity to provide substantial input into the process, in some cases as much as the manager. In these settings, supervisors evaluate their own performance, prepare for the appraisal, and actively participate in an appraisal discussion.

Figure 9 shows an appraisal process used in one organization. This approach maximizes supervisor involvement and essentially puts the efforts of the supervisor and the manager in the appraisal process on equal footing. In this example, both the supervisor (who is being appraised) and the manager receive the appraisal form at the same time. They are allowed approximately two weeks to gather information and complete the appraisal form. Then they are given a few more days to fully prepare for the discussion. As part of this preparation they gather any additional information to support performance results or to explain

Figure 9. Performance Appraisal Process.

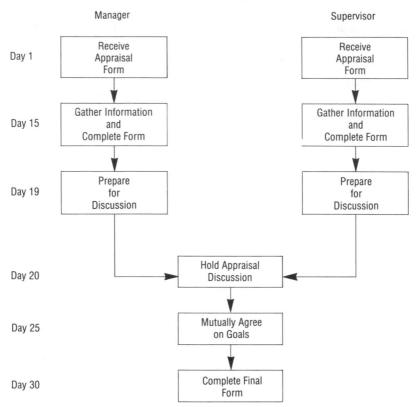

a lack of results. An appraisal discussion is held in an atmosphere of open, two-way communication. This particular company reports that the information on the two forms is usually very similar and that the separate assessments of supervisor performance closely parallel each other. In some cases, the manager's ratings are higher than the supervisor's. During the appraisal discussion they reach agreement on supervisory ratings, the results that were achieved, self-development needs, and other appraisal items. Then they agree on goals for the next period, particularly in areas where improvement is needed. Finally, the manager documents the complete appraisal process on a final copy of the form, which is reviewed by top management and becomes a permanent record of the performance appraisal.

This process seems to be quite involved, but the extra effort of getting supervisors involved can provide at least six distinct advantages:

- A more productive relationship is developed between manager and supervisor. Problems are more likely to be resolved, and solutions will be more readily accepted.
- Clearer boundaries of accountability are established. Each party may present information of which the other was unaware, leading to a more accurate appraisal.
- Self-motivation and initiative on the part of the supervisor are encouraged.
- Complaints, charges, and challenges to the appraisal process are minimized since supervisors will have a better understanding of their performance and shortcomings.
- Anxieties and frustrations are reduced significantly since supervisors have an ample opportunity to prepare for the performance discussion. Supervisors learn more about themselves.
- It makes legitimate a process that most supervisors are already involved in.

There are other advantages. Kaye and Krantz (1983, p. 34) have identified ten distinct advantages in their work with this type of performance appraisal. They characterize this approach to performance appraisal as a "win/win" approach in which everyone who participates wins.

This approach is not without its share of problems, however. It is time consuming in that both parties have to prepare for the appraisal process. Up to three forms have to be completed, and a lengthy discussion may be required. Also, for this approach to be effective, supervisors, as well as managers, should be trained in how to make the system work. And this training takes additional time and adds extra expense for the organization. Some supervisors, particularly those from an authoritarian background, prefer to be evaluated and are comfortable with minimum responsibilities in their own appraisal process. Some managers are also uncomfortable with this approach. They are reluctant to allow supervisors to rate themselves for fear of causing conflicts and disagreements on performance levels. They are concerned that supervisors will not be objective about their performance. Disagreement is a real possibility, and this could lead to confrontation and conflict.

But the advantages of this approach tend to outweigh the problems, as evidenced by the number of organizations moving toward more involvement on the part of their supervisors. One group of authors from a very respected consulting group predicts that "active involvement by employees in the appraisal process is here to stay" (Gelberd and others, 1983, p. 14).

Employee Ratings of Supervisors. Another issue receiving increasing attention is the use of feedback from the employees who report to the supervisor being appraised. At times almost everyone has wanted to give feedback to the boss. However, few programs are in place that allow any kind of formal or structured feedback on supervisory performance. If used effectively, feedback from subordinates can lead to improved supervisory effectiveness because subordinates are in a unique position to evaluate supervisory performance, particularly when that performance directly involves them. According to Hobson (1982, p. 8), "subordinate feedback to supervisors can serve to direct behavior, influence goals, and provide reinforcement as does feedback in the opposite direction."

Feedback from subordinates may not be suited for every organization, however. The extent to which it is well received varies considerably with individual supervisors. They must be open to constructive criticism, mature, and committed to personal improvement. The organizational climate must be one of mutual trust between management and employees, and there must be a strong top management commitment for improvement. Otherwise, the information will be ignored, or possibly there may even be retaliation from the supervisor for negative feedback. Also compounding the problem are general work group norms that look unfavorably on members who provide positive feedback to supervisors.

If this approach is suitable for the organization, however, there are a variety of ways in which feedback can be collected.

One is to use anonymous information that the supervisor collects on unsigned questionnaires. Another approach is to use a standardized instrument, such as an attitude survey, and to collect feedback periodically and systematically. This not only gives the current view of supervisory performance but will allow performance comparisons over time.

Employee feedback is an issue that should be considered in the design of the supervisory appraisal system. Although much research has been conducted on how managers rate supervisors, little has been reported on employees' ratings of supervisors. This will receive more attention in the future and may become another important element in formal supervisory performance systems.

Legal Considerations. Supervisors, like other employees, are protected by the laws that govern the employment relationship. There are two major types of legal concerns with performance appraisals. One involves state laws governing wrongful discharges, and the other includes the various fair employment laws at local, state, and federal levels.

A few years ago, employees working under no specific contract and not under a collective bargaining agreement could be discharged at any time, with or without just cause. This principle, known as the employment-at-will doctrine, has been recognized in all states for over a hundred years. In recent years, however, this doctrine has been eroding. Discharges without just cause have been severely limited by the courts, and now in a growing number of states employees cannot be fired unless it is for a just cause. Because of this, discharges of employees, including supervisors, should be supported with proper documentation. The performance appraisal can serve as the principle evidence on job performance to support the termination of a supervisor.

Antidiscrimination laws have had a significant impact on performance appraisal programs. Two of the most important ones are Title VII of the Civil Rights Act of 1964 and the Age Discrimination in Employment Act Amendments of 1978. These laws require that personnel decisions such as terminations, transfers, promotions, and demotions be based on job performance instead of on vague, subjective criteria. The Uniform Guidelines on Employee Selection Procedures, issued by the Equal Employment Opportunity Commission in 1978, require that performance appraisal programs be job related and based on clear and objective criteria. These guidelines also require that employers demonstrate the job relatedness of any device that is used in making employment decisions and has an adverse impact on members of any protected group. Thus, if an organization finds its performance appraisals do have an adverse impact, it must either stop using those appraisals, find an alternative procedure that eliminates the adverse impact, *or* validate the appraisal. Validation requires proof that the performance appraisal procedure gives results that are indicative of actual job performance (Kahalas, 1980).

Because of these requirements, the validity of subjective trait-based performance appraisals is almost impossible to defend. Behavior-based appraisals are also difficult to defend, but their validity increases if they are properly constructed around job-related criteria. However, specific quantitative standards as outlined earlier in this chapter are relatively easy to defend because they are objective and related directly to the job.

These legal considerations are among the reasons that performance appraisals are more and more making use of objective quantitative criteria or standards. Any organization developing a performance appraisal system should be prepared to defend that process if it is challenged. The use of clear, objective, job-related criteria to evaluate performance is crucial. If this condition is met, the organization will be in a much better position to defend its appraisal procedure.

Critical Incident Files. One fallacy in performance appraisals that extend for a period of a year or more is that there is a tendency for the most recent events to bias the appraisal process. Naturally, managers will remember those things that have happened most recently, particularly the negative items. Consistent, positive actions, as well as good overall results, may be overshadowed by a few negative events that occurred just before the appraisal discussion. One way to correct this problem is to have managers keep so-called critical incident files on each of their supervisors. These files contains exceptional items related to supervisory performance—both good and bad. An example of an exceptionally good incident might be as follows: "On January 23rd, Susan was particularly effective in resolving an employee complaint that might have led to a formal grievance had it not been resolved. The net result was a pleased employee and improved morale at the work station." An example of a negative incident might be as follows: "On July 15th, John failed to follow up on an urgent shipment scheduled to go out that day. An irate customer called later in the week and was highly critical of our failure to meet our promised delivery date."

Only exceptional items related to job performance should be placed in the critical incident file. After a few rounds of performance reviews, supervisors will come to realize that exceptional incidents are being noticed and documented. Because of this, they will try to keep the exceptions in the positive category.

Documentation. Another issue in performance appraisals is to determine the content and format of the documentation required. The critical incident files just mentioned will provide some of the documentation of supervisory performance. These files may be kept with the performance appraisal or used to supply information for the performance appraisal form. In either case, they are very important documents that add to the accuracy and completeness of the overall appraisal and are part of the complete documentation system. Most of the documentation of performance will be recorded on the performance appraisal form. Therefore, during the design of the form, the documentation issue becomes very important for four reasons:

First, documentation provides a permanent record of supervisory performance. Even the best of managers may forget details, and the organization cannot rely on their memories for a record of supervisory performance. Something as important as supervisory performance deserves to be documented thoroughly and accurately.

Second, documentation makes supervisors aware of what is on record concerning their performance. This is important both for good and bad performance. If supervisors have performed exceptionally well, then they are entitled to have that become part of their permanent record. Hopefully, this will enhance their career opportunities in the future. On the negative side, it is important for supervisors to know that their poor performance has become a matter of record. This puts additional pressure on them to try to overcome their deficiencies.

Third, documentation allows managers to support their personnel actions regarding supervisors—not only promotions and transfers but demotions and discharges as well. It is unlikely that a supervisor will be promoted to a job with more responsibility if he or she has no record of exceptional performance in previous assignments. Performance appraisals represent one of the best sources of information for evaluating a supervisor's potential for another assignment. The same holds true for transfers. Supervisors may be transferred to other assignments at their request or at the request of the organization. In either case, the performance appraisal provides the rationale for the transfer and may help support the actual move. Performance appraisals are also used to justify demotion or discharge of an employee. It is becoming increasingly difficult for an employer to discharge a supervisor without just cause, as noted earlier. The burden of proof is on the employer to ensure that there was just cause for discharge of a supervisor and that there is documentation to support the employer's claim.

Fourth, documentation will help defend the organization against discrimination charges. As also noted earlier, performance appraisal represents one of the areas of the employment relationship that has been challenged by discrimination charges and suits. The law clearly requires objective appraisals, and these cannot be made without complete and accurate documentation. Without a thoroughly documented performance appraisal, the employer is almost defenseless in a discrimination charge where performance is involved.

At the same time, effective documentation is time consuming, and it is difficult to obtain consistency within the organization. And if it is not done properly, documentation can be a liability rather than an asset. The organization must define the documentation requirements when considering time constraints and the information necessary to support the personnel actions in the organization. This is a very important issue that must be addressed early in the design of the performance appraisal system.

Communication. The final issue involves communication of the performance appraisal process. This is an important issue because much of the success of the appraisal process will depend on how well the manager and supervisor understand the process. Methods for communication range from verbal instructions for a performance appraisal form to elaborate policies, booklets, examples, training sessions, and meetings in which the organization explains the appraisal process in complete detail. The extent of communication will depend on the organization and the resources available. However, it is important to remember that the system will be understood only to the extent that information about it has been made available. Performance appraisal should never be treated as a secretive process with negative connotations. Rather, it should be set forth as a positive process that is good for supervisors, managers, and the organization.

Summary

This chapter presented a formal supervisory performance system that primarily includes job descriptions, performance standards, and performance appraisal. The organization will find it necessary to

- Review the supervisory job descriptions to see if they have been prepared in an acceptable format and accurately reflect job content. Although there are several ways to develop job descriptions, an especially useful and practical approach was presented in this chapter.
- Assess the feasibility of implementing a formal performance

standards program or other type of MBO program for supervisors. Performance standards represent an excellent way to
have clearly defined individual goals and targets for supervisors. The performance standards process outlined in this
chapter is not new, and it has been successfully implemented
in many different types of organizations, including government agencies.

- Examine the performance appraisal process for supervisors
  to see if improvements are necessary. Formal appraisal programs appear in almost all organizations in a variety of formats, yet they are not working very well. The various steps
  to revitalize an existing performance appraisal program were
  presented, and a number of important issues affecting the
  success of appraisals were discussed. These include timing,
  training, supervisory involvement, legal considerations, and
  documentation.

Several topics related to supervisory performance were
thoroughly discussed in this chapter; these range from the measurement of supervisory performance to various ways to communicate the appraisal process effectively. Few subjects are more
important than that of supervisory performance, and this chapter provides useful approaches to improve the individual performance of supervisors.

Suggested Readings

American Productivity Center. *Reward Systems and Productiv-
ity: A Final Report for the White House Conference on Pro-
ductivity.* Houston: American Productivity Center, 1983.
Blake, R. R., and Mouton, J. S. *Productivity: The Human Side.*
New York: AMACOM, 1981.
Connellan, T. K. *How to Improve Human Performance.* New
York: Harper & Row, 1981.
Giegold, W. C. *Management by Objectives: A Self-Instructional
Approach.* (3 Volumes) New York: McGraw-Hill, 1978.
Gilbert, T. F. *Human Competence: Engineering Worthy Perfor-
mance.* New York: McGraw-Hill, 1978.

Henderson, R. I. *Performance Appraisal.* (2nd ed.) Reston, Va.: Reston Publishing, 1984.

King, P. *Performance Planning and Appraisal: A How-To Book for Managers.* New York: McGraw-Hill, 1984.

Kirkpatrick, D. L. *How To Improve Performance Through Appraisal and Coaching.* New York: AMACOM, 1984.

Mondy, R. W., and others. *Supervision.* New York: Random House, 1983, 214–228.

Olson, R. F. *Performance Appraisal: A Guide to Greater Productivity.* New York: Wiley, 1981.

Phillips, J. J. *Handbook of Training Evaluation and Measurement Methods.* Houston: Gulf, 1983.

Sloma, R. S. *How to Measure Managerial Performance.* New York: Macmillan, 1980.

Watson, C. E. *Results-Oriented Managing: The Key to Effective Performance.* Reading, Mass.: Addison-Wesley, 1981.

5

Compensation:

Establishing Fair, Competitive, and Motivating Policies

Compensation, which includes pay and benefits, is a very important issue in all organizations today. (Until recently, pay was administered separately from employee benefits. But as benefits have grown, the line between pay and benefits has become blurred.) In addition, compensation figures heavily in the strategic management process. Some experts see the merging of reward systems, which are an important component of compensation, into the strategic management process that determines the direction of the organization (Greene and Roberts, 1983). In an important study involving corporate culture, chief executive officers voiced the need to establish an explicit set of values and then to communicate these values to their employees. They are doing this in part by structuring compensation to reinforce these values (Zippo, 1983).

Few things are more important to supervisors, or to all employees for that matter, than compensation. It determines their standard of living and social status and is an important form of recognition. It keeps them with organizations and makes them work hard. Supervisors exchange performance for rewards from the organization, as shown in Figure 10. As part

Figure 10. The Exchange Process.

of this exchange process, they are available to work for the organization, bringing with them their knowledge, skills, and ability. In exchange for their efforts and contribution they receive both compensation and noncompensation rewards. Compensation rewards appear to be more important and are described in this chapter. Noncompensation rewards are receiving increasing emphasis in organizations, however, and they include items such as working conditions, status, job structure, and developmental opportunities; all of these are discussed in other chapters.

A carefully planned and administered supervisory compensation system can have a tremendous impact on the organization, as well as on the individual supervisors, for at least four major reasons. First, supervisory compensation represents an increasingly costly investment for organizations. Supervisor salaries have increased significantly in recent years, primarily as a result of inflation and competitive pressures. In a typical organization the entire employee benefits package averages almost 40 percent of total payroll costs. When the expense of these benefits is combined with the costs of providing the necessary support services for supervisors, organizations find themselves making large expenditures to maintain and support the supervisory group. Because of this investment, it is important for organizations to manage the supervisory compensation system efficiently to maximize the return.

Second, an effective system will enable the organization to reward supervisors for their performance. Supervisors are eager to receive pay in proportion to their contribution. Yet too often organizations will position all supervisors at nearly equal levels and give them about the same increases each year. Periodic merit increases and direct incentive payments linked to performance can improve productivity in the organization, and such incentive plans are, in fact, becoming increasingly popular.

Third, effective, competitive compensation programs can boost the morale of supervisors, leave them with a good impression of the organization, and give them the feeling that they are being treated equitably. A supervisor's morale is important. If it is high, it will provide the impetus for outstanding results. But low supervisor morale will inhibit the efforts of others and cause the work unit's performance to fall short of expectations. It is difficult, if not impossible, to create an environment that motivates employees when the supervisors themselves are unmotivated.

Finally, an inadequate pay system is one of the reasons why supervisors leave an organization. Exit interviews conducted with departing supervisors reveal this to be the case in many organizations. If they think they are not being paid properly, supervisors will leave an organization, particularly if they have not been there long. Therefore, a competitive system can help keep supervisory turnover low and thus keep the organization stable and healthy.

This chapter is not intended to provide an organization with the information needed to design or develop a complete compensation system. Instead, it provides some useful approaches to deal specifically with supervisory compensation. Some aspects of supervisory pay should be treated no differently from the pay of other employees. However, there are a few problems unique to supervisors that will require action by the organization. The following actions should ensure that the organization is devoting proper attention to this important area and are explored in this chapter:

- developing a pay-for-performance philosophy
- considering the implementation of supervisory incentive plans
- maintaining an externally competitive system
- maintaining internal equity with other groups
- developing an effective approach to overtime pay for supervisory personnel

- communicating with supervisors to develop in them an adequate understanding of the compensation system

Types of Supervisory Compensation

Before we pursue the various issues regarding supervisory compensation, a brief review of the types of compensation is in order. Years ago compensation was a very simple matter that involved pay and a few benefits. Over time, pay and benefits have become so complex that there are almost as many types of pay and benefit programs as there are organizations. And their administration varies considerably with the type of organization and its use of consulting firms and outside benefit providers. The types of compensation can best be described by grouping them into categories as shown in Table 9, which lists the major types of compensation plans for supervisors. It is beyond the scope of this book to detail how each of these plans operates. But a brief description of each group should suffice. The Suggested Readings at the end of the chapter contains several books that do an excellent job of explaining compensation plans in detail.

Direct compensation is probably the most important part of the compensation package for supervisors. It is this component that will have the most immediate impact on job performance. Direct compensation includes base pay, plus any other types of short-term bonuses that are usually tied to performance. Compensation for time off is another important type of compensation. It includes benefits that are easily understood and that supervisors see as important. Most employees, including supervisors, realize the value of this benefit when they are enjoying a holiday or vacation and their salary continues to be paid. It is a low-cost, high-value item. Here, the primary concern is to remain competitive with other organizations.

Income continuation has become an increasingly important consideration, particularly during periods of business downturns and high unemployment. Unemployment insurance, supplemental unemployment benefits, and severance pay help protect supervisors from temporary job loss, whereas workers' compensation, Social Security, sick leave, and disability pro-

Table 9. Types of Supervisory Compensation.

Direct Compensation	Compensation for Time Off	Income Continuation	Deferred Compensation	Health, Accident, Liability Protection	Income Equivalent Payments
Base Pay	Holidays	Short-Term Disability	Social Security	Group Health Insurance	Counseling
Incentive Plans	Vacation	Long-Term Disability	Retirement Plans	Major Medical	Educational Assistance Programs
Production Bonus	Jury and Witness Pay	Workers' Compensation	Profit Sharing	Medicare	Subsidized Food Service
Christmas Bonus	Military Duty	Social Security	Thrift Plans	In-House Medical Services	Discounts on Merchandise
Special Performance Bonus	Funeral Leave	Accidental Death and Dismemberment	Tax Reduction Savings Plans (401K)	Dental	Physical Fitness
Safety Incentive Payments	Sick Leave	Unemployment Insurance	Savings Plans	Group Automobile	Professional Memberships
Commissions	Personal Leave	Supplemental Unemployment Benefits	Individual Retirement Accounts	Life Insurance	Professional Meetings
Overtime Premiums	Education and Training Assignments	Severance Pay	Stock Purchase Plans	Accident Insurance	Professional Journals and Publications
Shift Premiums		Sick Leave	Stock Option Plans	Travel Accident Insurance	Moving and Relocation Allowances
Suggestion Awards		Retirement Plans	Long-Term Performance Awards	Group Legal	Annual Physical Examinations
			Stock Appreciation Rights	Liability Coverage	Parking
					Low-Interest Loans
					Company Automobile

Source: Portions of this table are taken from Henderson, 1984.

grams protect supervisors from loss of income during periods of illness. In this category, as in the previous one, organizations need to maintain a competitive position. This type of compensation can improve morale and job satisfaction while building good feelings about the organization.

Deferred compensation is becoming an increasingly common form of payment. Deferred compensation is compensation earned in one year but paid at a future time. Savings plans, thrift plans, and profit-sharing plans are common benefits for supervisors. Other types of deferred compensation that were previously limited to executive-level employees are now being made available to supervisors. In many cases the levels of payout are tied to length of service. This helps the organization retain supervisors, since most plans provide that the deferred compensation will be forfeited or significantly reduced if supervisors leave. Deferred compensation provides employees with a long-range sense of security and has been useful in attracting new supervisors to organizations (Sibson, 1981, p. 32).

Health, accident, and liability protection is another area of tremendous growth and cost to the organization. These plans provide security and protection to the supervisor and his or her family. The variety and scope of plans are almost unlimited. They usually improve job satisfaction and can be an important element in recruiting new supervisors. Some of them are very basic, and are considered essential in any compensation package.

Income equivalent payments represent one of the most recent types of employee benefits. These include a miscellaneous collection of plans that either reimburse supervisors for expenses or pay for items of interest to supervisors. They are usually low in cost relative to the total cost of the compensation package, and their variety is almost without limit since they are tailored to the organization and the needs of the supervisory group. Many of them are related to discount purchases of the product made or service provided by the organization.

In summary, there are many types of plans that make up the total package of pay and benefits for supervisors. It has become an increasingly complex and costly area to administer. This chapter will focus on compensation plans that need to be examined regularly for their competitive position with other organizations, their relationship to supervisory performance, their cost to the organization, and their relationship to supervisory job satisfaction.

Elements of a Supervisory Compensation System

It is important to develop a basic understanding of all the different elements that make up the compensation system. A comprehensive supervisory compensation system will include compensation philosophy, compensation objectives, compensation policies, competitive strategy, job evaluation, performance measurement, pay structures and salary levels, system guidelines, incentives and bonuses, and communication. Regardless of the formal structure of the system, most of these elements will be addressed in some way or another. In detailed and elaborate systems, each element would be significant and might be presented as a separate policy or document in the complete salary plan.

Compensation Philosophy. An organization must develop and fine tune its philosophy on compensation for supervisors. In practice, the compensation philosophy for supervisors may not differ from that for other employees, although there are a number of supervisory pay issues that are unique and require the attention of top management. For some organizations, the philosophy may not be written but merely understood, at least by key managers. Others develop general statements that provide direction to the organization. They outline basic principles that the organization uses to guide its compensation plans and programs. They address such issues as pay for performance, cost-of-living increases, internal equity, external competitiveness, legal questions, and other issues where organizations may vary on their approach to compensation.

Compensation Objectives. Coming next are more specific statements that define the purposes of the compensation plan for supervisors. These specific objectives vary considerably with the type of organization and the organization's compensation philosophy. Some typical objectives are to

- attract employees to supervisory positions, either from within the organization or from outside sources
- keep supervisors from leaving the organization because of perceived unfairness and inequities in compensation
- reward supervisors for their performance and contribution to the organization
- maintain a competitive market position relative to supervisory salaries and benefits
- ensure that supervisors are paid in proportion to the difficulty and worth of their jobs
- comply with the various laws and government regulations affecting compensation matters
- provide a mechanism for consistent and fair administration of salaries and benefits for supervisory personnel
- control overall salary costs against planned annual budgets
- provide flexibility in supervisory compensation so that adjustments can be made to changes in both internal and external conditions that affect compensation

The objectives for a supervisory compensation system may not differ from the objectives of the overall compensation system for salaried employees. The objectives mentioned in the preceding list are fairly common for most compensation plans. In one study involving 277 compensation managers, the top three goals of compensation plans were to reward employee performance, remain competitive in the labor market, and maintain salary equity among employees (Freedman and others, 1982, p. 50). The words *rewarding, competitive,* and *equity* are very important terms that will be fully explored in this chapter.

Compensation Policies. After objectives come the policies that outline a framework for achieving an organization's objectives. Usually found in general policy manuals, compensation policies provide a foundation for the pay structure, define various responsibilities, outline the importance of the compensation system, and dictate how it will be administered. Policies outline how compensation for different employee groups is handled. For example, executive, managerial, supervisory, professional and technical, and clerical and hourly employees have different compensation needs, and each may require special consideration. Also, policies address the timing of performance reviews, pay increases, salary planning, and other important segments of the total compensation plan.

In practice, the organization's philosophy, objectives, and policies on compensation may be presented together as one part of the compensation system. Even though they are closely related, however, they remain three distinct issues that must be separated, at least in the minds of top management. Here is an example that gives a comparison of these issues, using pay for performance to illustrate the differences among them:

- *Philosophy.* This organization believes that an employee's compensation should be related to his or her contribution.
- *Objective.* This organization wants to provide direct bonus payments, based on work performance, to as many employees as possible.
- *Policy.* Incentive bonuses of 10 to 25 percent are available for all production and service supervisors based on the performance of the work unit in meeting predetermined standards.

Competitive Strategy. A very key part of a compensation system is to determine and maintain the desired competitive position for supervisors. The competition for supervisors may be limited to the local labor market, within the industry, or expanded to include regional and national markets. Along with the desired competitive position comes the mechanism for maintaining this position—a mechanism that usually involves salary and benefit surveys in the various labor markets. Organizations differ considerably in their approach to maintaining this competitive position. Some rely on small amounts of very subjective data while others collect detailed surveys with sophisticated analyses to arrive at desired salary levels in a full range of benchmark jobs. Because of its importance to supervisory compensation, this issue will be presented in more detail later in the chapter.

Job Evaluation. Another important part of a compensation system is the method by which jobs are assigned a specific pay grade or level. This job evaluation process provides a means for determining the relative importance or worth of supervisory jobs for pay purposes. While job evaluation systems vary according to the types of jobs and the organization's need, five basic approaches can be identified (Holley and Jennings, 1983, p. 312): point system, factor comparison, classification, ranking, and market pricing. The point system is the most frequently used approach and represents a quantitative method for establishing a supervisory pay grade. It assumes that there are a number of factors whose presence or absence should result in a greater or lesser value for each job in a family of jobs. Using job descriptions, job specifications, a predetermined rating scale, and salary surveys, point values are assigned for each of the jobs. Ranges of point value equate to pay levels.

The comparison method is similar to the point system in that jobs are evaluated by the use of compensable factors. This approach involves ranking certain benchmark jobs according to compensable factors to which dollar weightings will be assigned. The final result is a measurement scale that can be used for all jobs throughout the organization. Typical compensable factors in supervisory and management jobs are assets controlled, employees supervised, annual budget managed, opportunity for contribution, education and training required, technical knowledge required, experience needed, customer contact, public contact, stress experienced, difficulty of decisions, and interpersonal skill level necessary.

The importance of these factors varies considerably with the organization, the type of product or service delivered, and its philosophy, objectives, and policies regarding compensation. Factor comparison is a difficult and time-consuming process, but it gives a custom-designed approach for each organization.

The classification approach to job evaluation involves developing a predetermined number of job classes and fitting jobs into these classes. The different classes are differentiated on the basis of predetermined factors such as skills, responsibility, effort, working conditions, and education and training required. This is basically what the federal government does to establish pay grades. As new jobs are developed, they are slotted into one of the grade levels, ranging from GS-1 to GS-18. This kind of structure is relatively easy to develop and works best in larger organizations where there are a sufficient number of jobs to warrant using the system.

The ranking method, which is the simplest one, allows an organization to compare one job to another. The ranking is usually done on the basis of the overall importance of various jobs to the organization. It is used primarily with small organizations and ranks whole jobs rather than their various factors, as in other methods.

Market-based job evaluation systems simply involve determining what other organizations are paying for the same or similar jobs. Market averages are established, and additional points in the salary range are developed from these averages. For example, entry rates and maximum rates are usually established as a fixed percentage of the market average. This approach relies heavily on salary survey data and is useful when an organization places considerable importance on maintaining competitive salaries in the marketplace.

Performance Measurement. At the heart of any compensation system is the basis for making individual pay decisions. In most organizations, this is a function of the mechanisms that measure the performance of individuals or groups. This part of the compensation system determines what constitutes exceptional performance or marginal performance. Performance measurements allow compensation planners to remove much of the subjectivity present in individual pay decisions. The amount of emphasis on performance measurement depends on the extent to which an organization follows a pay-for-performance philosophy. Performance measurement includes such issues as the type of data collected, when it is collected, who collects it, and how it is interpreted. This may or may not tie directly into the performance appraisal process.

Pay Structures and Salary Levels. Another important part of the compensation system is to establish pay structures on the basis of the job evaluation system. These include the hierarchical job grade structure and salary ranges and progressions, as well as salary levels for each job grade. Such issues as the appropriate number of job grades, the amount of range spread, the degree of range overlap, and the relationship with other employee groups are addressed. Salary levels are determined by a number of factors. Competition and the organization's ability to pay are important considerations, along with changes in the cost of living and in general economic conditions. Various government regulations and the presence or absence of labor unions also affect the desired pay levels.

System Guidelines. Guidelines are usually furnished to managers so that they can administer the compensation system in a consistent and equitable manner. These guidelines outline when raises can be given and how much is allowed for a specific level of performance. Typical merit increases allowed for various levels of performance are shown below:

Performance	*Merit Increase Schedule*
Consistently exceeds standards	12 to 15 percent
Often exceeds standards	10 to 11 percent
Usually meets standards	7 to 9 percent
Partially meets standards	4 to 6 percent
Does not meet standards	0 to 3 percent

The allowable ranges are determined by the factors outlined previously. Guidelines describe how to handle the special issues of promotions, transfers, demotions, and job evaluations.

Incentives and Bonuses. If the organization subscribes to a pay-for-performance philosophy, then incentive and bonus plans are usually an important element in the total compensation system.

Because of the importance of this issue, and the increasing emphasis on incentive plans, they are discussed in more detail later in this chapter.

Communication. A final, but important, element in a compensation system is communications. This involves the variety of media used to inform supervisors and managers about the compensation system. One-on-one discussions, group meetings, benefit statements, procedure manuals, brochures, and booklets are a few of the methods that organizations have used to keep supervisors informed. This is a sensitive issue in some organizations since there is some debate over what should be communicated to supervisors. More details on this issue are presented later in the chapter.

Trends in Supervisory Compensation

Compensation practices have changed dramatically in recent years, and most experts indicate that more changes are in store for the future. Although there have been changes in the types and mix of individual benefits and pay practices, the most significant trends that have affected supervisory compensation are increased costs and value, pay for performance, flexible compensation, and increased government regulations. Each of these factors will have an impact on organizations designing pay and benefit programs in the future, particularly those involving supervisors.

Increased Costs and Value. By anyone's estimate, the cost of compensation has increased dramatically, and the real value of the compensation package has also grown significantly. Competitive pressures, inflation, and a variety of new and innovative compensation programs have increased the direct costs of compensation of supervisors. Probably more significant is the increase in that part of compensation generally regarded as benefits, both those required by governments as well as those voluntarily furnished by the organization. According to one report, there was a 19 percent real growth in the value of benefits from 1973 to 1981 (Carroll and Schuler, 1983, p. 6-18). This growth, which excludes the impact of inflation, includes pensions, capital accumulation plans, preretirement death plans, postretirement death plans, disability, total health coverage, and time off with pay. This growth is the result of a number of factors. Union and employee pressures have brought new benefits. Employees have come to regard many benefits as their right and to think that benefits should never be taken away but always added to. Until the advent of concessionary bargaining in the early 1980s, there was constant pressure at the bargaining table for new benefits or improvements in existing benefits. And as union employees gained benefits, so have nonunion employees. Improvements in legally required benefits, as well as increased government regulations, have boosted both benefit values and benefit costs. Inflation has taken its toll with benefits, particularly in the health care area, where there was a 94-percent increase in prices between 1973 and 1980 (Meyer, 1981, p. 2).

The rising costs of benefits have had a tremendous impact on organizations. In the current decade, employee pay and benefits have influenced everything from takeover battles to concession negotiations, while commanding more attention on the part of America's chief executives than ever before. Indeed all signs point to the fact that a company's very survival has become increasingly dependent on compensation issues (Salisbury, 1983). To combat this trend, many organizations are trying to hold the level of benefits constant and in some cases reduce them at the bargaining table. Cost containment features are being added to benefit plans, and educational programs are being implemented for employees to let them know the costs and value of their benefits. Specific ways in which employees can help the organization control costs in the future are discussed in these programs. In addition, organizations are looking at ways to increase the employee stake in benefits through increased employee contributions or reduced coverages. This question will present a significant challenge for organizations in the future and will have an effect on how the organization views the overall compensation package for supervisors as well as other employees.

Pay for Performance. One very important trend is the shift toward more emphasis on pay for performance in organizations. This is evident in all types of organizations and in almost every kind of setting, and it appears to be part of the overall attempt to influence individual performance in organizations. A recent study conducted by the consulting firm of Towers, Perin, Forster & Crosby, which involved 282 organizations, revealed some insights into changing attitudes about pay for performance (Walker, 1983). This trend was at the top of the list of issues about the changing nature of human resources in the business world. According to the study, "responses indicated increasing interest in merit pay, tying bonuses more closely to performance, basing salary scales on actual job content through job analysis, and providing more objective performance appraisals" (p. 4). Also, there is an interest in getting back to basics in performance management. The study indicated that there are few new tools for performance management, and the concern of respondents, therefore, was to make available tools work more effectively.

In the past there has been only a small difference in the percentage of merit increases available for exceptional performers as opposed to marginal performers. This might be acceptable when the average merit increase is relatively low—for example, in the 4- to 6-percent range that was experienced in the mid 1980s. However, as the average increase moves upward, the spread becomes less in relative terms. To overcome this situation, organizations are putting more pay-for-performance emphasis back into their merit programs. Greater spreads on the percent raise available are appearing. Merit programs with upper amounts in the 15- to 20-percent range are now appearing. On the lower side, the increase allowed for marginal performers is being reduced, and in many cases they are getting no raises at all.

Another study by the human resource consultants Drake, Beam, and Morin ("Performance Appraisals Reappraised," 1983) showed that many organizations are trying to strengthen the pay-performance link. This study involved 267 corporations and came to this conclusion: "Pay for performance is becoming a rallying cry for compensation systems designed in the 1980s as companies strive to trim the fat in wages and salaries" (p. 5). A leading expert in compensation has identified pay for performance as one of the major trends ahead in compensation (Ellig, 1983, p. 60). Experts from all types of organizations, participating in a White House Conference on Productivity, placed emphasis on this trend (American Productivity Center, 1983a). According to a final report for the conference: "Many of the current compensation systems in use do not focus on performance improvement, do not vary with performance, and do not reflect the special circumstances of different groups within an organization. Many compensation systems should be redesigned to correct these inadequacies" (p. 2). The conference report had two recommendations concerning pay for performance:

- Management and labor should work together to modify many of the current reward systems to increase their positive impact on performance and productivity. In some cases, this may mean dismantling some organization-wide systems that are no longer meeting the goals of the company or employees.
- Private and public sector organizations should seriously evaluate the potential application of tailored reward system approaches to compensation.

This trend toward more emphasis on pay for performance is becoming increasingly important to top management. One major study of 305 chief executive officers of industrial and service organizations, conducted by William M. Mercer, Inc., revealed that performance is the most important corporate value and that compensation systems should be designed to support it (Zippo, 1983, p. 43). Some of the specific findings were:

- Ninety-four percent of the chief executive officers believe that incentives are either very important or important in motivating high performers, while 92 percent consider incentives a key to rewarding performance accurately.
- Seventy-two percent say that pay for performance will become more important in reinforcing the values that are vital to their companies' success.

- Sixty-seven percent see a growing role for long-term performance-based incentives.
- Sixty-six percent believe that across-the-board salary increases will become less important.
- Seventy-seven percent of the respondents rated incentives as especially important in attracting new talent.

These trends are supported by the material in this chapter. Few of the approaches and ideas here represent new items or breakthroughs in performance management. Most of the tools and techniques have been around for some time but have not been used effectively and consistently. What is needed is for organizations to get back to the basics by concentrating on improving performance through compensation and appraisal systems.

Flexible Compensation. There has been growing interest in providing flexibility in compensation in both pay and benefits for some ten years now. Flexible compensation plans, frequently called cafeteria benefits, give employees some choice in selection of their form of compensation and help organizations control costs. Flexibility is provided in a variety of ways. In some cases employees are provided optional plans at a reduced cost that the organization is able to secure through a group effort. Another type of flexibility is to add supplements to existing plans to meet the needs of employees and their families. In this case the cost is usually shared by both the employer and the employee. The third type of flexibility allows employees to select how they will receive compensation. Employees can actually trade one of their benefits for another. In one organization employees are allowed to trade up to half of their yearly vacation for extra benefits or pay.

The idea has picked up some steam after a slow start. In one report in the *Wall Street Journal,* about eighty-eight organizations with a total of 500,000 employees now offer flexible compensation ("Flexible-Benefit Plans," 1983, p. 1). This same report projected that more than 200 concerns would have flexible compensation programs by late 1984.

Flexible compensation provides a vehicle for meeting the varied needs of supervisors with different family circumstances. A traditional fixed benefit plan does not necessarily satisfy the needs of a two-paycheck household, a single parent, or a single individual, all of which are common family arrangements these days. This flexibility lets supervisors manage their benefits and makes them aware of the costs and value of these benefits. This can lead to improvements in job satisfaction.

This trend is not without its critics. Some argue that the cafeteria approach to compensation adds more confusion to an already confusing issue. It is true that in some cases this approach can cause administrative problems and actually increase costs, since additional personnel may be needed to administer the plans. Comprehensive educational programs are needed to raise the employee understanding of benefits so that they can make intelligent decisions regarding them. These decisions are extremely important and can be disastrous if incorrectly made. Counseling programs may be necessary to provide one-on-one advice on how to make the best choice.

Increased Regulations. The 1970s witnessed strong government intervention in the area of pay and benefits for employees. No other decade has seen so much legislation, and it left some compensation planners wondering if this was the beginning of a long-term trend or just a temporary aberration. Unfortunately, it appears that more legislation is already on the horizon, both at the state and federal levels.

Probably the most significant individual piece of federal legislation was the Employee Retirement Income Security Act of 1974 (ERISA), which put stringent controls on benefit plans. ERISA provided new protections and guarantees for employees and their beneficiaries in the areas of pension benefit plans and welfare benefit plans, including health, accident, and death benefits. The percentage of companies with pension plans has declined slightly in the years since ERISA was enacted, and this suggests that the legislation has prompted some organizations to discontinue their pension plans (Lindsay, 1981, p. 64).

The Age Discrimination in Employment Act was amended

to extend the mandatory retirement age from sixty-five to seventy, and forecasters anticipate that mandatory retirement at seventy will be eliminated in the near future. The Pregnancy Discrimination Act of 1978 requires employers to treat pregnant female employees in the same manner as they treat disabled employees. The Social Security tax rates were increased dramatically during the 1970s, and the 1977 amendments to Social Security significantly reduced disability benefits, which caused the net amount payable from the typical employer-provided plan to increase.

The Tax Reduction Act of 1975 allowed for Tax Reduction Act Stock Ownership Plans (TRASOPs), which permitted a corporation to claim an extra 1 percent investment credit provided the company's tax savings were transferred to a TRASOP for investment in company stock. The Tax Revenue Act of 1978 and the Economic Recovery Tax Act of 1981 have greatly increased the attractiveness of capital accumulation plans. These laws encourage employers to adopt plans and employees to use them. The 1978 Tax Revenue Act allowed for deferred profit-sharing plans under Section 401(k). This is a major advantage, particularly for supervisors, since salaries are exempt from federal income taxes until withdrawal from the plan.

There has been increased interest in the issue of equal pay for equal work. Thus, the concept of comparable worth is based on the premise that employees should receive equal pay for work of comparable value. This concept will have an impact on the job evaluation process since it will cause more evaluations to be challenged in terms of job worth. All this could affect the evaluation of supervisory positions. Some may argue that supervisors should be paid more (or less) than engineers, for example. Such pressures will drive many organizations to market-based pay systems, using pay levels in the marketplace to establish the worth of new jobs (Ellig, 1983, p. 60).

In addition to legislation at the federal level, there has been an increased emphasis on laws and regulations affecting pay and benefits in almost every state. Combine these tendencies with state efforts to liberalize unemployment compensation and workers' compensation plans, and one can see why it is becoming more difficult for organizations to have consistent pay and benefit programs throughout the United States. Overall, laws and regulations have affected compensation significantly in the last few years, and this trend will probably continue in the future. Organizations will have to stay abreast of this trend and plan strategies to cope with it in the most cost-effective way.

Implications of Pay for Performance

Not every organization will or should develop and implement a pay-for-performance philosophy. This approach may bring more administrative headaches than the organization can effectively handle. And if not implemented and administered properly, it could even lower the morale of the supervisory group. However, the philosophy is based on sound motivational theories and an extensive base of research.

Performance-based pay systems are not inconsistent with probably one of the most controversial motivational theories, the Herzberg Two-Factor Theory of Motivation. Herzberg's research was very thorough and was conducted and replicated many times in the 1950s and 1960s. In his research, Herzberg identified two different sets of needs in employees: motivators and satisfiers (or hygiene factors). When present, motivators have an uplifting effect on employee performance; their absence, however, has little or no effect on performance. The satisfiers, when present, keep employees satisfied and content but will not necessarily lead to improved performance. Their absence, however, could lead to dissatisfaction and lower morale. The motivators, in the order of importance, are: achievement, recognition, the work itself, responsibility, advancement, and growth. The satisfiers, in the order of their strength, are: company policy and administration, supervision, relationship with supervisor, work conditions, salary, relationship with peers, personal life, relationship with subordinates, status, and security (Herzberg, 1968, p. 53). Some members of management have the mistaken belief that, according to Herzberg's research, money does not make a difference. This is not necessarily the case.

Since salary is a satisfier, Herzberg argues that the salary level it-self is not a factor that motivates individuals to high achieve-ment. It merely keeps them satisfied if it is at an acceptable level, and it will lead to dissatisfaction if it is perceived as inade-quate. However, if additional money is provided for exceptional performance, then money can be an effective motivator. Con-sider the top two motivators on Herzberg's list: achievement and recognition. According to his research, employees are moti-vated to improve performance when they are allowed to achieve and when they can see the results of this achievement. A pay-for-performance philosophy enhances the achievement aspect of motivation. How? One basic characteristic of a pay-for-perfor-mance philosophy is objective, job-related performance meas-ures. With this approach, employees know what they must accomplish and know when they have achieved their goal, whether it was established by themselves or someone else. The second motivator, recognition, is undoubtedly enhanced by this philosophy. There are many ways in which employees can re-ceive recognition, ranging from a simple pat on the back to a cash bonus tied directly to an outstanding accomplishment. Salary increases or bonus payments, provided for the recogni-tion of performance, can lead to higher levels of performance, according to Herzberg's theory. Thus, one of the most notable motivational theories does in fact support the pay-for-perfor-mance philosophy, at least to some degree.

One important theory of motivation that has received considerable attention in the 1970s and 1980s is the expec-tancy theory. Because this theory has typically demonstrated superior predictive validities in comparison to other theories, it is generally viewed as a dominant, if not the predominant, the-ory of work motivation (Mitchell, 1979, p. 243). This theory is based on the principle of expected value. Employees make choices about their contribution on the basis of the expected payoffs associated with their behavior and effort. The greater an employee's expectations, the greater the employee's motiva-tion to work hard. Similarly, the more highly an employee values a reward that can be obtained, the greater the employee's work motivation. Although there are many implications for practice from expectancy theory, three in particular warrant discussion (Kopelman, 1983, p. 62). First, the stronger the performance-reward relationship, the higher the organization-wide level of work motivation. Second, the stronger the performance-reward relationship, the more likely it is that high performing employees will be retained. Third, whereas rewards importantly influence satisfaction, it is the reward system that influences work motivation and job performance.

Research studies on the results of pay-for-performance programs have shown impressive results. One important book (Nash and Carroll, 1975, pp. 199–202) cited the results of five surveys encompassing more than 4,700 studies. The average increase in productivity after switching from time-based to output-based pay plans ranged from 29 to 63 percent with a median increase of 34.5 percent. More recently an extensive review of the literature found that, on the average, individual incentive plans increased output by 30 percent while group incentive plans typically increased output by 18 percent (Locke and others, 1980, pp. 363–388). Also, a comprehensive review of productivity experiments reported the results of seven studies that examined the effects of financial incentives. The results showed that performance increases ranged from 18 to 46 percent (Katzell and others, 1977).

The outstanding results of performance-based pay systems in individual organizations can be found throughout the literature. One important report described how IBM increased labor productivity in the manufacturing of typewriters by nearly 200 percent over a ten-year period (Vough, 1979, p. 2). According to Vough, one half of the increase in productivity was primarily due to two practices: pay for productivity—only for productivity, and promotion for productivity—only for productivity.

Many compensation experts and consultants have emphasized the relationship between pay and performance. Mitchell Fein, consultant to more than 500 companies, states that by any measure pay tied to performance is the most powerful motivator of improved work performance: "It is undeniable that from floor sweepers to presidents all (employees) raise their productivity when their pay is tied to productivity." And, similarly, John Miner concluded that whatever the literature one reads, the evidence of the motivating effects of contingent incentives is quite overwhelming (Kopelman, 1983, p. 63).

Still other experts differentiate among the motivating aspects of various types of compensation. Ellig (1984) presents a comparison of how various compensation elements rate in attracting, motivating, and retaining employees. Table 10 presents a summary of his results. According to Ellig, short-term

Table 10. Impact of Various Compensation Elements on Employees.

Compensation Element	Importance Rating		
	In Attracting	In Motivating	In Retaining
Salary	High	Moderate	High
Employee benefits	Low	Low	Moderate
Short-term incentives	High	High	Moderate
Long-term incentives	Moderate	Moderate	High
Perquisites	Low	Low	Moderate

Source: Ellig, 1984.

incentives have the highest prospects for motivating employees, whereas perquisites and employee benefits provide relatively low levels of motivation. Salary itself has only a moderate value in motivating employees because, according to Ellig, "Salary adjustments for outstanding performers are tempered by the lack of a downside risk in pay levels" (p. 26). It is also interesting to note that short-term incentives have a high value in attracting employees and a moderate value in retaining them. From this analysis it appears that the best approach to designing compensation programs to attract, motivate, and retain supervisors is to place emphasis on pay for performance in the salary plan while implementing short-term incentives. At all events, it is quite clear that pay for performance produces results. Thus, it is understandable why many organizations are moving toward this philosophy.

Establishing the Philosophy. Implementing a pay-for-performance program involves more than just establishing a merit system and developing bonus plans. It requires the development and implementation of a comprehensive philosophy on rewarding supervisors for their direct contribution and performance. This philosophy should focus on several major parts of compensation and contain the following elements:

1. *Current cash compensation is tied directly to the performance and/or contribution of supervisors.* With this philosophy, direct compensation is based on the performance of the supervisor's work unit and, whenever possible, on the direct contribution of the individual supervisor. Although not all the supervisor's effort can be directly related to its contribution to the bottom line, an organization with this philosophy will explore all areas to make the connection between pay and performance. All or most of the merit increase budget is allocated according to performance, with marginal or poor performers getting no increase, while supervisors with exceptional or outstanding performance records receive a significant merit increase. Also, incentives, bonuses, or other types of cash rewards are tied directly to objective performance criteria. This approach minimizes or eliminates across-the-board increases or cost-of-living adjustments that give all supervisors the same amount of increase.

2. *Performance appraisals determine the amount of salary increase.* The last chapter presented information regarding the timing of a performance appraisal relative to a salary increase. Some feel that the performance appraisal should be developmental in nature and thus removed from the decision-making process for merit increases. However, in an ideal pay-for-performance philosophy, the performance appraisal, or at least a major part of it, determines the amount of salary increase for the supervisor. This requires performance appraisal systems to contain an objective basis for assessing the supervisor's performance.

3. *Deferred compensation is related to performance.* There are a variety of deferred compensation plans designed to enhance the supervisor's overall pay and benefits package. To the greatest extent possible, deferred compensation plans should be related to the performance of either the individual supervisor, the department, the division, or the organization.

This places additional emphasis on getting the desired long-term results, either individually or collectively, and will encourage supervisors to make or support decisions that are in the best interest of the organization in the long run.

4. *The potential for contribution is an important factor in job evaluation.* Almost every supervisory compensation system has some logical way in which jobs are evaluated and assigned a pay grade. This usually involves a number of factors important to the job, either internal or external. In a pay-for-performance philosophy, a job's potential for contribution is an important factor in determining the relative worth of that position. A job that allows a supervisor to have a significant impact on the results of the organization is rated higher than one where potential is limited. This places the proper importance on the critical jobs in the organization.

5. *Objective, measurable criteria are established to determine the amount of bonus, incentive, or cash award.* This part of the philosophy appears obvious. However, there are many discretionary bonuses, particularly year-end bonuses, provided by organizations that are based on subjective criteria. Nonperformance factors such as attitude, effort, longevity, and political astuteness often provide the basis for determining the bonus as opposed to output, costs, and quality of work. In a pay-for-performance philosophy, there is little room for subjectivity in determining the amount of an award.

6. *The time lag between pay and performance is short.* Compensation is a reward for achieving results. The shorter the time lag between the pay for results and the achievement of those results, the greater the perception of the link between the two. A system of annual performance appraisals followed by merit increases does not sufficiently highlight performance and pay linkages. Therefore, short-term rewards are preferred over long-term increases.

7. *The magnitude of the reward for high performers is very significant.* There has been a tendency for the merit increases of both marginal and exceptional performers to cluster around the average amount of increase. The same situation exists for incentive or bonus payments. A greater pay-for-per-

formance link is likely if the rewards for high levels of performance are very significant. A 5- to 10-percent bonus spread may
not be nearly so effective as a zero to 20 percent spread. The
larger spread provides a significant reward for high levels of performance while the costs to the organization remain about the
same.

8. *Rewards focus more on individual rather than group
performance.* There are a number of effective plans that reward
a group for achieving certain targets. However, high levels of
performance can be achieved if they are linked directly to the
efforts of the individual. For supervisors, this includes plans
that relate directly to the supervisor's performance or that of
his or her work unit instead of plans based on departmental, divisional, or organizational results.

9. *Pay systems are kept as simple as possible.* Some pay-
for-performance programs are unnecessarily complex. Often
there are attempts to include as many of the factors that contribute to the overall results as possible. This desire to include
everything may reduce the effectiveness of plans by creating
confusion in the minds of plan participants. If supervisors cannot understand the system by which they are paid, then it is
unlikely to motivate them to achieve exceptional performance.
They need to see which performance measures determine their
pay so they can concentrate on the efforts that will yield them
the greatest rewards.

Problems with This Approach. Pay for performance is not without its share of critics, nor is it always easy to administer. This
approach requires a high degree of organizational commitment,
particularly on the part of management, to make it work. It is
more difficult to administer than a system not based on pay for
performance. For example, a system based on fixed cost-of-living adjustments, in which everyone gets the same increase, is
very easy to administer. Without the difficulty of administering
bonus plans, the overall compensation system for the organization becomes very simple to operate. Once the amount of adjustments is determined, it is simply a matter of changing the
payroll records to reflect the desired increase. There are no dis-

putes because every supervisor receives the same raise. There will be complaints, however, that high performers are not rewarded for their contribution while marginal employees are in effect rewarded for not performing.

Some critics argue that with most merit pay systems employees are unable to perceive a direct relationship between pay and performance (Lawler, 1981, p. 50), and they identify at least four factors that account for this problem. First, objective, comprehensive measures of performance are not always available in merit pay systems. Without these measures, salary increases are based on managerial judgement, and, as a result, they may be unfair, invalid, and even discriminatory. Second, organizations have traditionally kept salaries and pay practices secret. They have done an inadequate job of providing information about compensation systems, and when there is communication it is usually vague. As a result, supervisors come to question the credibility of the system and lose faith in merit pay. Third, the policies and procedures by which the merit pay systems are administered are usually complex and confusing. Therefore, supervisors find it difficult to see the relationship between pay and performance. This is reinforced when supervisors with marginal performance receive merit increases along with good performers. Finally, managers often create a negative perception of the connection between pay and performance. They are reluctant to recommend many large or small salary increases because they do not want to "deviate from the norm" too often. When small increases are given, managers sometimes downplay their involvement in the matter by saying that they tried to obtain a larger amount but failed. This suggests to supervisors that their salary increases are beyond the control of managers.

Inflation has taken its toll on merit pay systems, both in increasing the difficulty of administering systems and in rendering them ineffective in meeting their objectives. Inflation causes wages and salaries to increase, and organizations, in their zest to keep up with the competition, have had to dish out significant salary increases over the last few years. Unfortunately, many organizations have had to combine adjustments for inflation with merit increases. The result is a fully diluted merit system or, at best, a cost-of-living increase with a small variation for performance.

The size of an organization has an effect on merit systems. In large organizations it is more difficult to tie pay to performance since many supervisors may feel that their efforts have little impact on the bottom line of the organization. As a result, supervisors see themselves operating in an almost isolated world, and they are left wondering if their efforts really make a difference in achieving the organization's goals and objectives. When this is coupled with the traditional mistrust of large organizations, it is no surprise that many of the merit systems are perceived as ineffective and not directly related to performance.

In addition to the problems with merit pay, there are problems with bonus or incentive plans for supervisors. There is, first of all, the problem of placing too much emphasis on factors outside the control of supervisors. This can cause frustration and serve to demotivate supervisors instead of increasing their output. Also, the targets for the payout of a bonus must be clearly established and not be changed, at least during the time period established for the bonus. There is sometimes a tendency to gradually increase the target for a certain bonus, thus keeping a significant challenge in front of the supervisors. But this elusive target can eventually cause supervisors to give up and revert to an average level of performance. However, the payout targets may need to be adjusted when conditions warrant these changes, particularly in the case of targets involving factors outside the control of the supervisor.

Finally, in merit systems and bonus plans alike, inconsistent administration can cause serious problems. When managers do not follow the philosophy, goals, and procedures of the pay-for-performance system, then compensation may be perceived as being unfair, based on favoritism, and determined by the biases and subjective judgments of the management group.

These problems with merit pay systems and bonus plans should not prevent organizations from adopting a pay-for-performance philosophy. Even its critics will concede that a properly designed, carefully implemented, and effectively administered merit pay or bonus system will improve employee performance and boost morale. In practice, particularly with sophisticated compensation systems, the pay-for-performance philosophy is working better now then ever before. Organizations are removing many of the obstacles to these systems and are compensating supervisors for their direct contributions.

Supervisory Incentives and Bonuses

Supervisory incentive and bonus plans are an important part of the total compensation package for supervisors. These plans usually include direct compensation that is tied to predetermined performance criteria. The overall purpose of incentive plans is to motivate supervisors to achieve better than average results and maximum efficiency. Supervisors have a great deal of responsibility and in most organizations can have a tremendous impact on the results achieved by their work units. In most cases supervisors are rewarded for above-average performance and for achieving specific objectives. About 80 percent of all nongovernment, profit-oriented, public corporations have some form of bonus plan for managers, and almost half of all industrial companies provide a bonus plan for supervisors (Sibson, 1981, p. 242). These plans, which are appearing in increasing numbers, seem to be effective. Many of the same studies that support the pay-for-performance philosophy also support the increasing use of incentive and bonus plans, particularly for supervisors. These incentive plans come in a variety of formats and must be carefully designed to accomplish their objectives.

Types of Plans. There are several types of supervisory incentive and bonus plans, and their classifications vary in different studies and research works. *Individual performance plans* are tied to specific measurable criteria for the individual supervisor, and compensation is based on the extent to which he or she exceeds predetermined targets. These are quantitatively based and include output, costs, or other important factors under the supervisor's control. Bonuses are usually paid as a percentage of base salary, and they are designed to show a direct relationship between the amount of the bonus and the supervisor's performance.

A *work unit performance bonus* rewards a supervisor on the basis of how well the work unit has performed. In some respects this is no different from an individual performance plan since the supervisor's performance is determined to a large extent by the efforts and contribution of the employees supervised. However, a work unit performance bonus may tie a supervisor's bonuses directly to the performance of the employees in the unit. The supervisor receives a bonus when the work unit as a whole exceeds predetermined goals.

Profit-sharing plans represent an increasingly popular approach for rewarding groups of employees. The primary objective of a profit-sharing system is to instill a sense of partnership and teamwork into the organization. All employees, or specific groups of employees, receive a percentage of the profit above a predetermined level. In some plans, supervisors are eligible for a higher portion of the profit than nonmanagement employees are. In other plans all employees are eligible for the same share, usually calculated as a percentage of their base earnings. This type of plan clearly illustrates to supervisors and other employees the necessity for the organization to maintain a profit in order to be successful. It is one of the fastest growing methods of incentive pay.

Gain-sharing programs have also received a great deal of attention in recent years. They involve employees in improving the productivity and profitability of a work unit, department, or division. Employees are encouraged to find better ways to use labor, capital, materials, and energy in their unit. Gain-sharing plans have proved successful. For example, 74 percent of companies with group productivity plans rated their plans as successful in raising productivity. Estimates vary but there are probably between 500 and 1,000 gain-sharing plans in operation in the United States (American Productivity Center, 1983a, p. 14). Some operate under such trade names as Scanlon, Rucker, and Improshare. Each of these plans has specific formulas to determine the amounts paid out or deferred for future payouts. Gain sharing can contribute to a greater sense of common purpose and direction among all employees and supervisors when it is implemented in conjunction with increased participation on the job and small group discussions.

Year-end bonuses are usually discretionary bonuses based on the supervisor's performance relative to the work unit, department, division, or organization. They are typically tied in some way to the profits of the organization or unusual accomplishments of the supervisor. Year-end bonus payments may be based on a percentage of company profits, a fixed percentage of salary, or a lump-sum amount. Bonus payments can vary from year to year, depending on business conditions and the attitude of top management. Because of the uncertainty of the bonus and the somewhat subjective basis for payment, this type of incentive plan is not as motivational as other types. More than likely it will not increase the performance levels of supervisors, but it will increase their satisfaction with their jobs and the organization.

Cost reduction programs are very popular as bonus plans for either individuals or work groups. Under these plans, payments are based on actual cost savings and can be fixed dollar amounts or a percentage of the actual savings. One very well-known type of cost reduction plan is the employee suggestion system. This approach has been around for some time, but it is now being re-examined and revitalized by a number of major firms (American Productivity Center, 1983a, p. 12). Under the cost reduction approach, employees and supervisors are challenged to find ways to work in more intelligent ways, find alternative methods or procedures, reduce the cost of supplies and raw materials, or use any of the items that represent a cost to the organization more efficiently. Targets are usually established by means of historical cost data, and payments are based on the savings achieved by the supervisor or work unit.

An organization may use a combination of these bonuses since some of them are related to employee benefit packages and are available to all salaried or possibly all hourly employees.

Since direct incentives appear to motivate supervisors, the remainder of this section will be devoted to methods of developing incentive plans that provide a payout for the direct efforts of the supervisors.

Design Criteria. Supervisory incentive systems should be designed around the pay-for-performance philosophy outlined in the previous section. Much of what was said there also applies to the design of incentive plans. However, there are a number of actions that can influence the success of incentive plans, and these should be addressed during the plan design process. Thus, an organization should

1. incorporate a measure of performance that gauges true measures of success rather than measures that are primarily driven by inflation, accounting conventions, and other factors
2. balance measures of performance for both the short-term and long-term aspects of the work unit and organization
3. tailor the system specifically to the organization and to the individual supervisory jobs
4. provide information about the system so that supervisors understand it well enough to calculate their bonuses for a given level of results
5. base the plan on those factors that are measurable and within the control of the supervisor
6. secure input from the supervisors during the plan design process
7. set targets that are not impossible to achieve
8. develop some constraints around the plan so that supervisors do not receive inflated bonuses for work that is not the result of their own efforts

Measurement Criteria. Supervisory incentive plans should be designed to achieve results in the area that management considers most important. Although usually tied to improving efficiency, incentive plans can focus on one or more general areas, as shown in Table 11. The examples in the table show the variety

Table 11. General Measurement Criteria for Supervisory Bonus Plans.

Measurement Focus	Example
Productivity	An insurance claims processing supervisor receives a bonus based on the increase in claims processed per employee hour.
Costs	A mailroom supervisor in a large financial institution receives a bonus for reducing mailing and delivery costs.
Profitability	The supervisor of a small fast-food restaurant, which is part of a large chain, receives a bonus as a result of an improvement in the annual profit of the restaurant.
Quality	A computer assembly supervisor receives a bonus for reducing the number of rejects returned from customers.
Time savings	A programming supervisor for a large hospital complex receives a bonus for the early completion of a major programming project.
Service	An appliance repair supervisor of a large retail department store receives a bonus for reducing the time to respond to a service call.
Safety	A surface mining supervisor receives a bonus when the unit works for six months without an injury requiring medical treatment by a physician.

of performance data used in incentive and bonus plans. Depending on the type of organization and supervisory function, the plan could be designed to bring about planned improvements in one or more of these areas. It may be best to have a plan focus on only one area to keep things simple and understandable. However, to balance the job effort and to ensure that the supervisor focuses on all areas of responsibility, it might be necessary to focus on more than one area. For example, costs might be improved but only at the expense of quality, quality might be improved but profits might be reduced, or productivity might be improved at the expense of customer service. Whenever there are potential trade-offs, more than one factor may need to be considered in the plan design.

An important part of the plan design is to determine what specific items to measure in order to determine the amount of the bonus. Table 6 in the previous chapter shows typical measurement criteria that have been used in supervisory bonus plans. These represent hard data that are available in most organizations, and they are easily monitored. It is also very easy to assign dollar values to hard data, a step that is important in calculating payout on a bonus plan. When hard data are not available, less tangible and more subjective types of measurement criteria may have to be used. These soft data items are more difficult to measure and quantify, at least directly. Table 7 in the previous chapter gives some examples of soft data measurements. In some plans several soft data requirements are imposed as additional conditions for payout, while the level of payout is based on the hard data measurements. In this case the supervisor who qualifies for a bonus based on hard data measurements will be awarded the full amount of the bonus only if certain soft data standards have been met. Otherwise, only a portion of the bonus will be paid.

Supervisor Control. It is very important that items selected for performance measurement be largely under the control of supervisors if the plan has been designed to reward supervisors for obtaining above-average results from their individual efforts. Nothing is more frustrating to supervisors than to see a potential bonus go down the drain as a result of events totally beyond their control. The more control the supervisor has over the bonus, the more likely his or her performance will improve.

Supervisor Involvement. Unfortunately, a typical approach is to develop a plan in an atmosphere of secrecy and confidentiality so that plan participants will not have high expectations. This approach almost never works. An incentive plan cannot be designed in a vacuum. Input is needed from the group it is designed to motivate. A few organizations let supervisors participate in developing the supervisory incentive plans, although this is not a common practice. Supervisors are in a position to know which of their areas of responsibility will yield the greatest return. They can pinpoint problem areas and identify inequities. At a very minimum, supervisors should have an opportunity to review the incentive plan before it is finalized. The organization should listen to their concerns or complaints, as well as their suggestions for modifications. Also, supervisors who have input into the development of the plan are more likely to make it accomplish its objectives.

Establishing Targets and Payouts. Another critical part of the plan design is its target. There are two extremes to avoid here. First, a target should not be set that could be achieved without extra effort, otherwise the bonus becomes automatic and does not reward for exceptional performance. Second, the target should not be set so high that it cannot be obtained, because then the supervisor will simply ignore the plan. If the targets are periodically changed so that they become more difficult to achieve, supervisors will soon realize that the organization is playing a game, one that they will eventually lose. The targets should be realistic and should not be changed unless there is some justification for doing so.

Some supervisory incentive plans are developed to reward group performance while others are developed to reward individual supervisors. Group plans tie several work units together and make all the supervisors in one department (or division) eligible for a common bonus. The payout for achieving desired targets depends on the performance of other units in the department (division). In other situations, supervisory bonuses may depend on organizational performance. Although it might be argued that individual supervisory bonuses should not be paid when the overall organizational performance is down, the entire bonus should not necessarily be tied to the results of other units. A healthy approach is to have payout ratios heavily weighted to work unit results. For example, maybe only 30 percent of a supervisor's bonus should be affected by the performance of others; that is, departmental results might account for 20 percent while organizational results would account for another 10 percent, for a total of 30 percent. In this case, 70 percent of the supervisor's bonus would be tied to work unit results.

Individual plans motivate the supervisor and provide compensation directly related to the supervisor's contribution. Group plans have the added advantage of promoting cooperation to achieve a departmental or divisional objective. However, the trade-off is that supervisors may come to feel that others have too much control over their potential bonuses, and this may lessen their motivation.

Another approach to incentive payouts is to consider a variety of payout items from which the supervisor can choose. These cafeteria incentive plans recognize the individual differences among supervisors. Some supervisors may prefer one type of payout, others a different arrangement. These incentives are usually limited to short-range goals and may include items such as merchandise, gift certificates, vacations, trips, or time off with pay. This approach has the advantage of providing a range of potential payouts while allowing the supervisor to select the one that means the most to him or her. Although this kind of plan may be more difficult to administer than plans with cash payouts, it could get more performance per compensation dollars.

Plan Communication. It is important that incentive plans be thoroughly explained to supervisors and that they have a complete understanding of the system. Ideally, a supervisor should be able to calculate a bonus payment on the basis of results achieved over the period that the incentive plan was in effect. One organization requires supervisors to calculate a bonus from actual data before they are placed on the incentive plan. Many well-designed but complex plans fail simply because the supervisors do not understand them. In some organizations, the detailed mechanics of the plan are not revealed to supervisors. Only the final results are reported. This secrecy creates an air of mystery that can demotivate supervisors and destroy the positive effects of the plan. The principle of simplicity should be considered during each step in design of the plan. Anyway, it is almost impossible to have a measurement to take care of every item that could conceivably influence results.

Reviews and Revisions. Every supervisory incentive plan should be reviewed on a periodic basis to see if changes are necessary. Input for this review should come from supervisors and middle managers, as well as from human resources personnel. Changes should be implemented if the plan is not working properly or if adjustments are in order to improve its effectiveness. Adjustments in the targets during the period of the plan may be needed when there are changes in the market, production schedule, or other factors that are outside the control of the supervisor.

In summary, incentive plans are an excellent way to reward supervisors for their direct contribution to the organization's desired level of performance. Incentive plans can get more mileage for the compensation dollar than merit pay plans if they are developed properly, implemented effectively, and administered appropriately.

Competitive Considerations

Any compensation system must have mechanisms for keeping it externally competitive and internally equitable. This is particularly important for supervisors since an uncompetitive or inequitable pay system can result in an unfortunate number of turnovers. There are probably more groups—in and out of the organization—affecting the compensation of supervisors than affect the compensation of any other single group of employees. Figure 11 shows both the internal and external influences that will ultimately determine supervisory pay levels. Externally, the pay scales of supervisors need to be compared with those of other supervisors in the local labor market. Also, if appropriate, they need to be compared with those of other supervisors in the same type of business or service. Finally, survey data on a regional and national basis show trends in supervisory pay that are important if the supervisory group is highly mobile. Internally, there are four groups with whom a supervisor's pay level must be compared. First, there are the other supervisors in the organization. Next are the other professional employees, and particularly other staff employees whose main function is to support line supervisors. In addition, comparisons of a supervisor's pay with that of subordinates may be necessary to maintain a desired pay differential. And, finally, in some organizations a supervisor's pay relative to that of his or her immediate superior, the middle manager, is an important fac-

Figure 11. Groups Affecting Supervisory Compensation.

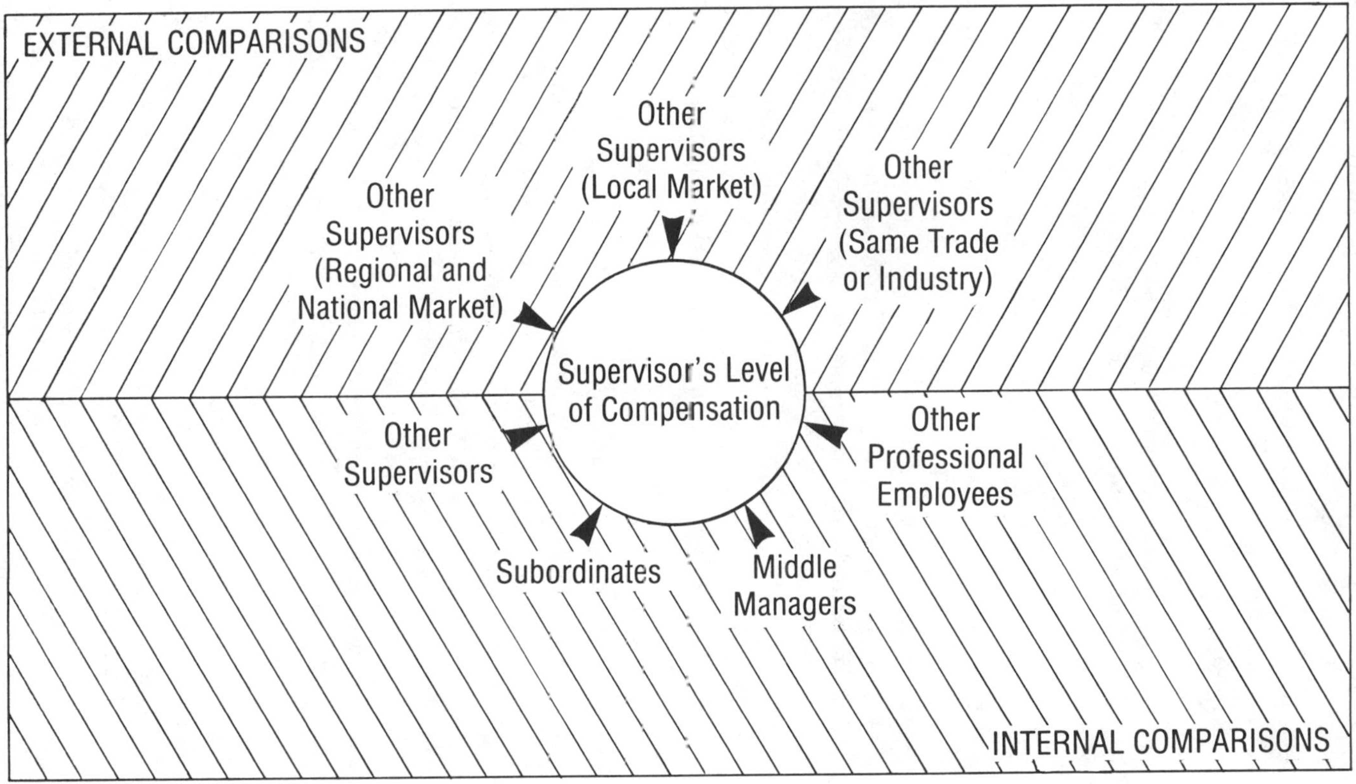

EXTERNAL COMPARISONS

INTERNAL COMPARISONS

Other Supervisors (Same Trade or Industry)

Other Supervisors (Local Market)

Other Supervisors (Regional and National Market)

Other Supervisors

Supervisor's Level of Compensation

Other Professional Employees

Middle Managers

Subordinates

tor. Ideally an organization would want to prevent the salaries of any of these groups from getting too far out of line with supervisory pay.

Local Comparisons. Although local competition may not be a factor in every situation, many organizations do compete with others in their locality in attracting supervisors, particularly if there are similar types of organizations in that area. Local surveys not only supply information that helps keep salaries competitive, but can have a tremendously positive impact on the supervisory group when the information is communicated to them. Supervisors will always hear rumors that supervisors are paid more or have a better bonus plan in another local organization. Without factual information the organization may not be able to counteract such rumors. An important part of a local survey is to identify the appropriate firms with which to compare supervisory salaries. After the survey has been conducted, the information can be used to make adjustments in the organization's salary plan.

Industry Comparisons. The second task is to examine data from organizations engaged in the same type of business or service. This is important to determine if pay differences exist among supervisors involved in similar work. For example, construction supervisors are compared with other construction supervisors, bank supervisors are compared with other bank supervisors, and so on. These surveys are usually available through industry, trade, or professional associations and can be very helpful in providing input to ensure that salaries are competitive for similar work.

Regional and National Comparisons. Finally, supervisory salaries may need to be compared with regional and national survey data. Data are usually available from professional services or special surveys conducted by compensation consultants. Survey data are usually presented regionally and expose geographical differences and even differences in rural and urban areas. National surveys are excellent for companies that operate on a broad, national scale and have supervisors in many parts of the country. Also, national survey data, when collected in a reliable and valid way, can be very helpful in communicating the competitive position to the supervisory group.

Developing a Strategy. Keeping the compensation plan competitive involves some strategic steps and decisions on the part of the organization. First, a planned position in the market must be established. For some organizations this is at the market average; that is, supervisors' pay is set equal to what is paid in the market, however that market is defined. Other organizations want to take the lead and be a certain fixed percentage above that market—for example, 10 percent above the market average. Still other organizations, for a variety of reasons, are satisfied to be a certain percentage under the market average.

Second, organizations must determine how often information is to be collected and reviewed. Some organizations prefer annual comparisons of their compensation scales with the market. Others look more often—some even continuously—and make adjustments as soon as significant evidence for change is uncovered. The timing depends on the rate of change of salaries in the market, as well as on the resources available for collecting the information.

The third step involves identification of the specific sources of information for supervisory compensation data. This includes selecting local organizations, identifying specific jobs for the survey, and outlining the types of data required from the survey. In many cases a sample of local companies is used for a local market survey, although in small communities all organizations of similar size may be included. Every effort should be made to keep the survey from being biased.

The fourth step involves the design of the actual method of collecting data. There are a variety of effective survey techniques, any one of which may be appropriate for the particular organization. Telephone surveys usually offer the quickest and least expensive method of collecting information. Mail surveys may be more suitable when more information is necessary. An onsite visit is another approach that can increase the reliability and accuracy of the information.

In the fifth step, the potential use of existing surveys is

examined. There are many organizations that conduct regional, national, and industry surveys. The Abbott-Langer Directory of Pay Survey Reports is the most comprehensive reference work currently available, and it covers a full spectrum of salary surveys (Rock, 1981). This report comes in three parts: U.S. survey reports not produced by the federal government, U.S. federal government survey reports, and non-U.S. survey reports. Other important surveys are conducted by the Administrative Management Society, the Executive Compensation Service, Management Compensation Services, the Hay Compensation Information Center, as well as the Bureau of Labor Statistics. The Executive Compensation Service offers one report that focuses directly on the supervisor's job: the *Supervisory Management Report*. Ranging from manufacturers of transportation equipment to banking institutions, this report shows a classification guide for every function of production first-line supervisors, service first-line supervisors, general supervisors, and office supervisory personnel. It includes data on cost-of-living allowances, working hours, and work shift differentials (Rock, 1984).

The sixth step determines how the survey data will be used. There are four principle uses of survey data to make adjustments in an organization's compensation system: job evaluation, salary ranges, merit increase budgets, and entry salary rates. A market-based job evaluation system uses survey data as a primary basis for determining the relative worth of a supervisor's job. Many organizations use survey data to adjust their salary range structures, possibly adjusting market averages and the rest of the structure along with those averages. Merit increase budgets quite frequently are determined on the basis of salary survey information. Finally, starting salary rates, particularly for new college graduates, are established through use of survey data.

A final step involves making all this information available to supervisors. It is important for supervisors to know that their pay system is competitive. As a general guideline, organizations should communicate as much information as possible—without revealing the individual input from other organizations—if the information supports their desired position in the market. This can have a tremendous impact on building credibility for the salary program and help supervisors understand what the organization is doing to keep salaries competitive. Without this information supervisors will have a tendency to think their system is not competitive.

Internal Equity

Supervisory pay should be examined for internal equity to ensure that supervisors are paid at a level consistent with comparable jobs in the organization and at a level that keeps supervisors at a proper differential with other groups of employees. It is one thing for supervisors to be convinced that they are paid appropriately when compared with other supervisors outside the organization. It is another matter for supervisors to consider their pay equitable when it is compared to that of groups with which they must work closely. Failure to address this issue properly can lead to morale problems and possibly reduce the effectiveness of supervisors.

Comparisons with Other Supervisors. The first task is to compare the pay scales of different groups of supervisors. This is more important when there are large numbers of supervisors. It may be necessary to pay some groups of supervisors more than others. It is not unusual for several different pay grades to be established for supervisors, and there are some valid reasons for these variances. For example, a supervisor of a low-skilled employee group such as the janitorial crew possibly should not be paid as much as a supervisor of x-ray technicians. Maintenance supervisors may need to be paid more than production supervisors if their function is seen as more critical and requirements for their job are more difficult to meet. Also, the scope of the job as defined in the job description in the previous chapter can have an impact on the supervisory pay level. A shipping supervisor with a small work crew may not need to be paid as much as a supervisor of an automated assembly line that represents an investment of $20 million. Some differences in supervisory jobs are taken into account in supervisory incentive and bonus plans. In these cases, anticipated total cash compensation, which includes incentive compensation, is used for internal equity comparisons.

Comparisons with Other Professionals. Another area of concern in internal equity is a comparison of supervisors with other professional employees, although the supervisor's work may not be related to, or even involved with, that of the other employees. Examples of jobs that may be appropriate to compare with that of supervisor are engineer, sales representative, accountant, buyer, personnel specialist, and statistician. All these are professional-level employees in an organization. The rationale for this comparison is that an organization does not want the salaries of its professional employees to get too far out of line with those of the supervisory group. A market-based system might ignore these differences, whereas internal equity comparisons should help guide the organization to develop an equitable system, at least as perceived by the supervisors. Even with a secretive salary administration plan, supervisors will have knowledge of the pay levels of other professionals. It is only natural to compare jobs and pay. Significant differences in pay may leave the supervisors wondering why they have chosen supervision as a career. This issue becomes more important in the case of professional staff employees who provide service and support to supervisors. These comparisons are sometimes ignored in an organization, and the result can be disastrous. Since these groups usually work closely together, supervisors may know the salaries of some of their counterparts in staff support organizations. Significantly higher pay levels for these employees will lower supervisory morale and can impair cooperation and teamwork between the two groups. The supervisor's job should command respect in the organization, and it is important that it command the proper level of compensation. A supervisor's pay should not fall below that of his or her professional counterparts in the organization, except for special cases where high levels of skills are needed. Consider this example: An organization recruits technical college graduates to enter a training program. The program prepares candidates to enter one of the following jobs: production supervisor, service supervisor, engineer, production controller, quality control technician, or field service representative. Candidates can have a choice of each of these jobs near the completion of the training program. In that organization the supervisor's job is regarded as the most difficult and challenging of all the positions. Yet the pay level is no better than that of the others. As a consequence the organization has difficulty enticing graduates to pursue supervisory jobs. In some cases it must resort to coercion to get a candidate to accept the job. The result is a high turnover rate for supervisory positions and increasing difficulty in attracting high-quality prospects for the job. An adjustment in the salary level of supervisors, coupled with the increased likelihood of a bonus, could make a considerable difference in the interest level for that job. Most new college graduates are not afraid of the difficult and challenging assignment of supervisor. They just want to be rewarded for their efforts.

Comparisons with Subordinates. The third area of concern is determining how to maintain pay differentials between supervisors and their subordinates. In too many cases supervisors receive the same pay as the highest-paid employee supervised, or even less pay. For example, a construction supervisor may have a weekly base salary that comes to less than the forty hours of pay that the top electrician, who is under his or her supervision, receives. This is particularly a problem in areas where there are highly skilled employees or in high-wage industries where the employees have had significant wage boosts through major contract settlements. If this problem is left unresolved, it can lower supervisory morale and discourage promising candidates from seeking supervisory roles. They might not see the potential reward for all the challenges and responsibilities of the job.

This problem needs to be addressed both in establishing the salary structure and in handling individual situations. The job evaluation process should take into consideration the potential for unusually high wages for employees in the work unit. This is the best time to remove inequities. More than likely, the factors that contribute to the high pay for the employees will also influence the pay level of supervisors.

Some organizations take care of this problem at the time of promotion by ensuring that the supervisor's pay level is adequately positioned above that of the highest-paid employees supervised. Promotional increases can be structured with enough flexibility to make these adjustments. Others try to take care of the problem through bonus plans that allow the supervisor to receive a significant bonus payment that places them above the highest-paid employees. One flaw in this approach is that in lean years the bonus may not be paid, and total supervisory income will suffer through no fault of the supervisor.

Still other organizations rely on other types of compensation, such as deferred compensation or special benefits available only to supervisors. These benefits provide extra incentive for employees to assume supervisory jobs, and they place the long-term total compensation of supervisors well above that of their employees. Unfortunately most supervisors are not long-range planners. They have a habit of looking at what they have in take-home pay as a measure of their compensation. Although they may understand the value of such benefits as deferred compensation and the potential for bonuses, there is nothing more convincing than immediate cash compensation.

And finally, some organizations prefer to ignore the problem, emphasizing the inherent value of the job and the nature of supervisory work as additional incentives to seek those responsibilities. More job security and better working conditions for supervisors than for nonmanagement employees are sometimes identified as substitutes for a fixed pay differential.

For organizations planning to maintain an adequate differential, the primary issue is determining the specific amounts. Various options are available, depending on the nature of the supervisory job and the type of employees supervised. One approach places the supervisor a minimum number of pay grades above the subordinate employees. This is more appropriate for supervisors who come under the same or similar job evaluation system as their subordinates. A policy of maintaining two pay-grade levels between the highest-graded employee in the unit and the supervisor is common. In other situations, a differential of three, four, or even five levels may be appropriate. A slight variation of this approach is to establish a minimum average differential so that the supervisory pay grade is at least a fixed number of levels above the weighted average of the pay grades of the employees supervised. This approach may be more realistic since it keeps the supervisory pay grade an adequate distance from the average of the grades of all employees instead of the grade of one employee who may be graded high for some unusual circumstance. For example, a data entry supervisor may have the following employee mix:

One data entry operator trainee (Grade 3)
Four data entry operators "B" (Grade 4)
Three data entry operators "A" (Grade 6)
One data coordinator (Grade 8)

A policy of maintaining the supervisor's pay three grades above the highest-graded employee would fix the supervisor's salary at grade eleven. A policy of three grades above the average grades of employees supervised would fix the supervisor's salary at grade eight, the same as that of the data coordinator. This may be the desired approach considering the specialized duties of the data coordinator.

A second approach is to set minimum differentials on base pay. The supervisor's base salary is placed at a fixed percent higher than the straight-time earnings of the highest-paid employee in the work unit. This figure may be 10 to 20 percent, depending on the level desired by the organization. This approach can be adversely affected by large amounts of employee overtime pay or large bonuses paid to the supervisor.

A third approach is to base minimum differentials on gross pay. This allows for employee overtime pay, as well as bonus pay for supervisors. In this case, the annual gross pay of the supervisor is a fixed percent over the gross pay of the highest-paid employee. Five to 15 percent is usually a healthy range for this differential. An annual adjustment may be necessary for this policy, based on the previous year's gross earnings, since the amount of overtime and bonuses cannot be accurately predicted for the coming year.

A fourth approach is to base minimum differentials on averages. In this case the gross pay or base pay of the supervisor is a fixed percent above the average straight-time pay or average gross pay of the subordinates. The organization must select either base or gross pay for making these comparisons. Fifteen to 45 percent is a healthy range for minimum differentials based on average employee pay. This approach might be more practical when there are a large number of employees at about the same wage level and only one or two individuals at a much higher wage level. The average of the entire group gives a more realistic comparison of the minimum differentials required.

An organization may choose to establish one, some, or all of these guidelines in developing the desired minimum differential. In one organization the following minimum differential policy was established for supervisors:

- The salary grade of staff supervisors will be at least two salary pay grades above the grade of the highest-graded salaried employee supervised.
- The base salary of production and service supervisors will be at least 20 percent greater than the straight-time wages of the highest-paid employee supervised, *and* the gross earnings of production and service supervisors will be at least 25 percent greater than the average gross earnings of all employees in the work unit.

This approach solves the problem of wage differentials, improves morale, and rewards supervisors appropriately for the job that they do.

Comparisons with Managers. At the upper end of the organization there is the issue of the minimum differential between supervisors and managers, although this question is usually not as serious as that of the differential between supervisors and their employees. If market-based job evaluation is used, salaries for middle managers are determined on the basis of competitive external rates. Nevertheless, in some organizations this differential issue is a concern and must be addressed either in establishing supervisory pay or establishing minimum pay levels for the middle-management group. The approach an organization takes would depend on whether its internal pay levels are heavily influenced by lower-level pay rates. If aggressive collective bargaining has resulted in high hourly rates, coupled with minimum differentials for supervisors, then a desired minimum differential between supervisors and managers may be a determining factor for middle-management salaries. In this case, negotiated hourly rates push up supervisory pay to the point where supervisors overlap with the middle managers. Upward adjustments may be necessary for the managers, and the same approaches used in establishing differentials between supervisors and their employees could be employed here. A serious question enters the picture with this issue: Where does the organization stop with this philosophy of minimum differentials? The answer lies strictly with the organization and its objectives. Obviously, at some point the pay for jobs must be determined solely by the job evaluation process. And managerial jobs have a greater variety of compensation, as well as noncompensation, rewards.

Overtime Pay Policies

Another perplexing supervisory compensation problem, related to minimum differentials, involves overtime pay. Supervisors usually acknowledge that they knew beforehand that their new job would involve more than forty hours a week. What they didn't expect were consistent periods of long work hours and no overtime compensation, while their employees, who continue to work fewer hours than they do, reap sizable overtime premiums. This problem is particularly serious in maintenance and support work where overtime is a normal part of the work schedule and the employees supervised are in relatively high wage brackets. What is overtime for their employees is routine for supervisors. A typical production maintenance unit, for example, may be on standby during regular shift time and then repair or replace equipment after normal hours. Supervisors are usually required to be on duty as long as any employees are at work. Because of unexpected breakdowns and unscheduled downtime, the problem can become quite serious. And if not handled properly, it can lower the morale of supervisors, reduce their efficiency, and leave them with a feeling that their compensation system is unfair.

Policies vary with organizations; they may range from no overtime for supervisors, regardless of how many hours they work, to the normal time and one half for each hour of work over forty hours. As with minimum differentials, this problem is unique in each organization. The philosophy, goals, or guiding principles of the organization ultimately determine the policy. Organizations opposed to paying supervisors overtime have some very legitimate arguments. They are reluctant to pay supervisors for something over which supervisors usually have control. Theoretically, a supervisor could schedule the work unit to work longer hours and thus enhance his or her own compensation through overtime pay. These organizations quickly point to the noncompensation rewards for supervisors, as well as other pay and benefits that are designed to reward supervisors and adequately compensate them for all their efforts. Paying supervisors overtime pay will cause problems for the payroll department and problems in administering other benefit plans. Finally, these organizations argue that if supervisors are paid overtime, the same as their employees, they then may identify more closely with workers than with management. These are good arguments, and there is no best way to handle the issue. The approach must depend on the organization. Nevertheless, there are some solutions that can help resolve this dilemma.

Solutions Without Pay. Ideally an organization would like to solve the problem without paying supervisors an overtime premium. If this is an objective, there are at least three approaches that may be appropriate for the organization. One is to prepare supervisors to manage their work unit so that overtime can be minimized. For example, they might be taught to delegate work so that their presence is not required when their employees are working overtime. This may require giving someone temporary responsibility for the unit or training others to assume additional responsibility when the supervisor is not present. In some cases it might be just a matter of developing coordination and scheduling skills in supervisors so that they can accomplish more during the normal work schedule.

A second approach is to establish a working foreman or group leader within the work unit. This group leader is typically an hourly employee who is paid a premium for functioning as a lead person and is compensated for overtime work along with other employees. This person does not have any responsibility for scheduling overtime but merely assumes part of the supervisory duties, particularly during periods of overtime work. This can be an inexpensive approach in that the overtime premium for the leader will be less than the overtime pay for supervisors, if they are in fact paid an overtime premium.

The third approach to resolving the problem without pay is to allow supervisors to take compensatory time off for the overtime hours worked. With this approach the manager keeps track of supervisory overtime and allows supervisors to take additional time off, usually on an hour-for-hour basis, over and above scheduled holidays and vacations. One problem with this approach is that in reality, with the supervisor's usual busy schedule, it may be difficult, if not impossible, for him to take compensatory time off and still effectively supervise the work unit. This problem is compounded in periods of high overtime when the compensatory hours increase significantly. Also, there may be a problem in getting someone to fill in for the supervisors while the compensatory time is taken. Like the other two approaches, this one is not flawless, but it does represent a workable solution to the problem without paying an overtime premium to supervisors.

Solutions With Pay. Some organizations prefer to pay overtime and must select a pay formula that will adequately compensate supervisors for their overtime work. The variety of approaches available is almost unlimited and may be influenced by local and state laws. Four variations are outlined below, beginning with the most liberal approach and ending with a conservative one:

- time and one-half pay for all hours worked over forty
- straight-time pay for all hours over forty
- half-time pay for all hours over forty
- straight-time pay for all hours over forty-five hours per week

An organization must select the pay plan that keeps costs at a minimum while adequately compensating supervisors for their excessive overtime efforts.

Communicating the Compensation Program

The importance of communication has been discussed several times in this chapter, yet probably no aspect of supervisory compensation is mishandled more frequently than communication. Supervisors, as well as other employees, are notoriously kept in the dark about pay practices. Many organizations keep their compensation systems secret and even do a poor job of communicating the small amount of information that they want their employees to have.

Communication is complex and confusing. Communication failures have probably caused more business problems than any other aspect of the management process. Because of this, it must be carefully planned and executed on a timely basis. In an organization the communication flow may be categorized as downward, upward, or lateral. In downward communication top management communicates to supervisors (and other employees) the organization's compensation philosophy, objectives, policies, procedures, and expectations. Through upward communication supervisors can keep top management informed about their concerns, misunderstandings, ideas, and suggestions about the compensation system. This feedback is important to ensure that supervisors have understood and accepted the message. Lateral communication often has compensation as its topic. Supervisors discuss with peer groups their concerns about and disappointments with pay practices. When their discussions are not based on solid information, this lateral communication will give a distorted picture of the compensation program.

Developing a trusting environment is an important task here. Supervisors are quick to compare their pay system, or at least what they know about their system, with what they hear about other systems. They form an opinion as to whether the system is fair, equitable, and motivational. It is important that they have accurate and reliable information. This can help build credibility and ensure that a trusting relationship is established between top management and supervisors.

Establishing a communication plan for compensation involves three general considerations. First, the organization must determine how open the pay plan will be. This involves identifying how much information can be efficiently communicated and what information can be appropriately released to supervisors. Second, communication objectives must be developed. Third, communication methods must be established. These methods may include a variety of effective communication media, or they may simply be the grapevine and rumor mill. These considerations must be addressed before communication details can be developed.

Openness of Pay Plans. The amount of information about compensation that should be provided to employees is a controversial issue. The approach ranges from one extreme to another. In some organizations everything about the pay system is communicated—individual salaries, salary ranges, pay grades, and policies and procedures. Nothing is kept secret. This will not work in some organizations but is typical of the approach used by government agencies and educational institutions. At the other extreme, some organizations reveal nothing to their supervisors but their own salary. No information is provided about the policies, procedures, ranges, or the basis for pay increases. A completely open policy would spell disaster for some organizations while a completely closed system would mean disaster for others. An organization must establish the position in between these two extremes that is best for it. When establishing the desired position, the organization must consider the concerns of supervisors (and other employees).

Supervisors usually want to know as much about the compensation system as they can. If the system is too secretive, it breeds distrust and a feeling that the company has something to hide. More positive than negative reactions can be generated from effective compensation communication, unless the system is unfair, inequitable, and uncompetitive. Before information has been communicated, supervisors have formed an opinion as to whether the system is fair and competitive with other companies. After the information has been revealed, their opinion is either confirmed or changed.

Supervisors want to know their exact performance requirements. This includes who measures them and their standing relative to predetermined standards or others in the department or division. In addition, they want to know the importance that the organization places on extra efforts and how they will be rewarded for such efforts. Supervisors want to know about their future job opportunities, including the possibility of promotions and transfers and the salary growth they can expect with those opportunities. Usually they are not asking for specifics but for a general indication of what levels of compensation they can achieve if they are willing to pay the price for those opportunities.

Changes to a more open system should be done at a gradual, calculated pace. Opening up a pay system is a very sensitive and difficult task for an organization, and successful implementation may depend on the timing and cautions observed. The process is virtually irreversible. Once a pay system is opened up, it is difficult, if not impossible, to move back to a closed system. Supervisors become accustomed to receiving certain information about pay; if it is suddenly stopped, they will have more distrust for the organization than if they had not received the information at all. This issue must be considered before any decision is made to release additional information to supervisors. One organization, a medium-size manufacturing facility, wanted to make its salary system more open and had hired outside consultants to help develop a strategy. An analysis of the current system revealed a number of inequities but there was also serious doubt about the company's competitiveness in the market-place. After this review the company decided to delay the decision to communicate additional information until it had had an opportunity to correct current problems. The moral of this story is, Do not provide information about the system unless it is in good working order.

The types of information communicated can vary considerably. The most common items are:

- philosophy of the compensation system
- objectives of the compensation system
- compensation policies
- how the organization maintains internal equity
- how the organization maintains external competitiveness
- basis for job evaluation
- salary structures (positions and ranges)
- pay range and position in the range
- salary grade
- basis for merit increases and pay actions
- supervisor's potential for salary growth

The last item is usually optional, but communicating the others would be consistent with the practices of most business and industrial organizations. They tend to be more conservative than government agencies, educational institutions, and nonprofit organizations.

Communication Objectives. A communication plan begins with objectives that identify the purposes for communicating compensation information. For the supervisory group, there are several objectives that may be established for this communications effort:

- *Improve job satisfaction.* A thorough understanding of pay practices should lead to improved satisfaction with the job and the organization. This assumes, of course, that the pay system is fair, equitable, and competitive.
- *Explain how the compensation system works.* It is important that supervisors have a thorough knowledge of the compen-

sation system so that its implementation occurs smoothly, without errors. The procedures and guidelines must be thoroughly understood so that supervisors can meet their responsibilities to administer the system properly.

- *Develop a consistent understanding of the compensation system.* It is one thing to know how the system works but another to develop a consistent understanding of it. Consistency is important to ensure that supervisors have the same message. Effective communication will help establish this consistent understanding. This is particularly important in a large organization where supervisors are removed from much of the policy-making process.
- *Enhance individual motivation of supervisors.* A compensation system, particularly one that is based on the pay-for-performance philosophy, can have a motivating effect on supervisors. An effective communication program will ensure that supervisors understand the rewards that they can expect to receive as a result of their individual efforts.
- *Prepare supervisors to answer questions about the compensation system.* Since supervisors have employees reporting to them, it is important that they be prepared to explain the pay system to their employees even if it is different from theirs. Quite frequently the compensation systems for supervisors and their employees are similar and have the same basic philosophy, objectives, and procedures.
- *Improve the organizational climate.* The compensation system is an important part of the organization's culture, philosophy, and style. It is important that supervisors know the role of compensation in the organization. This can occur only if it is properly communicated to supervisors.

These are only a sampling of the types of objectives that may be appropriate for making information about the compensation system available. The specific objectives will depend on the organization and what it wants its supervisors to know about pay practices.

Communication Media. A variety of communication media are available to communicate compensation information. The single

most important document for communicating the salary plan is
the *policy and procedure manual,* which describes how the plan
works and outlines how it is administered. In practice, most organizations do not distribute the salary policy and procedures
to supervisors unless their system is the same as the system for
nonmanagement employees. However, others will make it available to supervisors who do want to read it. In general the policy
and procedure manual details the objectives, the salary administration system, and specific instructions for administering the
plan.

Probably the most effective communication process is to
meet directly with supervisors, especially when the group consists of all the supervisors who report to a middle manager. In
this meeting, a compensation specialist (or the middle manager)
explains the compensation policies, procedures, and practices to
supervisors, leaving plenty of time for questions and answers.
The purpose is to let the supervisors know how the system
works and clear up any misunderstandings they may have. Other meetings, involving a larger group of supervisors, may be appropriate for broad and general compensation issues. One
organization presented to all supervisors the company's strategy to maintain competitive salaries. It revealed the results of
salary surveys without identifying what each company provided and then discussed the steps taken to maintain internal
equity. This kind of meeting is not directed at any one particular segment but is intended to educate the entire supervisory
group about the process of salary administration and to outline
what the organization has done and is planning to do to make
the system work. Another type of meeting involves one-on-one
discussions between supervisor and manager. They may discuss
those aspects of the salary plan that apply only to that supervisor. For instance, if the organization is committed to providing salary range data, information about other salary grades that
the supervisor has a likely possibility of achieving should be
discussed on a one-on-one basis.

Another very effective approach to communication is
through *brochures and booklets* designed for general distribution to the supervisors covered by the system. These brochures
usually back up the information discussed in general meetings

and are not as detailed and specific as the policy and procedure manuals. They come in a wide range of formats, ranging from single-page fliers to elaborate four-color brochures that detail the entire salary system. But an organization needs to exercise caution here, because anything appearing in writing will be construed to be policy and must be followed. Otherwise, the process may lose credibility.

Many organizations develop annual *pay and benefits statements* for their supervisors that outline the compensation levels they have obtained. They inform each supervisor of the personal benefits accrued during the year and summarize the amount of financial protection available through the various benefit programs. These statements are usually computerized and are fairly expensive to start up. Once implemented, they are easy to update and distribute each year. An important part of this statement is to communicate the employer's total cost for the compensation package. These statements are generally well received by supervisors and are becoming an important tool to improve satisfaction with the total compensation package.

A final communication medium is the *organizational publication.* This is used less frequently than any of the other approaches but nevertheless can be an effective medium. This approach can be used more readily if there is a publication designed especially for supervisors. This type of communication should not be a vehicle for winning supervisors over to the organization's philosophy. It should present policy, statistics, and general interest items designed to inform and educate supervisors.

In summary, the communication of compensation information is an important element in the compensation system. A variety of media are available for organizations to explain the system to supervisors. From maximum effectiveness, the communication must be carefully planned and executed.

Summary

This chapter fully explored supervisory compensation, which includes pay and benefits. It focused on types and elements of supervisory compensation, trends in supervisory compensation, pay for performance, considerations of equity and competitiveness, and communication. Organizations must

- Examine the various elements of existing compensation systems, as described in this chapter, to ensure that all parts are functioning adequately.
- Keep abreast of the trends in supervisory compensation, as outlined in this chapter, and make adjustments when necessary.
- Explore the feasibility of increasing the organization's commitment to the pay-for-performance philosophy. The characteristics of an ideal philosophy were presented, along with the problems in this approach.
- Evaluate the feasibility of implementing supervisory incentive and bonus plans, a type of compensation that is becoming more popular. Several plan design factors were outlined.
- Take the necessary steps to keep the compensation system competitive. Comparisons with local industries, as well as regional and national comparisons, may be necessary.
- Ensure that the compensation system is internally equitable when considering salaries of other supervisors, staff and professional employees, subordinates, and managers. Also, overtime pay policies may need to be adjusted to allow for supervisory overtime pay where there are serious inequities between supervisor salaries and wages of employees.
- Communicate the compensation system effectively through a variety of media.

Several effective approaches that can help organizations meet these challenges were presented in this chapter. Compensation is a very important issue that can have a significant impact on performance. The issues of open pay plans were discussed, along with communication objectives and communication media.

Suggested Readings

Armstrong, M., and Lorentzen, J. F. *Handbook of Personnel Management Practice*. Englewood Cliffs, N.J.: Prentice-Hall, 1982.

Berg, J. G. *Managing Compensation.* New York: AMACOM, 1976.

Carroll, S. J., and Schuler, R. S. (Eds.). *Human Resources Management in the 1980s.* Washington, D.C.: Bureau of National Affairs, 1983.

Foulkes, F. K. *Personnel Policies in Large Nonunion Companies.* Englewood Cliffs, N.J.: Prentice-Hall, 1980.

Henderson, R. I. *Compensation Management: Rewarding Performance.* Reston, Va.: Reston Publishing, 1979.

Holley, W. H., and Jennings, K. M. *Personnel Management: Functions and Issues.* New York: Dryden, 1983.

Nash, A. N. and Carroll, S. J., Jr. *The Management of Compensation.* Monterey, Calif.: Brooks/Cole, 1975.

Rock, M. L. (Ed.). *Handbook of Wage and Salary Administration.* (2nd ed.) New York: McGraw-Hill, 1984.

Sibson, R. E. *Compensation.* (Rev. ed.) New York: AMACOM, 1981.

Vough, C. F. *Productivity: A Practical Program for Improving Efficiency.* New York: AMACOM, 1979.

Yoder, D., and Heneman, H. G., Jr. (Eds.). *ASPA Handbook of Personnel and Industrial Relations.* Vol. 2: *Motivation and Commitment.* Washington, D.C.: Bureau of National Affairs, 1975.

6

Communication:

Improving Relations Among Supervisors, Employees, and Upper Management

No book on supervisory effectiveness would be complete without a chapter devoted to communication. Communication nearly always appears at the top or close to the top of any list of problems confronting organizations. Communication is at the very heart of the supervisor's job, and it is implicit in all aspects of the supervisory role. One study showed that supervisors spend 90 percent of their workday reading, writing, listening, and speaking (Christenson and others, 1982, p. 99). The supervisor must communicate with employees, peers, and management and in some cases with third-party representatives who are either internal or external to the work environment. It is important for several reasons that the organization focus on developing effective communications with the supervisor. First, effective communication helps ensure that supervisors will feel a part of the management team. It promotes understanding of the organization's mission and goals and focuses attention on the supervisors' efforts to accomplish objectives. This is particularly true for confidential information shared with supervisors that is not essential to their jobs. Although they may not need to have this information, they will appreciate management's trust and confidence in sharing it with them. However, communication is not a one-way process, although the focus sometimes is on providing information to supervisors. An organization must have two-way communication and listen to what supervisors are saying and take their suggestions in a sincere and trusting manner. This can increase supervisors' feeling of participation in the decisions that affect their work unit. Gathering input prior to a change in policies and procedures can increase supervisors' awareness that their input is helpful and is really needed by the organization.

Second, effective communication will improve supervisory morale and build loyalty. Supervisors want to be in the know. They want to have information concerning their organization, department, and work unit. Because of their responsibility they have a right to receive information in advance of the employees in their work unit. It is particularly demoralizing for supervisors to be left in the dark and to receive important information through the grapevine or rumor mill. Informed supervisors become more cooperative and successful, especially if they are encouraged to express their ideas and management is responsive to those ideas. Effective communications can stimulate interest in the organization, build loyalty toward it, and develop pride in work. In these times when it is difficult to foster loyalty, organizations need to focus on those activities that will increase loyalty, particularly for the supervisory group.

Third, effective communication will improve supervisory effectiveness. It helps create an environment that will enhance productivity and improve efficiency. An uninformed supervisor is an ineffective supervisor. Effective communications and productivity go hand in hand. One author who devoted an entire book to the relationship between communication and productivity argues strongly in favor of face-to-face communication as a tool for improving efficiency and productivity (D'Aprix, 1982a). Leaders must see and feel what their followers are experiencing; otherwise, they become out of touch. Conversely, a lack of communication can hamper the smooth flow of the work unit's operation and hinder productivity in the organization.

Fourth, effective communication improves the organization's image. Informed supervisors make better representatives of the organization in their outside contacts. In numbers alone they are important, since they represent the largest group of management employees. They are usually involved in a variety of civic and community activities, and they speak with authority for the organization whether they realize it or not. Supervisors can be important resources when they are aware of the organization's goals, plans, and activities, as well as of sensitive issues that may involve the organization. This is particularly important for organizations that are frequently under the critical eye of the community or regulatory agencies, such as public utilities. Supervisors can help considerably if they are equipped to handle critical comments or counter unjustified attacks on the organization.

Fifth, effective communication can defuse potential problems. Work slowdowns, strikes, grievances, discrimination charges, and even law suits sometimes result from poor communication, particularly on the part of supervisors. One labor expert cited lack of communication as one of the causes of strikes and presented the following comment from an employee as typical of how communications can influence labor relations: "There is a big communication gap between corporate and the plants. They never let you know what is going on in the company. It starts with top management, who don't really initiate communications down the line to any extent or follow through on any information they do send out" (Imberman, 1981, p. 45). On the positive side, several organizations have credited good, open communications during contract negotiations as being the single most important ingredient in avoiding a work stoppage. One organization published regular bulletins for employees during negotiations and prepared supervisors to hold meetings with employees to discuss issues on the bargaining table. As a last step, the company handed out its final offer to the union just prior to the contract vote. Supervisors, in small group meetings with employees, explained the company's final position and answered questions from the employees. These actions were credited by management as being an important factor in having two successive favorable contract votes.

Finally, effective communication is a major part of

the supervisor's basic job responsibilities. Supervising is virtually synonymous with communicating. Too often managers and supervisors see communication as an extracurricular activity, not an inherent ingredient in their actual job duties. Almost any analysis of the supervisor's job, however, will identify communication as the dominant portion of the duties. In one major study involving first-level supervisors at AT&T, most of the fourteen principal duties of supervisors were found to relate directly to communication (Macdonald, 1982, p. 20).

Therefore, for all these reasons it is important that organizations focus on a good communication system to keep supervisors informed and at the same time establish frequent, open, two-way communications with them. This chapter outlines specific methods and techniques that an organization can pursue to improve communication with supervisors.

Supervisory Communication Process

Communication is not just a message sent or received. It is a process by which meanings are exchanged among individuals or groups through some organized system of words, symbols, or signs. Whether or not the receiver understands the intended message depends not only on the sender but on the medium by which it is sent, the attitude of both the sender and the receiver, and a variety of obstacles that can influence the process. A basic model of the communication process usually contains the following steps:

1. *Sender formulates the message.* The sender is the person who originates the particular communication. At times, the supervisor is the sender; at other times, the receiver.
2. *Communication method is selected.* The sender selects the way the message is to be communicated. A variety of choices is available, either written or oral.
3. *Message is transmitted using the chosen method.*
4. *Message is received.* The receiver is the person or persons who should receive the message, as the sender intended.
5. *Receiver interprets message.* A variety of factors can influence the understanding and interpretation of the message.

These steps are used—either consciously or unconsciously—each time a message is transmitted. During this transmission, there are many barriers that can have a significant impact on the communication. Attitudes, perceptions, prejudices, environment, position, ability, stress, and timing are only a few of these.

Information Flows. From the supervisor's standpoint, information flows in five general directions: organization wide, downward, upward, laterally, and externally. Organization-wide communication represents messages that are sent to all employees (or supervisors) in the organization, whether written or verbal. Organizational publications, bulletins, announcements, video tape messages, and other standardized communication media are effective in getting the same message out to every individual in the organization. Downward communication goes from the top of the organization to the bottom, usually through the chain of command. This may be ineffective, however, since many of the meanings and much of the content of the communication may be distorted as they go down the organization. One study showed that about 80 percent of the message has been lost by the time it reaches the lower-level employees (Reber and Terry, 1975, p. 148). Upward communication is not as common in organizations as it should be. This involves feedback from the employees in terms of their attitude, concerns, perceptions, suggestions, and ideas. The extent of upward communication depends on the willingness of the organization to accept this information from lower-level employees. Lateral communication occurs in every organization and is necessary to get the job done. Also, it is the primary vehicle for rumors. Employees talk with each other, and supervisors talk with other supervisors. Information is transmitted officially and unofficially throughout the organization. Lateral communication is probably the most inefficient way for information to pass since it may be distorted and based on faulty assumptions. External communication may not be a part of every supervisor's job, but it is becoming a more frequent occurrence. Customers, suppliers, competitors, and government agencies may need to communicate directly with supervisors. The effectiveness of this communication can be very important to the organization. Organizations need to recognize the different flows of information and address each one when considering improvements in communications that involve supervisors.

Unique Role of the Supervisor. Supervisors have problems unique to their position when it comes to communication. Their perspective is and should be different from the perspectives of those at the top of the organization and those at the bottom. Top management expects supervisors to be the experts in the processes of their work units, to know what is happening in the organization, and to keep it informed. Nonmanagement employees who work for the supervisors look to them as their preferred source of information. They want their supervisors to keep them posted on important news, goals, plans, directions, problems, and issues influencing the organization. Employees expect their supervisor to be an excellent communicator, to level with them, and to establish two-way open communications. In short, supervisors provide a connection between management and the operating level where the work is done.

Among peer groups supervisors must communicate across the organization. As mentioned in Chapter One, a supervisor must communicate with a wide variety of individuals and is sometimes caught between diverse groups in the organization. Figure 12 shows the various groups with which a typical supervisor must communicate to make the job function in an efficient manner.

In addition to the typical problems associated with communication, supervisors may have increased communication problems in certain situations. For example, communication problems are magnified when:

- The supervisor is considerably younger than the employees supervised.
- The supervisor is new to the organization and is dealing with an old-timer in the organization.
- The supervisor is a woman, and the employees are men who may resent her.
- The supervisor is a member of an ethnic minority group dealing with employees in an ethnic majority group.

Figure 12. Communication Flows for the Supervisor.

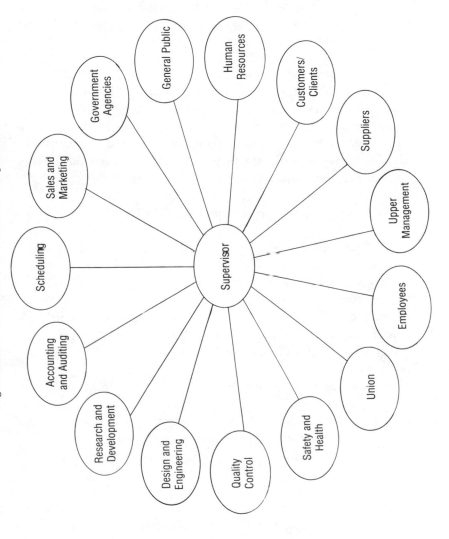

- The supervisor has been promoted from the ranks and must now supervise longtime friends and "buddies."
- The supervisor is minimally educated or trained, and employees are better educated or more highly trained.
- The supervisor has a college degree, but none of the employees do.

In each of these situations, because of the uniqueness of the relationship, the supervisor will have special problems (St. John, 1983). Supervisors may need special training, coaching, and counseling in how to minimize the difficulties in these unique situations. Otherwise, supervisors may become ineffective by aligning themselves too much with employees and thus creating an us-them syndrome.

Supervisory Communication Trends

Communication with employees is a constantly changing process. Our changing society and business environment constantly generate new information that must be communicated to employees. In addition, new and innovative communication techniques bring new ways in which organizations can improve communications. Coupled with all these changes are three very distinct trends that affect supervisors.

- Employees want more dialogue with their supervisors and top executives.
- The supervisor is in the best position to communicate with and influence employees in the work setting.
- Employees want to have more information about the performance of the organization.

These trends have a significant impact on management and present important challenges for the organization. The evidence for these trends comes from many research studies. One major study conducted by the Opinion Research Corporation (Morgan and Schiemann, 1983, p. 17) involved some 250,000 employees in approximately 200 of the organizations for which Opinion

Research Corporation (ORC) has conducted employee surveys since the 1950s. According to this study, three categories of nonmanagement employees—professional, clerical, and hourly employees—want to receive information from their immediate supervisor. Seventy-eight percent of the professional, 73 percent of the clerical, and 59 percent of the hourly employees identified the immediate supervisor as the preferred source of information. What is disturbing, however, is that the study showed that, for the first time since ORC has been conducting these surveys, the grapevine is rated as the number one current source of information, while it ranks the lowest as the preferred source. Employees are getting information from the grapevine and the rumor mill but prefer to get it from their supervisors. What is also disturbing in the study is that no more than four in ten employees at any organizational level felt that their companies were doing a good job of letting them know what was going on in the company. ORC had four major recommendations:

- Regular meetings between management and employees should be held throughout the organization, and managers (supervisors) should be trained to conduct these meetings effectively.
- Top management should not limit its contact with employees to formal meetings but should rather maintain regular day-to-day contact with them.
- Managers and supervisors should be made accountable for communicating effectively, which can be accomplished in a number of ways (for example, building communication goals into the performance evaluation process).
- Top management should ensure that supervisors have the information they need to communicate with their employees.

The ORC results almost duplicated a study conducted earlier by the International Association of Business Communicators and Towers, Perrin, Forster & Crosby. This survey involved nearly 46,000 employees in forty organizations. One part of the survey asked employees to rank fifteen sources of information—both as current and as preferred sources of information. The immediate supervisor was ranked as the number one current source and preferred source, while the grapevine was ranked as the number two current source (Foltz, 1981, p. 13).

It is no secret why employees prefer to receive information from their immediate supervisor. To most employees supervisors represent the organization. They are management and what they say is interpreted as official. Supervisors have frequent contact with employees and are always present to explain or interpret information. Coupled with the fact that the supervisor is a member of the management team, this accessibility puts the supervisor in the best position to get messages across and exert influence on employees. Most changes and new programs implemented by organizations are more effective if they are implemented *through* the supervisor—not *with* the supervisor. It is important that supervisors be a part of any major communication effort, regardless of how complex or confusing an issue may be.

One of the strongest endorsements for showing that employees want more information about the performance of their organization comes from a recent White House Conference on Productivity (American Productivity Center, 1983a). The conference involved top leaders from business, government, labor, and education. Their final report on reward systems and productivity contained this key recommendation: "Private industry, particularly large- to medium-size firms, should be encouraged and guided toward sharing business performance information with employees at all levels throughout the firm."

Too frequently employees complain about not knowing the direction in which the company is heading—its goals, objectives, plans, and particularly the problems and issues it faces. This information sometimes appears in the headlines when the company is facing a crisis, perhaps a controversial environmental issue, or is involved in negotiations with the union. Some employees, particularly those associated with larger companies, complain that they find out more about what is going on in their organization in the newspaper than they do through official communication channels. This kind of environment breeds distrust, reduces loyalty, and generally results in an ineffective work force.

The White House report recommended that companies share information in the following general areas:

- cost of production (or operating costs for service organizations)
- business plans
- operating floor information
- personnel-related information
- customer information

In the IABC and TPF&C study mentioned earlier, 90 percent of the employees were very interested or interested in receiving information on productivity improvement, while 79 percent were very interested or interested in receiving information on financial results. What may come as a surprise is that 87 percent were very interested or interested in knowing more about the competitive position of the organization (Foltz, 1981, p. 13). From these results it is obvious that employees are eager to know more about their organization's performance.

Few executives will not agree that employees do a more effective job when they know the importance of their work and how it fits into the business. Also, employees want to know to what extent their future wages and job opportunities are dependent on the success of the organization. Yet organizations are still reluctant to provide this information to employees. They feel that it will generate negative reactions and create more problems than if it had not been communicated. There are, however, numerous examples of companies that do share this information: Honeywell, General Motors, Fairchild Instruments, NEC Electronics, to name a few. Their results have been very positive, and there were none of the negative effects that are sometimes feared (American Productivity Center, 1983a, p. 5).

Establishing an Effective Communication System

Employees expect open, accurate, and timely communications from their supervisors and their organizations. Effective communication is not something that is implemented as a one-time project or program. It must be established and developed over time. It may have a variety of labels. Some call it "open" communications, others "positive" communications. The words *candid, two way,* and *feedback* usually enter into the description of an effective communication system. There is no one system that will be effective for all organizations. As with many aspects of the management process, communications must be tailored to the needs of the organization. However, the following ingredients appear to be common to most effective communication systems:

1. *Effective communication requires a variety of media.* No organization can rely on a single communication technique to satisfy its communication needs with employees and supervisors. It must use a combination of verbal and written communications, with some targeted for general-interest audiences while others are narrowly focused on specific groups such as supervisors. This is an important point that many organizations overlook. They rely on the chain of command and the in-house publication to do all the communicating. This is an unfortunate mistake and leaves employees and supervisors in the dark about many of the things they need to know.

2. *An effective communication system will place emphasis on face-to-face communication.* As was reported earlier, employees want more dialogue with supervisors and managers. Face-to-face communication builds credibility and allows employees to get the facts straight from the source. It allows them to clear up misunderstandings and can help build loyalty to the organization. It cannot serve as the only type of communication because it is time consuming, but it can serve as a primary technique for providing information to supervisors and other employees.

3. *An effective communication system focuses on the supervisor.* In some organizations communication skills are used as part of the requirements for supervisory selection since oral communication and written communication are typical job dimensions. Supervisors are in the best position to influence employees and shape their attitudes, and the supervisor's role in communicating with employees should never be undermined.

To help ensure that this does not happen, three important rules must be observed. First, supervisors should receive information before their employees do. Second, supervisory input should be secured if it is practical. Their reaction to, and evaluation of, the information may be very helpful in identifying potential problems. Third, whenever feasible, the information should be developed for supervisors to disseminate to employees. This is very important in improving the credibility of supervisors while at the same time building supervisory loyalty and commitment to the organization.

4. *An effective communication system will present bad news as well as good news.* It is painful for management to communicate bad news, particularly through official communication channels. Naturally, management wants to be positive, and it wants to present a positive image even when all is not well. However, employees are sometimes smarter than management gives them credit for being. They sometimes know what is happening or can anticipate what will happen. Unless they receive some official communication, their facts may be distorted and they will not always have the complete picture. Employees will eventually come by the information, and it is best for them to hear it from the organization first and to have all the facts at hand. In organizations that have tried to present unpleasant information to the employees, the results have usually been positive. Employees understand and appreciate frankness. One organization had never presented any bad news in the official company magazine in its seventy-five-year history except for announcing employee deaths. In an experiment the company presented a story on housekeeping that showed many problem areas and included an unsightly photograph of one of its facilities on the front cover of the magazine. The results were surprising. The magazine editor received many positive comments about the company's efforts to improve housekeeping and its willingness to talk about this sensitive issue. As a result of this special communication and increased emphasis on housekeeping, the situation improved.

5. *An effective communication system faces issues rather than avoids them.* How many times have organizations in their

official communication channels or members of top management responded with "no comment" to a very sensitive question? While this response may be appropriate in a few isolated cases, it is usually best for the organization to face an issue and set forth its position. This is particularly true for larger organizations in small communities where they are under the close scrutiny of the local media. One city's largest employer never responds to the local media about anything in the organization nor does it communicate very effectively with employees. Comments for the media about what is happening on a particular issue usually come from the union president or district representative of the international union. In this case the organization is missing an opportunity to build credibility and loyalty for the company. Instead, it is allowing the union to build loyalties.

6. *An effective communication system will anticipate potential problems and prepare communication plans for them.* Organizations must consider the communication aspect of almost everything they undertake. Whether it is good or bad news about the company, a new program or plan, or a changing direction, communication plays an important part in the planning process. The message must be carefully planned in advance and communicated in a timely way. The communication media must be flexible so that they can be adjusted to the changing needs of the target audience.

7. *Effective communication requires much effort and is time consuming.* Communication is something an organization must do constantly. It is never complete. It must become a routine part of the duties of all management and particularly supervisors. An organization can never relax and let its guard down. Otherwise, problems will develop through misunderstandings and misinformation.

8. *An effective communication system will have involvement and support of the top management group.* In the most effective systems, top managers regularly meet with employees at various levels. They set an example in communication with their open, frank, face-to-face discussions, and they give positive reinforcement to supervisors who are good communicators —reinforcement that includes financial rewards and incentives.

In short, they expect good communication, require it, and reward it while at the same time setting an example for others.

The methods of communicating with supervisors vary widely. The types of media used to communicate with supervisors include:

Organization publication, newspaper, or magazine	Problem-solving meetings
Special publication for supervisors	Work unit meetings
News bulletins	Staff meetings
Press releases	Open discussion meetings
Memos	Audio/telephone messages
Reports	Video presentations
Organizational charts	Bulletin boards
Handbooks	Letters
Policy manuals	Annual reports
Procedure manuals	Open-door policy
Training programs	Attitude/opinion surveys
	Pay inserts

Although a few of these are specifically focused on supervisors, most are used to communicate with all employees. This chapter will focus only on the items directly related to supervision that have the most impact on the organization. These are the meetings conducted with supervisors, special publications targeted for the supervisory group, and work unit meetings that are usually conducted by supervisors.

What to Communicate

The specific content of communications with supervisors will naturally depend on the type of organization and its goals. There are two general categories of information. First is the information necessary if the supervisor is to function effectively on the job. This is the need-to-know type of information that is job related and must be communicated on a timely basis so that supervisors know what must be done and how it must be done. The second general category is information that is not absolutely necessary but can be helpful to the supervisor. This is a nice-to-know type of information that, if communicated, will make supervisors feel that they are part of the organization. When communicated regularly, it helps build loyalty, improves the management identification of supervisors, and raises their morale. This category includes confidential and sensitive information that may not be communicated to the entire organization. Many organizations stop short in their communication efforts and fail to provide this type of information to supervisors. Eight major groups of information are discussed next. The first four are in the need-to-know category while the last four are in the nice-to-know category.

Work Unit Information. Supervisors must have information about their work unit. The information can come from the top of the organization, laterally from staff support groups, and upward from employees in the work unit. Supervisors need to know work unit results and the costs associated with their efforts. They must know operating and quality standards and schedule changes, as well as other important items that will have an impact on their work unit.

Organizational Policies and Procedures. Another important kind of information involves the policies and procedures of the organization. These represent the "rules of the game." Supervisors need to understand them thoroughly and to know the rationale for their existence. Ideally, the supervisory group should provide input into their development. Also, the organization must secure supervisory support to enforce these policies and procedures. Otherwise there will be many inconsistencies, and the effectiveness of the organization will be hampered. Included in this group are work rules, pay practices, and employee benefits.

Organizational Changes. Supervisors need to have information about most organizational changes to function effectively on the job. It is also important for supervisors to understand why changes are taking place, if this can be communicated to them. Anticipated organizational changes are probably the number one subject of the grapevine in the organization. Whether they involve changes in the structure, reporting relationship, or individual employees, it is important that supervisors learn about these changes before their employees do. It is embarrassing to supervisors for employees to bring to their attention changes that are expected to take place in the organization. It lowers respect for the position and eats away at the credibility of supervisors.

Organizational Problems and Concerns. Organizations are notorious for not informing supervisors about serious problems the organizations face. Too often lower-level management is shielded from the facts surrounding a serious problem. In turn, organizations destroy their own credibility, and they may find it difficult to get supervisors to believe them in the future. Whether the problem involves sagging profits, plant closings, major layoffs, or public confrontations, supervisors should be informed about the problem and what the organization plans to do about it. Refusal to discuss these issues will cause the grapevine to grow. Supervisors, as well as employees, will use their imaginations to fill in the missing information. The best supervisors may leave the organization. No doubt there is risk in divulging sensitive information, and this may make the problem even worse. However, at least some information can usually be provided. Frank, open responses can do much to keep the confidence level high, and they might also help in mustering the forces necessary to solve the problem.

Organizational Plans. Supervisors want to know about the mission, goals, and plans of their organization. They have much at stake in the future of the organization, and they want to know where it is going. They want to learn about these matters through official channels, particularly before the other employees find out about them. They want information about new acquisitions, major capital expenditures, and other important topics in which they have a vital interest. In some cases it may not be feasible to divulge all the plans to supervisors. However, most organizations can communicate more than they do now. Face-to-face communication with top management is an impor-

tant way to discuss the future of the organization with supervisors.

Organizational Performance. The progress being made by an organization, as well as the outlook for the future, is another area
of importance to supervisors. In a publicly held organization,
financial information is usually communicated through the
company's annual report. In a closely held or private organization, however, supervisors may have little opportunity to know
how well the organization is doing and particularly how it compares with other organizations. This policy may need to be re-
evaluated. Some financial or performance information should
be provided to supervisors. This can be done without revealing
the important financial numbers that the organization may not
want to release. It is understandable why some organizations
want to avoid disclosing earnings and profitability figures. However, they must be willing to share some of their confidential information with supervisors. Otherwise the loyalty and commitment may not be there.

Customer and Client Information. Every organization wants its
managers to appreciate its customers and clients even if its managers do not interface directly with them. The existence of most
organizations depends on their ability to satisfy customers and
clients. Supervisors should know about changes in major clients
and customers and why the changes have occurred. They may
need to communicate this information to their employees, particularly if the employees have contact with customers and
clients. Also, supervisors should know about new services
planned or new products under development and how they will
be integrated into the sales and marketing function in the organization.

External Environment. The final kind of information to communicate to supervisors involves those issues outside the organization that can have an impact on its future. The external environment's impact on business has increased dramatically in
recent years. Information on economic trends, the local busi-

ness environment, and the political climate can be helpful to supervisors. The organization needs an informed and educated group of supervisors. They must understand the many complex issues that can have an impact on the organization and the work unit. They must understand why we have government regulations and government intervention into the normal functions of an organization. And giving this kind of information provides an excellent opportunity to align supervisors with top management in support of specific issues outside the organization.

The categories discussed here are broad but contain the types of information supervisors either need to know or would like to know about the organization. Information should be provided routinely through a variety of channels. This information can increase the effectiveness of supervisors, make them feel a part of the management team, boost their morale, and improve their commitment to the organization.

Meetings with Supervisors

From the evidence presented earlier, it should be apparent that face-to-face meetings represent an important and essential way to communicate with supervisors. Although there can be a variety of meetings, three important types of regular meetings should be held with supervisors: periodic staff meetings, problem-solving meetings, and small group discussion meetings with top management.

Staff Meetings. Staff meetings represent the typical chain of command meeting where information flows from the top down. They are usually held weekly or monthly, depending on the organizational setting. Middle managers meet with their supervisors to discuss departmental progress, changes in work schedules, procedures and policies, new major projects, organizational plans and changes, and any other actions that may affect the department. This type of meeting is essential to mold the supervisors in a department into a cooperative team. It will ensure that they all receive the same message, and this is important when the information is to be passed on to nonmanagement employees. A frequent complaint among supervisors is that their staff meetings are boring and uninteresting. This provides a challenge for managers to make the meetings stimulating, secure supervisory input, and be willing to discuss all the types of information mentioned earlier. Probably more than any other kind, this type of meeting serves as a review of progress in the department and as a means to discuss other items that are important to improve the efficiency and effectiveness of the department.

Problem-Solving Meetings. Occasionally, supervisors should be assembled to disseminate helpful job-related information and to discuss problems confronting the organization. These meetings are different from regular off-the-job training programs where employees attend one-half-week to two-week training sessions. They also differ from the task force problem-solving meeting in which supervisors are asked to solve a particular problem. They are usually held monthly and allow the organization to discuss issues with a large group of supervisors and obtain limited feedback. A variety of topics are appropriate for this meeting:

Absenteeism	Labor negotiations
Turnover	Legal issues
Grievance trends	Quality problems
Affirmative action	Customer complaints
Equal opportunity employment	Productivity declines
Employee benefit abuses	Employee theft
Safety and accident performance	Sabotage and vandalism
Industrial health and hygiene	Alcoholism/drug abuse
Housekeeping	Inventory shortages

One organization was having a problem with time card errors. It met with all the supervisors in several groups to discuss the problem, review policies and procedures, and offer suggestions on how the problem could be corrected. Supervisors provided their ideas, and the potential solutions were collected, edited, and distributed to all supervisors. As a result of this meeting, time card errors were reduced significantly.

Small Group Meetings with Top Management. Small group feed-back sessions allow the organization to resolve complaints and problems facing the supervisory group, while keeping lines of communication open with top management. All supervisors have gripes and grievances, yet they usually have no methods available to resolve them. Informal, frank discussions can allow supervisors to express their feelings in a nonthreatening environment, usually to a member of top management. These meetings come in a variety of formats and have catchy names such as "face to face," "skip level," "table talk," "speak out," "person to person," "open up," "rap session," and "meet the executives."

These meetings should be conducted in a trusting atmosphere with open communication. Supervisors should feel that there will be no retaliation for their comments and that management will listen to their complaints. In one organization with about 100 supervisors, the chief executive regularly meets with them, skipping two or three levels of management. He carefully explains why he is doing it: to keep in touch with the feelings of the supervisors and to boost their morale. In this setting the emphasis is on two-way communication and not necessarily on resolving issues. It is unlikely that this chief executive will take any significant action as a result of the meetings, although he may explore issues identified in the meetings at an appropriate time with other key managers in the organization.

Some may wonder why supervisors, who are usually considered part of the management group, deserve this kind of special attention. The answer lies in their unique role in the organization and their potential impact on organizational performance. An unhappy and complaining group of supervisors will not achieve the results desired by the organization. Differences need to be aired and resolved so that supervisors can concentrate on getting results through their employees. Meetings with top executives make supervisors feel that they are an important part of the management group. If handled improperly, however, these meetings can easily turn into unmanageable gripe sessions that will adversely affect the organization. To obtain maximum results, the following guidelines should be used:

1. *The purpose of the meeting should be thoroughly ex-*

plained. Supervisors, middle managers, and top managers must understand the purpose of these meetings. This can alleviate anxieties, particularly if certain levels of management are left out. It also helps to avoid misunderstandings about the scope of this type of communication.

2. *Guidelines must be developed.* Policies, procedures, and meeting guidelines need to be clearly outlined and discussed with all levels of management. Changing rules in the middle of the process can do more harm than not having the meetings in the first place.

3. *The organization should consider removing the second level of management.* It is important that supervisors feel free to discuss issues directly with upper management. Sometimes the middle manager is the problem. Because of this it may be necessary to remove the level of management just above supervisors. This skip-level technique has been successful in developing a feeling among supervisors that someone at the top of the organization is willing to listen to them. On the negative side, this approach can create anxiety in middle managers, particularly the insecure, nervous ones. They may feel that top management is circumventing their authority and spying on their department. Clear communication, up front, can help alleviate these concerns and keep managers from becoming overly concerned about the process.

4. *The meeting must be conducted in confidence.* Supervisors must understand that their comments will be kept confidential. Otherwise, the information will be filtered, and frank comments will not be provided. This is a credibility test for top management. A few supervisors will not trust top management regardless of what is said. Most, however, will believe management if it states that no comments will be tied to any one individual. A trusting climate is essential for this process to work effectively.

5. *Supervisors must feel that the process will accomplish something worthwhile.* Some supervisors will immediately see the advantages of this type of meeting. Others may not. Airing complaints is not the primary purpose of the meeting. It is designed to improve relationships, keep supervisors informed, and

resolve problems and differences before they become more serious. Supervisors must be convinced that action will be taken as a result of what is said before they will be willing to open up with top management.

6. *Top management must take action.* When major issues are brought to the attention of top management, particularly issues that have not been identified in the past, some action must be taken. The issues raised by supervisors will usually have some substance. They may represent problems that need to be resolved. Changes in policies or procedures may be in order. As soon as supervisors see some action as a result of these sessions, they take on increased importance for supervisors, and the sessions will be more fruitful in the future. Of course, in a given instance the conclusion may be that no investigation of action should be taken. In this case, it is important to communicate why no action is planned. Otherwise the exercise may come to be considered a waste of time.

7. *The most skillful communicator should handle the initial meeting.* Supervisors are reluctant to bring up issues at the beginning of this type of communication program. It may take a skillful discussion leader to bring out issues for group discussion. Possibly the best communicator in top management, or a member of the human resources staff, would be the appropriate person to kick off the meetings. After the first few meetings, discussions should become routine, and other members of top management may need to conduct them.

In summary, small group discussion meetings with supervisors can produce excellent results for an organization. Their focus is on problem solving, grievance resolution, and building relationships between supervisors and top management.

Implementing Work Unit Meetings

Small group meetings for the work unit conducted by the supervisor have become an important source of information for employees, as well as a tool for organizations to build morale and increase productivity. Several studies, including the one by Opinion Research Corporation (ORC), have shown that this is the source of information preferred by employees and one that develops positive employee relations while building an effective two-way communication system. In the ORC study, 56 percent of clerical and 61 percent of hourly employees identified their supervisor as their preferred source of information (Morgan and Schiemann, 1983, p. 17). In the IABC and TPF&C study, the immediate supervisor was ranked as the preferred source of information while small group meetings were ranked second (Foltz, 1981, p. 13). This clearly shows the importance of direct communication with the supervisor. In increasing numbers, organizations are not only encouraging supervisors to hold regular group meetings with their work unit but requiring them to do so.

Work unit meetings differ from typical group meetings. They are conducted with nonmanagement employees who are usually at the lowest educational level in the organization and are probably among the poorest communicators. Also, they are conducted by supervisors who may not be as skilled at holding meetings as higher-level managers. They are usually implemented to enable employees to share ideas and opinions and resolve differences. The issues discussed in, and the results obtained from, these meetings can be very critical to the organization. Two-way open communication is essential for the process to work.

Many supervisors, particularly those in the industrial sector, are not accustomed to holding group meetings with their employees. They have an inherent fear that they will not be able to answer employee questions or that employees will turn hostile and the meeting get completely out of control. Also, they have the normal uneasiness about making presentations before groups. While supervisors may initially lack the confidence and poise to accomplish this task in a professional manner, the necessary skills can be developed in them. Positive reinforcement from middle managers, as well as initial success from the implementation of the meetings, can inspire supervisors to turn this communication medium into a very productive activity. In organizations where meetings have become a way of life, supervisors have learned how to hold effective meetings with employees, and success stories are plentiful. Organizations are missing an excellent opportunity if they fail to utilize this type of communication. According to one author, failure to conduct face-to-face discussions with employees is costing America dearly in efficiency, productivity, and the will to compete (D'Aprix, 1982b, p. 32).

Objectives. The objectives developed for work unit meetings depend on the particular organization. The degree of openness in communication, the educational level of employees, and supervisory communication skills will all have an impact on the objectives. Among the more common objectives are to

1. disseminate information of interest to employees in the work unit.
2. air complaints and informal grievances among the employees
3. resolve problems facing the work unit
4. identify potential problems and prevent them from affecting the work unit
5. remove impediments to efficiency and effectiveness in the output of the work unit
6. secure employee input into decisions that will affect the work unit
7. improve the cooperative spirit and teamwork among employees
8. build commitments to organizational viewpoints and management actions
9. gauge employee reactions to organizational programs, plans, and activities

Although it may be unusual for an organization to have every one of these objectives for their small group meetings, it is common to find a variety of purposes for undertaking this type of communication activity. Some of the objectives will require more employee input than others. For example, objective eight may not require employee input, while objective nine involves employee input almost exclusively. The best approach may require a balance of the two types of objectives.

Issues. Several issues must be addressed by the organization
when implementing work unit meetings. The approach adopted
for each of the following issues will depend on which of the objectives listed in the preceding paragraph have been selected, as
well as on the communication environment in the organization.

• *Location.* Meetings can take place in the work unit, the
supervisor's office (if there is one), at a nearby meeting room,
or at an offsite motel. Some organizations have built special
meeting rooms near work areas specifically for this purpose. The
best results may be achieved when employees are allowed to
stay in or near their own work environment. This is where they
feel most comfortable and are more likely to open up and voice
their opinions and ideas on the meeting topics.

• *Group makeup.* Just who is involved in these meetings
is a very important issue. In some organizations the entire work
group participates. In others, because of the large numbers involved and production-scheduling difficulties, only part of the
group may attend. When this is the case, it is important that
members of the group be rotated so that all employees eventually participate. The common approach is to have a fixed percentage of the employee work group attend the meeting (25
percent for instance) and have members rotate, leaving at least
one or two from one meeting to the next to allow for continuity. Another possibility is to divide the work unit into two or
more groups and hold separate meetings so that all will participate. But this could cause some confusion in follow-up discussions at a later time since what is said in one meeting may not
be said in another.

• *Outsider attendance.* A representative of the human resources department usually attends the meeting along with the
supervisor's immediate manager. The number of outsiders should
be kept to a minimum since their presence may detract from
the group activities and inhibit employee input. In some cases a
higher-level manager may attend as well as other staff specialists. Interaction with management above the supervisory level is
important to employees. In these situations the supervisor may
be absent while the middle manager conducts the meeting with
the employees. If not handled properly, however, this approach

can lower supervisory morale since supervisors may start to think their authority is being undermined or their ability to supervise is being questioned. However, this approach may be necessary if there are problems in the work unit that appear to be focused on the ability of the supervisor.

- *Topics.* The topics selected will relate directly to the objectives of the meeting. The variety of topics that can be used in work unit meetings include:

Organizational performance
Work unit performance
Work unit goals
Operating costs
Problems facing the work unit
Potential problem areas
Employee complaints
Announcements of interest to work unit
Progress reports on major projects
Suggestions for improvements in work unit
Production and schedule changes

New procedures for the work unit
Changes in organization policies
Changes in work rules
Explanation of management actions
Planning social/recreation events
Employee benefit changes
Ideas for reducing costs
Employee reaction to programs/plans
New products/services from work unit

The topics should be of interest to the employees and at the same time important to the organization. Also, the topics presented for the supervisory problem-solving meeting may also be appropriate to discuss with employees since they deal with issues involving employees. The topics should be planned in advance and in some cases even announced to the employees before the meeting. Usually time is allotted for other items, such as complaints and problems. To stimulate constructive discussion, it may be necessary to ask employees to submit topics or questions anonymously.

- *Discussion format.* The way in which the discussion is initiated and conducted is important to the success of a work unit meeting. Employees should be made to feel at ease and relaxed. Although this is a formal process, it should be conducted as an informal two-way discussion. The supervisor or meeting leader will have to initiate the discussion and keep it on target. In the early stages of this process, it might be appropriate to plant thought-provoking questions in the group. After employees become accustomed to these meetings, they will usually begin to open up and provide very useful and valuable input.

• *Duration.* Work unit meetings are usually held during regular working hours and employees are paid while they attend. A few organizations conduct them after hours and pay employees overtime. The meetings should be long enough to accomplish the objectives but short enough to keep employees from becoming bored. Durations in the range of thirty minutes to one hour are typical. The length may vary, depending on the extent of discussion and the quality of input from employees. The cost of lost productivity is a factor to consider in establishing the length of the meetings. It may be too costly to have all employees stop work for two hours for each meeting, although the results could easily overshadow the costs. Meetings after work, which employees are not paid to attend, may be an alternative but will usually not generate the needed enthusiasm.

• *Follow-up.* Another important part of this process occurs after the meeting. Employees will bring up items for which the supervisor will not have answers. It is important for these items to be investigated and the information ultimately supplied, particularly if it has been promised. More information on follow-up is presented later in this section.

• *Facts versus opinions.* Facts should be communicated while opinions are minimized. Although it may be necessary for the supervisors to provide opinions on a particular issue, it is best to stick with information that can be verified. Undisputable facts are convincing and difficult to challenge, whereas opinions may turn off the group.

Implementation. The introduction of work unit meetings for organizations not currently conducting such meetings can represent a significant challenge. Supervisors need a thorough explanation of the rationale for this type of communication process.

If feasible, supervisors should be involved in developing the mechanics of the process and resolving the issues discussed in the preceding list. Some organizations try work unit meetings on a pilot approach and collect information on their success or failure. Tangible evidence of success can ease the resistance to change as the meetings are implemented across the organization. Supervisors are less reluctant to participate willingly in this activity when they see what others have achieved. It may be helpful to show supervisors the results achieved in other organizations, as documented in research studies and reports that can be found throughout the literature.

The biggest task in implementation is to gain supervisory acceptance and to get supervisors enthusiastic about making this activity work. More than in any other communication activity, the efforts of the supervisor will make the difference in the success or failure of work unit meetings. The extent of past group meeting activity, of any type, will raise or lower the amount of resistance among the supervisory group. In some organizations supervisors conduct weekly or monthly staff meetings. Also, weekly safety meetings are common. Supervisors with this kind of experience will usually have the confidence and the poise to conduct the meetings, although work unit meetings—as described in this section—are considerably different from a typical staff meeting or safety meeting where the information all flows one way.

In unionized locations it is important to discuss this communication technique with union leadership. Otherwise, it may perceive this as a ploy to circumvent the grievance procedure and undermine the union's role in the organization. Although they may be unenthusiastic, most unions will accept this approach to communication because they can see in it a way to resolve grievances without resorting to the time-consuming process of the written protest. The organization must be careful to ensure that antiunion information is not allowed to surface in the meeting or to become part of the discussion.

If work unit meetings are to become a way of life in the organization, some ground rules must be established. Some organizations have developed policies and procedures that outline how, when, and where the meetings will be held. Others go further in specifying the exact length of the meetings and in dictating how participating employees' time will be charged. Forms for documenting the discussion and for recording meeting attendance are sometimes used.

Training Supervisors. Another important step to help make this type of communication work properly is to prepare supervisors to conduct meetings. A training program may help supervisors understand the mechanics of meeting dynamics and improve their skills at planning the meeting, gathering information, presenting information, handling employee reactions, and providing follow-up after the meeting. Emphasis is usually placed on handling different types of personalities, ranging from the overly talkative employee to the employee who will never voluntarily give any input. The objectives of one such workshop were to

- explain to supervisors the need for work unit meetings with employees
- develop the skills needed to conduct effective meetings
- show supervisors how to plan, schedule, coordinate, and follow up on group meetings
- build the supervisor's confidence in his or her ability to handle problems that may occur during group meetings

In this workshop the supervisors were involved in a full day of training. Each had an opportunity to conduct a simulated group meeting, have it videotaped, and receive constructive feedback on how the process might be improved. The participants for the simulated group meetings were employees trained in predetermined roles that were designed to reflect typical meeting settings.

Staff Support. Staff support, usually from the human resources department, may be necessary to make work unit meetings operate smoothly in an organization. Staff employees usually develop the policies and procedures outlined in earlier sections. In some cases they may attend the meetings and help supervisors with planning and scheduling. Still another possibility is to have staff employees develop issues for meetings. For example, an organization may be interested in receiving feedback from employees on a new benefit plan that was recently implemented. Supervisors may be asked to solicit feedback in the next meeting they conduct by means of a prepared list of questions. When these are collected throughout the organization, they provide a realistic assessment of employee reaction to the new plan.

An important area where staff support is usually necessary is in the follow-up on meetings. Frequently, questions are raised during meetings that are beyond the scope of the supervisor's responsibility or expertise. Staff support employees can usually secure the information. In most cases, the human resources department receives the request for additional information and is responsible for getting it back to the supervisor. The meeting form shown in Exhibit 5 can be used not only to document what happened in the meeting and who was there but to assist in the follow-up process. Part of the form has a section where the supervisor lists questions for which additional information is needed. After being reviewed by two levels of management, this form is forwarded to the human resources department, where a specialist secures the required information and provides it to the supervisor. In most cases the information is readily available and is sent directly to the supervisor. This type of follow-up assistance not only is helpful to employees but improves the morale of supervisors since it gives them easy access to information they need to pass along to employees.

Conditions for Failure. As with any new program, work unit meetings can easily fail if they are not implemented properly and managed and monitored effectively. Top management must show its support for this activity, possibly by setting the example for conducting this type of meeting with supervisors. Also, it is important that management monitors the results, frequently checks on the progress of work unit meetings, and provides positive reinforcement to supervisors to continue this process. A number of conditions can cause this process to fail:

Exhibit 5. Group Meeting Record.

GROUP MEETING RECORD

(To be completed by the supervisor within 24 hours of the meeting)

DEPARTMENT   SUPERVISOR   DATE SUBMITTED

INSTRUCTIONS:
1. The purpose of this record is to help you better summarize the success of your group meeting and to help you determine what action, if any, you should take as a result of the meeting. This record will also help to keep your general supervisor, manager, and division manager aware of the progress of your meetings and other information which may be valuable to them.
2. Please complete this meeting record **within 24 hours** of the close of the meeting and forward to your immediate supervisor.
3. Please provide accurate and concise information for all areas requested.

4. The back of the record may be used if additional space is required.
5. It is recommended that you keep a copy of each completed record for your use as a guide for future meetings, and as a reminder of activities and problems encountered in past meetings.
6. When the record has been signed by your department manager it will be forwarded to your division manager for review.
7. A copy of this completed record will be kept on file for six months following the meeting.

Date & Time
of Meeting? _____

How many
attended? _____

Length of
meeting? _____

Where was
meeting held? _____

Briefly describe the subjects covered:

_____
_____
_____
_____

List questions that came up for which you need additional information:

_____
_____
_____
_____

Note any problems you encountered:

_____
_____
_____
_____

Did anyone other than your employees attend the meeting? Yes _____   No _____

If so, who was it? _____

Other comments: _____
_____
_____
_____

SUPERVISOR SIGNATURE   GENERAL SUPERVISOR   DEPARTMENT MANAGER SIGNATURE

WHEN COMPLETED FORWARD TO DIVISION MANAGER.

- unclear motives for conducting meetings
- lack of trust between management and nonmanagement employees
- inadequate support for the process by upper-level management
- retaliation against employees who make negative comments
- open criticism of employees for their suggestions or ideas
- incorrect information being disseminated in the meeting
- inadequate supervisory preparation
- lack of sincerity in the way the meetings are conducted
- failure to follow up on the issues raised by employees
- avoiding the sensitive issues rather than facing them head on
- failure to change meeting format and content regularly

These can be easily avoided if the issues in this section are addressed appropriately by the organization and steps are taken to avoid the causes of failure.

Supervisory Publications

Supervisors need timely information from official sources. They need it to make decisions, to keep employees informed, and to respond adequately to pressing job situations. To meet this need, many organizations have established a publication specifically for supervisors. This official medium from the organization to the supervisor adds an extra dimension to the communication effort. It can help keep supervisors informed and build their loyalty to the organization. The format and content may vary considerably, but the following principles may serve as guidelines in establishing this type of publication:

- *The information should be factual and newsworthy.* It should not be a voice for management or an outlet for expression of opinion. It should contain verifiable facts and other information of interest to supervisors.
- *The information should be presented on a timely basis.* Occasionally, if not regularly, important news should be announced in this publication, ahead of other sources such as

the grapevine. This builds interest and a desire to read the publication as soon as it is received.

- *The information should be accurate.* There is no better way to lose the credibility of a publication than to present incomplete statistics, erroneous conclusions, or excessive errors. The information should be carefully screened for accuracy and for consistency with other official records of the organization.

- *The information should be provided directly to supervisors.* Ideally, the publication should be mailed or delivered to supervisors rather than sent through the chain of command. This may be one of the few items that supervisors receive for their use only, since much of the other information available to them is available to others in the organization. Although it may be sent on a personal and confidential basis, occasionally the publication may also contain information that should be passed on to employees.

- *Both good and bad news must be reported.* The publication's credibility will suffer if it is restricted to good news only. Carefully selected statistics showing only positive trends will further erode credibility. The publication should present data even when they point to negative trends. Negative trends can bring attention to problem areas, and the long-term impact of publicizing them may be positive.

- *Information should be presented in a consistent manner.* Statistics should be presented in the same format in successive issues. Otherwise they will do nothing but confuse the readers. Consistent formats enable the information to be quickly absorbed, understood, and compared with what has happened in the past.

The subjects presented in the publication may vary considerably from one organization to another. The information should be important to the supervisor and help improve performance. It should provide help in answering questions often asked by the employees. The topics suitable for problem-solving meetings described earlier are also appropriate for this newsletter.

The name of the publication is very important. It should

reflect the intended audience by having the word *supervisor* or *supervision* in the title. This emphasizes that it is specifically designed for supervisors. Also, it should contain a descriptive word to illustrate the type of communication. Exhibit 6 presents a name generator with combinations that can be used to develop an appropriate title.

Exhibit 6. Supervisory Publication Name Generator.

First Name(s)	Second Name
Supervisor's	Newsletter
Superintendent's	Report
Foreman's	Bulletin
Manager's	Flash
Group leader's	Update
Leader's	Infogram
Head nurse's	Message
Government supervisor's	Memo
Staff supervisor's	Memorandum
Department head's	Bugle
Section leader's	Messagegram
	Review
	Communique

Sometimes an audit may be appropriate to gauge the effectiveness of this publication. Audits can involve telephone surveys, mailed questionnaires, or face-to-face interviews with all or a selected sample of supervisors to see how often and how carefully they read the publication. The publication should be under frequent review for potential changes. Otherwise, even though different news is presented, it will become routine and may be easily overlooked. A redesigned format with new types of information can help keep readers' interest high. In some organizations, special issues are published to draw additional attention to a particular topic.

Improving Supervisory Communication Skills

Many organizations have developed programs to improve communication skills for their supervisors. Because of the importance of communication and the serious consequences of communication failures, an investment in supervisory training in communications can realize a significant return to the organization. Improvement in communication skills usually centers on five distinct areas: listening, speaking, writing, reading, and body language.

Listening. Failure to listen is a frequently occurring communication problem, and it can be particularly destructive when supervisors fail to listen to employees. Complaints are common from employees about management's failure to listen to them. From a study of labor relations comes a typical employee comment that summarizes their frustration: "Suggestions and ideas should be listened to by the company. Maybe we have something worthwhile and important to say or to contribute. Most of us have been here for a long time. Once in a while, it may be worthwhile to listen to the operator. He stands by the machine every day. He sees the work close up. He must know something that the guys upstairs can't learn out of a book. Why doesn't someone try listening to us?" (Imberman, 1981, p. 45).

The problem of listening is inherent in our communication structure. Individuals are capable of understanding speech at a rate of about 600 words per minute, yet most people speak at only 100 to 140 words per minute. Thus, the brain enjoys a considerable amount of idle time while someone is talking. Rather than use this time to understand the speaker's idea better, minds tend to wander, daydreaming may take over, and the receiver becomes distracted. Once the mind is on some other subject, the speaker's message will be lost (Christenson and others, 1982, p. 108).

Attitude surveys have revealed poor listening habits among supervisors. The approaches taken by organizations to improve the listening skills of their supervisors vary. In some cases managers coach and counsel supervisors on their listening habits. Other organizations adopt special programs to encourage supervisors to improve listening skills. They have adopted terms such as *assertive listening* and *active listening* to bring attention to the problem. Guidelines, checklists, and lists of do's and don't's are sometimes distributed to supervisors to help them

improve listening skills. Still other organizations provide training in listening skills. In some cases it is integrated with regular
communication skills training while at other times it is handled
as a separate course. A program called Effective Listening was
developed and marketed by Xerox Learning Systems. It has significantly improved the listening skills of the supervisors who
have taken it.

One thing is certain. Effective listening takes a concen-
trated effort on the part of the supervisor. Since few people
have to do as much communicating in their jobs as supervisors,
organizations should invest in improving their listening habits.

Speaking. Improving oral communication is another important
area of communication skills development. Oral communication
consumes more supervisory time than written communication.
One study revealed that almost 90 percent of a supervisor's
communication is through speech, by far the most common
kind of human communication and probably the most effective
for conveying ideas, opinions, facts, and feelings (Macdonald,
1982, p. 122). Most of the attempts to improve supervisors' oral
communication center on upgrading the way they conduct
meetings with their employees. However, some organizations
also concentrate on improving supervisor's skills in making formal presentations. Quite often supervisors are required to make
presentations before peer groups, upper management, general
audiences, or even outside groups. External training programs
such as the Dale Carnegie course rely heavily on confidence
building in preparing their participants to make presentations
before groups. Other programs focus on thorough preparation,
establishing an agenda, the mechanics of the presentation, and
securing feedback from the audience. Both of these approaches
have achieved promising results. Good oral presentation skills
can make the difference in supervisory career advancement because such skills are highly visible. Their cultivation is an important part of the growth and development of supervisors.

Writing. Another crucial communication skill for supervisors is
writing. Supervisors write memos, letters, notes, and reports.

They must complete forms for their organization, such as accident investigations, inventory variances, disciplinary records, performance appraisals, and production reports. Although good writing is a skill that seems to come naturally for some people, it is not an inherent ability. It can be learned. Just as oral presentations are important to success, writing can have considerable impact on a supervisor's advancement. Too often managers decide that a supervisor lacks ability on the sole evidence of a poorly written report. Somehow poor writing is seen as linked with ability and intelligence, although this is not necessarily true. And effective writing does not necessarily correlate with level of education. Some colleges and universities are turning out graduates who have not mastered the skill of writing clear, concise, grammatically correct sentences and paragraphs. When these people enter management, they often continue to turn out reports, letters, and memos that are confusing, ambiguous, and at times meaningless. As a consequence the recipients of these muddled messages frequently do not know what to do or may follow an incorrect course of action (Macdonald, 1982, p. 140). Conversely, some supervisors without high school educations write clear and understandable letters and memos. Effective writing is not easy, nor is it the most comfortable of disciplines for an action-oriented supervisor who prefers to deal with people face-to-face. Yet, it is a necessary part of the job, and its importance is growing as supervisors are continually bombarded with additional requirements for written reports and responses.

There are a variety of approaches available to improve written communication skills. On-the-job training from the manager can be very helpful in improving these skills. In fact, more and more managers and executives are demanding better writing skills from their supervisors. They are excellent communicators and demand no less from their subordinates. For many supervisors, formal training in effective writing may be in order. Internal workshops to improve written communication skills are common. Outside seminars and local community education programs are readily available. In addition there are many workbooks, self-instruction programs, and textbooks on business writing. There is little reason for supervisors to struggle with poor writing skills and have their careers stifled by this deficiency. It is one area that definitely can be improved.

Reading. Another area where communication skills can be improved is that of reading habits and practices. Although this is not as critical as the other areas discussed, it can be an important skill for supervisors whose jobs require much reading. This problem is more serious at higher levels in the organization because of the voluminous amount of written communication sent to upper management. Nevertheless, some organizations attempt to improve the reading skills of supervisors through training programs in rapid reading and speed reading. Some of these courses have produced impressive increases in reading speed and comprehension. One problem is lack of continued improvement. Unless the skills developed in the training program are practiced and reinforced on a regular basis, reading speed and comprehension can fall back to the previous levels.

Body Language. In recent years, increasing attention has been given to body language and other forms of nonverbal communication. Body language refers to physical signals by means of which people can communicate information without words. Subconsciously or consciously people use one or more components of body language in their communication process. Space is one component. How close one person stands to another is an indication of the tone of the conversation. Social communication usually takes place within a four- to eight-foot range. Friendly conversations usually take place within eighteen inches to four feet (Ray and Eison, 1983, p. 166). It is important for supervisors to observe employees' private space. Invading their space makes them feel uncomfortable and hampers communication. Posture is another type of body language. A person who is bored may slump enough to embarrass the other person. An individual's posture is usually relaxed in nonthreatening situations but might tighten up and become rigid when that person is threatened. Touch is another type of body language that can be misunderstood. It usually has negative connotations, and supervisors are often cautioned about touching other employees. Physical appearance, hand gestures, eye behavior, and facial expressions are other types of body language that can send signals to employees. Improved communication will occur when supervisors are aware of the impact of body language and know how to interpret it. Some organizations conduct training programs on body language to teach supervisors to use it to their advantage.

Special Issues in Supervisory Communication

To make this chapter complete, a few special issues need to be addressed. These include the grapevine, confidential information, and communication between staff and line. Each of these areas can create problems for the supervisor.

Working with the Grapevine. The grapevine, or rumor mill, presents a unique challenge for organizations. It exists in every type of organization. Regardless of what is done to try to eliminate it, it cannot be killed. If it is suppressed in one area, it springs up in another, and in some organizations it seems to thrive and grow at will. In the Opinion Research Corporation study mentioned earlier, employees said their primary source of information was the grapevine (Morgan and Schiemann, 1983, p. 17). Yet, at the same time, they said it was their least preferred source.

While formal systems of communication occasionally break down, the grapevine seems to always operate speedily and efficiently and without any particular regard for the truth. And the supervisor is often caught in the tendrils of this treacherous growth. Because of their unique role, supervisors must learn to deal with it constructively, or they will be consumed by it. The grapevine can ruin reputations, hamper effectiveness, damage credibility, and in some cases even destroy careers.

The grapevine works for several reasons. Employees need and want to have information about the organization and the people in it. If they do not receive it from official sources, they will resort to other channels such as the grapevine. It always seems to be convenient, and most rumors carried through the grapevine have some substance to them. Some students of the grapevine have claimed that 70 to 90 percent of the information passed along it is correct (Timm, 1980, p. 74). Unfortunately, however, in many cases the facts are distorted, and the information is incomplete. Rumors get started when there has been a selective omission of information. Bits and pieces are communicated, but there are many holes in what is presented. Employees and supervisors are left to use their imaginations to fill the gaps. Rumors are sometimes caused by poor timing of official communications. Quite often official announcements are preceded by unofficial announcements from the grapevine. The grapevine will explain why an announcement is made when the official announcement had no explanation. And finally, the information carried on the grapevine is usually considered important to both the sender and the receiver. It is information affecting them and their jobs. They want to know it, and they think they have a right to find out about it. If it turns out to be insignificant or unimportant, however, it often dies on the grapevine.

The challenge facing supervisors is to learn to work with the grapevine and minimize it as a source of information for employees. This involves a few specific actions on the part of supervisors:

1. *Provide information regularly to employees.* Face-to-face work unit meetings, as described earlier, represent an opportunity to provide employees with information that they want and need to know. This is an excellent way to counteract the grapevine.

2. *Plan the timing of communication to anticipate the grapevine.* As most managers will confess, this is difficult to do. Official announcements will be anticipated by the grapevine in spite of an organization's deliberate efforts otherwise. This presents an interesting challenge for the organization. Using the supervisory group, the organization should purposely try to anticipate the grapevine, even if such an attempt involves extra effort. In some organizations critical and important announcements are handled in a very confidential and secretive manner to eliminate the grapevine's impact until they are ready to be

officially communicated. These announcements are handled
through the supervisors and sometimes involve a meeting of top
management with all the supervisors—offsite if necessary—to
explain the upcoming announcement. Then the supervisors are
allowed to make the announcement ahead of the grapevine.
This improves the credibility of the supervisors and puts them
solidly ahead of the grapevine as the employees' primary source
of information.

3. *If the rumor is harmful, try to stop it.* Sometimes the
grapevine will carry a vicious rumor that may be damaging to
the organization, department, or even specific employees. When
this is the case, the supervisor should collect the facts surrounding the situation, bring the employees together, and stop the
rumor. Unfortunately, many times the supervisor will be caught
in the middle of the situation without knowing the facts. In
these cases the organization should supply the supervisors with
the pertinent facts and encourage supervisors to communicate
them directly to employees as soon as possible.

4. *Downplay the significance of the grapevine.* In meetings with employees, supervisors should downplay the significance of information from the grapevine. They should discourage employees from participating in it. Whenever possible,
rumors should be discredited, and at times the supervisor may
want to consider disciplinary action for those who start them.
This, of course, can be a very delicate area since the supervisor
must have the necessary facts to take disciplinary action.

5. *Test the grapevine occasionally.* Supervisors must
know what is going on in the work unit. They need to know
their employees and their problems and concerns. They must be
aware of the grapevine and the culprits involved in its growth
and development. It may be helpful for the supervisor to test
the grapevine with planted information to identify the key play-
ers, determine how fast it works, and assess the extent of distor-
tion. Staying attuned to this process can help the supervisor
"manage" the grapevine and eventually minimize its impact as a
source of information for employees.

Handling Confidential and Sensitive Information. Obviously
there are certain types of information that cannot be shared

with supervisors. Although they may feel they should be allowed to receive it, sensitive information about new product plans, competitive marketing strategies, potential acquisitions, or the sale of assets may need to be kept secret until plans are finalized and the effort is well underway. Also, there are times when plans for new programs being developed are incomplete and therefore should not be discussed with anyone. In these situations communication must be handled carefully by the organization.

The ideal approach is to communicate honestly and diplomatically without damaging the department or organization. Supervisors should be prepared to accept that certain types of information cannot be released to them or to others. Sometimes they must simply have enough trust and confidence in the organization to wait for the final word on what is happening. They may need to be reassured that the organization will benefit by the move or that no one will be adversely impacted, if that indeed is the case. There should be an explanation as to why the information cannot be released. If it would involve a breach of company policy to answer a particular question, then this should be explained. If it is a confidential or sensitive item whose disclosure would hurt the organization or destroy its competitive position, then this should also be explained to supervisors. If it has become part of the rumor mill, it may be appropriate to bring employees together to discuss the situation without divulging details. Supervisors should be encouraged to ask questions about things heard but not yet released as official information. A positive approach to these situations will ensure that no harm is done by not disclosing details. This will continue to build the trust and confidence of supervisors in the organization.

Communication from Staff to Line Supervisors. Some of the most disruptive and poorly executed attempts at communication are found in the memos and requests for information from staff to line supervisors. Staff groups are dependent on the information supplied by line management, and they often complain when line supervisors do not respond to their requests. Supervisors are extremely busy individuals with many demands placed on them. And there appear to be too many requests for input and information from staff groups. For this reason, requests for information should be kept to a minimum and, when needed, should be handled in the most efficient and effective manner.

In many organizations a memo from a staff department requesting information, particularly if it is not routinely supplied information, will be ignored by the majority of supervisors. Some supervisors base their actions on this philosophy: If the information has not been requested before, it is safe to ignore the memo on the first request. Some will ignore all the memos until they are absolutely convinced they have to supply the information.

A more effective approach is to have the request for information come from a line manager. The staff department then reviews the request with him or her, explains the purpose of the information and why it is needed, and prepares the memo for the manager's signature. Even if the information is to be sent directly from staff departments and line supervisors realize that the staff initiated the information, they will be more likely to respond to the memo since the request comes from a manager in the chain of command. It can be dangerous for supervisors to ignore a request from top management, since they depend on it for future promotional considerations as well as compensation actions. This effort, although simple, has the added feature of ensuring that line and staff groups are working together in their efforts to secure necessary information from supervisors. Also, it is a way to prevent staff members from sending unimportant and frivolous requests to supervisors. If they must meet with senior management to discuss the information that they need and get a manager's signature on the memo, then their request will have to involve something worthwhile and important. Otherwise they will not secure top management's endorsement.

Summary

This chapter covered the important issue of supervisory communication. It focused on the communication process, communication trends, establishing an effective communication system, what to communicate, meetings with supervisors, work unit meetings, supervisory publications, improving communication skills, and special issues in communication. To have effective communication, the organization must

- Ensure that supervisors understand the communication process and their role in it. Fundamental concepts were presented here, along with recent trends and special issues in supervisory communication.
- Examine the present communication climate to see if it is appropriate and meets the needs of supervisors. In addition, the various types of information communicated to supervisors, as outlined in the chapter, should be reviewed periodically.
- Keep supervisors informed on important issues through a variety of meetings. Staff meetings, problem-solving meetings, and small group meetings with top management are all effective ways to keep supervisors informed.
- Prepare and encourage supervisors to conduct regular work unit meetings with their employees. These meetings can be the most important part of the communication process. The issues that must be addressed to make work unit meetings successful were explored.
- Explore the feasibility of developing a special publication for supervisors. This may be a productive and efficient method of direct communication with supervisors.
- Improve supervisory skills in the actual process of communication. Supervisory training in listening, speaking, writing, reading, and body language may be needed to enhance the communication process.

Special attention to all these areas should result in a tremendous improvement in supervisory communication.

Suggested Readings

Burgoon, M., and others. *Small Group Communication: A Functional Approach.* New York: Holt, Rinehart and Winston, 1974.

Christenson, C., and others. *Supervising.* Reading, Mass.: Addison-Wesley, 1982, 98–128.

de Mare, G. *Communicating at the Top.* New York: Wiley, 1979.

Imundo, L. V. *The Effective Supervisor's Handbook.* New York: AMACOM, 1980, 72–93.

Keys, B., and Henshall, J. *Supervision.* New York: Wiley, 1984, 159–184.

Lesly, P. *How We Discommunicate.* New York: AMACOM, 1979.

Lindo, D. K. *Supervision Can Be Easy!* New York: AMACOM, 1979, 37–83.

Mondy, R. W., and others. *Supervision.* New York: Random House, 1983, 156–173.

Ray, C. M., and Eison, C. L. *Supervision.* New York: Dryden, 1983, 128–175.

Timm, P. R. *Managerial Communication: A Finger on the Pulse.* Englewood Cliffs, N.J.: Prentice-Hall, 1980.

Towers, Perrin, Forster & Crosby. *Case Studies in Organizational Communication.* New York: Towers, Perrin, Forster & Crosby, 1975.

7

Decision Making:

Improving Skills, Delegating Authority, and Removing Constraints

Few managers will argue about the need to improve supervisory decision-making abilities. However, while organizations want supervisors to make better decisions, they still impede the decision-making process with unnecessary constraints and restrictions. It is also true, of course, that supervisors are not always prepared to make decisions. This chapter therefore focuses on three major issues:

- The authority supervisors are provided in the structure of their jobs. This varies considerably among organizations and is generally less than what it should be.
- The growing number of constraints placed on supervisors that hinder their freedom to manage. The number and complexity of policies, procedures, labor contracts, and laws have grown considerably in recent years.
- The extent of supervisor preparation to improve decision-making skills and ability. Few organizations devote time to prepare supervisors for decision-making.

Most organizations assume that their supervisors have the necessary authority to perform their jobs since top management rarely receives complaints about this issue. But a lack of complaints does not necessarily mean that there is not a problem. Most observers will agree that supervisory authority has gradually eroded over the years. Surveys and studies have repeatedly identified eroding authority as one of the major problems facing supervisors. Supervisors usually want all the authority they can get with minimum restrictions and controls. But from the viewpoint of top management, there must be controls, and some decisions must be moved up in the organization beyond the scope of supervisors and even middle managers. An important question addressed in this chapter is how much authority supervisors need to meet their responsibilities and get the desired results.

The issue of supervisory preparation is a perplexing one for organizations. Many organizations argue that supervisory participation in the decision-making process should be strictly limited because they are unable to provide much meaningful input for decisions. If this is true, however, it may be the result of a lack of training or a lack of experience that can only be achieved through actual involvement in the decision-making process. Supervisors learn from the decisions they make. Their increased involvement becomes a continuous learning process that will improve the quality of their future decisions. Also, preparing supervisors to make better decisions may be fruitless if the organization does not change its decision-making limits for supervisors. Otherwise, they may be prepared to perform something that they are not allowed to do. Therefore, supervisory authority must be increased at the same time supervisory preparation for decision-making is undertaken.

Additional emphasis on improving the decision-making ability of supervisors can reap significant benefits for the organization. First, it should make supervisors more effective and improve the output and quality of the work unit. Excessive constraints and restrictions inhibit the contribution of the supervisory group, and a lack of authority to make timely decisions can hinder the effectiveness of supervisors. However, increased authority will not help unless supervisors are prepared to handle it. An investment in training supervisors to make decisions, coupled with clearer expectations from management, can improve the quality of decisions and ultimately improve the effectiveness of supervisors.

Second, increased decision-making ability should boost the morale of supervisors while improving their identification with management. Providing ample authority will help improve job satisfaction just as a lack of authority will cause frustration (Frangipane, 1979). Supervisors must feel that they have the tools and support necessary to perform their jobs effectively. An increased role in the destiny of the organization will cause supervisors to identify more closely with management than with their employees. In fact, decision-making authority is one of the key areas that separate management from nonmanagement employees. Improved morale, satisfaction, and management identification have the added benefits of making supervisory jobs more attractive for prospective candidates.

Finally, improving the decision-making ability of supervisors can help streamline the organization and relieve upper management of some of the pressures to make decisions. Supervisors with adequate levels of authority and the preparation necessary to make decisions can cut through the bureaucracy that is often characteristic of large organizations. They can meet their responsibilities and get the desired results without conferring with various staff support personnel and multiple layers of management. As a result, action can be taken swiftly and decisions made on a timely basis. One of the attributes of excellent companies identified by Peters and Waterman (1982, p. 15) is that they are operated with lean staffs and without multiple layers of management and supervisors are given the necessary authority to accomplish their tasks. Increased decision-making authority at the supervisory level relieves middle management and upper management of many of the detailed decisions that may be inappropriate for their scope of responsibilities. Middle and upper management can spend additional time on the more meaningful and productive parts of their jobs —developing plans, goals, and objectives. It is not uncommon to find situations in which supervisors have to constantly check for approval at the next level of management. This unnecessarily complicates the job of middle management while hampering the effectiveness of supervisors. The long-range net effect of giving increased decision-making authority to supervisors is to eliminate some levels of management in larger organizations and at the same time streamline the organization to the point where staff departments can possibly be reduced. There is evidence now that the middle level of management is shrinking while the supervisory level is growing (Bittel, 1980, p. 603).

For these reasons, it is important that an organization assess the decision-making status of its supervisors and make improvements if they are warranted. Of course, increasing supervisory authority is not without its share of potential problems. Increased authority for unprepared supervisors can result in chaos. There are many actions that need the approval of staff support personnel and upper management, and there are a variety of decisions that do not and should not have supervisory input. Changes in this area should be approached with caution; careful planning and training may be a necessary part of the process.

The Decision-Making Process

It is important for supervisors and organizations to understand the process by which decisions are made in an organizational setting. Both the supervisor and the organization can then take steps to improve that process, if improvement is needed. This section begins with a model of decision making, explores the factors affecting decision making, and examines the various types of decision makers.

Decision-Making Model. Many of the decisions in organizations are made without much thought or preparation. Some are routine, spontaneous, and become integrated into the job responsibilities. Others are based on intuition with little logic applied to the process. However, there are times when the impact of decisions is significant and the problems are serious enough to warrant a thorough analysis of the situation. A general framework is needed that the supervisor can use to arrive at an optimal decision. There are a variety of models available, all of which involve the logical, sequential steps of identifying the problem, gathering information, and choosing the appropriate solution. The model presented in Figure 13 and described in what follows

Figure 13. Supervisory Decision-Making and Problem-Solving Model.

1. Fully Describe the Problem or Decision

2. Gather Relevant Information from All Sources

3. Itemize Potential Causes, If It Is a Problem

4. Select the Most Likely Cause

5. Identify Potential Solutions

6. Evaluate Each Solution and Select the Most Appropriate One

7. Develop a Plan of Action

8. Explain the Decision and Secure Commitment

9. Implement Decision

10. Follow Up

is more detailed than some models found in the literature. But it is usually best to have a detailed model for complicated and confusing issues that call for thought-provoking ideas. For simple and straightforward problems and decisions, the model can be shortened by tailoring it to the specific situation and omitting inappropriate steps. The model can be used to solve a complex problem or to make a major decision. In these cases, action must be taken, but it is unclear what has caused the problem or which action is best for the decision at hand. The model should be executed on a timely basis to avoid a crisis situation since decision making under stress is not a desired approach. Here are the steps for this model.

1. *Fully describe the problem or decision.* It is important that the supervisor have a thorough understanding of the decision to be made or the problem to be solved. This includes symptoms of the problem, the individuals involved, the magnitude of the problem or decision, and its impact on the work unit. It may be a problem that is important to top management or important to the supervisor. It may be a problem related to work unit performance or individual performance. It may be a problem related to commitments within the organization, or it could involve external factors. An incomplete description could result in solving the wrong problem or implementing a decision that is not on target. There should be some differentiation between minor problems and major ones. Minor problems do not warrant time-consuming considerations, while big ones should be considered in detail.

2. *Gather relevant information from all sources.* An obvious second step is to get all the facts, that is, to gather documents, records, performance data, and, most importantly, employee input. Information may come from customers, suppliers, government officials, employees in another department, or even other organizations. Information may be collected through interviews, observations, or surveys. It may be appropriate to involve middle and top management. In the absence of appropriate data, supervisors may have to make assumptions about the problem. The importance of securing input from employees in the work unit for decisions affecting their unit or for problems in which they are involved cannot be overemphasized.

3. *Itemize potential causes if there are problems.* The objective of this step is to generate as many ideas as possible of what might be causing the problem. It is likely that a few probable causes can be identified. Employee input may be valuable here, particularly if employees are directly involved in the problem situation. The chances are they know what is causing the problem and may have some potential solutions in mind. Input from specialists and others well informed on the subject may also be helpful.

4. *Select the most likely cause.* Each of the potential causes should be investigated to see if it is a likely cause. This may require securing additional data, checking other records, and getting additional input from other individuals who may be involved. This is a fine-tuning process in which the supervisor focuses on the most likely cause.

5. *Identify potential solutions.* The objective of this step is to generate as many potential solutions as possible. There are usually several approaches to correcting a problem or several decisions that can be made regarding a particular situation. Some recommend that at least three alternatives be developed to avoid an either/or possibility. These should be listed with not much thought given to the quality of the solution or the appropriateness of the decision. Most decisions will involve some type of trade-off, and there is usually a point where the cost of obtaining extra information exceeds its value. Employee input may be appropriate to improve the quality of potential solutions. Utilizing established procedures for solving a problem is a definite plus.

6. *Evaluate each solution and select the most appropriate one.* The result of this step will be the identification of the best way to make the decision or to solve the problem. Each potential solution is evaluated in terms of its appropriateness, feasibility, and likelihood of correcting the problem or making the most effective decision. This may involve the careful weighing of alternatives while considering the impact of each potential solution or course of action. Supervisors should always consider the possibility of making no decision or taking no action, and they should not insist on being right in every situation, since this is obviously impossible. Supervisors should be prepared to be wrong sometimes. Employee input may also be appropriate for this step.

7. *Develop a plan of action.* Once a decision has been selected, a plan of action should be developed to implement the decision or to correct the problem. This involves determining what will be done, by whom, and at what time. A pilot test or trial run may be appropriate if the decision involves many individuals and its impact is uncertain.

8. *Explain the decision and secure commitment.* It is important that those involved in implementing a decision and those who will be affected by the decision thoroughly understand the situation and the basis for the decision. Supervisors are faced with three courses of action: They can avoid explaining the decision at all, they can explain the decision before it is implemented, or they can explain it after it is implemented. (Of course, if those individuals affected by the decision are involved in the decision-making process, no formal explanation will be needed.) Without an explanation, misunderstandings can hamper the implementation process and keep the supervisor from achieving the results expected. Making decisions without giving explanations develops suspicion, fosters hostility, and reduces confidence and respect, not to mention support and acceptance. It is very important for the supervisor to secure commitment from all those involved. Commitment leads to ownership, which is very important even if the employees had very little to do with making the decision.

9. *Implement the decision.* An obvious next step is to implement the decision or the solution to the problem. The implementation phase of a decision is far more important for success than is the correctness of the decision itself. This involves following the detailed steps in the action plan and monitoring the process to ensure that it is accomplished on time and as expected. This may be as simple as announcing the decision and making the necessary changes at that point, or it may consist of a process that involves many individuals and steps over a long period of time.

10. *Follow-up.* The final step in the decision-making process is follow-up. At some predetermined date, the supervisor should conduct a follow-up to ensure that everything was completed on time and with the results expected. This should improve the accuracy of future decisions. Successes can be analyzed for general solutions that might work in other situations. Too often, supervisors and managers stop short of this important step. It is essential to complete the full implementation of the decision-making and problem-solving process.

Factors Affecting Supervisory Decision-Making. As the model clearly indicates, there are many factors that influence the decision-making process and, for that matter, determine whether a logical approach is even necessary. The following describes the important factors that can inhibit or enhance the decisions made or the problems solved by supervisors.

1. *Type of decision.* Obviously, routine decisions will not need a formal approach. However, complex problems or important nonroutine decisions that can have a significant impact on the work unit may require a formal approach to ensure that quality is maintained in the decision-making process. There is no specific rule as to when a formal approach is needed. The answer lies with the style of the supervisor and the importance of the decision to be made or the problem to be solved.

2. *Nature of the work.* Some work groups are involved in functions that are critical to the success of the organization. Other work groups are perhaps involved in routine, repetitive, and redundant processes that, although necessary, may not be essential to the survival of the organization or to its everyday functioning. Thus, decisions made by a supervisor in a critical work group such as accounting or financial control may be more important to the organization than those made by a supervisor of a clean-up crew for a construction firm.

3. *Degree of acceptance by employees.* It is extremely important to have a decision accepted by those whom it affects or who will be responsible for putting it into effect. Some decisions, such as developing new work practices and procedures, require high acceptance by employees. Others, such as initiating new products and services, may require little employee acceptance for the decision to be implemented successfully.

4. *Top management support.* The degree of support that top management lends to the decision-making process can affect the quality of decisions. If top management prefers intuitive, informal decisions as opposed to decisions developed within a logical framework, then that is what they will get. Management must communicate its expectations and requirements in decision making and provide reinforcement when supervisors follow the desired course of action.

5. *Documentation.* Some organizations, particularly larger ones, require detailed documentation of problems solved or de-

cisions made. In others documentation is less structured and may not have such strict requirements. It is very important to have a certain amount of documentation, but excessive documentation can be counterproductive.

6. *Authority and responsibility.* The amount of authority or responsibility given to supervisors can vastly affect the decisions they make. Job descriptions usually detail to some extent the amount of authority that supervisors have to make decisions affecting their work units.

7. *Resources available.* The extent to which information is available in an organization can affect the quality of its decisions. Many decisions or solutions to problems require high-quality data. Inadequate records, constraints on securing input from other groups, or lack of resourcefulness on the part of the decision maker can hinder the decision-making process significantly.

8. *Time limits.* Finally, the timing of the decision is extremely important. A quick decision may preclude use of a systematic, logical, decision-making process. In this case, the judgment, intuition, and experience of the decision maker become crucial. However, when there is ample time, decision making can take on a more logical and formal character.

While there may be others, these factors can greatly influence the approach to decisions, the quality of decisions, and the formality of the decision-making process in an organization (Mondy and others, 1983, pp. 39–44).

Types of Decision Makers. It is sometimes useful to analyze supervisors in terms of their decision-making style. Several styles are differentiated here, but a particular supervisor's style may represent a combination of them.

1. *Impulsive decision makers* make fast decisions. For them, it is more important to make a quick decision than to analyze the quality of the decision. These supervisors will often act before taking time to think through the situation. They give little consideration to the facts or to the attitude and input of others. They realize that decisions must be made, and they are willing to make them in record time.

2. *Deep thinkers* become absorbed with a problem; if left alone long enough, they will probably solve it. They prefer to work alone, and they give much thought to a situation, analyzing it in their own minds in many different ways before making a decision or devising a solution. They are low-pressure individuals who rarely get excited or upset.

3. *Procrastinators* put off decisions until it is too late. The problem has either resolved itself or gone away, or the organization has missed a chance to capitalize on an opportunity. They operate on the theory that most problems will solve themselves if you wait long enough. They will never make a decision unless they are forced to and then only at the last minute.

4. *Politicians* tend to make decisions that will not offend anyone, particularly those who can influence their own careers. They will straddle the fence on issues, taking a stand only when they must and then with a very low profile. They like to avoid controversial issues and stay clear of conflicts.

5. *Risk seekers* enjoy making decisions, particularly those in which the stakes are high. They actively seek opportunities to make changes and make things happen. These are usually high-energy, high-achieving individuals who are best suited for dynamic, changing organizations.

6. *Risk avoiders* want to avoid making changes unless there is a pressing reason for them. They prefer stable organizations with little or no growth. These supervisors are best suited for bureaucratic organizations and may be particularly comfortable in a government setting.

7. *Naive decision makers* underestimate the impact decisions may have on others. They take the attitude that everything will eventually work out and that each person responsible will naturally do what he or she should do to make the decision work or to solve the problem. Their naive assumptions usually get them into trouble, and the result can be dangerous for the organization.

8. *Researchers* spend too much time on analysis and data collection. They want to have every fact and consider every possibility before taking an action or trying to solve a problem. This is sometimes referred to as "paralysis by analysis"; the

supervisor becomes bogged down in the numbers and loses sight of the purpose of decision making.

9. *Biased decision makers* are prejudiced in their opinions and attitudes about practices, individuals, and functions in the organization. They tend to make decisions based on prejudgments, disregarding objective information that can be or has been assembled. These supervisors can cause serious problems for the organization.

Middle managers are in a much better position to coach and counsel their supervisors when they are aware of the supervisors' approach to decision making. Realistically, supervisors will use a combination of different styles. Rarely is one style absolutely the best, and any one of them may be valid for a particular situation. A safe approach is to avoid extremes and damaging tactics. Additional insights into this question can be found in Bittel (1980, pp. 595-596) and Boyd (1976, pp. 324-325).

How Authority Is Obtained

Authority is usually defined as the *right* to command, expend resources, and influence behavior. Power is the ability of one person to influence another. Authority differs from responsibility, which is the accountability for reaching objectives through proper use of resources and adherence to organizational policy. Authority is necessary to carry out responsibilities (Terry and Rue, 1982, p. 34).

There are several ways to classify the different types of authority. To distinguish between formal and informal authority is one approach. Formal authority is that which is given to the supervisor and informal is that which is earned over time. (The terms *official* and *unofficial* are sometimes substituted for *formal* and *informal*.) In other cases, authority is divided into line and staff authority. Line supervisors have direct control over employees, while staff supervisors do not have direct control and must persuade others to meet their responsibilities. Staff authority supports and advises line authority. But a better approach is a classification based on the source of authority, since this provides more insight into how supervisors can increase the amount of authority they have.

It is not uncommon to find certain supervisors in an organization wielding much more authority than others, although they are all at the same job level. These supervisors are allowed to make decisions and provide input on a variety of issues, and in some cases they have more clout than middle managers. These varying degrees of authority can be best explained by examining the various sources of authority. There are a number of ways in which supervisors receive authority to perform their jobs. To a large extent, the amount of authority supervisors have depends on their function, responsibilities, performance, expertise, behavior, and trust, each of which is described in the paragraphs that follow.

1. *Function.* Some functions in an organization gradually take on more importance than others, and supervisors of those functions come to have more inherent authority. In recent years quality assurance groups, operations audit teams, product design groups, and research and development departments have become more important to an organization's success. In addition, a few traditional functions such as financial control and human resources development have increased their influence markedly over the past ten years. These shifts in organizational authority by function will continue to occur, and supervisors involved in those functions will have more authority than others since they will have the ability to influence others significantly (Imundo, 1980, p. 105).

2. *Responsibilities.* Much of the supervisor's authority is based on his or her job responsibilities. This authority is the only legal authority that supervisors possess. It represents the decision-making limits inherent in the job and the control that supervisors exercise over the employees who report to them. Some supervisory jobs command more authority than others. The assets controlled, the number of employees supervised, and the annual budget managed help determine the amount of supervisory authority. Supervisors exercise their authority in making job assignments, giving instructions, rewarding employees, and taking disciplinary action. Authority is exercised in almost

every phase of the relationship between supervisor and subordinates.

3. *Performance.* Supervisors have authority based on their individual performance. Top performers in the organization command respect and are able to influence others. They have the ability to get things done and make things happen. Because of this, others respect their opinion even though the supervisors are not in the legitimate chain of command. Other supervisors, and even managers in the organization, will seek their guidance and direction and call on them to solve organizational problems, even those outside their normal scope of responsibility. This type of authority is developed over time through consistent high levels of performance by a supervisor.

4. *Expertise.* Supervisors have authority based on their expertise, which is a function of their skills, knowledge, and ability. Supervisors with high levels of competence are valuable to the organization, particularly if they share their knowledge and skills with others. They are very knowledgeable about their work unit, technical processes, and organizational goals and objectives. They are usually labeled technical experts and may have such credentials as advanced degrees or professional certifications. They have a consistent pattern of knowing what to do at a given time. Because of this, they exert much influence over others. Some of these supervisors bring this authority with them at the time of promotion. In other cases it is developed on the job through years of repeated successes and accomplishments in the work unit, as well as through off-the-job study.

5. *Behavior.* Supervisors also have authority based on their behavior or actions toward others in the organization. They have certain traits, habits, and characteristics that have developed over time; that is, supervisors look, feel, believe, think, act, and react to events and other employees in certain ways. If this behavior is positive, supervisors can begin to attract others and influence their behavior. Other employees, supervisors, and even managers will exert extra efforts to respond to their requests. This may be a direct result of the interpersonal skills possessed by supervisors and how they use them in dealing

with others. Supervisors with high amounts of this type of authority treat others with dignity and use empathy in their personal interactions. This type of authority is used as a supplement to, not a replacement or substitute for, other types of authority.

6. *Trust.* Finally, there is authority based on trust. This refers to the quality of relationships between supervisors and those with whom they have regular contact. Supervisors with high degrees of this kind of authority work with people in an open and honest way. They have no ulterior motives or hidden agendas. Other individuals know where they stand and will trust these supervisors and their actions. They have the best interest of others in mind, as well as that of the organization. Once this trust is lost, however, it is difficult to regain. Some supervisors never fully develop an adequate level of trust to get others to do what needs to be done.

Increasing Supervisory Authority

Having authority is one thing, using it is another. Effective use of authority can have a significant impact on work group performance. Employees can either support, comply with, or resist the actions of supervisors (Yukl and Taber, 1983, p. 38). Employees who support their supervisor are enthusiastic about meeting his or her requests. They accept the goals of the supervisor and the work unit and exert maximum efforts to accomplish them in a productive and efficient manner. Compliance will ensure that the job is done but not with the enthusiasm and maximum effort that comes from supportive employees. Employees will go along with the leader's request because they think they must, but they usually will not achieve high output and increased efficiency. Resistance hampers the output of the work group. Employees either outwardly or inwardly resist the efforts of the supervisor and may work against his or her directions. Absenteeism, slowdowns, sabotage, and delays are typical reactions of employees who have decided to resist the efforts of the supervisor.

The reactions of the work group to different types of authority may vary. The use of authoity based on function or the responsibilities of the job will almost always get compliance from the work group. However, support is not always guaranteed, and employee resistance can also develop. Authority based on performance or expertise is likely to secure support from the group. Employees want to learn from the person who has demonstrated high performance or is regarded as an expert in a particular process. Compliance is likely when this authority base is used; however, resistance may occur if this authority is used improperly, since some employees react negatively to high performers and experts. Authority based on behavior or trust is also likely to secure the support of the work group. Compliance usually will follow but is not guaranteed. It is unlikely that there will be any resistance to the authority based on the trust established by the supervisor. It is important to remember that support can easily be obtained through use of each of these types of authority if it is exercised in a commonsense manner.

Decision-Making Limits. The exact amount of legal authority that a supervisor possesses is not always clear. The vagueness of supervisory authority sometimes results from the conflicting demands and requirements of the job or from the fact that supervisory duties are defined in a variety of documents. The job description is probably the most important document for defining the authority given to supervisors, although it is often incomplete and not specific enough. Policy manuals sometimes contain additional details about authority for supervisors as it relates to making decisions and giving approval. Procedure manuals and employee handbooks also contain information about the authority granted to supervisors. In addition, past practices, not necessarily committed to writing, can either provide the supervisor with increased authority or eat away at his or her present authority base. And, finally, oral commitments can impact the authority base. For example, supervisors may be told that they have the authority to make certain types of decisions not made by others in the past and not prohibited by some policy or procedure. Conversely, supervisors may be told that they cannot make a decision without approval of a higher level of management, even though there is no specific regulation that forbids them making the decision.

To compound the problem, the legal authority of supervisors is rarely spelled out for them in sufficient detail. Their manager may outline what kind of authority they have but give few or no details. As a result, supervisors make faulty assumptions and draw improper conclusions about the kind and degree of authority that goes with their jobs. They learn through trial and error and from other supervisors what they can or cannot do.

One effective approach to clearing up the confusion about authority is to develop a document that clearly defines the decision-making limits for supervisors. This should be a comprehensive list developed from all the sources of formal supervisory authority. It must be carefully examined to see if it is consistent with good management practices. Exhibit 7 represents an example of such a document. It outlines the varying degrees of authority delegated to the supervisor. It is easy to understand and use. When discussed with supervisors, it can improve their morale and give them a greater sense of accountability for the destiny of their work units.

Delegation from Managers. One important way to increase supervisory authority rests squarely with middle managers; that is, managers can delegate some of their authority to the supervisory group. From a practical angle, this approach gives supervisors additional authority without major changes in policies or procedures. This can have a positive impact on supervisors and increase their job satisfaction. It gives them a chance to have more meaningful work and provides them with an opportunity to learn and grow on their present jobs. In addition, it prepares them for more responsibility in the future.

Delegation is usually defined as the assignment of decision-making responsibilities to a subordinate in an organizational setting (Ford, 1983, p. 3). Delegation skills are important for an effective middle manager. In extreme cases, delegation can make the difference between success or failure for the manager. Every organization has its share of managers who will not

Exhibit 7. Supervisory Decision-Making Limits.

Actions	Decision-Making Parameters		
	Complete Authority	Inform After Decision	Submit for Approval
Employment/Employee Relations			
Give permission for absence (up to five days)	✓		
Give permission for absence (more than five days)		✓	
Grant leave of absence			✓
Prepare vacation schedules	✓		
Handle employee complaints		✓	
Reduce staff	✓		
Select employees for layoff		✓	
Promote employees		✓	
Demote employees		✓	
Transfer employees to another department			✓
Hire additional employees			✓
Select new employees	✓		
Labor Relations			
Issue verbal warnings	✓		
Issue written warnings		✓	
Suspend employees		✓	
Discharge probationary employees	✓		
Discharge regular employees		✓	
Settle grievances with union (first step)	✓		
Settle grievances with union (after first step)			✓
Compensation and Benefits			
Set starting rate (within policy limits)		✓	
Determine incentive allowances	✓		
Merit increase (budgeted)		✓	
Merit increase (unbudgeted)			✓
Job content changes		✓	
Job classification changes			✓
Grant paid personal leaves (up to three days)		✓	
Grant paid personal leaves (more than three days)			✓
Explain employee benefits	✓		
Explain pay policy	✓		

Exhibit 7. Supervisory Decision-Making Limits, Cont'd.

| | Decision-Making Parameters | | |
Actions	Complete Authority	Inform After Decision	Submit for Approval
Training and Education			
Send employees to internal training programs	√		
Send employees to external training programs		√	
Request that new training programs be developed		√	
Approve tuition refund requests			√
Select and develop a replacement			√
Safety and Health			
Send employees to the first-aid station	√		
Investigate the cause of accidents		√	
Determine if an employee should be sent to a doctor	√		
Notify family of accident victim	√		
Correct unsafe conditions	√		
Establish standards for housekeeping	√		
Conduct safety meetings	√		
Enforce safety and work rules	√		
Job Assignments			
Assign duties to employees	√		
Change job assignments	√		
Set work schedules		√	
Change work schedules		√	
Determine when output is stopped due to abnormal situations		√	
Authorize overtime	√		
Determine individual performance standards	√		
Purchasing			
Purchase supplies for work unit (under $2,000)	√		
Purchase supplies for work unit ($2,000 to $5,000)		√	
Purchase supplies for work unit (over $5,000)			√
Requisition tools	√		
Purchase capital equipment			√

(continued on next page)

Exhibit 7. Supervisory Decision-Making Limits, Cont'd.

Actions	Decision-Making Parameters		
	Complete Authority	Inform After Decision	Submit for Approval
Quality			
Determine if material should be scrapped	✓		
Set quality standards			✓
Resolve customer complaints		✓	
Equipment and Materials			
Authorize equipment setup changes	✓		
Make purchase versus repair decisions on equipment			✓
Stop jobs in process	✓		
Approve maintenance and repair work	✓		
Authorize substitutions of raw materials		✓	
Change operating procedures			✓
Change layout of work unit			✓
Determine inventory levels		✓	
Accounting/Control			
Approve petty cash expenditures	✓		
Approve payroll records	✓		
Establish budget for the work unit			✓
Approve charges against the work unit's budget		✓	
Approve production records		✓	

Definitions:

   Complete Authority—Supervisor makes decision with informing or consulting with manager.

   Inform After Decision—Supervisor makes decision and informs manager of the decision.

   Submit for Approval—Supervisor submits recommendation to manager for approval.

delegate job duties. For a variety of reasons (or excuses), they refuse to let their supervisors do any part of their job. Consequently, while they work long hours, they actually reduce their own effectiveness. This approach also creates problems for supervisors. They may come to think that their manager does not trust them with job assignments. As a result, supervisory morale is lowered, and there is increased reliance on the boss to get the job done.

The effectiveness of the delegation process is a function of several factors. The following list outlines the important conditions that must exist for effective delegation from manager to supervisor.

1. *The organizational climate must support delegation.* Organizational policies and procedures must allow the middle manager enough latitude to delegate authority down to the lowest, most effective level. It is not unusual to have a manager who successfully practices delegation characterized by his peers and top management as a lazy person who avoids work. This negative perception of delegation will inhibit delegation efforts and ultimately stifle the process. There is a false notion held by some managers that the higher a manager's position in the organization the more hours he or she must work. This obviously is not the case. Some of the most successful managers are those who work relatively short hours, delegating many of their assignments to their subordinate managers and supervisors. A healthy, positive attitude toward delegation is necessary if managers are to pass some of their duties on to the supervisory group.

2. *Supervisors must have the ability to handle the tasks delegated to them.* This basic condition is almost too fundamental to mention. However, in practice it is often overlooked. Assignments are given to supervisors when they are not prepared to accomplish them. They may not have the training, skills, or resources necessary to successfully handle a project. This is particularly true when tasks are "dumped" on supervisors without an explanation of what is to be done and how it is to be accomplished.

3. *The supervisor must have a positive attitude about assuming additional responsibilities.* Not all supervisors will welcome additional assignments from the middle manager. They may perceive the work as being asked to do the boss's job without the compensation that the boss receives. In this case delegation will be unwelcome and unwanted. The result will be loss of

morale and possibly less-than-desirable end results. The supervisor must understand that delegation is an opportunity to learn more about the organization and grow in his or her present job. Because of this, it may be best to target specific supervisors for delegation assignments, those who are eager to learn more and who want additional responsibilities. Also, it is important to examine the impact of delegation on the work load of the supervisor. If delegation causes unusual hardships, then reassignment of present duties may be necessary to maximize its effectiveness.

4. *The middle manager must be emotionally secure and stable in the job.* When delegating authority becomes a threat to security, serious problems can develop. Every organization has insecure managers. They fear that supervisors may take their jobs. (If this is a realistic possibility, it will probably happen anyway.) An unwilling delegator may sabotage the efforts of supervisors when forced to delegate assignments. He or she may need special counseling or coaching to overcome this fear.

5. *Delegation takes time to practice effectively.* Probably the most common reason given for managers' failing to delegate is that it takes more time to show someone how to handle a task than it does to do it oneself. For a one-time assignment this may very well be the case. However, the manager and the organization may be saving time if supervisors will have to repeat the task in the future. Delegation is a time-consuming process, one that may require a heavy commitment up front, but it will also have lasting results.

The success of delegation will depend on all these factors. Usually the first step in this process is to concentrate on those activities that can be most easily delegated. This can be accomplished by outlining the significant duties performed by the manager and the supervisor. One format, adapted from an approach suggested by Bittel (1980, p. 146), involves listing activities in the following categories:

1. tasks that managers must do
2. tasks that managers should do but that supervisors could assist them in doing
3. tasks that managers could do but that supervisors could also do if given the opportunity

4. tasks that supervisors should do but that managers could help them do in an emergency
5. tasks that supervisors must do

Placing the current duties and responsibilities of managers and supervisors into these categories may reveal some likely areas for delegation. The tasks with maximum delegation potential are those listed in the third category, which will probably account for a large number of activities.

After the activities are identified, it is best to delegate a whole job if that is feasible. The supervisor should be allowed to complete it without middle-manager involvement and then have the final results monitored. Constantly checking on progress while giving unrequested advice and counsel is not true delegation. It is merely dumping tasks on a supervisor without giving him the authority or freedom to complete them. Another important part of the delegation process is to address the authority and responsibility issue. Typically, the manager will keep the responsibility for the work that is delegated. However, it is customary to give the supervisor authority to exercise whatever controls are necessary to accomplish the task. It is difficult, if not impossible, for a supervisor to accomplish a task without authority over the individuals who are needed for its completion. Effective delegation requires the manager to state clearly what is to be done. Misunderstandings can easily creep into the delegation process because the activity is new to the supervisor, whereas it may be routine for the manager. An area must be selected that is easily measured so that progress can be monitored and documented. This gives the supervisor a feeling of fulfillment while showing the middle manager some tangible results of the delegation process.

In summary, delegation is an important responsibility of middle managers. Delegating authority to supervisors to accomplish tasks normally completed by middle managers is an effective way to develop supervisors while also improving their morale and job satisfaction. At the same time, the effectiveness of middle managers can be enhanced.

Awareness of Supervisory Authority. As noted earlier, supervisors do not always have a clear understanding of their authority. An organization may need to develop in supervisors an awareness of their authority and how they may improve it in the future. Here are five specific techniques for doing so:

1. *Publish guidelines on authority.* An earlier section outlined how specific decision-making limits can be developed for supervisors. This is a way to communicate authority limits that leaves little room for misunderstandings and lets supervisors know exactly where they stand (see Exhibit 7). In lieu of a document that sets decision-making limits, authority can be detailed in the supervisory job description or in special publications designed for the supervisory group. One organization published a booklet on the job of supervisor that detailed all its major responsibilities and outlined its authority.

2. *Discuss authority in meetings with supervisors.* General supervisory meetings provide an appropriate place to discuss the question of authority, particularly when they focus on instances in which authority has been misunderstood or improperly used. Such meetings provide an excellent forum to discuss increases in or reductions of decision-making authority for supervisors. They should allow for two-way communication and give supervisors the opportunity to ask questions and get clarifications. In one organization purchasing limits were increased for supervisors for purchases not requiring additional approval. This change was discussed in general meetings with supervisors, and an explanation for it was given. As a result, it had a positive impact on the group.

3. *Discuss authority in training programs.* Supervisory training and leadership programs provide an excellent arena for discussing the problem of authority. It is here that supervisors may complain about their lack of authority. They may complain that they are expected to do their job but are not given the necessary authority. These complaints can be appropriately addressed if part of the training program is devoted to the subject of supervisory authority. Ideally, this segment could be conducted by a line manager who is one or two levels above the supervisory group. A straightforward discussion could clear up misunderstandings and leave a positive impression on the supervisory group.

4. *Encourage middle managers to discuss with supervisors the proper use of authority.* Middle managers should be prepared to discuss how authority should be effectively used and how supervisors may obtain additional authority in the future. This could be discussed in response to complaints from supervisors that they do not have the authority they need to accomplish their jobs effectively. One-on-one coaching may be appropriate to handle problem areas or to clear up isolated cases of misunderstanding.

5. *Make comparisons with other organizations.* Regardless of the lack of authority supervisors think they have, there are usually other organizations in which the situation is worse. Without revealing enough specifics to alienate another organization, it may be helpful to discuss examples of supervisors who have even less authority. In one organization, where supervisors had complained about the constraints placed on them by their labor contract, discussions were held with them to highlight examples of constraints that existed in another local organization. After this discussion the supervisors had a better appreciation for their level of authority. This approach can be dangerous if it is not handled properly, since it can destroy relationships with other organizations. However, it should be appropriate to discuss items that are a matter of public record, such as a labor agreement.

Profit Center Concept. Many organizations have resorted to placing supervisors in autonomous units called profit centers. (A profit center is a unit whose profit contribution can be clearly pinpointed.) This pushes decisions down to the lowest, most effective level and enables supervisors to operate their work unit as if it were their own company or firm. The American Management Associations (AMA) actively promoted this concept in their seminars for top management in the 1970s and called it the unit president concept. This approach involved establishing decentralized departments for lower-level management groups. Establishing the profit center concept involves four important criteria:

1. *Operating parameters.* Parameters must be established within which the supervisors are allowed to operate. Figure 14

Figure 14. Profit Center Concept.

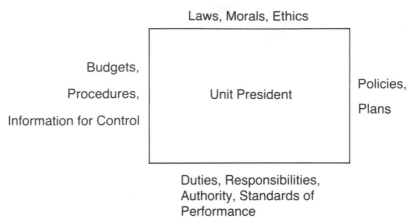

shows the general parameters established in the AMA's unit president concept. Supervisors are bound by laws, morals, and ethics on one side; by policies and plans on another side; by duties, responsibilities, authority, and standards of performance on another; and finally by budgets, procedures, and information necessary for control on the fourth side. Overall, these parameters provide a general framework within which a supervisor can operate.

2. *Minimum control.* Supervisors should have minimum restrictions with much autonomy and authority to perform their tasks. They should have as much freedom as possible, approaching that of a president of a small division or a manager of an independent retail store.

3. *Expected results.* Supervisors should be given bottom-line targets that they are expected to achieve. They should be rewarded for achieving those targets and receive additional incentives for beating the targets. Standard efficiency measures, profits, and return on investment are potential criteria for measuring the expected results.

4. *Training/preparation.* Supervisors must be trained to make decisions and know how to achieve the expected results. This may involve programs apart from those contained in traditional training and education programs for supervisors.

Although the profit center concept may not be appropriate for all organizations, it should at least be given serious consideration to see if it might be applicable in a particular organization.

Removing Decision-Making Constraints

The constraints placed on supervisors are often confusing, complex, and excessive. Supervisors sometimes misunderstand why the constraints exist. Moreover, constraints often originate from several different sources and unnecessarily place obstacles or barriers in the way of supervisors who are trying to successfully manage their work units. Constraints can significantly affect the morale of supervisors. When constraining conditions have existed over a long period of time, supervisors come to think they go with the territory—that they are an inherent part of the supervisor's job. This attitude can be improved if the organization makes an aggressive effort to minimize the impact of constraints.

Constraints are usually necessary, at least to a certain degree. Almost always constraints are developed with good intentions. Some mechanisms must exist to provide consistency and define the ultimate limits of decision-making authority. Certain things must be done in a specific way, probably in what is perceived to be the most effective way. Unfortunately, because of isolated problems, poor work practices, and shortsighted supervision, constraints that entangle the supervisor in a web of unnecessary controls and restrictions may gradually develop. The four general areas of constraints addressed in this section include labor agreements, organizational policies, work unit constraints, and legal controls.

Labor Agreements. Supervisors in unionized locations often correctly think that labor agreements put them at an inherent disadvantage. Negotiators (for both sides) have stripped supervisors of much of their authority. Rather than always dealing directly with employees, supervisors have become more dependent upon, and are quite often a target of, the union. It has become increasingly difficult to hire or fire without union involvement.

Hiring often has to come from the union list; firing has to follow a strict interpretation of the contract, often requiring a number of warnings to the employee in question. Layoffs are normally by seniority, not according to productivity. Disciplinary action has been formally taken away from the supervisor's judgment and has been reduced to written procedures (Sasser and Leonard, 1980, pp. 115-116). This situation may not be characteristic of all unionized locations, but it is common in far too many organizations. Unions, in their desire to become more involved in decision making, and organizations, with their concern for contract settlements without work stoppages, have slowly negotiated away supervisory rights. What can be done about the situation at this time? The answers are not easy.

For organizations without unions, this dilemma should strengthen the rationale for remaining nonunion. A primary reason why organizations maintain nonunion status is to give their supervisors freedom to manage their units without the unnecessary controls and restrictions inherent in third-party interventions. Nonunion supervisors should be reminded of the plight of their fellow supervisors in unionized locations, particularly those that have very restrictive work contracts.

When an organization does find itself with a new union, it should immediately consider the constraints placed on supervisors. It is in developing the initial agreement that many organizations unnecessarily complicate the supervisor's job. The contract should be brief, focusing on economic issues, if possible. Each part of the contract should be closely scrutinized to ensure that the supervisor's authority is not unnecessarily restricted. This is particularly important with the management rights clause. An example of an effective rights clause appears in Exhibit 8.

Obviously, the union will also have standard contracts that it will try to implement. For example, the union may argue that the supervisor should notify the shop steward about planned overtime. However, as the organization grows and overtime becomes routine, it may unnecessarily complicate the supervisor's job if he has to inform the shop steward each time. Alert management negotiators can prevent many future problems by keeping the contract trim and unrestrictive.

Exhibit 8. Sample Management Rights Clause.

Except as otherwise provided in this agreement, the company retains all the rights and functions of management that it has by law, the exercise of which shall not be subject to arbitration. Without limiting the generality of the preceding statement, these rights include:

   a. Direction and arrangement of work forces and the structure of the management organization of each unit, including the right to hire, suspend, discharge, transfer, and relieve employees from duty because of lack of work, or other legitimate reasons.
   b. Assignment of employees to specific jobs and making changes in the structure and content of jobs.
   c. Enforcement of work rules and regulations now in effect and those that may be issued from time to time.
   d. Disciplinary action for employees.
   e. Determination of products to be manufactured, work processes used, and services rendered.
   f. Location of the business, including establishment of new units, and the relocation or closing of old units.
   g. Determination of financial policies, including accounting procedures, inventory methods, and sales prices.
   h. Selection of employees for promotion to supervisory, managerial, and professional positions.
   i. Control and use of plant property.
   j. Determination of quality standards and procedures.
   k. Scheduling of operations, number of shifts, and work times.
   l. Right to subcontract work to outside vendors as management deems necessary.

It is further agreed that the preceding detailed enumerations of management rights shall in no way be deemed to exclude any other management prerogatives that may not have been specifically enumerated.

This philosophy should be part of all contract negotiations: Keep the supervisory authority base intact and keep the contract free of unnecessary complications. It is unlikely the union will strike over these issues if the organization remains firm in its approach. It is also not unthinkable to change an existing contract that seems to impose excessive controls on the supervisors or to mandate inefficient work practices. In recent years unions have been willing to listen to proposals to make organizations more efficient, even if this means giving up some rights they have negotiated in the past, provided that these proposals are presented with logical, reasonable arguments. The outcome of these negotiations may depend on the trust existing between the parties and the union's ability to understand how the practices in question unnecessarily restrict efficiency. This action should be an option for consideration during preparation for negotiations should changes in contract language be desired. The timing may be right for the union to accept the language changes.

Organizational Policies. Another group of constraints placed on supervisors are those that result from organizational policies. Personnel and human resources policies, which represent a major segment of these policies, are in place for every organization. In nonunion organizations they usually replace the labor agreement and are strictly enforced. Typical areas for these human resources policies include

employee selection	employee records
new employee orientation	equal employment opportunity
human resource development	and affirmative action
compensation	disciplinary action
employee benefits	safety and health issues
performance appraisal	general work rules

Other policies are developed and disseminated by staff support groups—for example, purchasing, technical services, and finance and accounting. In industrial settings, additional policies may originate from production control, engineering, quality assurance, and maintenance. These policies are sometimes developed with little or no regard to their potential impact on the supervisory group. They are usually developed in response to isolated problems involving a few supervisors. As a result, the entire supervisory group is punished for the actions of a few. This is not meant to imply that all policies are unnecessary or are developed without regard to the supervisor. However, in many cases, they could be far less restrictive while accomplishing the same ultimate result.

The way in which these organizational policies evolve deserves careful attention. For example, one organization was experimenting with company-wide group meetings for its employees, something the company had never practiced before.

The organization made the decision with little or no input from supervisors. First came an announcement encouraging supervisors to hold group meetings. When no meetings were held, the organization established a policy requiring one meeting each month. Still only a few meetings were held. Then the company required supervisors to document in detail what had happened in their meetings. This allowed top management to see who was having meetings and who was not. Many of the supervisors still did not conduct meetings, and eventually they were reprimanded or chastised for not following policy. These problems might have been avoided by training supervisors in the group-meeting process, showing them the results that could be achieved, encouraging them to participate in the process, and supporting their efforts. This would not necessarily guarantee success but would probably achieve more positive results than the other method.

What can the organization do about the policies that affect supervisors? First, there should be a review of the current status of policies that require supervisory input or place restrictions on supervisory actions. This review can be accomplished by asking six questions:

1. Why were the policies created?
2. What impact do they have on supervisory morale?
3. Do they improve or impede efficiency?
4. Are they necessary now?
5. What would happen if they were removed or changed?
6. How can they be removed or changed?

Frank answers to these questions can help determine whether policies should continue or be changed.

Second, the rationale for each policy should be explained so that supervisors can understand why it is necessary. Quite often, when supervisors know why something is needed, they will be more likely to perform the task willingly and with better results. In one organization the supervisor of customer service representatives had to furnish detailed information on customer reactions, customer complaints, and problems encountered.

This represented a significant portion of the job, yet the supervisor could see little or no use for the information that was being furnished. As a result, the task became very annoying to the supervisor, and the information he provided was usually incomplete. Eventually management discussed with the supervisor why the information was needed and how it was used. After this discussion the supervisor's attitude improved, and he consequently provided the information with little or no resistance and with more thoroughness than before.

Third, there must be a close working relationship between supervisors and the staff group developing policies. Each should have a clear understanding of the other's role. In one organization, supervisors spend time in staff support groups to see how the information is generated and why the policies are needed. Likewise, staff support employees spend time with line supervisors to understand the impact of their policies. This not only develops a better understanding of the process but improves the actual working relationship between the two groups. (Staff and line relationships are discussed further in Chapter Nine.)

Work Unit Constraints. Possibly the most important constraints affecting supervisors are those that immediately affect the work unit and the employees in the work unit. These include any constraints or obstacles in the immediate work environment that restrict or inhibit the supervisor's or employee's ability to perform their jobs effectively. According to O'Connor and others (1984, p. 92), these constraints can be grouped into the following categories:

1. lack of tools and equipment
2. unavailability of materials and supplies
3. inadequate preparation
4. improper work environment
5. lack of required services and assistance from others
6. lack of time to perform a task
7. lack of job-related information
8. inadequate budgetary support

Although these situational job constraints are being recognized increasingly as factors that limit improvements in productivity (Peters and O'Connor, 1980, p. 391), few organizations have yet implemented constraint reduction programs in order to improve productivity. The result is that employees become dissatisfied and frustrated, the supervisor experiences unnecessary stress, and the work unit's profitability and productivity suffer. One approach to improve the situation is to determine the value (or the average per-person gain in performance) that would occur if the constraint were reduced or removed. This figure is then converted to a dollar value. The next step is to estimate the number of employees who will be affected by reducing or removing the constraint and the length of time it will take for a positive impact to be realized. The third and final step is to determine the cost of alleviating the constraining condition. A cost-benefit analysis can then be performed to see if it is cost effective to make the change. Reductions in work constraints may represent a major undertaking for the organization but can have significant payoffs in improved productivity and profitability. It just might be the most fertile area for improving productivity in the organization.

Legal Controls. Finally, there have been an increasing number of laws and government regulations that have had a direct impact on supervisors, and the trend seems to be toward additional controls. Probably the most significant regulations are those dealing with fair employment practices. The Equal Employment Opportunity Act and Age Discrimination Act, as well as other federal and state laws and executive orders, have placed demands directly on supervisors. They must ensure that each personnel action—including selection, promotion, transfer, discharge, and performance appraisal—is accomplished without discrimination. Supervisors are frequently named in charges and suits involving violations of discrimination laws and regulations. Basic employment standards are outlined in the Fair Labor Standards Act, which sets restrictions on hours of work, minimum age for employment, and when and how overtime pay is calculated. Also, particularly for nonunion companies, the National Labor Relations Act covers employment practices and employee relations at the work place and lists a number of unfair labor practices that supervisors cannot engage in. There are many safety and health regulations contained in the Occupational Safety and Health Act and the Mine Safety and Health Act. These outline safety standards, reporting requirements, and controls on supervisors at the work place. Other laws may be more significant to a particular industry or organizational setting.

This section is not intended to explore the details of these various laws and regulations. The important point here is that organizations are experiencing more and more outside interference that has a direct impact on the supervisor's freedom to manage the work unit. There are differing arguments as to whether all these laws and regulations are necessary. Nevertheless, they do exist and supervisors must learn to live with them.

An organization must help supervisors develop a thorough understanding of all the laws and regulations that affect them. They must know what they should or should not do to comply with them. Organizations must by all means always adhere to the regulations, even if they are inconsistent with their philosophy. Otherwise, the organization may face heavy fines, adverse public reaction, and reduced employee morale. The penalties are too severe for organizations to ignore.

Another part of the strategy is to develop a productive relationship with the agency involved in administering the regulation. An effective working relationship can improve understanding of the law and remedy problems that may exist, particularly in gray areas where interpretation of the law is necessary. Some agencies are available on a consulting basis to help an organization comply with their regulations.

Finally, organizations should not give up in their attempts to change existing regulations or prevent further regulations. Most regulations are created with good intentions. They are designed to prevent problems, but, unfortunately, all organizations come to be penalized for the actions of a few. Businesses and industries, in particular, should examine themselves to ensure that they are doing their jobs properly, within a framework that is ethically and morally correct in society. Otherwise, additional regulations will be forthcoming. It is certainly proper for the organization to encourage supervisors to contact their elected officials to express their opinions about government regulations and to help prevent their proliferation in the future. Possibly if all organizations did this, many unnecessary regulations could be avoided, and supervisors would not have the problems they face now.

Summary

This chapter explored several important areas of decision making that have a significant impact on supervisory performance. The focus was on the freedom and ability of supervisors to make decisions. To improve supervisory decision making, the organization must

- Examine the formal decision-making process at the supervisory level to see if it needs improvement and if supervisors are prepared to make the decisions necessary to be successful on the job.
- Review the amount of authority granted supervisors to see if additional authority is in order.
- Analyze the constraints placed on supervision to see if they are excessive and, if so, explore ways to minimize their impact.

Lack of authority, coupled with unnecessary constraints, creates supervisory frustration and breeds inefficiencies. The mere possession of increased authority does not necessarily mean that supervisors will exercise it. But just knowing that they have the freedom to manage their units can have a positive impact on their performance.

Suggested Readings

Bittell, L. R. *What Every Supervisor Should Know.* (4th ed.) New York: McGraw-Hill, 1980.

Boyd, B. B. *Management-Minded Supervision.* (2nd ed.) New York: McGraw-Hill, 1976, 319–340.

Christenson, C., and others. *Supervising.* Reading, Mass.: Addison-Wesley, 1982, 218–241.

Engel, H. M. *How to Delegate: A Guide for Getting Things Done.* Houston: Gulf, 1983.

Keys, B., and Henshall, J. *Supervision.* New York: Wiley, 1984, 64–83.

Lewis, P. V. *Managing Human Relations.* Boston: Kent, 1983, 162–182.

Mondy, R. W., and others. *Supervision.* New York: Random House, 1983, 34–48.

Steinmetz, C. L., and Todd, H. R., Jr. *First-Line Management: Approaching Supervision Effectively.* (3rd ed.) Plano, Tex.: Business Publications, 1983, 78–101.

8

Participative Management:

Successful Programs Involving Supervisors

While the previous chapter focused on decision-making authority and ability, this chapter explores participative management, which is the process of involving employees at different levels in making decisions that affect their work area and jobs. The nature and extent of employee and supervisory involvement will be covered in this chapter. Participative management is practiced by everyone to a certain extent. The problem lies in determining how much participation is necessary or to what extent a lack of participation can be demotivating to supervisors.

Few managers will argue about the merits of participative management. Yet, in practice, many organizations are still reluctant to fully implement this process. Organizations usually want supervisors and their employees to contribute ideas and suggestions to make improvements, but formal approaches to accomplish this are sometimes missing. This chapter will focus on three major issues:

- The extent to which supervisors are allowed to participate in the major decisions affecting a department or division. Supervisors have much experience and ability and are valuable resources to top management in operational and strategic decisions.

- The extent to which supervisors are allowed to involve their employees in making the decisions that affect their work unit. Employees have many suggestions and ideas that can improve the quality of the decisions made at the work unit level.
- The role of the supervisor in the implementation and operation of various employee participation programs. These programs, which have gained increased acceptance in the 1970s and 1980s, bring new challenges to the supervisor.

Increased attention to participative management with supervisors can realize important benefits for the organization. First and most importantly, there should be better decisions made with input from the supervisor. Lack of participation in decisions makes supervisors less interested in improving productivity and quality. Many studies have shown that group participation can increase the quality of decisions (American Productivity Center, 1983a, p. 6). From a logical point of view, it makes sense to allow supervisors to participate in decisions that affect the employees, work processes, and procedures of their work unit. Almost every organization can uncover frightening examples of decisions made at the top of the organization—with no input from supervisors—that later proved impossible to implement. Possibly a new piece of equipment will not tie in with other equipment, employees are not prepared to administer a new procedure, or the decision has created a serious morale problem in the work unit. At this point it is usually too late to reverse course. The damage has been done to the bottom line or to employee morale or to both.

Second, increased involvement in decision making should improve supervisory morale, motivation, and identification with management. Very few things are more irritating to supervisors than having their suggestions ignored. They rightfully believe that they can make important and worthwhile contributions to the organization. Thus, to have their input ignored is demoralizing to them. Moreover, not permitting supervisors to more fully participate in decision making destroys an opportunity to give supervisors rewards that serve as powerful motivators. The act of participation is a reward. It provides a sense of achievement and accomplishment. Increased input into decisions will cause supervisors to identify more closely with management. They will feel that they are important, contributing members of management. This improved morale, increased motivation, and management identification not only helps supervisors but makes the job more attractive for prospective candidates.

Third, increased participation in decisions can prepare supervisors for future job opportunities. Decision making is an important skill for higher-level management jobs. Increased involvement in the decision-making process will prepare supervisors for more responsibility and expanded roles should they become available. One organization, for example, was faced with the dilemma of what to do with a very autocratic production manager who had responsibility for manufacturing a successful product line. He had achieved a reputation for low-cost performance and efficiency. In recent years, however, costs had begun to increase and the product line's profitability to deteriorate. Management felt that part of the problem was the manager's autocratic style. He ignored the input of his supervisors and never allowed them to be part of any decisions affecting the department. He told them what to do, when to do it, and how to do it. His philosophy filtered down throughout the department, and his supervisors ignored the input of their employees. Inefficiency began to creep in. The company therefore made an abrupt change by replacing the autocratic manager with one who was very participative in his management style and had been successful in another department. The new manager's philosophy was almost the exact opposite of the previous manager's. The new manager pushed decisions down to the lowest, most effective level and got his supervisors involved in most of the decisions affecting their department.

Having made this change, management anxiously waited for the results they had expected. Unfortunately, the performance of the organization continued to deteriorate. Costs increased and output slipped. The reason was pinpointed later in an analysis of the total operation: In the transition from one management style to another, the supervisors had not known how to change course. The new manager forced them to make decisions that they had not made before. They had never been asked to provide input so they did not know how to do it. They made many mistakes and had to learn through trial and error. Meanwhile, the department suffered. The autocratic management style had failed to develop supervisors who could assume additional responsibilities and adapt to changes in the organization. It is revealing that none of the supervisors in the department was considered as a potential replacement for the autocratic manager. They were not perceived as being strong leaders, which was probably a result of their lack of active involvement in the management of the department.

Finally, increased input into decisions will improve commitment to those decisions. Once a decision is made, the supervisor is charged with the responsibility of making it succeed. The supervisor must be deeply committed to implementing the decision successfully. Supervisory participation in the decision-making process increases "personal ownership" on the part of the supervisor and thus increases his or her determination to make a plan work. Responsibility for the decision gives the supervisor the satisfaction of knowing that something he or she has helped decide will make a significant difference in the organization. This increases loyalty to the organization and develops pride while ensuring that decisions are implemented successfully. Also, when employees below the supervisor level are allowed to participate in decisions affecting the work unit, their commitment is also increased.

For all these reasons, it is important for an organization to consider a more formal approach to participative management at the supervisory level and below. It may not be the answer to all problems—and there may be other approaches equally effective under the right circumstances—but it is a proven technique that can produce significant benefits for organizations.

Participative Management Fundamentals

Many organizations have turned to participative management techniques to help boost productivity and improve employee relations as well as to solve a variety of problems facing the organization. For some it was a timely move that produced favorable results. For others, participative management fell short of expectations and did not produce the desired results. This section explores the fundamental issues of participative management and how it works in organizations. Throughout this section, the focus shifts back and forth between the setting in which supervisors participate with managers to make decisions affecting the department to the setting in which employees participate in work unit decisions with supervisors.

Basic Concepts. The fundamental premise of participative management is that many employees want to share in the decision-making process and that they often have the ability to help develop better decisions. This process is a natural area of concentration for the supervisor. Supervision usually involves getting work done through other people, and employee involvement in decision making is an excellent way to help accomplish the work of the unit through the employees. The degree of participation allowed often reveals the leadership style of a manager or supervisor. Participative management is the opposite of autocratic management, which centralizes decision making and allows employees to have little or no input into decisions affecting the work unit.

When participative management is initially discussed with supervisors, they often develop unrealistic fears and misconceptions about the process. They fear that it may lead to some form of industrial democracy in which employees vote on issues. Industrial democracy has made significant strides in Europe, particularly in West Germany, where federal laws provide for codetermination, which allows employees to have approval over issues affecting the work unit and even the organization as a whole. In the United States, participative management rarely includes approval authority, and it does not circumvent any of the hierarchial levels of authority in the organization. Supervisors retain the control necessary to run their work units but receive valuable input from employees.

Status of Supervisory Participation. Sometimes top management has an illusion that participative management is functioning in an organization when it is not. Ask any chief executive if his or her organization practices participative management, and you will usually get a yes response without much hesitation. To think otherwise would almost be un-American. Top executives like to think that their organizations are managed in the most effective way, involving input from all levels of employees and, specifically, from supervisors. The problem lies in the extent to which the process is actually used. Even the most authority-oriented manager will hedge when questioned in this area. One conversation with an autocratic manager went something like this:

> *Question:* Do you practice participative management?
>
> *Response:* What do you mean?
>
> *Question:* Do you get your supervisors involved in the decisions affecting their jobs?
>
> *Response:* I always get information from the supervisors when I need it.
>
> *Question:* Do you always get them involved in important problems or decisions facing your department?
>
> *Response:* I get them involved when it's appropriate for them to be involved.

From that series of questions and responses, it is difficult to pinpoint the actual degree of participation on the part of the supervisors in the organization, although it is probably very small.

Because of the elusive nature of participative management, it is important for the organization to assess how well the process is working, particularly regarding the issue of supervisory participation. The quiz shown in Exhibit 9 provides useful input for determining the extent to which supervisors are participating in decisions affecting their work units. It is designed to be administered to supervisors and can be quickly completed and tabulated.

More detailed surveys than the one shown in Exhibit 9

Exhibit 9. A Quick Participation Quiz for Supervisors.

Place a T for true or an F for false by each of the statements below. If the statement is neither true nor false, pick the one that is closest to the correct answer. Please answer on the basis of the situation in your own organization.

_____ 1. I feel completely free to go to top management about decisions that affect my work unit.

_____ 2. The vast majority of authority and influence in this organization rests with top management.

_____ 3. Top management appreciates and uses our suggestions for improving the organization.

_____ 4. There is very little cooperation and teamwork in my department, division, and organization.

_____ 5. All the supervisors in my department (division) meet regularly to review the progress toward our goals and objectives.

_____ 6. I play an important part in making the decisions about important issues affecting my work unit.

_____ 7. Supervisors and other professional personnel are seldom asked for their opinions before decisions are made.

_____ 8. When a problem needs solving, a manager involves all the supervisors in the department to find a solution.

_____ 9. All the supervisors in my department (division) are committed to achieving the department's (division's) objectives.

_____ 10. Top management often makes decisions without explaining them to the supervisory group.

_____ 11. Major decisions affecting my work unit require my input before they are adopted.

_____ 12. Supervisors are encouraged to think for themselves and to suggest ways to improve the organization.

_____ 13. There is more independent effort than teamwork on the part of supervisors in this organization.

_____ 14. Supervisors receive regular feedback about their performance relative to their departmental objectives.

_____ 15. I feel that I am a part of the management of this organization because of the input I have into decision making.

Source: Adapted in part from a quiz developed by Velma Lashbrook that appeared in Juechter, 1982.

are available, and others could be easily developed specifically for an organization. However, this brief quiz can provide considerable insight into how participation is working in the organization, from those who should know best. The most desired answers are:

1.	T	6.	T	11.	T
2.	F	7.	F	12.	T
3.	T	8.	T	13.	F
4.	F	9.	T	14.	T
5.	T	10.	F	15.	T

Each correct answer is worth 1 point, giving a range of potential scores from 0 to 15. The results can be interpreted this way:

Score
Range   *Explanation*

13–15 *High participation.* This range indicates that participative management has been firmly established in the organization and that supervisors are closely involved in decisions that affect their work unit as well as the organization as a whole. Supervisory morale should be very high.

10–12 *Moderate participation.* This range indicates that participative management has made considerable progress in the organization but that there is still some room for improvement. Although supervisors are not involved to the fullest extent, participation is good and morale should be high.

7–9 *Some participation.* This range indicates the emergence of some efforts to initiate participative practices. But several areas need developing, and there is considerable room for improvement. Because supervisors are not utilized nearly to the extent they should be, their morale suffers.

4–6 *Low participation.* This range indicates a lack of appreciation for the input of supervisors and the values of participative management. Supervisory morale is probably very low. Major organizational pressures may be required to shift focus to more involvement from the supervisors.

0–3 *No participation.* This range probably does not exist in American organizations today. It would be difficult for an organization to be effective—or even survive—with this extreme lack of participation from supervisors.

Advantages of Participative Management. As briefly described earlier, there are several advantages to the participative management process. Although these will vary with the degree of participation, the employee relations climate in the company, and the types of decisions in which supervisors are involved, there are five important overall advantages:

1. *Better decisions.* Participative management enables managers and supervisors to utilize more resources and therefore increase the chances for better decisions. A climate of participation in the work unit can help break down the barriers to upward communication that exist in many organizations. This opens up an avenue of information that can enhance the quality of decisions. A skillful group leader, who has the ability to sort out good ideas from bad ones, can solicit meaningful input from employees. Quite often, employees in a work unit are more knowledgeable about work-related issues than the supervisor. To ignore this input is to forsake a powerful source of information that can make a tremendous difference when decisions are made. Exercises frequently used in management training programs vividly show how groups can achieve greater progress toward a goal than an individual manager or supervisor can. Many research efforts are available that show how the quality of decisions is improved through the group process when compared to independent actions (Croft, 1984).

2. *Increased acceptance.* Probably the most important advantage of participative management is that it improves acceptance of decisions by the group that must live with them. It is important to remember that the supervisor's responsibility in decision making does not stop when the decision has been made. It must be implemented successfully, and the biggest stumbling block to successful implementation is usually lack of acceptance by employees. Any action that can increase such acceptance will positively affect the outcome of the decision. Employees who have provided input will more readily accept the final decision even if they think it will have an adverse impact on them. Otherwise, they can cause the decision implementation to fail or to be much less effective than it could be.

3. *Increased creativity.* Participative management allows

the organization to tap the mind of virtually every employee. Working together, supervisors and employees can come up with innovative decisions. Many important, creative ideas have been the result of group input rather than of the independent thoughts of an individual.

4. *Increased employee motivation.* Participative management can raise morale and motivate employees. Participation in the various steps of the decision-making process provides an important source of job satisfaction and a new feeling of purpose and meaning in work. Supervisors like to feel that their ideas are important and are sought by the organization. When they regularly provide input into the problems and decisions of the work unit, they have a much greater feeling of identification with the company and with its goals and objectives. They develop a personal stake in the success of the department, division, and organization as a whole. Problems and decisions become the property of the work group, not of management. More difficult problems provide an ever-greater sense of satisfaction. Employees like to have a challenge, and solving a problem and successfully implementing the solution provides a meaningful sense of responsibility for them.

5. *Employee development.* A final important advantage of participative management is that employees learn and grow through the process. It provides them with an opportunity to utilize new skills and helps them to reach their maximum potential. They can also learn from other employees who are providing input. Participative management, when compared to "just taking orders," helps individuals to become more mature and responsible.

With all these advantages, organizations should logically place increased emphasis on participative management. Yet many of them are reluctant to share decision making with supervisors, let alone with all employees. But as productivity issues increasingly demand the attention of top executives, more emphasis will necessarily have to be placed on this important process.

Disadvantages of Participative Management. As with most other management processes, participative management has some disadvantages:

1. *Time.* When input is solicited from several people as opposed to an individual making a decision, there will be significantly more time involved. The amount of additional time will depend on the type of decision and the group discussion skills of the manager or supervisor. An unskilled group leader can waste precious time by letting employees discuss issues without providing meaningful input. However, participative management offers a potential time savings during the implementation phase of the decision. The time for communicating and implementing a decision should be shortened when employees have been involved. When they have not been involved, the decision must be thoroughly explained and, in some cases, even "sold" to the employees.

2. *Costs.* The participative management process may generate more costs than individual decision making. Because the employees' time is valuable, participative management can represent a significant cost to the organization. In addition, for many organizations it may result in lost production or output while the group provides input to help make the decision. This cost factor is important and must be considered before the process is encouraged. However, a more effective and better decision could easily outweigh the additional costs of the group decision-making process.

3. *Conflict avoidance.* In some group decision-making processes, a phenomenon known as *groupthink* may hinder the quality of the decision. Employees infected by groupthink are willing to reach a consensus at all costs in order to avoid conflicts. It is characteristic of cohesive groups whose members are very sensitive to the feelings of one another. For them, it is highly important to reach a consensus even if it is the wrong one. This process, if allowed to occur in a group, can lower the quality of the decisions made and defeat the purposes of participative management.

There may be other disadvantages to participative management in a particular setting or situation. However, these three disadvantages seem to be the most common ones. It is a process that offers much promise with only a few potential drawbacks. And these disadvantages, although important, should not prevent the organization from practicing participative management with supervisors or employees.

Implementing Participative Management

Participative management is always being practiced at least to some extent in all organizations. It is not a question of no participation or full participation. Figure 15 shows a scale of potential degrees of involvement in decision making. They range from one end of the scale, where there is no participation, to the other extreme, where the manager permits subordinates to function within limits they define themselves. The left side of the scale represents the autocratic style of management in which the manager makes the decision and announces it. There is little or no consideration of what subordinates may prefer or think about the decision. On the other side of the scale the manager has essentially delegated the decision-making process to the supervisors. This represents an extreme degree of group freedom that would probably not be found in a formal organization. In reality, an organization's practice will very likely be somewhere between these two extremes.

Another way to examine the degree of participation necessary is to analyze situations in which participation is crucial. The two primary aims of participative management are to improve the acceptance of the decision by those it will affect and to improve the quality of the decision. If the group leader is the most knowledgeable expert in the decision-making process, then it is important to have a high degree of input from the group leader, as well as from the employees, to keep the quality of the decision high. Also, when there is a high concern for acceptance, there must be a high degree of participation from members of the group. Figure 16 shows the trade-offs of different possibilities of quality and acceptance. One axis shows the concern for quality of the decision, while the other shows the concern for acceptance. When there is low concern for both, almost any convenient method of decision making would be ap-

Figure 15. Degrees of Participative Management.

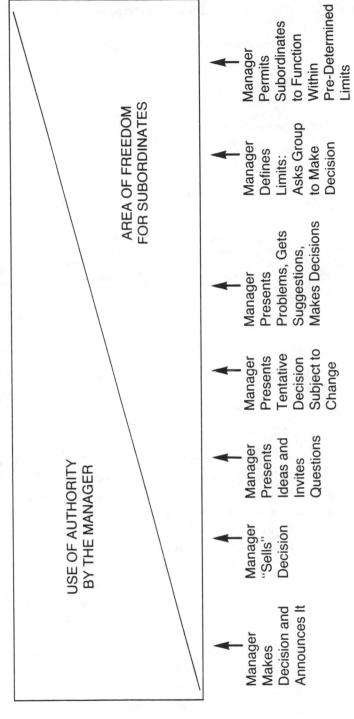

USE OF AUTHORITY
BY THE MANAGER

AREA OF FREEDOM
FOR SUBORDINATES

Manager
Makes
Decision and
Announces It

Manager
"Sells"
Decision

Manager
Presents
Ideas and
Invites
Questions

Manager
Presents
Tentative
Decision
Subject to
Change

Manager
Presents
Problems, Gets
Suggestions,
Makes Decisions

Manager
Defines
Limits:
Asks Group
to Make
Decision

Manager
Permits
Subordinates
to Function
Within
Pre-Determined
Limits

Source: Adapted from Tannenbaum and Schmidt, 1958, p. 97.

Figure 16. Preferred Decision-Making Approaches.

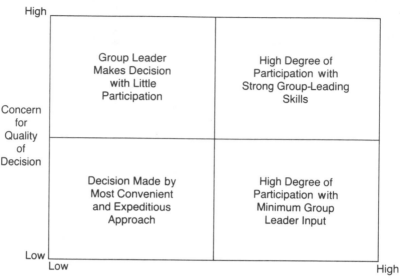

propriate. Conversely, when there is a high concern for both quality and acceptance, there should also be a high degree of participation with significant input from the group leader. This also requires a high degree of discussion-leading skills in the group leader.

When there is high concern for quality, but low concern for acceptance, there should be strong input from the group leader with minimal involvement of the employees. Possibly only the key employees should be involved, that is, those with the most information on the issue or problem. When there is high concern for acceptance and low concern for quality, there will be need for a high degree of participation wth minimum group leader control and input. It is important for all members of the group to contribute to the final decision even if it is not an optimal one.

Approaches to Participative Management. Just as there can be varying degrees of input by employees into the decision-making process, there are a variety of ways in which this input can be secured. Some of the most common approaches to participative management are outlined in the following paragraphs.

1. *Work unit meetings.* Routine meetings conducted by the supervisor provide an excellent environment for practicing participative management. Problems, decisions, and issues facing the work group can be thoroughly discussed and ample input secured from all members of the work unit. (These types of meetings were discussed in Chapter Six.) At the next level up in the organization, departmental meetings involving supervisors provide the same kind of atmosphere in which to solve problems facing the department.

2. *Committees.* Most organizations use committees to some extent. Committees come in many different formats with a variety of responsibilities. They are usually temporary in nature and allow employees to provide input, advice, and counsel to solve a problem, make a decision, or analyze the results of the work unit. Committees may function in a work unit or a department, or they may cross functional lines throughout the organization. Committees at the work unit level are typically involved in safety, quality control, productivity improvement, and equal employment opportunity issues.

3. *Brainstorming.* Once a problem has been identified and analyzed, brainstorming can be used to generate ideas that will help provide a solution to it. Group members are free to offer ideas without criticism, and no judgment is rendered on the quality of any of the suggestions. Employees are encouraged not only to contribute ideas but to suggest how other ideas can be turned into better ideas.

4. *Nominal grouping.* The nominal group technique allows group members to generate ideas by silently jotting down their thoughts about a specific issue, problem, or decision. There is no verbal interaction between the group members. After all the ideas have been solicited, they are integrated to generate a complete list. This list is then distributed to the group members, and they are asked to secretly vote for the five solutions that they think are most significant and should receive the highest priority. The data are then tabulated and presented to upper management. This approach lacks the interac-

tion that is characteristic of the other techniques, but it allows the group to focus on the issues without getting sidetracked by excessive discussion and other distractions.

5. *Delphi Technique.* Another approach similar to nominal grouping is the use of a Delphi technique to collect and tabulate the opinions from group members without discussion or debate. In this approach the individuals independently complete a questionnaire regarding the problem, issue, or decision. The questionnaires are tabulated and the information fed back to all the group members. Group members then fill out another round of questionnaires and receive additional feedback. This process is repeated until there seems to be significant agreement among the panel members. A final report is prepared to present the results of this process. This technique is best used to get a consensus of experts on the future direction of the organization or the markets and technology within which it operates.

These five techniques represent common ways a supervisor can secure input from employees. For additional information, see Lewis (1983, pp. 169-172). Other approaches to secure employee input are found in formal employee participation programs, which are discussed later in the chapter.

Target Areas for Participative Management. Although participative management is important to virtually every aspect of the supervisor's job, there are some areas where it is more important and necessary. The areas that can yield the greatest payoff for participative management are those that are important to both the organization *and* the members of the group. Typical target areas are (1) productivity improvement, (2) equipment purchases, (3) procedure changes, (4) work method changes, (5) work scheduling, (6) quality standards and control, (7) training and education needs, (8) organizational communication, (9) human resources programs, (10) employee benefit changes, and (11) union negotiations.

Conditions for Successful Implementation. The benefits of participative management outlined earlier are only potential benefits. They will not be realized unless participative management is successfully implemented and becomes a way of life in the organization. There are certain conditions that must be satisfied for this management practice to be successfully implemented:

1. *Information openness.* The organization must be open with its information, particularly with information needed to solve problems and make decisions. There must be a willingness to discuss this information with groups of supervisors or employees. An air of secrecy and extreme confidentiality will dampen the spirit and enthusiasm of those involved in the participative approach.

2. *Nonthreatening atmosphere.* Employees and supervisors must be allowed to voice opinions, give suggestions, and provide input without the threat of retaliation or criticism. Otherwise, employees will be reluctant to contribute to and participate in the process.

3. *Employee relations climate.* The overall climate in the organization must be good if implementation is to be successful. It will be difficult for participative management to work if there are serious problems with employee morale that show up in excessive complaints, grievances, turnover, absenteeism, and tardiness. This process is not a tool to change the organization. It is principally a technique to improve decision making and the acceptance of decisions. It cannot and will not correct major deficiencies in the employee relations climate.

4. *Limits of decisions.* The decision-making limits should be well defined. Obviously, the group cannot be allowed to alter work rules that affect other departments, change company policy, or modify union contracts. They must stay within predescribed limits, or their efforts will be fruitless.

5. *Employees' ability to make a contribution.* The basic premise of participative management is that employees have useful suggestions that can improve the quality of decisions. This assumes that they possess the skills, knowledge, and ability to make a meaningful contribution to the discussion. If they lack these prerequisites, the participative approach will become frustrating and appear to be hopeless. Employees may soon give up, realizing that they are unable to make a productive contribution.

6. *Employees' ability to communicate.* In addition to

having skills, knowledge and ability, employees must be able to express themselves in an understandable manner. In organizations where the educational level is very low and communication skills are weak, it may be difficult for employees to feel comfortable communicating their thoughts and ideas to higher management. Generally, the better the communication skills the employees have, the more workable the process will be.

7. *Timed implementation.* Participative management must be implemented on a gradual basis over an extended period of time, particularly if it represents a significant change in management practices. Employees resist change. The new process must be thoroughly explained, and employees or supervisors must see the advantages of their participation.

8. *Union cooperation.* Where participative management is practiced in unionized locations, a new element enters the picture. The extent of union cooperation can determine the success or failure of the new process. Unions are usually skeptical of an employee participation program. They see it as a threat to their existence and as a subtle way for organizations to try to remove unions or lessen their impact. If union cooperation turns into union resistance, the result could be disastrous. In the early stages of implementation, the union must be involved and thoroughly understand the process. This can reduce their resistance and might even secure their cooperation.

9. *Examples/role models.* Supervisors or managers charged with the responsibility to make participative management work at their level must see a demonstration of the process from their superiors. Top managers must serve as role models to show others how to make the process work effectively. They should practice, encourage, and reinforce the use of the participative approach. Even more importantly, supervisors need to see and hear about successful applications of the process at their level. Otherwise, they may wonder if the process is worthwhile and if it really works.

10. *Education and training.* Any successful implementation of participative management must include a means to prepare the individuals who will be involved in the process. Group leaders must be trained in discussion-leading skills. Ideally, they

should be able to practice these skills and learn how to effectively secure input from a varied group. They must be rewarded for successful applications of participative management and receive counseling and coaching when they fall short of management expectations. In addition, in some cases, it may be appropriate to train employees in how to provide meaningful input into group discussions. Lack of thorough preparation on the part of those involved will keep participative management from being as effective as it can be and cause frustration in those individuals who are responsible for making it work.

Supervisor and Employee Participation Programs

No chapter on participative management would be complete without a discussion of the growing number of employee participation programs in place throughout the United States. Their impact has been significant, and they represent an important challenge for the supervisor. The previous section outlined the conditions necessary to successfully implement participative management. The same conditions must exist for employee participation programs to work successfully. However, when formal programs are implemented for working-level employees, a new set of issues must be faced. Supervisors are sometimes unprepared for the changes that these participation programs involve. They may be skeptical about their purpose and may feel threatened by their existence. The supervisors' role often shifts from that of expert to that of listener. When supervisors are not involved in implementing programs in their work units, they may feel further threatened and see this exclusion as a vote of no confidence in their ability. As a result, they may react with increased skepticism and defensiveness. These problems can be overcome if the organization focuses on the supervisor's role when implementing these programs. This section briefly outlines the typical employee participation programs, the supervisor's role in these programs, and the preparation necessary for success.

Types of Programs. The most common type of worker participation program is the *quality circle* or *quality control circle.* Quality circles originated in Japan and were first reported in use in the United States in 1974 by the Lockheed Corporation. The purpose of the quality circle is to improve communication between employees and management and solve work-related problems. The members of the circle are usually employees who come from a common work area. The leaders are usually first-level supervisors. However, in a growing number of cases, one of the employees in the work group is chosen as the leader of the circle. The size of the groups varies but usually is between eight and twelve employees. The circle may define its own parameters, or they may be established by the organization. It usually focuses on work unit problems and deals with a wide range of concerns, including cost, productivity, quality improvement, and employee morale. Facilitators and coordinators of the program are usually trained, and sometimes the group members are too. They typically meet once a week and usually have no monetary incentives (Harmon, 1984). Quality circles are not limited to industrial settings. They have had widespread use with significant results in government, financial institutions, hospitals, and other service industries. Supervisors see them as effective in improving their relationship with employees, working conditions, quality of work, productivity, and employee performance (Zahra, 1984).

Following closely behind quality circles are the *quality of work life* (QWL) programs implemented to improve work environments and increase employee job satisfaction. QWL groups focus on issues such as job security, meaningful work, responsibility, participation in decision making, safety, and industrial health. Their primary goal is to make human labor both productive and meaningful. The QWL structure and the approaches used to accomplish group goals are similar in many ways to those characteristics found in quality circles. Supervisory participation is extremely important. Supervisors hold regular meetings with members of the QWL team. Goals are defined, and special facilitators (or supervisors) are trained to secure maximum input from employee. Although the approaches are of a "soft" nature, they have generated some hard results.

One study of twelve QWL programs reported results that ranged from substantial dollar savings and productivity improvements to reductions in absenteeism and turnover (Bernstein, 1983).

Some organizations have developed groups or teams to focus on *productivity improvement*. The format and structure of these teams are very flexible and vary with the organization. The worker participation programs typically focus on the cost of producing the product or the output of the work group. Some of these teams receive monetary incentives or a share of the cost savings. There are a number of standardized plans (Scanlon, Rucker, and Improshare, to name just a few) that have produced significant results in the organizations in which they have been implemented (Gorlin and Schein, 1984).

The variety of other programs is only limited by the creativity of the organizations that have implemented them. Some custom-designed programs have catchy names, such as the CHAMPS (Cooperative Hourly and Management Problem Solving) program at Reynolds Metal Company. The program at Koppers, called PRIDE (Productivity, Reliability, Innovation, Dedication, and Effort), recognizes employees whose ideas and extraordinary efforts make Koppers a better company. Regardless of the nature or scope of the programs, their primary aim is to improve the current state of affairs at the work plant. These improvements, however, can themselves generate problems for supervisors unless their role is clearly defined and they are given the proper preparation.

Supervisors' Role. In formal employee participation programs, supervisors have four distinct and important roles. First, they should be responsible for implementing the program in their work area. In many cases they are the initial group leaders, or at least they are the key individuals in the implementation. When quality circles became widely used in Japan in the early 1960s, the key individual was the foreman. It is important that supervisors have an active and important role in the process, otherwise it may undermine their supervisory role.

Second, supervisors need to be the experts on the mechanics of the participation program being implemented. They must understand how the program should work, why it was installed, and what results should be obtained. Supervisors should know the details of the program and be regarded as experts by the work unit.

Third, the supervisors must be supportive of the process. No major program of change will succeed without support of the supervisors. The degree of their participation, encouragement, and endorsement will be a key factor in whether or not employees are fully involved. This is a particularly critical issue when programs are conducted by individuals other than supervisors. In this case, supervisors may come to think that they have lost the confidence of management.

Finally, supervisors have a significant role in documenting the results. These programs are designed to secure results, and the only way the organization will know whether a particular program was a success is to document what has happened or what has changed as a result of it. The supervisor has important responsibilities in documenting measurable changes and tracking the program results.

Supervisors' Preparation. As with any other program, supervisors must be thoroughly prepared to make an employee participation program work. This involves three significant activities: initial indoctrination, involvement in the design, and special training. At the onset of a major change effort, supervisors should have an explanation of the organization's plans. This typically represents a sales pitch to supervisors to explain why the organization is placing emphasis in this area. It may be appropriate to test the climate with supervisors and even with employees to make sure that the organization is prepared for the program. It is important to show supervisors what results have been achieved in other organizations and what benefits they will receive as a result of the program.

The importance of the involvement of supervisors in the development of an employee participation program cannot be overemphasized. Among other things, this gives the supervisory group the chance to make helpful ideas and suggestions in the design of the program. If their input is ignored, however, they will not feel that they have a part in it and will not consider it to be their program.

The training provided for supervisors is very critical. Quite often, this new program will include a need for new skills, and, unless supervisors are prepared, the program may be doomed. They need to have their role specifically outlined, and the organization should tell the supervisors what is expected of them. In addition, the problems and successes of other organizations need to be clearly outlined. There is little need to learn through trial and error when similar organizations have tackled the same problem. Training in group-leading or conference discussion skills is one of the most important activities in the training phase. Many supervisors are not skilled at leading discussions and must sharpen these skills to achieve maximum results from the effort. Also, in some programs, helping skills need to be developed; that is, supervisors must be trained to give positive feedback, provide counseling, and resolve complaints and conflicts.

Organizational Support. Supervisors should be provided ample organizational support to ensure success for the effort. Direct assistance, guidance, advice, and counsel should be provided from staff support groups involved in the process. This typically includes departments that go under such names as human resource development, human resources and personnel, accounting and control, quality assurance, quality control, systems design, industrial engineering, and methods engineering. Depending on the nature of the program, other staff groups could be involved. The key role of staff support is to provide assistance as necessary to the supervisory group as it struggles with implementation. Supervisors need strong middle-management support to make the program successful. Managers must reinforce supervisors' efforts, let them know what the organization expects, and provide assistance. Also, top management support, public and private, will make it clear to supervisors that the organization is fully committed to the program. Finally, the organization must plan a measurement strategy so that results can be documented. In some cases, elaborate evaluation and measurement systems are developed, and data are collected through typical performance measures, attitude surveys, and participants' ratings.

Summary

This chapter explored several important areas of participative management, including the supervisor's role in employee participation programs. Fundamental concepts of participative management were introduced, along with the essential ingredients for successful implementation. Participative management is a proven approach to increase productivity, improve morale and job satisfaction, and enhance the working relationship between employees and supervisors. The organization is left with the challenge to

- Examine the formal processes for involving supervisors in decisions that affect their immediate environment and determine if changes are necessary.
- Assess the extent to which employees are allowed to participate in decisions impacting their jobs and encourage supervisors to tap this potential source of ideas.
- Ensure that supervisors are thoroughly involved in the development and implementation of formal employee participation programs such as quality circles, should they be introduced in the organization.

Few people will take issue with the merits of participative management. Yet it appears that this approach to decision making and problem solving is far from common practice in organizations. No doubt there is room for improvement in this area.

It may appear that some of the advice in this chapter contradicts previous advice. The last chapter recommended that organizations give supervisors more authority and influence while this chapter suggests that they yield some of their authority and influence to their employees through the participative decision-making process. But there is really no contradiction here. In any participative decision-making activity, at least as it is practiced in the United States, final authority still rests with the ranking member of the work group, in this case the supervisor. Although supervisors should secure input, suggestions, and ideas from employees, they have the ultimate authority to make decisions and to ensure that they are implemented effectively.

Suggested Readings

Bittel, L. R. *What Every Supervisor Should Know.* (4th ed.) New York: McGraw-Hill, 1980.

Blake, R. R., and Mouton, J. S. *Productivity: The Human Side.* New York: AMACOM, 1981.

Christenson, C., and others. *Supervising.* Reading, Mass.: Addison-Wesley, 1982, 218-241.

Duncan, W. J. *Organizational Behavior.* (2nd ed.) Boston: Houghton Mifflin, 1981, 163-213.

Ivancevich, J. M., and others. *Organizational Behavior and Performance.* Santa Monica, Calif.: Goodyear, 1977.

Nash, M. *Managing Organizational Performance.* San Francisco: Jossey-Bass, 1983, 255-334.

Ouchi, W. *Theory Z.* Reading, Mass.: Addison-Wesley, 1981.

Pascale, R. T., and Althos, A. G. *The Art of Japanese Management: Applications for American Executives.* New York: Simon & Schuster, 1981.

Reber, R. W., and Terry, G. E. *Behavioral Insights for Supervision.* Englewood Cliffs, N.J.: Prentice-Hall, 1975, 89-119.

Sasaki, N., and Hutchins, D. *The Japanese Approach to Product Quality: Its Applicability to the West.* Elmsford, N.Y.: Pergamon Press, 1984.

Schlesinger, L. A. *Quality of Work Life and the Supervisor.* New York: Praeger, 1982.

Shaw, M. E. *Group Dynamics: The Psychology of Small Group Behavior.* (2nd ed.) New York: McGraw-Hill, 1976.

Warrick, D. D., and Zawacki, R. A. *Supervisory Management.* New York: Harper & Row, 1984, 182-205.

Zander, A. *Making Groups Effective.* San Francisco: Jossey-Bass, 1983.

9

Organizational Support and Recognition:

Helping Supervisors Do Their Jobs Better

The support given by an organization to its supervisors is of great importance. It involves a variety of areas, and the degree to which each of these areas is appropriately addressed in an organization can have a significant bottom-line impact. Organizational support for supervisors focuses on five important issues:

- The degree to which the organization provides job security for supervisors and keeps them meaningfully employed during fluctuating periods of work. Supervisors represent important resources and should be made to feel that their jobs are secure as long as their performance is satisfactory and the organization can afford to keep them on the payroll.
- The manner in which supervisors are treated when they cannot perform satisfactorily and must be removed from their jobs. There are a variety of approaches to this sensitive issue that can both prevent damage to the organization and maintain the supervisor's self-esteem.
- The proper role of support services for supervisors. Much attention has recently been focused on the size, purpose, and

effectiveness of staff support groups. It is important for supervisors to receive genuine, helpful assistance from staff groups, and several effective approaches are available that can help the organization improve this support.

- The positive reinforcement and recognition provided to supervisors for accomplishing significant milestones or achievements or for performing in an exceptional manner. Supervisors, like any other group of employees, want recognition when they perform well. As a whole, organizations appear to lack adequate recognition programs for their supervisors.

- The extent to which supervisors are considered part of the management team. Management identification is necessary for supervisors to fulfill their role as management's representatives on the front line. Yet, in reality, a large number of supervisors identify more closely with their employees than with management.

Effective organizational support is needed for all employees regardless of their jobs. However, because of the unique role of supervisors and their potential impact on performance, organizations should focus extra attention on this group to ensure that it is provided with proper support.

Improved organizational support can have a positive impact on supervisory performance and on the attractiveness of the job itself. First, this support can increase the effectiveness of supervisors. Establishing cooperative relationships, improving job security, and providing recognition for accomplishments are factors that will enhance the supervisor's ability to perform in an exceptional manner. Few will argue that job insecurity hampers the effectiveness of any person. Recognition from the organization, including top and middle management, can be a powerful source of motivation for the supervisory group. (This chapter distinguishes recognition from performance appraisal, which was explored in Chapter Four.) Creating a harmonious, cooperative team can also improve the effectiveness of supervisors. Constant turmoil, conflict, and disagreement can do nothing more than create inefficiencies for the organization.

Second, improved organizational support can increase

supervisory job satisfaction and morale. Supervisors are special employees and must be treated that way. Positive reinforcement and recognition, improved job security, effective approaches to handle substandard performance, and management identification all help improve the job satisfaction of supervisors. Lacking these enhancements, they would be perceived as no more important than any other group of employees. Yet, as has been clearly demonstrated, their role is unique and their impact on the organization can be crucial. When the organization treats supervisors as indispensable members of the management team, there is an uplifting effect on the morale of the group. Its members feel good about their role in the organization and what they can accomplish.

Third, improved organizational support can increase the attractiveness of the job of supervisor. The status and success of the job in the future will depend on the quality of candidates attracted to the position. Other employees may aspire to become part of the management team when supervisors are clearly perceived as members of management and receive special attention. Positive reinforcement from the organization, especially from upper management, can also increase the attractiveness of the job. Employees want to be a part of something that clearly stands out in the organization.

Fourth, improved job security, coupled with more effective ways to deal with unsatisfactory performance, will reduce a supervisor's resistance to change. This resistance can reduce the organization's ability to adapt to changing markets in a competitive environment and to implement new products and services. Supervisors worried about their jobs will want to protect their own turf and will be reluctant to agree to any changes in their current work environment. They may see automation, new methods, and improved processes as ways to eliminate them or their jobs. Conversely, supervisors who are secure in their jobs will welcome innovation. They will see it as an opportunity to progress with the organization and help it succeed.

Finally, improved organizational support will increase the overall teamwork of the organization. It is important that supervisors work effectively with other members of management, and there must be a healthy, productive relationship between line functions and staff functions. Positive steps to improve or enhance the staff support provided to supervisors in the organization will result in a more cohesive group. Strong management identification, instilled in the minds of supervisors, will make them feel that they are part of management, and this in turn will build up the spirit of cooperation and teamwork needed for the success of the organization.

Improving Supervisory Job Security

Supervisors should not have to be overly concerned about job security. They have enough problems in carrying out their full range of responsibilities to worry about the stability of their future employment. Such concerns are amplified in an organization where there is an air of secrecy and a lack of information about future plans, goals, and problems facing the organization. When a decline in the organization is apparent, supervisors begin to worry about their fate. They reach conclusions based on how the organization has handled these situations in the past. If there have been unfair and inequitable applications of policies in times of layoff, concern over job insecurity will be even greater. Supervisors will see themselves as being powerless and having little or no control over their own destiny. This makes for a very unhealthy environment, and the best supervisors may leave the organization for one that is committed to preserving the continuity of employment, at least for supervisors.

Handling Supervisory Reductions. Organizations usually show their true colors during periods of economic downturn. Unfortunately, many supervisors are placed on temporary layoffs even though top management knows that the department, plant, or division will probably return to previous staffing levels in the near future. This short-term thinking can have disastrous long-term consequences. Many organizations speak of their commitment to protect supervisors from layoffs, but actions speak louder than words. Supervisors need to see convincing evidence that they will be retained during difficult periods. Although they resent it, nonmanagement employees, particularly those with very little seniority, may expect to be laid off as business turns down. Supervisors expect—and rightfully so—to remain employed during slumps. They want the organization to take care of them during this temporary period, and in the long run, the organization will be much better off if it preserves the continuity of the supervisory group. Supervisors represent a significant investment for the organization. Their effectiveness can be multiplied several times through their employees. They are valuable assets that should be retained during economic downturns. Some very prestigious organizations, including IBM, Delta Air Lines, and Hewlett-Packard, have adopted this approach. They do not consider retaining supervisors an extra expense but an investment in the future. Also, with today's cost of layoffs, retaining supervisors is becoming an attractive cost-savings alternative. Severance pay, higher unemployment compensation taxes, continuation of health and other benefits for a period of time after layoffs, administrative costs, and legal fees have staggering financial implications for organizations.

Obviously, there are some situations in which supervisory layoffs are necessary. An organization with serious problems and little or no hope of returning to previous employment levels may have to consider supervisory layoffs as part of the drastic restructuring necessary to keep the organization healthy. In this situation survival is the issue. Also, when there are plant closings, which may wipe out an entire work force, the organization may be left with few options for its supervisory group.

What is needed is a positive approach to find productive alternatives for supervisors during periods of displacement. This basically represents a full employment practice for supervisors without a binding policy statement. The possibilities are almost unlimited but usually can be grouped under one of the following general categories:

1. *Fill-in assignments.* Supervisors are used to fill in for other supervisors or other salaried employees in departments, sections, or plants unaffected by the temporary downturn. This is a common practice. These fill-in assignments cover normal va-

cancies created by vacations, jury duty, sick leave, or other significant time-off periods. This practice requires advance planning and the cooperation of other sections, which can usually be obtained.

2. *Alternate work assignments.* Supervisors are used to perform needed work assignments such as maintenance, repair, or cleanup. One firm uses supervisors during downturns to conduct audits, tabulate inventory, or perform other necessary accounting and control functions. Another firm places supervisors over work crews to repaint all facilities, something that must be done periodically anyway.

3. *Special projects.* Supervisors are used on special projects where their assistance is not essential but can be very beneficial to the organization. Examples of these projects include analyzing a persistent quality control problem, solving a work flow bottleneck in the department, assisting a sales representative in handling a customer complaint or in improving customer relations, and assisting the engineering group on design or redesign projects. These are not make-work assignments, but projects to which supervisors can make meaningful contributions.

4. *Training.* Supervisors take part in training activities to improve their skills and increase their knowledge in areas that will be helpful for them in their jobs in the future. These activities may include formal classroom training as well as on-the-job training in other departments and sections of the organization. One organization increased the staff of its training department so that it could provide a full array of training programs for supervisors during an economic downturn. These programs had been planned for a future date, but their implementation was stepped up to take advantage of the idle time of the supervisory group.

5. *Eliminate subcontracting and temporary employees.* Functions that can be performed by the current work force and are now being subcontracted can possibly be redirected to the internal work force. Also, temporary employees can be eliminated to make work for the permanent employees. The ease with which this can be accomplished depends on the commitments made when subcontracting was planned or temporary

employees were hired. One major manufacturer subcontracts entire support functions during peak times and brings them in-house during slumps.

6. *Outside activities.* Supervisors are assigned to worth-while community and public service assignments. One organiza-tion loans supervisors to a health care agency while another pro-vides supervisors to assist local government in their field of expertise. Charitable fund drives such as the United Way, as well as public service campaigns, are another source of useful activity for displaced supervisors. They not only provide meaningful assignments but give the organization favorable public and com-munity relations exposure.

7. *Retirement or extended vacations.* Letting supervisors use all their accumulated vacation time is a very simple and workable alternative to layoffs. If it is is feasible, giving them additional vacation time, in advance, may also be appropriate. From the supervisor's viewpoint, these are certainly better alter-natives than being laid off without pay. Also, for those who are eligible, increased incentives for early retirement may be appro-priate. Many organizations have given bonuses for a specified time period to allow older employees an opportunity to retire early with more pay than they would otherwise receive. How-ever, the trend toward early retirement has been reversed due to the Age Discrimination Act, inflation, and increased uncertainty about the Social Security system and the economy. Because of this, early retirement of supervisors may not be a viable option for some organizations.

8. *Relocation.* A final approach is to move displaced su-pervisors to other locations. Relocation has become very expen-sive, however, averaging somewhere in the range of $30 to $40 thousand for each family moved. It may be too expensive for the organization to relocate large numbers of supervisors. How-ever, for key supervisors with long service records, this cost may be an investment in the future, since these valuable employees will very likely make significant contributions at another location.

With some creativity organizations can usually find useful or productive alternatives to a reduction of the supervisory work force. This will keep supervisors on the payroll, making a contribution or learning something new, while they wait for their previous jobs to return. They will represent a prepared supervisory team ready for a new challenge as soon as the work load increases. Without the continuity of an intact supervisory group, much of the capability of the organization will be lost, and it will not have the loyalty and commitment of supervisors in the future. But one caution is in order: An organization must be careful not to assign supervisors to perform work that is normally done by hourly employees when there are restrictions on this activity. Some union contracts specifically prohibit supervisors from performing bargaining unit work.

Handling Prior Work Unit Seniority. For supervisors promoted from within the work unit there is another important job security issue: departmental seniority. This is particularly important for industrial concerns in which seniority is a major factor in promotions, layoffs, and transfers and employees with the most seniority are sometimes promoted to supervisory jobs. Supervisors accepting a promotion from within the work group will naturally wonder what will happen to them if they are unable to perform the job satisfactorily. Many of them would like to be able to move back to their previous jobs. Unfortunately, this may not be an attractive alternative if there are restrictions on how seniority is treated after promotion to a supervisory position. Consider this situation: A company's union agreement calls for the loss of departmental seniority for any employee promoted to a supervisory job. The employee with the most seniority is promoted to supervisor but for some reason cannot perform the job satisfactorily. The employee has a long service career with the company and wants to return to his old job. Yet, according to the seniority rules, the supervisor would go back to the work unit without any departmental seniority. The first reduction in the work force would mean the former supervisor might face layoff. Obviously this situation would be detrimental to the organization and to the employee. Supervisors should have the security of knowing that they can return to their old jobs if their venture into management is not successful. This approach can help attract top-notch employees who otherwise might not want to give up their seniority to become part of the management group.

An organization facing this issue has four basic alternatives. First, it can simply allow departmental seniority to be lost when employees are promoted to supervision. But, as the example in the preceding paragraph illustrates, this is the least attractive approach and one that can cause severe problems for the organization. Often unions prefer this approach because they look upon employees promoted from the bargaining unit to management as traitors who have turned against their fellow union members. They feel no obligation to restore their seniority and provide them with rights over employees who remained in the work unit.

Second, departmental seniority can be retained for a set period of time, usually six months or one year. If the supervisor remains in the job after that time, seniority is lost. This provides a probationary period and allows newly promoted employees an opportunity to get a feel for their jobs. Before the end of this period, supervisors may return to their previous jobs without losing seniority. One problem with this approach is that the probationary period may not be long enough. Also, supervisors may have to be returned to their previous jobs at a later time through no fault of their own. In this case supervisors still suffer unnecessary hardships because of the loss of departmental seniority.

Third, departmental seniority can be frozen at the time of promotion. This seems to be a fair approach in that supervisors retain previous departmental seniority if they return to their old jobs in the work unit. From a seniority viewpoint, nothing is gained and nothing is lost in their move to supervision.

Finally, departmental seniority can be allowed to accumulate while the employee is in the supervisory job. While this approach is the best one for the supervisor and probably for the organization, it is difficult to get unions to agree to this type of seniority arrangement. When it becomes a reality, however, supervisors gain an added sense of security from knowing that they are accumulating department seniority in case they need or want to return to their old jobs. This is an ideal situation that should be the goal of organizations in their collective bargaining agreements.

The question facing many companies, however, is what to do about the current situation. Obviously if there are no contract restrictions, as in a nonunion company, it is relatively easy to change the current seniority arrangement to one that is more attractive for supervisory promotions. Unfortunately, some organizations are bound by very restrictive labor contracts that prohibit reinstating prior seniority to supervisors who are placed back in the bargaining unit. This restriction may well be an important item to include on the agenda for the next negotiations. Sometimes a union negotiating team will agree to management proposals for changes in seniority rules. After all, some members of that team may want to become supervisors in the future. By all means the organization should resist any future efforts to restrict provisions for reinstating seniority to employees promoted out of the bargaining unit.

Communicating Job Security. Providing information about job security is almost as important as the practices adopted by the organization to relieve job insecurity. Supervisors should know what to expect of the organization, particularly during a downturn. In addition they should know how the organization plans for peak work loads that may affect employment stability in the future. Several approaches to communication may be appropriate. The organization should consider developing and publishing a statement of policy regarding supervisory layoffs. If the practice of the organization is to plan and schedule work so that supervisory layoffs are avoided, then supervisors should know this. Such a policy statement should be carefully worded so that it does not represent a binding employment contract unless that is the intention. Some type of policy statement can probably do more to boost morale of the supervisory group than any other single action regarding job security. Also, some organizations have developed handbooks or manuals exclusively for supervisors. Statements or explanations of job security may be appropriate for these documents. In addition, personnel and human resources policy and procedure manuals should contain information about how supervisors will be treated during downturns or reductions in the work force.

Job security should be discussed at the time of promotion. This should be highlighted as a benefit for assuming the supervisory assignment. The manager and/or human resources executive should explain the policy and what it means to the supervisor. Examples of what might happen to the supervisor should there be a downturn would be very helpful, particularly if they were compared to what might happen if the supervisor remained in his or her previous job.

When a reduction is inevitable, it is important to discuss its implications with supervisors. Management should address the issue of lack of work and, specifically, what courses of action will be taken as the work load decreases. This can help remove the anxieties of supervisors. When they know they are secure, they can focus their attention on what to do with the remainder of the work force. The importance of taking this action cannot be overemphasized. Nothing is more demoralizing to an organization than for management to remain silent on the destiny of supervisors when a cutback has become necessary. The best supervisors may leave the organization while the others may simply give up.

Confronting Substandard Performance

Not all supervisors can or will succeed in their jobs. Inevitably there will be those whose performance is unacceptable or whose dissatisfaction with their jobs is so obvious that it becomes detrimental to employee morale and the organization. It is important for the organization to respond quickly to this situation because of the impact that supervisors can have on the performance of the organization and on the employees they supervise. Their visibility is high. They set an example for others, and in many cases they are role models for prospective supervisory candidates. Their ineffectiveness cannot be tolerated and must be confronted early.

Possibly this issue could be settled through better supervisory selection and training. Chapter Two outlined the problems that can result from a poor selection of supervisory candidates. In addition, it presented a number of approaches that can help ensure that the right candidate is selected for the job. Chapter Three outlined the requirements of successful supervisory training programs and showed how important it is to build skills in supervisors early so that they can gain the confidence they need on the job. Sometimes a lack of training at or near the time of promotion can be the precipitating cause of a supervisor's failure.

When a supervisor's performance does not meet expectations, the organization should immediately provide counseling by the middle manager, with possibly some assistance from the human resources staff. This may provide the incentive for the supervisor to improve or correct deficiencies in his or her skills. Continuous coaching from the middle manager may be necessary to build the supervisor's confidence. These managers are in the best position to assess performance and discuss how the supervisor may change to improve performance in the future.

When it becomes obvious that the problem cannot be corrected, the organization can take a variety of approaches to remove the supervisor from the job. There are several important considerations in selecting the approach. First, action should be taken as soon as possible. Too many times ineffective supervisors are allowed to flounder and sink, destroying themselves and their work unit in the process. Second, the dignity and self-esteem of the supervisor should be maintained, particularly if part of the responsibility for failure rests with management. Third, the organization must keep in mind that other supervisors, as well as potential supervisors in the organization, will be watching closely. If the substandard performance of a supervisor is obvious to the others, they will usually want their organization to take action to correct the problem. They do not want an ineffective supervisor to drain the organization. Conversely, they would like to see a fellow supervisor treated humanely and fairly because they may fear that they will be in a similar situation in the future.

There are seven basic approaches to this question:

1. *Discharge.* Although this is presented first, it is the least desired approach. In fact, however, this action is taken by far too many organizations when faced with poor performance. Supervisors are discharged and placed on the street even though they may have many years of experience and may have been wrongfully placed in a supervisor's job. This solution should be used as a last resort when no other alternatives will work. However, if the reason for removing a supervisor is serious enough, then discharge may be the appropriate action. For example, if the supervisor is guilty of dishonesty or illegal activities, then discharge may be the only alternative open to the organization. Also, when the supervisor has tried but lacks the required skills or ability for the job and cannot be logically fitted into the other approaches, then discharge may be the best course of action.

2. *Lateral transfer to another department.* Depending on the reason for his or her poor performance, a lateral transfer to another department could be an appropriate approach to salvaging an ineffective supervisor. Problems in adjusting to a particular management style, getting along with the employees in a work unit, or cooperating with peer groups could possibly be resolved with a transfer to another section or location. In one organization, a supervisor was having a difficult time adjusting to an autocratic manager. He was unable to please his boss, although, according to others, he had the potential to make a good supervisor. He was transferred to another department with a manager who had a different leadership style. As a result, he was successful in the new assignment. This approach needs to be carefully examined to ensure that the supervisor can succeed in the new location. Whatever caused the failure may surface again. However, a change from a distasteful situation can sometimes spark a renewed determination to succeed in a new assignment; the person involved may feel that this is his last chance to make it in supervision.

3. *Transfer to a nonsupervisory professional job.* Supervisors with the necessary expertise might be transferred to a professional assignment. If the substandard performance was the result of the supervisor's inability to lead and motivate employees,

then a professional nonsupervisory job, where there are no employees to be supervised, might be an appropriate alternative. In one company a data-processing specialist was promoted to supervisor of computer operations. When she failed to succeed on the job, she was transferred to a programming assignment where she was not required to supervise employees. The new assignment was an important one, and her loss of status was minimal. The employee was able to maintain her confidence and did not feel that she had been damaged by the experience of failing in supervision.

4. *Demotion to the previous job.* Another approach is to send supervisors back to their old jobs. Although this approach is usually not recommended, it can be appropriate for certain situations. Supervisors may ask to return, and sometimes they can do so gracefully without damaging the organization or other employees. An important concern is the attitude of the supervisor. A poor attitude may lower the morale of the work group and damage the organization. In one organization an experienced machinist asked to be moved back to his old job after an unsuccessful try as supervisor. The employee was given his old assignment and was even congratulated on his efforts in the supervisory assignment. In this case the department manager made a point of recognizing the long service of the employee and discussing how he could help as a machinist. The former supervisor brought an excellent attitude to a situation that could have been very distasteful.

5. *Demotion to another department.* Sometimes it is better to consider placing supervisors in another department and not back in their old work unit. This is particularly appropriate if a supervisor will feel embarrassed and humiliated to return to his old work unit after failing in the supervisory role. When moving to a new group, even though in a similar job, the former supervisor can start fresh with renewed dedication. In one case, a quality control inspector was promoted to inspection supervisor and failed on the job. Instead of discussing alternatives, he asked to be allowed to go back to his former job. But the organization saw the possibility of adjustment problems and so placed the former supervisor back into the same job but in an-

other plant. The impact of this transition on the individual was minimal.

6. *Prepare for a new job.* A somewhat expensive approach is to prepare the supervisor for another job in the organization. This may not be practical because of the educational costs involved. However, it may be appropriate for supervisors with long service records who could make valuable contributions in another job if they had the necessary skills. In one organization an engineer was promoted to plant-engineering supervisor, failed in the assignment, and then assumed the job of technical buyer in the purchasing department after completing a comprehensive course on purchasing policies and practices. This was considered a better approach than moving the engineer back into an engineering slot in his former department. The employee brought much-needed skills and knowledge about the technical aspects of the items he would be responsible for purchasing.

7. *Outplacement.* A growing trend in many organizations is to provide outplacement services to supervisors who cannot function in the job. This includes assistance in finding another job, counseling and coaching in job-hunting skills, and in some cases providing the travel allowances needed to conduct a job search. This may be appropriate for long-service supervisors whose ineffectiveness in the job was so serious as to preclude other internal placement possibilities. Removal is then in the best interest of the individual as well as of the organization, yet the organization may still want to provide assistance. In one example a nursing supervisor was provided outplacement assistance when she failed in her assignment. Her ineffectiveness and dissatisfaction with the organization, as she struggled with the supervisory assignment, left the organization with no alternative but to remove her entirely. It was felt she would be detrimental if she remained, and outplacement was the best alternative available. She was provided assistance in relocating and found a job at another hospital. The transition left both the individual and the organization with positive feelings about the way the situation was handled.

Improving Staff Support for Supervisors

In order to discuss the role of staff support and analyze its impact on supervisors, two definitions are in order. *Line* functions in an organization are those that are directly concerned with obtaining the organization's goals or objectives. Without them there is no organization. In a manufacturing firm, production and sales are the two line functions. *Staff* functions in an organization are those that are indirectly concerned with achieving the organization's goals and objectives. They assist, support, or help the line functions. Examples of staff functions include accounting, human resources, industrial engineering, purchasing, facilities services, production control, data processing, and office services. Accounting would be considered by many to be an essential part of a manufacturing firm. However, it is not *absolutely* necessary for the firm's existence.

What is line for one organization may be staff for another. In a hospital complex the line functions might be the nursing activities. In a manufacturing firm, the medical department, which might be staffed with nurses, would be considered a staff department. In some organizations, of course, it is difficult to distinguish between line and staff. Also, many of the staff functions actually support other staff functions as well as the line function. The human resources development (HRD) department (a staff department) may develop as many training programs for staff support employees as it does for line employees. To make a fine distinction between the two groups might imply that the HRD department serves only one group. However, since there is a distinction between the groups in most organizations and the staff function's *primary* role is to help line organizations, the distinction will be retained in this chapter. Also, staff will be described in its role of supporting supervisors. These supervisors may work in the line organization or be supervisors of staff functions.

Staff support functions exist in almost every type and size of organization. Even a small office with five sales representatives will have a staff support person, typically a secretary or office manager. There is nothing wrong with having staff. In an effective organization, both line and staff are necessary. Problems surface when the staff is not fulfilling its intended purpose, particularly if it is not supporting supervisors the way it should. All staff functions are created with good intentions. But somewhere along the line many of them—but not all—grow too large or become ineffective. Staff groups are designed to provide service, assistance, information, advice, change, control, and auditing. All these functions are useful, and they have logical and productive places in organizations. However, a number of problems can develop when staffs discharge these functions.

Problems with Staff Groups. These problems, which have evolved gradually, have created serious problems in some organizations. Ineffective, misdirected staff support can be detrimental to supervisors and can even deal a fatal blow to an organization in today's competitive environment. These problems do not exist in every organization, but organizations should not wait for them to occur. They may develop when there is a change in organizational purpose, particularly if supervisors look upon the change as unnecessary. Supervisors usually welcome the services performed by staff groups unless they think they can perform them more efficiently themselves. Supervisors also usually respond well to staff support if they think it is helpful and if they can decide whether or not to seek it. But staff functions can easily create ill feelings when they are forced on the supervisor. This problem reaches serious proportions when a staff group goes from giving advice to exercising control or when a permanent service department is established and the supervisor has little control over that service.

Too often staff support groups continue to grow in size without having any apparent effect on the success or profitability of the organization. Staff support groups begin to depend on each other. They generate forms and procedures and have meetings with each other. One staff support group is used to justify the existence of another. Staffs can easily grow out of proportion and add greatly to the overhead of the organization. Also, as staff support groups grow, so does the unnecessary burden placed on supervisors and managers. In some way or another they must spend time with the staff group because it generates requests, paper work, procedures, plans, or policies.

Staff support employees have a unique role. They must be expert at what they do to win the respect and credibility of the line organization. In too many cases, however, incompetent, misdirected staff members have destroyed the credibility of the staff function and reduced the effectiveness of the organization. Supervisors expect staff support personnel to be professionals and provide services and assistance as outlined in their initial charter. Anything short of excellence in their conduct will hinder the staff's ability to function effectively in the organization. Fortunately, it is not uncommon to find productive working relationships between supervisors and their staff support personnel. Where this exists, it is usually the result of a very capable staff's perceiving its role properly and developing an effective relationship with supervisors and managers, particularly those in the line organization.

Fundamental misunderstandings about each other's roles, function, purpose, jobs, and working environment can lead to problems between staff support employees and the groups they must support. Supervisors, particularly line supervisors, do not always have an understanding of why staff functions exist. There may be little explanation when additional staff is added and no communication when the staff's responsibility and influence are increased. Supervisors have very little opportunity to see what is done by the staff organizations and the end use of the staff efforts. Often, supervisors feel that staff members should be the first to go in a layoff. In addition, little information or counsel is given on how the two groups should work together. Staff specialists have little understanding of what impact they have on the supervisors they support, and they do not always understand the frustrations and anxieties of the supervisor's job. This lack of understanding on both sides—staff and line—results in an inhibiting and sometimes discouraging atmosphere that can lead to a decline in organizational effectiveness.

Because of these problems, staff groups have difficulty in working with the supervisors they are supposed to support. Line and staff conflicts have become a way of life in many organizations. Although some of it occurs naturally because of the conflicting goals of different groups, there is no reason for an organization to accept anything short of productive working relationships. The next section focuses on solutions to the problems of staff groups, how staff can support supervisors, and how conflicts can be resolved.

Solutions to Staff Support Problems. Most will agree that there is a need to achieve productive relationships between staff support groups and supervisors, but specific approaches to the problem are not always undertaken. Most organizations rely on common goals and the inherent ability of supervisors and staff to achieve the desired levels of effective support. But this may be short of what is needed. Organizations may need to examine the quality and appropriateness of support services to see if improvements are in order. The following actions are workable solutions to staff problems:

1. *Staff function review.* The organization should periodically review staff functions to see if their role is consistent with what was intended or what is proper in today's environment. Possibly a staff support function that provides control could be changed to one that provides advice or auditing. An effective way to accomplish this staff review is to list all the staff functions and indicate the initial reasons for their creation. Next, indicate the types of roles that the staff is currently seen as fulfilling. Third, list the roles that the organization prefers the staff to undertake in the future. If it is found that either the perceived role or intended role is different from the preferred role, changes will be necessary in staff functions.

2. *Staff performance appraisal.* Another approach to improving the effectiveness of staff groups is to have their performance appraisals and salary increases determined to a certain extent by the supervisors and managers whom they support or serve. This involves securing a performance rating or assessment of the staff group from a supervisor who receives support from it. This performance rating can serve as the basis for the performance appraisal or be used as one input into the overall ap-

praisal of an individual staff member. In addition, this could help determine the next salary increase for the staff group.

If staff support personnel know that their future career and potential salary increases will be determined by those they are supporting or serving, they are likely to provide better support. Unfortunately, prejudiced supervisors could easily use this technique to destroy an individual rather than help improve staff services. In some situations, where staff and line must work closely together, the evaluation process could be two-way. However, in most settings, two-way evaluations are not practical since staff support is there to serve the line organization at its pleasure.

As an alternative, supervisors could be asked to provide a performance rating of an entire staff group—a rating that would then reflect the performance of the entire group and could possibly influence the amount of salary increase it receives. Opponents of this process will argue that the supervisors and managers of other departments do not always know if staff support employees are doing a good job. While this may be a valid argument, such managers and supervisors certainly should know the value of the support provided to their own work unit. When a staff support person is seen as ineffective or his support is considered useless to the work unit, then a problem exists that must be rectified. The process described here will certainly bring it into focus and direct the proper attention to it.

3. *Staff location.* The location of the staff can make a significant difference in its effectiveness. There are two issues here: one is the staff's physical location and the other is its position in the organizational structure. Physically, the staff should be housed near the division, department, or plant it serves. Ideally, it should be housed in the same building with the groups it supports. Townsend (1984, p. 229) tells the story of the corporate office expansion at Avis. For years, while he was chairman, he kept the headquarters staff housed in 30,000 feet of floor space in one building. Eventually, but with much hesitation and only after much insistence from his executives, he decided to let several units move outside the main headquarters building into neighboring buildings. But Townsend only let a

profit center move, not a staff support group. As he states, if accounting ever moved out, it might "take out [its] frustration in empire building before you realize what's happening." The position of the staff support functions on the organizational chart is another important issue. In a typical organizational structure, many decentralized units have staff support groups that report to a plant manager, division manager, or division president. These staff support groups may have indirect-reporting relationships to corporate office staff counterparts but receive their direction and leadership from a local executive. This helps ensure that staff employees focus on their role of supporting the other groups, particularly the line supervisors.

4. *Selection standards for staff employees.* Staff employees must be effective at their jobs if they are to be successful. They must build credibility and respect among their "clients." This may require an organization to adopt high standards for people who move into staff support functions. They must possess not only the technical skills necessary for the staff specialty but also good communication and interpersonal skills. It is unfortunately true, however, that overly aggressive and ambitious employees can turn staff departments into fiefdoms. Staff employees should not be authority oriented but should focus on influencing others through their knowledge and expertise.

5. *Improving communication.* Many of the problems of staff groups come from a simple lack of understanding of the roles of line and staff, with both groups sharing the blame. The typical line viewpoint of staff members is that

- they are ineffective and do not know what they are doing
- their advice and counsel are not very useful
- they delegate blame while trying to grab credit for everything that is done
- they fail to communicate and keep the line and organization informed
- they fail to see the overall objectives of the organization

At the same time, staff groups say of members of the line organization that

- they do not understand the reasons for the staff function
- they do not utilize staff services effectively
- they resist any new ideas or changes in the organization
- they do not get staff involved in problems and issues when they should be involved
- they do not give the staff enough authority to accomplish its objectives

Some of these misconceptions on both sides can be overcome through positive attempts to communicate the role and function of each. Organizations must communicate the role of staff groups and encourage staff and line organizations to work closely together to achieve common organizational goals. When the staff's role is changed, the nature of that change should be made known to the organization with proper explanations. Information about staff expansions or reductions should be given, along with reasons for the actions. Staff departments should be made aware of the problems they create for the supervisors whom they support. Plans and programs initiated by staff groups need to be carefully explained to the supervisors and managers who will be affected by them. Supervisory meetings to discuss the relation between line and staff and the role of staff departments may be appropriate.

6. *Staff measurement systems.* When management by objectives (MBO) was first implemented, it was primarily aimed at essential line functions. Measurement of success was relatively easy for these functions. As MBO became more successful and measurement systems more sophisticated, however, the process spread to staff support groups. The implementation of MBO for staff groups can help improve staff services and the relation between line and staff. With measurable goals and objectives, the organization, including line supervisors, can readily determine the staff's accomplishments, and the staff can be held accountable for results.

It is possible to achieve much success with this approach, and measurement systems can be developed for virtually every staff function. An interesting example involves IBM's approach to staff measurement (Charon and Schlumpf, 1981, p. 8). Their

approach, called common staffing systems or functional performance systems, measures differences in productivity over time
and between the same functions in different organizational
units within IBM. The system was designed with the following
parameters:

- It had to be simple and understandable.
- It had to be seen as a management aid.
- It had to enable comparisons between units.
- It had to have a sound data base structured to permit track-
  ing over time.
- It had to identify efficient and effective areas of perfor-
  mance.
- It had to measure work load in meaningful terms.

The first problem was to prepare descriptions of all the
tasks performed. IBM identified fourteen general functions that
would be measured, including personnel, finance, production
control, procurement, general services, and facilities services.
For each of the functions, a group of activities was identified.
They ranged from as few as 4 in some functions to as many as
17 for manufacturing and engineering, with about 140 activities
identified overall. Next, approximately sixty work-related indicators were listed, including items such as indirect manpower,
purchasing dollars, square feet, transactions, and installed equipment. From these, various productivity ratios were developed
and used for comparing plants and measuring improvements in
productivity over time. For many of the functions, a norm index was developed to show what level of performance or output would be appropriate under normal conditions. IBM is very
pleased with this system and reports that it is used for three specific purposes: productivity comparisons, resource planning,
and productivity tracking.

The solutions just discussed focus on the problems of
staff and how staff groups can be changed or altered to improve
the support they provide. They assume that line and staff conflicts are caused principally by the staff organization, but this is
far from the case. Many of the differences between line and

staff are caused by the unwillingness of the line organization to accept the role of the staff and work with it in an effective manner. Both groups must learn to work together. Therefore, while the issue of line and staff cooperation is complex, it can be resolved or minimized by examining a combination of these approaches.

Providing Recognition for Supervisors

An important part of organizational support is to provide recognition for supervisors, particularly when they have done an excellent job or when the achievements of their work unit should be brought to the attention of others. In practice, many of the items covered in previous chapters provide recognition for supervisors. Training, performance appraisal, compensation, communication, decision-making capacity, and participative management all have the secondary effect of providing recognition for supervisors. This section goes beyond those topics and outlines what organizations can do to specifically improve rewards for supervisors. It focuses on nonmonetary rewards, the role of top management in providing recognition, public recognition from the organization, and middle-manager reinforcement.

Principles of Recognition. There are many ways in which supervisors can be recognized for their contributions. Recognition is an act or gesture of appreciation to a supervisor who has reached an important milestone. It is a very powerful motivator. The interesting thing about recognition is that the way recognition is provided (style) is just as important as the type of recognition (substance). A particular kind of recognition may be very pleasing and effective in itself; however, if it is given improperly, it can actually have a negative impact. According to Phillips (1982, p. 14), there are five basic principles of giving recognition:

1. *Recognition must be timely.* This is important but often overlooked. Outstanding results should be recognized as soon as possible after they are achieved. If a manager mentions an achievement a month after it occurred, the impact might

even be counterproductive. The best time to reward someone is right after he or she has performed a praiseworthy action.

2. *Recognition must be appropriate for the achievement.* The size of the reward must be matched with the accomplishment. A free cup of coffee or a lunch for a supervisor who has broken all previous company production records would certainly not be an appropriate reward. A bonus or gift, along with public recognition, might be more fitting.

3. *Recognition must be perceived as worthwhile.* Although a manager may think a reward is appropriate, the supervisor may not look at it that way. In one organization, a supervisor was selected to be a United Way representative as a reward for doing an outstanding job. The supervisor did not perceive it as a reward but instead as punishment. In his eyes it was not a worthwhile form of recognition.

4. *Most recognition should be done in public.* The old saying "Reward in public, criticize in private" is usually the best rule to follow. In most cases, supervisors should be given praise and recognition in the presence of fellow supervisors and possibly before an audience of top managers. This lets others know what they have accomplished and that the managers and organization are pleased with that performance.

5. *Recognition must show sincerity.* If a manager hands out a reward merely because of policy or past practice, its impact will be either minimized or negated. It must be done in an honest and sincere manner.

The other part of recognition involves substance, that is, the types of recognition that can be used effectively to recognize supervisors for their efforts. Although there are many possibilities, here are a few common ones:

- promotions
- transfers
- merit increases
- bonuses
- special assignments
- special training programs
- commendation memos
- service awards
- community or task force assignments
- dinners or receptions
- announcements in meetings
- weekend trips
- organizational publications
- special thanks

This list is by no means exhaustive but should stimulate a few ideas about possible ways to recognize supervisors. The remainder of this section outlines what top management, the organization, and middle managers can do to provide recognition to supervisors.

Top Management Support. No group is more important to supervisors than the top management of the organization. Most supervisors strive for recognition from top management and will even settle for an occasional acknowledgment from them. Top management actions in this area will have a lasting effect and can have a strong motivational impact. They can improve the performance, job satisfaction, and organizational loyalty of supervisors. Before taking action, top management must know which supervisors are performing at their best, which deserve special recognition, or which just need a special thanks for completing several years of service. This may become a problem in large organizations with several layers of management. Some executives designate someone to remind them of supervisors who deserve special attention or recognition. The human resources executive is a logical choice for this assignment. In most organizations performance information generated through routine reports can identify supervisors who deserve special attention. If this is not available, then someone may be needed to inform top management. Here are a few simple, yet effective, approaches for providing this kind of recognition:

1. *Visits.* A personal visit from a top executive who mentions an accomplishment or offers congratulations can provide a powerful stimulus for the supervisor. Personal visits are time consuming but if planned properly they can be very effective and even rewarding for the top executive. It gives him or her a chance to keep in touch with supervisors, find out what is on their minds, and observe their environment and work setting.

2. *Calls.* A phone call from a top executive can also have a significant impact on supervisors, almost the same as that of a personal visit. Just realizing that a top executive took the time to phone does much for a supervisor. Calls should be planned and executed on a timely basis soon after important accomplishments and special events. If this method is used too often,

however, it loses its effectiveness and becomes just another routine way of communicating with supervisors.

3. *Personal notes.* Similar to visits and calls, a personal note to a supervisor is another effective way to provide recognition. When the personal note highlights achievements, it makes it clear to supervisors that someone in the organization cares and is watching their performance. Executives who take the time to visit, call, or write will be long remembered as effective executives in the organization.

4. *Memos.* Memos to supervisors, as individuals or as a group, can be another effective approach to highlighting accomplishments. It is unusual for supervisors to hear directly from top executives. Most of the communication they receive comes from staff support groups or their immediate middle manager. However, memos directly from the chief executive or other top executives, with appropriate copies to others in the chain of command, can have a motivating effect on supervisors. One effective approach is to send a memo to all supervisors in a department or division when they have achieved excellent results. Although this approach does not single out one individual, it reinforces that the team, working together, has reached outstanding goals.

Organizational Recognition. One of the most effective kinds of recognition is public recognition. This way, all of management, including the supervisor's peer group, and in some cases the entire organization, will know about the contributions of the supervisor. The following approaches can be very effective in providing public recognition:

1. *Publicizing accomplishments in organizational publications.* Almost every organization has some type of in-house publication designed to distribute news and other information to employees. This is an excellent way to highlight achievements, particularly those of the supervisory group. Providing recognition should be one of the goals of the internal publication, and articles about outstanding achievements should be planned regularly. Production records, outstanding quality attainments, and increases in efficiency as well as accomplish-

ments in the area of employee relations are excellent topics to include in the publication, particularly when they can be tied to a work unit or individual supervisor. In one organization a particular work unit had broken all previous records for days worked without a lost-time accident. The story was highlighted in the company's publication, along with appropriate background information on the supervisor. Photographs of the entire work unit and the supervisor were included. This effort showed supervisors that the organization supported and recognized their efforts.

2. *Management newsletter.* As mentioned in Chapter Six, some organizations have a special publication for the management group. In some cases this is designed specifically for supervisors. If this publication is available, it makes an ideal medium for disseminating information about achievements of the supervisory group. In fact, this is usually one of the fundamental purposes for having the management publication. In one management newsletter, a special column called "Outstanding Achievement" is used to highlight outstanding supervisory performance. Each month at least one supervisor is highlighted. Of course this method cannot be used to excess, and it must highlight accomplishments worthy of special recognition.

3. *General meetings with supervisors.* Another excellent opportunity to recognize supervisors is provided by the regular meetings of the management group. Many organizations conduct these meetings on a periodic basis and include recognition of outstanding supervisory performance as one of the regular items on the agenda. Although many supervisors shun this kind of publicity, particularly among their peer group, they will appreciate top management's concern for their performance. It helps build credibility and respect for supervisors who have made significant achievements, and it motivates them to repeat their achievements. One organization devotes the first few minutes of each monthly meeting to recognizing major accomplishments, outstanding performance, significant records, and unusual efforts above and beyond the call of duty. The candidates for recognition are submitted by middle managers or identified by the human resources department from the organization's

official records. One supervisor was recognized for working over twenty-four hours on a project to meet a difficult deadline.

4. *Staff meetings.* Regular staff meetings are held in most departments. They represent an excellent setting in which to recognize supervisors in the department who have outstanding accomplishments. This can improve teamwork and motivate supervisors to repeat their good performances in the future. But some caution must be exercised so that the same supervisor or supervisors do not always dominate the limelight, possibly causing resentment among other supervisors.

5. *Panel discussions.* Although not appropriate for all organizations, panel discussions are sometimes conducted to give supervisors an opportunity to explore an issue, problem, or program. Supervisors who have developed expertise in a particular area may serve on the panel to analyze the issue, offer solutions to the problem, or explain the new program. One organization was having a serious problem with employee absenteeism. The company invited a group of four supervisors with the best absenteeism records to meet with other supervisors in a panel discussion. They were asked to explain how they achieved their results and how others might do the same.

6. *Success stories.* Similar to panel discussions, unusual success stories should be publicized in the organization by using the variety of media already described. This will ensure that an outstanding performance that had a significant impact on the organization receives proper recognition throughout the organization. An actual situation in a manufacturing firm illustrates the value of providing this kind of recognition for supervisors.

A production unit had achieved outstanding results through the efforts of a team of two supervisors. These results were in the form of key bottom-line measures, such as a reduction of absenteeism, employee turnover, lost-time accidents, grievances, and scrap rate and an increase in unit hour, a basic measure of individual productivity. The supervisors achieved these results by applying the basic skills taught in a supervisory training program. This was mentioned at the beginning of the presentation made at a monthly meeting for all supervisors. Using a panel discussion format, the two supervisors outlined what they had done to get their results. The comments of the supervisors were published in a pamphlet for distribution to all the other supervisors through their department heads. The title of the publication, "Getting Results: A Success Story," reflected their accomplishments. On the inside cover the specific results were detailed, and additional information on the supervisors was provided. A close-up photograph of each supervisor taken during the panel discussion was included on this page. The next two pages presented a summary of the techniques used to secure the results. The pamphlet was used in staff meetings as a discussion guide to cover the points raised in the panel discussion. Top executives were also sent copies. In addition, the discussion was videotaped and used in subsequent training programs as a model of successful supervision. The pamphlet also served as a handout at these training programs.

From all indications, the recognition was effective. Favorable responses were received from all levels of management. Other supervisors began to use more of the approaches presented by the two supervisors. Top executives asked the HRD department to prepare and conduct similar meetings. This was the beginning of a continuing program called "Supervisory Success Stories" (Phillips, 1983b, p. 273).

7. *Service awards.* The typical service award program includes a gift for an employee for completing five years of service and in five-year increments thereafter. Employees usually have the opportunity to select the gift, which typically includes the organization's name, logo, or trademark, along with the number of years of service. Although service award programs usually involve all employees, it is particularly important to fully recognize the supervisors with long service records, possibly before an audience of upper management and fellow supervisors. Too many organizations fail to take enough time to handle a service award ceremony properly. It is an important milestone when someone has worked twenty years for an organization. Although the performance of these supervisors may not always have been outstanding, their job tenure is valuable to the organization. They deserve, and expect, proper recognition. The extra effort to make this event a special occasion will help the manager gain

loyalty and commitment from these supervisors. Top management must set the example and require other managers to make maximum use of the service award program. In one organization, managers and supervisors are given guidelines for handling the awards ceremony. Various suggestions are presented, along with a few minimum requirements. For instance, thirty-five-year award recipients should at least have a special dinner in their honor. These guidelines are sent to the manager, along with the service award.

Middle-Manager Reinforcement. Although it is important to have support from top executives and public recognition from all parts of the organization, nothing is more motivating for supervisors than to have their performance recognized by their immediate manager. In most organizations middle managers will have the most impact on the supervisor's career advancement and pay increases. Many of the opportunities for public recognition just described will be more meaningful for a supervisor if the middle manager is involved.

Middle managers are in a unique position to reinforce significant achievements and accomplishments and to provide recognition for outstanding results. Supervisors need daily feedback on how they are doing, and no kind of formal recognition or reward program can take the place of that. But quite often, middle managers do not take the time or know how to give positive reinforcement. To remedy this, some organizations train middle managers to use positive reinforcement and feedback (PRF) to keep their supervisors motivated. The following agenda represents one such training program:

- the importance of PRF
- the theory of PRF
- PRF techniques
- when to use PRF
- follow-up after PRF
- a model of an effective use of PRF
- skill practice
- critique of skill practice
- on-the-job application

Middle-management recognition of supervisors need not be limited to verbal comments. It may be appropriate to document exceptional performance separately and apart from the performance appraisal and place it in the supervisor's personnel file. A random search in the personnel files of most organizations will reveal few, if any, documents related to outstanding performance. But it may be common to find notes, memos, and reports that outline examples of poor performance. Managers want to make sure they are thoroughly covered when there is a performance problem, but they do not take the necessary time to document outstanding achievement. It may be just as important to document outstanding performance, however, since this has a very positive impact on supervisors. First, the very act of giving recognition leaves a lasting impression. Second, the fact that the manager will take the time to document achievement is further evidence of the manager's awareness of the results that have been achieved. Third, the fact that the documentation is becoming part of the personnel files provides a feeling of security for the supervisors, since they know that their next manager will have some written evidence of their accomplishments.

This is a powerful tool that is underutilized in most organizations today. Of course, this approach will not be effective if it is used too often. If every little item of performance is documented, then the end result may be counterproductive. Also, reports of oustanding achievement may cancel previous reports on supervisors who have a documented record of poor achievement in the past. In practice, this cancellation may be appropriate. However, if the organization does not want to override prior records, then the record of exceptional performance could also mention the previous problems.

Making Supervisors Part of the Management Team

Most people in business regard supervisors as part of company management. Yet supervisors do not always see it that way themselves. Recent studies provide some disturbing information here. The National Survey of Supervisory Management Practices, discussed earlier (Bittel and Ramsey, 1982, p. 36), represented responses from over 8,000 supervisors in 564 different organizational units in thirty-seven states. Only 40 percent of supervisors responding to this survey regarded themselves as part of management while 19 percent felt closer to their employees than to management.

The problem often seems to be one of divided loyalty. In the eyes of employees, supervisors are members of management. They expect them to identify with management and represent management. However, supervisors may feel closer to employees, often because they were once part of that group. When organizations treat supervisors no differently from other employees, the problem becomes worse. And occasionally, of course, supervisors may actively take the side of employees against management. To argue that supervisors must identify with management does not mean that supervisors should not empathize with their employees. On the contrary, supervisors should support their employees when they are right. Being loyal to management does not mean blind obedience to it.

Without proper alignment with management, however, supervisors cannot fulfill their responsibility as management's representative on the front line. How can a company ensure that it has the loyalty of supervisors? One executive summarizes it this way, "Treat supervisors as if they are a part of management and they will identify with management." Although this is easier said than done, there are a number of actions that will provide support in the transition process and on the job after promotion. Many of the recommended actions presented in earlier chapters will help supervisors identify with management. These include

- training supervisors to be managers (Chapter Three)
- providing the same or similar compensation programs for supervisors as for other managers (Chapter Five)
- establishing special communication programs for supervisors (Chapter Six)
- improving supervisory authority and decision-making ability (Chapter Seven)
- involving supervisors in important decisions for the organization (Chapter Eight)

In addition to these actions, there are four other ways in which organizations can help make supervisors identify with the management team.

Changing the Job Title. If supervisors are considered members of management, maybe they should be labeled as such. Titles such as foreman, group leader, head nurse, or section coordinator may imply a closer association with working-level employees than with management. Even the title of supervisor may be a mismatch. Many organizations are changing the title of supervisor to that of manager because the job not only involves supervising employees but quite often involves managing a work unit and in some cases a profit center. This practice is common for supervisors in professional and technical areas. For example, the manager of an accounting unit may actually be a first-level supervisor but is rarely called a supervisor. But there seems to be much reluctance to make the change across the board. As Drucker (1974, p. 394) indicates, "The fact that we are reluctant to call the supervisor a manager, even though his job fits the traditional definition better than the jobs of people who hold higher and much more important positions in the executive hierarchy, only demonstrates that the definition accentuates the secondary rather than the primary." Maybe it is time to consider changing all supervisory job titles to manager.

Management's Representative. Another effective way to clear up misunderstandings about the status of supervisors is to designate supervisors as official management representatives for their department or area of responsibility. This should involve more than just verbal commitments or statements of philosophy. It should include visible signs that the organization has officially designated supervisors as management representatives. One organization constructed signs in each work area stating, "If you need additional information on . . . , see your management representative." Also, forms that require supervisory approval have signature spaces labeled "management representative" instead of "supervisor." Inviting supervisors to meetings that were traditionally reserved for other managers may also help them to identify with management.

In other cases, supervisors who serve on committees are designated and referred to as representatives of management. In many organizations, it is common practice for supervisors to be included on a rotating basis in labor contract negotiations. They become a part of the management negotiating team. This clears up any doubt about where their loyalty should lie. Other possibilities include listing supervisors as management representatives in telephone books, manuals, and directories. Some organizations publish a management directory that lists all members of management, from first-level supervisors to top executives, including addresses and home phone numbers. These actions, although simple, can ensure that supervisors feel they are part of the management team.

Membership in Management Associations. One of the most effective ways to improve management identification and provide support for supervisors is to have them actively participate in a management association. There are three major associations available for supervisory participation: the National Management Association (NMA), the International Management Council of the Young Men's Christian Association, and the American Management Associations (AMA). At AMA individual memberships are available, as is chapter membership for students at colleges and universities through the Society for the Advancement of Management, a division of AMA. The International Management Council makes membership available through city chapters. At NMA, individual memberships and city chapters are available, although the majority of members come from special chapters in organizations. While all three vary in their approach, the NMA is the most promising in that it offers a full array of programs and services to promote professional management among supervisors and also provides opportunities to develop leadership skills.

Founded in 1925 under the guidance of Charles F. Kettering, famed inventor and industrialist, NMA, a nonprofit organization, has become the world's largest management association, with a membership of almost 70,000 supervisors and managers in 255 affiliated chapters. It has representatives from over 1,200 organizations. NMA is dedicated to the development and recognition of management as a profession and to the promotion of the American free enterprise system. Management chapters in NMA devote at least 75 percent of their activities to the development of the managerial skills of their members. The chapter concept provides the maximum opportunity for personal and professional growth to occur in the management team, both individually and collectively. NMA offers opportunities in four major areas: (1) educational resource materials; (2) leadership, growth, and development; (3) communication among the management team; and (4) development of the image of the manager.

NMA's primary target audience is first-level supervisors, who make up the majority of the membership. The secondary audience is middle managers and professional employees in affiliated organizations. Organizations with as few as twenty professional and managerial employees can benefit from the chapter concept. Below that number it is best to consider individual memberships or a city chapter membership. Additional information on NMA can be obtained from its national headquarters at 2210 Arbor Boulevard, Dayton, Ohio 45439.

Professional Certification. In 1975 the Institute of Certified Professional Managers was created to provide for certification of members of management. The institute has four purposes:

- To recognize management as a profession
- To provide direction for study in the supervisory and management field
- To provide a critical, third-party evaluation of managerial competence
- To recognize demonstrated competence in the managerial field

Certification requires a combination of education, experience, and successful completion of a series of three examinations. Although the name of the institute implies that it is for managers, many certified professional managers are from the first-level supervisory group. Many of the materials used to prepare for the examination focus on supervisory skills. Professional certification represents an excellent way for an organization to recognize supervisors as being part of the management team and give them an opportunity to demonstrate their competence in supervisory and managerial skills. Additional information can be obtained from the Institute of Certified Professional Managers, James Madison University, Harrisonburg, Virginia 22807.

Although these steps are aimed at aligning supervisors with management instead of with their employees, it is important that the organization not create a two-class system. Supervisors must respect the dignity of their employees and treat them as equals in most aspects of their job. Supervisors should not begin to think in terms of "us" and "them" or "we" and "they." All employees, including management, have the same ultimate purpose, and that is to make the organization succeed. However, supervisors are charged with the responsibility of representing management for the organization. They must identify with the goals, philosophy, and mission of the organization and see that the expected results are achieved. The actions outlined in this section are necessary to ensure that supervisors thoroughly understand their role and function in the organization.

Summary

This chapter explored a variety of issues concerning organizational support and recognition for supervisors. It focused on job security, substandard performance, staff support, supervisor recognition, and management identification. Supervisors are very special employees who need to receive adequate support, assistance, and recognition from management and the entire organization. They should not have to be unnecessarily concerned about the security of their jobs as long as they perform in a satisfactory manner, and they should know that they are part of the management team. The organization is left with the challenges to do the following:

- Take steps to ensure that supervisors are employed during temporary work reductions.
- Develop effective ways to confront substandard performance and gracefully remove supervisors from their jobs when it is apparent they cannot perform satisfactorily.
- Examine and improve, if necessary, the staff support services provided to supervisors.
- Provide appropriate management and organizational recognition for supervisors when they reach significant milestones or perform in an outstanding manner.
- Ensure that supervisors understand that they are part of the management team.

These actions are necessary if supervisors are to be effective in their jobs, understand their role as management representatives, and be aware of the benefits as well as the challenges inherent in supervisory assignments.

Suggested Readings

Foulkes, F. K. *Personnel Policies in Large Nonunion Companies.* Englewood Cliffs, N.J.: Prentice-Hall, 1980.

Hirschhorn, L., and Associates. *Cutting Back: Retrenchment and Redevelopment in Human and Community Services.* San Francisco: Jossey-Bass, 1983.

Katz, D., Kahn, R. L., and Adams, J. S. (Eds.). *The Study of Organizations: Findings from Field and Laboratory.* San Francisco: Jossey-Bass, 1982.

Keys, B., and Henshall, J. L. *Supervision.* New York: Wiley, 1984.

Koontz, H., and O'Donnell, C. *Essentials of Management.* (2nd ed.) New York: McGraw-Hill, 1978, 218–238.

McConkey, D. D. *Management by Objectives for Staff Managers.* New York: Vantage, 1972.

Pascale, R. T., and Althos, A. G. *The Art of Japanese Management: Applications for American Executives.* New York: Simon & Schuster, 1981.

Peters, T. J., and Waterman, R. H., Jr. *In Search of Excellence.* New York: Harper & Row, 1982, 306–317.

Vough, C. F. *Productivity: A Practical Program for Improving Efficiency.* New York: AMACOM, 1979.

10

Developing and Implementing
a Comprehensive
Improvement Program

Throughout this book, many of the problems, concerns, challenges, and opportunities for supervisors have been explored. Now it is time to reflect on the impact all this material has on the supervisory job. What emerges clearly is that the supervisor of the future will be very different from the supervisor of the past. A new profile of the supervisor is coming into view. In some organizations the supervisor's job has already changed dramatically, although in others the traditional supervisory role has yet to be challenged.

The description of the supervisor of the future is essentially a review of this book, chapter by chapter. The new supervisor:

1. Functions as a *team leader* and *resource person.* Chapter One discussed the problems and frustrations of the supervisor and how the supervisor's job has changed. It outlined the need for role redefinition and described the new supervisor as a team leader and resource person, not an authority figure.

2. Is *selected* for the job on the basis of important and essential requirements. Chapter Two illustrated the importance of the proper selection of supervisors and outlined some successful approaches to this issue. Supervisor selection is becom-

371

ing more scientific and professional than it was in the past. Factors that affect the selection process, as well as sources of new supervisors, were thoroughly discussed. A complete selection system was presented that, when operating effectively, can prevent many of the problems caused by inadequate and incompetent supervision.

3. Is thoroughly *trained* for the challenges and tasks of the job. Chapter Three outlined practical successful approaches for providing training for both new and experienced supervisors. The supervisor's job is too difficult and demanding to learn completely through trial and error. A comprehensive approach to supervisory training is necessary to prevent future supervisory problems and bring success in the job quickly. Factors that influence the success of supervisory training were presented.

4. Maintains high *performance standards* and receives regular *performance* feedback. Chapter Four focused on the development of a formal supervisory performance system. It explored the basic issues of job descriptions, performance standards, and performance appraisals. There is no place in a professional supervisor's job for vague and nebulous performance standards. Supervisors must understand their job duties, know what is expected of them, and receive feedback on how well they are doing.

5. Receives competitive *compensation* based on performance. Chapter Five explored the important issues of supervisory compensation, including types of compensation, recent trends in compensation, and the basic requirements for a successful and competitive compensation system. Supervisors are no longer among the lowest-paid professional employees, but improvements are still needed. Few things are more important to supervisors than their pay, and direct correlations between compensation and performance can motivate supervisors to high levels of achievement.

6. Receives *communication* on important organizational issues and keeps his or her employees informed. Chapter Six presented the complicated and misunderstood issue of supervisory communications. It outlined what should be communicated to supervisors and how it should be communicated. It ana-

lyzed the basic communication problems supervisors face, including problems in communicating with their employees. Organizations cannot afford to keep supervisors in the dark. Constant attention to this important area will help alleviate many future problems.

7. Has the freedom, authority, and ability to *make decisions* and manage the work unit with minimum interference. Chapter Seven outlined a basic decision-making process and explored the sources and use of authority. Supervisors cannot function effectively with severely restricted authority and decision-making ability. This chapter showed how constraints can be removed from supervisors' jobs, giving them the freedom to manage their work unit with minimum interference from others, whether inside or outside the organization.

8. *Participates* in key organizational decisions and allows employees to participate in decisions affecting the work unit. Chapter Eight explored participative management in the sense of both allowing supervisors to be more involved in decisions and encouraging them to solicit meaningful input from their employees. Supervisory and employee input is valuable; participation can help make the work unit more productive and the organization more effective. Although participative management is not the answer to all problems, it is a promising way to improve productivity, job satisfaction, and morale.

9. Receives positive *organizational support* as a key member of the management group. Chapter Nine discussed the various support mechanisms in the organization that can impact supervisory performance. Supervisors must have positive support and assistance to be effective. Adequate job security, effective ways to handle unsatisfactory performance, helpful staff support, recognition for outstanding performance and achievements, and making supervisors members of the management team were the major elements of organizational support presented in this chapter. This effective support for the supervisory group is a final ingredient for making the supervisor an important and contributing member of the management team.

These essential characteristics give a profile of the supervisor of the future. It is an ideal that most organizations should strive to achieve. Some have made great progress toward it, while others still fall far short. The remainder of this chapter outlines how an organization can come closer to approximating this ideal—the supervisor of the future. The recommended approach involves five simple steps:

1. Determine the current posture of the supervisory staff.
2. Set priorities for improving this posture.
3. Develop a plan of action.
4. Communicate the improvement to supervisors and all other members of the organization.
5. Evaluate progress and make adjustments.

These steps are appropriate for any organization. Of course, the process may be complex in large organizational settings, relatively simple and easy to accomplish in smaller organizations. And not every organization will or should be interested in implementing a major improvement program for supervisors. Some organizations have made much progress in this area and have little need to do anything else. In others, problems exist only in a few isolated areas. But in some cases major improvement is necessary throughout the organization. A carefully planned program for change may then be in order.

Determining the Current Posture

Although some areas for improvement might be easily identified, an important step in assessing the current status of supervisors in an organization is to gather information from two main groups. First, managers and executives above the first level can provide an excellent assessment of the supervisors' situation and identify their problems. Second, information collected directly from supervisors can provide input about their problems, attitudes, and concerns.

Management Input. The management of the organization—from middle managers to chief executive—should provide information about the current status of supervisors. Input can be secured through meetings, discussions, interviews, or surveys. One of the most effective means is to have management complete a confidential survey about its supervisors. The survey can gauge the extent to which the organization is committed to improving the supervisory job and can assess the status of programs and actions designed to bring about this improvement. The survey in Appendix B is designed to measure the organizational commitment to supervisors. It is appropriate for any level of management above the supervisory group, the target audience for improvement. It covers all the major topics discussed in this book, and it is designed to focus on each of the previous chapters.

National Survey of Supervisory Management Practices. One of the most effective ways to assess the current status of supervisors in an organization is to use a standard survey developed specifically for this purpose. While there are many standard surveys designed to check the attitude of supervisors, none is as comprehensive as the National Survey of Supervisory Management Practices. It focuses not only on attitudes but on problems faced by supervisors and the organizational practices that have an impact on supervisors. The survey was developed by Lester Bittel and Jackson Ramsey of the Center for Supervisory Research at James Madison University in Harrisonburg, Virginia. They have been gathering data since 1981, and the data base now includes information on more than 10,000 supervisors in over 600 organizations. The survey accurately reflects the demographics of the over 2,000,000 supervisors in the United States. Organizations represented include those in the areas of manufacturing, construction, mining, banking, insurance, communication, transportation, utilities, health care, education, government, retailing, wholesaling, data processing, and distribution. The data base is continuously being expanded, and any organization wishing to participate can do so by contacting the Center for Supervisory Research. The participating organization coordinates the survey and is charged a very nominal fee to have the data tabulated and reported by department or section.

The purpose of the survey is to develop data that will help managers (and the organization), now and in the future, to carry out the following tasks:

1. Determine an optimum degree of organizational and administrative support for supervisory work.
2. Assess the intensity of operating pressures and problems as they affect supervisory efforts and perceptions.
3. Compare, against a large average, the attitudes of the organization's supervisors toward their work and their careers.
4. Judge the sensitivity of their supervisors toward employee motivations and work conditions.
5. Consider the significance of the supervisors' own judgments of their performance capabilities.
6. Design and structure better supervisory roles in their organization.
7. Devise and implement more effective supervisory selection procedures.
8. Conceive of, and put into place, more relevant supervisory training and development programs.

The survey instrument is essentially self-administered and contains 149 multiple-choice questions of fact, opinion, and self-evaluation. Most responses are obtained from assembled groups of supervisors under carefully controlled conditions. As a result, the survey return represents a nearly 100 percent response rate. The results found in the first report, which includes over 6,000 supervisors, have a 99-percent chance of being an accurate reflection of the population represented by the sample and any segment of that sample when compared with another sample.

The principle hypothesis of the survey was that supervisors who agreed or were directed to participate would respond to a self-administered questionnaire in such a manner as to generate a useful and substantial library of collective information about themselves and their jobs. The mass of data collected by the survey bears out its hypothesis. For question after question, the distribution of responses is narrow enough to demonstrate a remarkable consistency of conditions and viewpoints yet varied enough when examined segment by segment to provide evidence of significant differences according to a number of demographic classifications.

This survey represents a highly significant contribution to research on supervisory conditions, practices, problems, and attitudes. In several places throughout this book, the latest survey results have been quoted, and these results show a need for attention in most of the areas outlined here. For additional information on how to obtain the survey report or to participate in the survey, contact the Center for Supervisory Research, School of Business, James Madison University, Harrisonburg, Virginia 22807.

This endorsement of the National Survey of Supervisory Management Practices is not intended to reflect on the quality of other surveys conducted with supervisors. The Opinion Research Corporation, Science Research Associates, Towers, Perrin, Forster & Crosby, the Research Institute of America, and Hay Associates, among others, have attempted to gather information about supervisory attitudes and problems. However, the National Survey of Supervisory Management Practices focuses on the subject of, and the material contained in, this book. It is highly recommended, not only as a resource work but as a tool to gauge the current status of supervision in an organization.

Developing New Surveys. Some organizations prefer a custom-designed survey to administer to supervisors. Before discussing the advantages of this approach, it is important to understand its pitfalls. First outside norms are not available with which to compare results. The results have to be judged against what top management perceives as appropriate or desirable. There is no way for managers to know how their supervisors compare with others in the same industry or in a similar organizational setting. Second, custom-designed surveys are expensive. In many cases an organization would be reinventing the wheel. Effective surveys are available that can meet the needs of almost any organization. In addition, a mechanism for collecting, tabulating, and analyzing data would have to be developed, whereas with existing surveys this is usually developed by the survey supplier. Third, the results may not be as reliable and valid as with existing surveys. Many of the commercially available surveys have been tested for reliability, consistency, accuracy, and validity. They usually work well, and the results can be trusted.

Now for the advantages of a custom-designed survey. First, regardless of the quality of an existing survey, it will not exactly fit an organization's requirements. Naturally, when a survey is designed to cut across organizations and industries its usefulness in any particular setting will be compromised. Second, a custom-designed survey will explore the issues that are important to the organization and will penetrate deeply into the areas of primary concern. Third, custom-designed surveys may have more receptivity with supervisors. They may be impressed by the fact that the organization has taken the time to develop a survey for them instead of administering an outside, third-party survey. Moreover, supervisors like to think that their problems and concerns are unique and not at all the same as those of any other organization.

Regardless of which approach is used, surveys can be very useful if they are administered properly and are responded to appropriately. This book makes no attempt to present the basics of attitude survey design or the principles involved in effectively administering surveys. Many other books do an excellent job of providing this information, and some of them are listed in the Suggested Readings at the end of this chapter. However, it is important to briefly point out some of the conditions for successful surveys of the supervisory group. First, the survey should be thoroughly explained to supervisors. They will probably be pleased with what the organization is attempting to accomplish but will understand the survey only if it is thoroughly explained to them. This will help ensure that input is complete and quality data are obtained. Second, it is best to survey all the supervisors unless a very carefully controlled and valid sampling procedure can be devised. It is important to have an accurate reflection of all supervisory attitudes, concerns, and problems. Third, it is important to let supervisors know that action will result from the survey, if the results show that action is necessary. The survey results should be communicated to the supervisors, and there should be some discussion of planned actions in the future. With this explanation up front, and with the follow-up discussions and actions, the entire experience will be a pleasant one for supervisors. Fourth, it may be appropriate to have supervisors involved in the design of the survey if it is a custom-designed one. They may be able to bring out some issues not previously identified, and their participation will help ensure their acceptance of the survey. And finally, the survey must be conducted in a confidential and anonymous manner. Supervisors must be convinced that what they say will not be traced to them and cannot be used in retaliation at some later date. Some organizations use third-party consultants to conduct surveys, refusing to be involved in any handling or tabulating of the data. Some go to the extreme of locking up the data and having the consultant remove it immediately from the premises. Extreme steps may not be necessary, but at least some indication that the information will be kept confidential and anonymous is essential.

Setting Priorities

After the data have been collected, analyzed, and presented in a format for management to understand and use, it is time to set priorities. This is often a confusing step in the process. Not everything can be done at the same time. The organization must determine which areas need action now, which are less urgent, and which need no action at all. One approach is simply to do nothing if the data reveal no significant problems. If this is the case, it should be communicated to supervisors with appropriate explanations. However, for most organizations some improvements will be needed. There are five important factors that should be considered in selecting the areas for initial action:

1. *Items that represent major differences from what was expected.* When norms are used and the current organizational data on supervisors show significant deviation from the norms, this may pinpoint an area for attention. An area for immediate

attention may also be identified when the internal status of supervisors deviates significantly from what management expected. Suppose, for example, top management thought that supervisors knew what was expected of them, yet the results from the data revealed that this was far from the case. This might be an important area to tackle.

2. *Items important to top management.* Naturally, some items will have more importance in the eyes of top management than others, and these might warrant some initial attention. For example, if management is deeply concerned about the caliber of training provided to supervisors, and there are significant differences in what was expected and what was reported, then this might identify an area for consideration. But top management might not think it important for supervisors to identify with top management, and so results in that area might take on a low priority.

3. *Items important to supervisors.* It would obviously be appropriate to concentrate on items that are important to supervisors—for example, a report that there are serious problems in pay policies. Conversely, supervisors may report that they are not being involved in decision making but may in fact not place very much importance on increasing their decision-making role.

4. *Items that can show a significant return.* From a return on investment standpoint, items that can impact the effectiveness of the organization should be tackled first. In this category would be a conclusion that there are so many constraints placed on supervisors that they are ineffective in performing their jobs. However, other items may not have very much impact on the organization's overall effectiveness—for example, a report by supervisors that they are last to find out about anything because of poor communication.

5. *Items that are feasible and practical for implementation.* Some items may be impractical to fix while others can be readily changed. This must be considered when selecting items for immediate attention. For example, significant problems with pay practices may have to be resolved over time and may not be placed on the initial list of actions. Also, a very restrictive labor contract may be difficult, if not impossible, to change.

Using these five factors, the organization can select priority items. It may be appropriate to go back to the supervisory group with a potential set of improvements and have them help determine the priorities. This same process could be conducted with the management group. The result of this step is to arrive at a manageable number of actions that can be undertaken. Some organizations develop a short-term list and a long-range list. The long-range items are those that the organization will tackle over the next three to five years, while those on the short-term list will need immediate attention.

Developing a Plan of Action

The next step is to develop a detailed plan to bring about the necessary changes. Some changes may be made immediately and will not require any planning to complete. For example, a quick policy change could rectify complaints about supervisors' lack of authority in purchasing materials and supplies. In most instances, however, it will not be enough to simply institute a new policy, revise an old policy, or implement a single new program. Most changes will involve a series of actions that must be gradually set in motion over several years. This can best be accomplished through an organized plan involving the *what, who, when, how,* and *where* of each action. Exhibit 10 shows a sample form for developing this action plan.

Objectives must be set for each of the items. This defines *what* is to be done. These objectives should be measurable, precise, clearly written, and achievable.

The responsibilities define *who* should accomplish the objective as outlined on the plan. The human resources function may have the prime responsibility for coordinating the overall improvement plan, although many of the actions will be completed by others, including the supervisors. In addition to human resources, other key managers may have significant coordinating roles, and the responsibility of each manager must be clearly designated.

A timetable indicates *when* things will be done. Some will be accomplished quickly while others will take a considerable amount of time. The more detailed the steps—with completion

Exhibit 10.

SUPERVISORY IMPROVEMENT PLAN

PLANT/DIVISION/DEPARTMENT _____ RESPONSIBLE EXECUTIVE _____ DATE _____ PAGE ___ of ___

OBJECTIVE	ACTION ITEMS	PERSON RESPONSIBLE	TARGET DATE	ACTUAL DATE

dates tied to each step—the more likely it is that the item will stay on target. It is important to take action soon and to have some visible signs of progress.

The mechanics of reaching the objectives show *how* the action plan will be accomplished. They detail specific steps for completing each objective. These steps may involve policy changes, training programs, new procedures, manual revisions, or meetings.

The location of each of the items indicates *where* it will happen. Changes may be necessary in only one division, department, or plant. However, many of the actions may involve organization-wide changes.

It is important that the organization be committed to achieving the items on the action plan. Otherwise, it will be a fruitless exercise and the object of ridicule by the supervisory group.

Communicating the Improvement

The next step in the process is to communicate the planned improvements to all who will be involved in or affected by the change. It is important that management above the first level have a clear understanding of what is taking place, why it is being done, and what actions will be taken in the future. But the key group for communication is the supervisory group. It may be appropriate to again use the *what, who, how, where,* and *when* approach in making this important communication. In terms of *when,* it is best to communicate with supervisors as soon as possible. If priorities can be established and action plans developed soon after the results of the survey are known, then it may be appropriate to wait until both of these steps are completed before communicating with supervisors. However, if there is a significant time lag beteween receiving the results and developing action plans, it may be best to have two introductory meetings with the supervisors, one to discuss the findings and the second to explain what will be done.

Determining *what* to communicate involves four major areas. First, the unedited results are communicated so that supervisors will know both the collective results and the results by department and division. Second, supervisors should know the priorities for actions established by management and receive an explanation of why these priorities were selected. Next, action plans should be discussed. The amount of details given will depend on the items. For some, little detail may be necessary—perhaps only a discussion of the final outcome and when it will be achieved. For others, particularly very serious problems, more detailed reports on the action plans may be appropriate. Finally, what management expects from supervisors should be communicated, if the organization has specific expectations. If supervisors are expected to have a significant part in making an improvement, and most likely they will, then management should outline what they expect from the supervisory group.

Who should be involved in the communication process is another important issue. Top executives over the target supervisors should certainly take part. Division managers (for a division), plant managers (for a plant), or the chief executive officer would also be appropriate participants. Their involvement would show the importance that the organization places on this process. For convenience, part of the communication might be handled by other key executives, including the top human resources manager.

The *where* and *how* of communication go together. It is recommended that initial communications involve meetings with supervisors. These may be large group meetings held away from the work area and possibly even in locations away from the organization's facilities. Subsequent communications on progress may be made through special memos and newsletters or in supervisory staff meetings. Overall, communication may be just as important as the actions taken, because misunderstandings can easily develop if supervisors are not aware of planned actions and the progress made.

Since much of the material may be sensitive and confidential, it should be communicated only to supervisors and other managers and executives in the organization who have a need to know. Other employees not directly involved in the effort, even key professional employees, should not necessarily receive the information. Receiving it may make them wonder why management has focused special attention on supervision and not on the rest of the work force.

Evaluating Progress and Making Adjustments

A final part of the implementation process is to routinely monitor its progress and make adjustments when necessary. Too often, programs are planned and implemented with great fanfare and then quickly forgotten. Other things happen, managers get busy, and attention is directed to different areas. It is easy to allow a well-designed plan to meet a quick and untimely death.

One way to ensure that plans are completed on time is to place many of the action items into the goals of the various groups involved. These goals could be short-term departmental objectives or individual performance standards:

- The human resource development department might be involved in implementing training programs for supervisors.
- The employment department might be involved in improving the supervisory selection process.
- The compensation department might be charged with the responsibility for redesigning pay practices for supervisors.
- The purchasing department might be involved in revising policies on the requirements for supervisory approval.

The organization may need to hold status meetings to assess what has been done and to determine if a replanning of strategy is necessary. Progress reports should be generated and communicated to the management group and to supervisors. Depending on the seriousness of the initial problems or the magnitude of improvement needed, periodic reports from a top executive may be appropriate to keep everyone informed as to what is being done and the results achieved. When much of the improvement has been completed, it may be appropriate to revisit management and supervisors to see if they are aware of the results that have been achieved. The same surveys conducted initially could be administered again to see if there have been improvements, as perceived by the target group. After all, supervisors, and other members of management, must be aware that the situation has changed for there to be lasting improvement.

Conclusion

This book has presented an argument for wide-ranging changes in the role and work of supervisors. Not every organization will need improvement in each of the areas presented. Some items are more important and carry a higher priority than others. Each organization must assess its current posture and develop new policies, programs, and management practices to make the necessary improvements. The need for change will not always be apparent. The status of supervisors as seen by management may not reflect the viewpoint of the supervisors themselves. Input directly from supervisors may be necessary to form a clear picture of the present situation. The research presented here strongly suggests the need to raise the status and prestige of supervisors, as well as to take action to improve their effectiveness. There can be no doubt that supervisors are key individuals whose impact on an organization can be multipled several times through the efforts of their employees. The supervisor's role has changed greatly since the middle of the century, and experts agree that it will change even more radically in the future. Thus, organizations will be forced to adjust to a continuing series of changes if they want to have the best supervisors for their money.

This book contains virtually all the information necessary to begin creating the supervisor of the future. Much of the beauty of the approach outlined here lies in its simplicity. There is no need to make the process overly complex. Moreover, its systems orientation allows various aspects of the job to be tackled simultaneously so that improvements in one area are not made at the expense of other areas. Collectively, this material, when implemented, should provide the key to eliciting a whole new range of contributions from the supervisory group.

Adding zest and new dimensions to the supervisor's frustrating job can be a rewarding process that will have an immediate, positive impact on an organization. The supervisor's personal productivity should be improved since many of the impediments to his or her success will simply disappear. Supervisors will remain on the job longer since they will encounter less difficulty and frustration. Also, other employees in the organization may come to actively seek the job because of its increased attractiveness. This should help ensure that an ample supply of qualified candidates is always available.

For those organizations just beginning to focus attention on this group, the road will be long and hard. There will be much to be accomplished and it will take time. For those that have already made some progress, the future is still laced with challenges to make additional improvements.

Suggested Readings

Backstrom, C. H., and Hursh-Cesar, G. D. *Survey Research.* (2nd ed.) New York: Wiley, 1981.

Dillman, D. A. *Mail and Telephone Surveys: The Total Design Method.* New York: Wiley, 1978.

Henerson, M. E., and others. *How to Measure Attitudes.* Beverly Hills, Calif.: Sage, 1978.

Oppenheim, A. N. *Questionnaire Design and Attitude Measurement.* New York: Basic Books, 1966.

Patton, M. Q. *Practical Evaluation.* Beverly Hills, Calif.: Sage, 1982, 139-185.

Phillips, J. J. *Handbook of Training Evaluation and Measurement Methods.* Houston: Gulf, 1983, 64-92.

Stone, E. F. *Research Methods in Organizational Behavior.* Santa Monica, Calif.: Goodyear, 1978, 61-86.

Thierauf, R. J. *Management Auditing: A Questionnaire Approach.* New York: AMACOM, 1980.

Zemke, R., and Kramlinger, T. *Figuring Things Out.* Reading, Mass.: Addison-Wesley, 1982, 155-180.

Appendix A

A Day in the Life
of a Supervisor

The following is a factual account of one day in a supervisor's work schedule. Nothing has been changed except the supervisor's name. The company, a medium-size manufacturing firm, will remain anonymous. The setting is a foundry unit where metal is melted and poured into molds to make castings. The specific job is that of molding unit supervisor, which represents an ideal setting to illustrate the frustrations facing first-level supervisors. Experienced supervisors and managers will no doubt find these frustrations familiar. Supervisor candidates will see the challenges involved in this key job. Other technical and supervisory personnel who provide support functions should once again be reminded by this account of the scope and difficulty of the jobs of the supervisors they assist.

The foundry unit selected has been in operation for many years. Much of the equipment is old, as evidenced by the occurrence of a substantial number of breakdowns throughout the day. Hourly employees are on an incentive system—that is, they receive base pay plus a bonus, depending on the number of good pieces produced over and above a predetermined number. They are represented by a major union. The supervisor is on a production bonus based on controllable cost components.

Note: Portions of this description originally appeared in Phillips (1980).

388

For Pete Johnson, the workday began at 5:45 A.M. with a quick check of the inspection records to see whether all the previous day's production had been weighed and checked. The foundry was quiet, with only a handful of employees working. A glance at the production schedule showed what should be run that day at which stations. Remembering that one of his employees had to go to court that day, Johnson made an adjustment in the work schedule by moving one of the other operators to the missing employee's location.

Checking the equipment, he noticed that a leaky valve at one of the stations had not been repaired. It had been reported on the previous afternoon, and the night shift maintenance supervisor had assured him that it would be repaired. Johnson hastily looked for the unit maintenance millwright and asked him to repair it. Johnson fumbled through the desk drawer and cabinets until he found a rebuilt valve and gave it to the maintenance mechanic, who proceeded to install it.

Johnson spoke to almost all the people as they arrived, asked them how they were doing, and carried on informal conversations with them. They all responded in a friendly manner. He made a quick trip to the time card rack to see who already was present. When he returned, he performed miscellaneous adjustments on the machines to get ready for the daily production. Johnson then received word that one of his long-service employees would be absent because his son had had an auto accident the night before. The news disturbed Johnson since the employee was a dependable one who had not missed a day in a long time. Because Monday was a holiday, he would not be eligible for holiday pay if he missed work today (Friday). The company's policy requires an employee to work the days before and after the holiday to receive pay for it. Johnson made a decision to shift operators to cover for the absence.

Close to starting time, the employees began to man their machines. Johnson made his rounds among employees, patting them on the back, making small talk, and kidding with them. He noticed, however, that the maintenance employee had changed the valve on the wrong machine. When asked about it, the millwright told Johnson that he had said machine 14, but Johnson insisted he had told him machine 13. It was an obvious communication problem. The mechanic slowly began to correct the situation. Instead of changing valves, however, he went to the shop to get a new one. The delay meant there would be downtime charged to that operator, and Johnson felt frustrated, particularly since the problem was something he had asked maintenance to handle the day before. When the shift finally began at 7:00 A.M., Johnson was two employees short, but he had enough to handle the planned production for that day.

At 7:05 A.M., a minor breakdown occurred, and Johnson jumped in to solve the problem. The wheel on the conveyor system had jumped off the track—a problem regarded as a minor breakdown. The millwright stood by and watched while two supervisors worked furiously to get it back running. It took them only about two to three minutes, but precious time had been lost. That kind of breakdown occurred at least seven or eight times during the day. During all the minor breakdowns, the unit millwright usually stood by, watching the supervisors make the repairs, rather than doing them himself. When asked about this situation, Johnson said that the supervisors could make the minor repairs but that the millwright should help with major breakdowns.

About 8 A.M., one of the sand recovery conveyor systems clogged up and spilled foundry sand everywhere. The crew quickly shut down the system and began to repair the unit while the department head stood by, watching. Dust was all over the unit, and it was hard even to see. The department head went to look for the maintenance men, but, in the meantime, Johnson and one of the other employees isolated the trouble and fixed it themselves.

Johnson made a trip to inspection at 8:20 A.M. to see if the run for the previous day had been weighed and checked. It was the second check he made that day to ensure that his employees would not be shorted on their production. Since they were paid on a piece-rate incentive basis, if their paycheck was less than what they expected they would go to the payroll department and ask for an explanation. Johnson found some mistakes that inspection had made, but, after conferring with the inspection supervisor, he accounted for all the discrepancies.

Returning to the work unit at approximately 8:30 A.M., he found that one of the large conveyor drives had stopped suddenly. Maintenance men were called to the scene, and they came in a hurry. After they had observed and checked the conveyor system, the trouble was spotted and repaired in about fifteen minutes. During that time, all stations were down, and all employees had to be paid downtime. That type of breakdown occurred two or three times that day, and maintenance had to make some minor makeshift repairs rapidly. In the meantime, both employees who had been absent earlier reported for work and filled out the crew for the day.

Problems developed at the cupola, and there was not enough molten iron available to prevent a delay in production. When the cupola problems had been straightened out, an additional iron pourer was needed to catch up with the work. Johnson took one of his other employees, trained in several different jobs, and let him do iron pouring for about forty-five minutes. This job carried a higher classification than his regular assignment, and Johnson asked him if he wanted to record the forty-five minutes as an iron pourer. The employee declined. That attitude is an indication of the cooperation Johnson has with his work group. Members are flexible and do not mind moving to different jobs. The substitute for the iron pourer worked on three different jobs that day, took them all in stride, and seemed anxious to do a good job.

About 9:15 A.M., Johnson took a fifteen-minute break with two other supervisors. They discussed some of the problems they were having at work, plus a few personal problems. After his break, Johnson made a trip outside to the scrap pile to see whether all the iron that had been counted as scrap really was scrap. He also checked the scrap to see what had caused it. Some of the scrap had resulted from the cleaning process, and some castings had been damaged by the conveyor system, a situation out of the control of the operator. The inspection team was cooperative. Although it charged the scrap to the unit, it would not charge it to the employee when it could be determined that the reason was beyond the control of the operator. That action once again pointed out Johnson's never-ending concern that each employee be paid properly for the work he produced. It was reflected all day long, in all his activities.

Johnson received the incentive calculations around 11:00 A.M. These gave an analysis of the previous day's production and showed what each employee would be paid. He promptly passed these on to the individual employees.

About 11:20 A.M., a large, revolving cleaning bin stopped turning. An immediate call was sounded for the maintenance crew, which quickly converged on the scene. The crew sized up the situation within four or five minutes and determined that it was a major breakdown that would require a substantial amount of welding. Johnson immediately let his employees go to lunch a few minutes early, hoping that the breakdown would be repaired during the lunch period.

After lunch, the maintenance crew said it would take at least thirty more minutes for the repair, although the crew was working furiously. Five maintenance mechanics, a lift truck operator, and a supervisor were working on the damaged cleaning bin. Meanwhile, all the units were idle, and the employees moved outside the foundry to wait for the repair to be completed. Johnson summoned the department head to stand by in case the breakdown continued much longer. If the breakdown continued until 2:30 P.M., it would be more economical to send the employees home and scratch the rest of the day's production, keeping only a few employees to help clean up. Just to be on the safe side, since it was payday, Johnson went to the personnel office, picked up paychecks, and distributed them to the employees.

In the next few minutes, it became evident that the breakdown was going to continue longer than had been predicted. The question about sending the work crew home became more pertinent. Johnson conferred several times with the department head to determine who should stay if the crew was sent home. They had to be sure that the most qualified senior employees were chosen. Plans were quickly mapped out. The amount of production achieved was secondary to their concern that they would have to send their employees home without pay that afternoon.

As time passed, the employees continued to accumulate downtime, a costly situation for the company. The maintenance personnel were making progress and said they might have the unit repaired in time to achieve additional production that day. Johnson quickly made the decision to give the employees a fifteen-minute break at 12:45 P.M. rather than wait until 1:25 P.M., the normal break time. Most of them would not take a break anyway because of the length of the downtime, but to be on the safe side, he personally instructed each one to take a break so that nobody would take it after production resumed. Shortly after 1:00 P.M., the unit was put back into operation and full production resumed.

Johnson met with the timekeeper and gave him his time log for the total hours of the day's production. Periodically through the day, he glanced at the lineup and checked production by the individual machines. Occasionally, he ordered additional cores which were used in the production process. Also, the machines had to be changed periodically for a new production run.

Periodically, Johnson conferred with the time-study engineer. And, on that particular day, the engineer showed up to make a spot audit on one of the jobs. Johnson also conferred regularly with the production scheduler for the unit. He had a very good working relationship with the support personnel and was able to get most of the things he wanted. He asked others for assistance in such a way that he rarely was turned down.

Now and then, Johnson glanced at two employees from the construction department who were painting the overhead railing around the top floor of the unit. He had written a detailed letter to his department head and the construction manager, pointing out what they needed to do to stay in compliance with the requirements set by the Occupational Safety and Health Act. Immediately after the letter was received, the construction department placed someone on the unit to repair or replace the items on the list. When Johnson asked his boss why he got such support, the department head said it was because he was doing such a good job and was sincerely interested in complying with the OSHA requirements. That assessment points out Johnson's ability to get others to assist him and to utilize the support personnel available to him.

When one of the employees in the shakeout area (where the sand is removed from the castings) complained that he needed a muscle relaxer, Johnson sent him to the dispensary. He knew the difficulty of the shakeout job and had been trying to get the pay on the job increased because of the hard work involved. The company even had tried to automate it, but with no success. He compared the daily posting sheet of production for the previous day, and it showed that the iron pourers made approximately $10 per day more than shakeout employees. The iron pourers did not work as hard, but their work required more skill.

The daily schedule had called for production of a small number of large castings. The machines were set up, molds were made, and the iron was poured. Those particular castings could not be run through the regular cleaning process. They had to be pulled off the conveyor system, put in a temporary storage area, and cleaned by a separate process. The procedure didn't occur very often, but when it did Johnson usually had someone standing by to pull the castings off the conveyor. On this occasion, he did the job himself. It took about thirty minutes to pick them up after the shakeout process.

Throughout the day, Johnson communicated with his employees and gave them recognition when they had done an outstanding job. They seemed to appreciate his attention, and they carried on friendly conversations with him. Johnson had an excellent work crew, and he said he would "match his crew against any other in the foundries." He treated them as individuals, and he was concerned about their welfare. When any member of the crew was sick and in the hospital, he sent a fruit basket. However, he was cautious about being too friendly with his employees since some might try to take advantage of him. But he knew those situations are the exception rather than the rule.

Because of the breakdown, there was no afternoon break, and Johnson missed the opportunity to collect his thoughts over a cup of coffee. Throughout the day, he worked at a furious pace, checking on the operation and talking with different employees. Except for lunch and break, there was no sitting down. Minor breakdowns kept him running from one end of the unit to the other. Near the end of the work shift, Johnson made his rounds to remind all the employees that Monday was a holiday. Some had forgotten.

As the shift phased out, Johnson made his rounds to check on final production and compliment the employees on the job they had done. He compared the production with what they had been supposed to produce. Overall, the production for the day was a disappointment. When the two hours of downtime were taken into account, however, the output had been very good. It was approximately 80 percent of what had been produced the previous day. Five or six maintenance employees had worked on the unit for two hours, and that time would be charged against the employees' cost bonus. Also, probably during the night or over the weekend, five or six maintenance employees would be needed to make permanent repairs on the cleaning bin, almost guaranteeing a washout on the supervisor's cost bonus. This had happened frequently. His maintenance budget sometimes was completely used up because of the condition of the equipment. That, he felt, was not under his control, and he was disappointed because of it.

Johnson took a few minutes to repair a knee pad. Doing so would save the expense of a new one on the budget—an example of the positive effects of a cost bonus system. Johnson made preliminary plans for the next day's activities; he got some patterns organized, helped to clean up the unit, and made sure that all equipment and gas had been turned off.

At 3:30 P.M., Johnson left the unit to go to the locker house, and he reflected on the day. It had not been a very good one. Maybe the next workday would be better. It was the end of a day that had begun ten hours earlier, a hectic and challenging day for a foundry supervisor. It had become clear during the day that the job of a foundry supervisor is a tough one. It requires skill, capability, and intelligence, as well as a lot of energy and muscle. It's a tiring job in a tough environment.

Appendix B

Management Commitment Survey:

Determining Organizational Support for Supervisory Effectiveness

The following questions are designed to measure the extent of organizational commitment to the needs, desires, aspirations, and status of first-level supervisors. Please circle the response that comes closest to describing the situation in your organization.

1. In this organization, the supervisor's job is
   a. not attractive and is rarely sought by any outstanding candidates
   b. not any more attractive than other professional jobs, and an average number of candidates seek the job
   c. considered very attractive and is sought after by high-potential employees
2. In the last ten years, the supervisor's job has
   a. not been examined for potential improvements
   b. been changed in a few routine ways to adjust to shifts in the organization
   c. been completely restructured to improve its effectiveness

396

3. In this organization, the supervisory style
   a. is authoritarian with autocratic overtones
   b. provides firm leadership and direction to employees
   c. emphasizes team leadership, providing support and resources to employees
4. Supervisory selections are primarily based on
   a. technical skills, seniority, and attitude
   b. perceived knowledge of supervisory duties, appearance, work experience, and attitude
   c. job-related information gathered from interviews, exercises, simulations, and background checks
5. Supervisors are selected by
   a. the manager who has the vacancy
   b. the combined decision of at least two levels of management in the area where the vacancy occurs
   c. the combined input of a variety of staff and line personnel with a final review by top management
6. the sources of new supervisors are
   a. internal departmental promotions only
   b. formal supervisor trainee programs
   c. a combination of external recruits and internal promotions
7. Training for new supervisors
   a. is informal, mostly through trial and error, as the supervisor learns on the job
   b. consists of an initial indoctrination, followed by on-the-job training
   c. involves a variety of methods, from indoctrination to skill training, with planned follow-up
8. In general, supervisors are trained
   a. in an outside seminar when a deficiency is identified
   b. through a progressive series of formal training and education programs
   c. through a variety of activities, including classroom training, outside seminars, self-study, on-the-job coaching, special assignments, and projects
9. Career counseling is provided
   a. only to nonsupervisory personnel
   b. to a few selected supervisory personnel

      c.   to all supervisors who have the potential for, and are interested in, advancement

10.   Job descriptions for supervisors
      a.   have been developed for a few jobs
      b.   have been developed but are not revised regularly
      c.   have been developed and are regularly revised to accurately reflect current job content

11.   Written objective performance standards are developed for
      a.   none of our supervisors
      b.   a few production-oriented supervisors only
      c.   all supervisory personnel

12.   Supervisory performance appraisals are
      a.   conducted sporadically and involve only a part of the supervisory group
      b.   one-way discussions, conducted once a year for all supervisors
      c.   effective, two-way feedback sessions, conducted at least annually and reviewed by the next level of management

13.   Supervisor's salaries are kept competitive by
      a.   comparing them with the salaries of supervisors in the local market
      b.   comparing them with the going rate in local markets and also measuring them against industry and national survey data
      c.   comparing them with a variety of external local and national survey data as well as making internal comparisons

14.   The supervisor's cash compensation
      a.   is frequently less than that of the employees they supervise, when considering overtime pay
      b.   is occasionally less than that of the employees they supervise, when considering overtime pay
      c.   is almost never less than that of the employees they supervise, when considering overtime pay

15.   Supervisory salary increases are based on
      a.   across-the-board increases
      b.   a combination of cost-of-living adjustments and across-the-board increases

  c. a merit pay program that rewards supervisors for their performance

16. Supervisory bonus plans are in place
  a. for none of our supervisors
  b. for a selected group of production-oriented supervisors
  c. for the majority of the supervisory work force

17. In regard to understanding compensation practices, supervisors
  a. know very little about the basis for their pay or salary ranges
  b. have some understanding of their base pay but not of their total compensation package
  c. have a complete understanding of their compensation program, including salary range and the potential for salary increases

18. Supervisors usually find out about important items
  a. from their employees, the grapevine, or other unofficial communication channels
  b. at the same time as other employees, through official written communication
  c. in advance of the general work force, through both verbal and written communication

19. Supervisors provide a vital link when communicating to all employees
  a. almost never
  b. at times when a special occasion arises
  c. frequently, at regular employee group meetings

20. Employee small group meetings conducted by supervisors are
  a. impractical and unproductive for this organization
  b. used at a few locations, at the discretion of supervisors
  c. used as a regular part of the two-way communication process between management and employees

21. In this organization, employees would rate the supervisor as
  a. the worst source of communication
  b. just another source of information, not any more important than any other source
  c. the most important and reliable source of information about the organization

22. Regarding the control of the work unit, supervisors have
   a.   very limited control over their unit's performance and
        output
   b.   control over most of the things for which they are
        evaluated by management
   c.   almost total control over the unit's output and per-
        formance
23. In the past fifteen years, supervisory authority
   a.   has eroded as a result of additional policies, union
        agreements, and internal changes
   b.   has been affected very little by internal policies, union
        agreements, or other forces that the organization can
        control
   c.   has improved through changes in management poli-
        cies and practices
24. In regard to decision making, supervisors are
   a.   rarely encouraged to make decisions and are not
        trained in the decision-making process
   b.   encouraged to make decisions but receive no specific
        direction or training
   c.   encouraged to make decisions and have received train-
        ing in how to make effective decisions
25. Supervisors are involved in decisions that affect their work
     unit and their jobs
   a.   occasionally, when it is convenient
   b.   routinely in certain areas
   c.   in almost every instance
26. Employee input into decisions affecting the work unit
   a.   is not secured
   b.   is accepted when initiated by employees
   c.   is encouraged and sought regularly by supervisors
27. In economic downturns, supervisors
   a.   must be placed on layoff when the number of other
        employees is reduced
   b.   are the last to go when a department or plant is re-
        duced
   c.   are never placed on layoff unless organizational sur-
        vival is at issue

28. When supervisors consider their own status, do they
    a. closely identify with the nonmanagement employees and rarely take the view of management
    b. at times consider themselves as representatives of management while at others as mediators between management and employees
    c. closely align themselves with the goals and missions of management and clearly consider themselves a part of the management group
29. The supervisor's job is perceived to be
    a. a highly skilled, craftsman-level job in the organization
    b. a respectable coordination and control position
    c. a well-respected element of the management team
30. Supervisory accomplishments are
    a. occasionally mentioned directly to the supervisor
    b. acknowledged by the supervisor's middle manager and brought to the attention of others
    c. regularly recognized by several levels of management, using a variety of approaches
31. Conflicts between line and staff groups at the supervisory level are
    a. frequent and devastating, but a necessary factor in this business
    b. regular, but constructive at times
    c. infrequent and not disruptive
32. Staff support for supervisors is
    a. inadequate and perceived to be ineffective on the part of the line organization
    b. minimally acceptable, when considering staff's role
    c. very positive and productive

The "C" response is the most desired one for each statement. "B" is preferred to "A." Sufficient data are unavailable to make comparisons between organizations. It might be more appropriate to analyze responses to specific statements or to compare total scores to what the organization expects.

References

Abboud, M. J., and Richardson, H. L. "What Do Supervisors Want from Their Jobs?" *Personnel Journal,* June 1978, pp. 308–334.

American Productivity Center. *Reward Systems and Productivity: A Final Report for the White House Conference on Productivity.* Houston: American Productivity Center, 1983a.

American Productivity Center. "Putting the Work Ethic to Work." Productivity Brief, No. 31. Houston: American Productivity Center, 1983b.

American Society for Personnel Administration. *Employees Selection Procedures.* Survey No. 45, Bulletin to Management. Washington, D.C.: Bureau of National Affairs, 1983.

Bernstein, P. "Using the Soft Approach for Hard Results." *Business,* April-June 1983, pp. 13–21.

Bittel, L. R. *What Every Supervisor Should Know.* (4th ed.) New York: McGraw-Hill, 1980.

Bittel, L. R., and Ramsey, J. E. "The Limited, Traditional World of Supervisors." *Harvard Business Review,* July-August 1982, pp. 26–36.

Bittel, L. R., and Ramsey, J. E. "What to Do About Misfit Supervisors." *Management Review,* March 1983, pp. 37–43.

Bolles, R. *What Color Is Your Parachute?* Berkeley, Calif.: Ten Speed Press, 1978.

Boyd, B. B. *Management-Minded Supervision.* (2nd ed.) New York: McGraw-Hill, 1976.

Bureau of National Affairs. *Performance Appraisal Programs.* PPF Survey, No. 135. Washington, D.C.: Bureau of National Affairs, 1983.

Butler, R. J., and Yorks, L. "A New Appraisal System as Organizational Change: G.E.'s Task Force Approach." *Personnel,* January-February 1984, pp. 31–42.

Carroll, S. J., and Schuler, R. S. (Eds.). *Human Resources Management in the 1980s.* Washington, D.C.: Bureau of National Affairs, 1983.

Charon, K. A., and Schlumpf, J. D. "How to Measure Productivity of the Indirect Work Force." *Management Review,* August 1981, pp. 8–14.

Christenson, C., and others. *Supervising.* Reading, Mass.: Addison-Wesley, 1982.

Cook, D. D. "Foreman: Where Theory Collides with Reality." *Industry Week,* April 6, 1981, pp. 74–80.

"Corporate Career Development Programs Are Alive and Well." *Management Review,* January 1984, p. 53.

Croft, J. "Ten Ways to Communicate for Change." *Supervision,* May 1984, pp. 9–10.

D'Aprix, R. *Communicating for Productivity.* New York: Harper & Row, 1982a.

D'Aprix, R. "The Oldest (and Best) Way to Communicate with Employees." *Harvard Business Review,* September-October 1982b, pp. 30–32.

Doud, E. A., Jr., and Miller, E. J. "First-Line Supervisors: The Key to Improved Performance." *Management Review,* December 1980, pp. 18–24.

Drucker, P. F. *The Practice of Management.* New York: Harper & Row, 1954.

Drucker, P. F. *Management: Tasks, Responsibilities, Practices.* New York: Harper & Row, 1974.

Drucker, P. F. "Twilight of the First-Line Supervisor?" *Wall Street Journal,* June 7, 1983, p. 32.

Ellig, B. R. "What's Ahead in Compensation and Benefits." *Management Review,* August 1983, pp. 56–61.

Ellig, B. R. "Total Compensation Design: Elements and Issues." *Personnel,* January-February 1984, pp. 22–30.

"Flexible-Benefit Plans." *Wall Street Journal,* December 27, 1983, p. 1.

Foltz, R. G. "Communique." *Personnel Administrator,* July 1981, pp. 13–86.

Fombrun, C. J., and Laud, R. L. "Strategic Issues in Performance Appraisal: Theory and Practice." *Personnel,* November-December 1983, pp. 23–31.

Ford, R. C. "Delegation Without Fear." *Supervisory Management,* July 1983, pp. 2–8.

Foulkes, F. K. *Personnel Policies in Large Nonunion Companies.* Englewood Cliffs, N.J.: Prentice-Hall, 1980.

Frangipane, L. J. "First-Line Supervisors Say of Middle Managers: There's Lots of Room for Improvement." *Management Review,* May 1979, p. 46.

Freedman, S. M., and others. "The Compensation Program: Balancing Organizational and Employee Needs." *Compensation Review,* second quarter 1982, pp. 47–53.

Gelberd, L. B., and others. "Self-Appraisals: The Next Stage in Performance Evaluations." *Supervisory Management,* May 1983, pp. 9–14.

Gellerman, S. W. "Supervisory Training: Key to Productivity!" *BNAC Communicator,* Bureau of National Affairs, 1981, Fall, p. 2.

Gorlin, H., and Schein, L. *Innovations in Managing Human Resources.* New York: Conference Board, 1984.

Greene, R. J., and Roberts, R. G. "Strategic Integration of Compensation Benefits." *Personnel Administrator,* May 1983, pp. 79–82.

Harmon, J. F. "The Supervisor and Quality Control Circles." *Supervisory Management,* February 1984, pp. 26–31.

Henderson, R. I. *Executive, Managerial, and Professional Compensation.* Reston, Va.: Reston Publishing, 1984.

Henerson, M. E., and others. *How to Measure Attitudes.* Beverly Hills, Calif.: Sage, 1978.

Herzberg, F. "One More Time: How Do You Motivate Employees?" *Harvard Business Review,* January-February 1968, pp. 53–62.

Hobson, C. J. "Why Employees Should Rate Supervisory Effectiveness." *Supervisory Management,* September 1982, pp. 8–11.

Holley, W. H., and Jennings, K. M. *Personnel Management: Functions and Issues.* New York: Dryden, 1983.

Imberman, W. "How to Enjoy Not Having a Strike." *Management Review,* September 1981, pp. 43–47.

Imundo, L. V. *The Effective Supervisor's Handbook.* New York: AMACOM, 1980.

Jerdee, T. H., and Calhoon, R. P. "Training Needs of First-Level Supervisors." *Personnel Administrator,* October 1977, pp. 23–24.

Juechter, W. M. "The Pros and Cons of Participative Management." *Management Review,* September 1982, pp. 44–48.

Kahalas, H. "The Environmental Context of Performance Evaluation and Its Effect on Current Practices." *Human Resource Management,* Fall 1980, pp. 32–40.

Katzell, R. A., and others. *A Guide to Worker Productivity Experiments in the United States 1971–75.* New York: New York University Press, 1977.

Kaye, B., and Krantz, S. "Performance Appraisal: A Win/Win Approach." *Training and Development Journal,* March 1983, pp. 32–35.

Keavenly, T. J., and Jackson, J. H. "Propensity for Career Change Among Supervisors." *Human Resource Management,* Fall 1977, pp. 13–15.

King, P. "How to Prepare for a Performance Appraisal Interview." *Training and Development Journal,* February 1984, pp. 66–69.

Kirkpatrick, D. L. *A Practical Guide for Supervisory Training and Development.* (2nd ed.) Reading, Mass.: Addison-Wesley, 1983.

Kopelman, R. E. "Linking Pay to Performance Is a Proven Management Tool." *Personnel Administrator,* October 1983, pp. 60–68.

Lashbrook, V. J. "New Training Programs: To Buy or Build." *Training Magazine,* November 1981, pp. 53-55.

Lawler, E. E. "Merit Pay: Fact or Fiction?" *Management Review,* April 1981, pp. 50-53.

Lazer, R. I., and Wikstrom, W. *Appraising Managerial Performance: Current Practices and Future Directions.* New York: Conference Board, 1977.

Lea, D., and Leibowitz, Z. B. "A Mentor: Would You Know One if You Saw One?" *Supervisory Management,* April 1983, pp. 32-35.

LeFlufy, R. "HRD and the Economy: What Must Change?" *Training Magazine,* April 1983, p. 58.

Levine, H. Z. "Consensus: Supervisory Training." *Personnel,* November-December 1982, pp. 4-12.

Lewis, P. V. *Managing Human Relations.* Boston: Kent, 1983.

Lindsay, F. D. "Employee Benefits, Then and Now." *Nation's Business,* August 1981, pp. 64-68.

Locke, E. A., and others. "The Relative Effectiveness of Four Methods of Improving Employee Performance." In K. D. Duncan and others (Eds.), *Changes in Working Life.* New York: Wiley, 1980.

Luthans, F., Lyman, D., and Lockwood, D. L. "An Individual Management Development Approach." *Human Resource Management,* Fall 1978, pp. 1-5.

Macdonald, C. R. *Performance-Based Supervisory Development: Adapted from a Major AT&T Study.* Amherst, Mass.: Human Resource Development Press, 1982.

"Management Development: How GAO Does It." *Personnel,* July-August 1983, pp. 58-60.

Meyer, M. *Profile of Employee Benefits.* Report No. 813. New York: Conference Board, 1981.

Miner, M. G., and Miner, J. B. *Employee Selection Within the Law.* Washington, D.C.: Bureau of National Affairs, 1978.

Mitchell, T. R. "Organizational Behavior." In M. K. Rozenweig and L. W. Porter (Eds.), *Annual Review of Psychology.* Vol. 3. Palo Alto, Calif.: Annual Reviews, 1979.

Moffatt, T. L. *Selection Interviewing for Managers.* New York: Harper & Row, 1979.

Mondy, R. W., and others. *Supervision.* New York: Random House, 1983.

Morgan, B. S., and Schiemann, W. A. "Why Internal Communication Is Failing." *Public Relations Journal,* March 1983, pp. 15–17.

Moses, J. L., and Byham, W. C. (Eds.). *Applying the Assessment Center Method.* Elmsford, N.Y.: Pergamon Press, 1977.

Myers, M. S. *Every Employee a Manager.* New York: McGraw-Hill, 1970.

Nadler, L. *Corporate Human Resources Development: A Management Tool.* New York: Van Nostrand Reinhold, 1980.

Nash, A. N., and Carroll, S. J., Jr. *The Management of Compensation.* Monterey, Calif.: Brooks/Cole, 1975.

Northrup, H. R., and others. *The Objective Selection of Supervisors.* Manpower and Human Resources Studies, No. 8. Philadelphia: Industrial Research Unit, Wharton School, University of Pennsylvania, 1978.

O'Connor, E. J., and others. "Work Constraints: Barriers to Productivity." *Personnel Administrator,* May 1984, pp. 90–98.

Overbeke, J. E. "Foreman—Who'd Want the Job?" *Industry Week,* April 28, 1975, pp. 30–39.

Pajer, R. G. "Performance Appraisal: A New Era for Federal Government Managers." *Personnel Administrator,* March 1984, pp. 81–89.

"Performance Appraisals Reappraised." *Management Review,* November 1983, p. 5.

Peters, L. H., and O'Connor, E. J. "Situational Constraints and Work Outcomes: The Influences of a Frequently Overloaded Construct." *Academy of Management Review,* 1980, *5,* 391–397.

Peters, T. J., and Waterman, R. H., Jr. *In Search of Excellence.* New York: Harper & Row, 1982.

Phillips, J. J. "How to Improve Management Support for Supervisory Training Programs." *Training and Development Journal,* August 1978, pp. 23–26.

Phillips, J. J. "A Day in the Life of a Foundry Supervisor." *Foundry Management and Technology,* July 1980, pp. 40–48.

Phillips, J. J. "How Cross-Training Leads to Effective On-the-Job Development." *Training Magazine,* July 1981, pp. 35-37.

Phillips, J. J. "Rewarding Employees Effectively: Substance and Style." *Supervision,* November 1982, pp. 14-20.

Phillips, J. J. "How to Keep from Getting Burned on an Outside Seminar." *Supervision,* November 1983a, pp. 7-10.

Phillips, J. J. *Handbook of Training Evaluation and Measurement Methods.* Houston: Gulf, 1983b.

Phillips, J. J., and others. "Skills of an Effective Foundry Supervisor." *Foundry Management and Technology,* August 1980a, pp. 35-40.

Phillips, J. J., and others. "Using the Assessment Center System Approach." *Foundry Management and Technology,* September 1980b, pp. 97-106.

Plachy, R. J. "Appraisal Scales That Measure Performance Outcomes and Job Results." *Personnel,* May-June 1983, pp. 57-65.

Ray, C. M., and Eison, C. L. *Supervision.* New York: Dryden, 1983.

Reber, R. W., and Terry, G. E. *Behavioral Insights for Supervision.* Englewood Cliffs, N.J.: Prentice-Hall, 1975.

Rendero, T. "Supervisory Selection Procedures." *Personnel,* March-April 1980, pp. 4-9.

Robinson, J. C. *Developing Managers Through Behavior Modeling.* Austin, Tex.: Learning Concepts, 1983.

Rock, M. L. (Ed.). *Handbook of Wage and Salary Administration.* (2nd ed.) New York: McGraw-Hill, 1984.

St. John, W. D. "Successful Communication Between Supervisors and Employees." *Personnel Journal,* January 1983, pp. 71-77.

Salisbury, D. L. "The Corporate Stake in Employee Benefits." *Enterprise,* August 1983, pp. 18-19.

Sasser, W. E., Jr., and Leonard, F. S. "Let First-Level Supervisors Do Their Job." *Harvard Business Review,* March-April 1980, pp. 113-121.

Schoenfeldt, R. C. "The Foreman's Job as Perceived by His Wife." *Supervisory Management,* September 1980, pp. 9-15.

Sibson, R. E. *Compensation.* (Rev. ed.) New York: AMACOM, 1981.

Siegel, A. L. "Employee Attitude Survey Reveals Some Clear Messages for Managers and Supervisors." *Management,* Spring 1980, pp. 13–15.

Simpson, D. B. "Supervisor Assessments Can Be a Developmental Tool." *Personnel Administrator,* June 1983, pp. 55–56.

Tannenbaum, R., and Schmidt, W. "How to Choose a Leadership Pattern." *Harvard Business Review,* March-April 1958, p. 97.

Terry, G. R., and Rue, L. W. *Supervision.* Homewood, Ill.: Irwin, 1982.

Timm, P. R. *Managerial Communication: A Finger on the Pulse.* Englewood Cliffs, N.J.: Prentice-Hall, 1980.

Townsend, R. *Further Up the Organization.* New York: Knopf, 1984.

"Training in Organizations." *Training Magazine,* October 1983, pp. 41–53.

Vough, C. F. *Productivity: A Practical Program for Improving Efficiency.* New York: AMACOM, 1979.

Walker, J. W. *Human Resource Issues, Strategies, and Programs.* New York: Towers, Perrin, Forster & Crosby, 1983.

Wortman, M. S., Jr., and Sperling, J. *Defining the Manager's Job.* (2nd ed.) New York: AMACOM, 1975.

Yoder, D., and Heneman, H. G., Jr. (Eds.). *ASPA Handbook of Personnel and Industrial Relations.* Washington, D.C.: Bureau of National Affairs, 1979.

Yukl, G., and Taber, T. "The Effective Use of Managerial Power." *Personnel,* March-April 1983, pp. 37–44.

Zahra, S. A. "What Supervisors Think About QCs." *Supervisory Management,* August 1984, pp. 27–33.

Zemke, R., and Kramlinger, T. *Figuring Things Out.* Reading, Mass.: Addison-Wesley, 1982.

Zippo, M. "CEOs Setting Compensation and Other Values to Reinforce Corporate Culture." *Personnel,* November-December 1983, pp. 42–44.

Index

411